GOVERNANCE AND ISLAM IN EAST AFRICA

Based at the Aga Khan Centre in London, the Aga Khan University Institute for the Study of Muslim Civilisations is a higher education institution with a focus on research, publications, graduate studies and outreach. It promotes scholarship that opens up new perspectives on Muslim heritage, modernity, religion, culture, and society. The Institute aims to create opportunities for interaction among academics and other professionals in an effort to deepen the understanding of pressing issues affecting Muslim societies today.

Exploring Muslim Contexts

Series Editor: Farouk Topan

This series seeks to address salient and urgent issues faced by Muslim societies as they evolve in a rapidly globalising world. It brings together the scholarship of leading specialists from various academic fields, representing a wide range of theoretical and practical perspectives.

Development Models in Muslim Contexts: Chinese, 'Islamic' and Neo-liberal Alternatives
Edited by Robert Springborg

The Challenge of Pluralism: Paradigms from Muslim Contexts
Edited by Abdou Filali-Ansary and Sikeena Karmali Ahmed

Cosmopolitanisms in Muslim Contexts: Perspectives from the Past
Edited by Derryl MacLean and Sikeena Karmali Ahmed

Ethnographies of Islam: Ritual Performances and Everyday Practices
Edited by Badouin Dupret, Thomas Pierret, Paulo Pinto and Kathryn Spellman-Poots

Genealogy and Knowledge in Muslim Societies: Understanding the Past
Edited by Sarah Bowen Savant and Helena de Felipe

Contemporary Islamic Law in Indonesia: Sharia and Legal Pluralism
Arskal Salim

Shaping Global Islamic Discourses: The Role of Al-Azhar, Al-Madina and Al-Mustafa
Edited by Masooda Bano and Keiko Sakurai

Gender, Governance and Islam
Edited by Deniz Kandiyoti, Nadje Al-Ali and Kathryn Spellman Poots

What is Islamic Studies? European and North American Approaches to a Contested Field
Edited by Leif Stenberg and Philip Wood

Muslim Cultures of the Indian Ocean: Diversity and Pluralism, Past and Present
Edited by Stéphane Pradines and Farouk Topan

Governance and Islam in East Africa: Muslims and the State in Kenya and Tanzania
Edited by Farouk Topan, Kai Kresse, Erin E. Stiles and Hassan Mwakimako

edinburghuniversitypress.com/series/ecmc

Governance and Islam in East Africa

Muslims and the State in Kenya and Tanzania

Edited by Farouk Topan, Kai Kresse, Erin E. Stiles and Hassan Mwakimako

EDINBURGH
University Press

IN ASSOCIATION WITH

THE AGA KHAN UNIVERSITY
(International) in the United Kingdom
Institute for the Study of Muslim Civilisations

Edinburgh University Press is one of the leading university presses in the UK. We publish academic books and journals in our selected subject areas across the humanities and social sciences, combining cutting-edge scholarship with high editorial and production values to produce academic works of lasting importance. For more information visit our website: edinburghuniversitypress.com

We are committed to making research available to a wide audience and are pleased to be publishing Platinum Open Access editions of the ebooks in this series.

© Farouk Topan, Kai Kresse, Erin E. Stiles and Hassan Mwakimako 2024, 2025 under a Creative Commons Attribution-Non-Commercial-Non-Derivatives licence

Edinburgh University Press Ltd
13 Infirmary Street
Edinburgh EH1 1LT

First published in hardback by Edinburgh University Press 2024

Typeset in Goudy Oldstyle by
Cheshire Typesetting Ltd, Cuddington, Cheshire

A CIP record for this book is available from the British Library

ISBN 978 1 4744 8297 4 (hardback)
ISBN 978 1 4744 8298 1 (paperback)
ISBN 978 1 4744 8299 8 (webready PDF)
ISBN 978 1 4744 8300 1 (epub)

The right of Farouk Topan, Kai Kresse, Erin E. Stiles and Hassan Mwakimako to be identified as editors of this work has been asserted in accordance with the Copyright, Designs and Patents Act 1988 and the Copyright and Related Rights Regulations 2003 (SI No. 2498).

Contents

Acknowledgements   vii
Map of eastern Africa   ix

    Introduction   1
    Farouk Topan, with Kai Kresse, Erin E. Stiles and Hassan Mwakimako

PART I: POLITICS

1. An Islamic Interpretive Strategy for Exploring Grassroots Governance in Northern Kenya   25
   Mark LeVine

2. The Kenyan State and Coastal Muslims: The Politics of Alienation and Engagement   49
   Jeremy Prestholdt

3. Counter-narrativity as Peace, Love and Unity: Citizenship and Belonging in a Kenyan Muslim Counter-radicalisation Programme   69
   Halkano Abdi Wario

4. Beyond Vicious Circles in the Kenyan Post-colony? On the Value of Discursive Space   92
   Kai Kresse

5. Islam, Politics and the Limits of Authority in Mainland Tanzania, 1955–1968   112
   James R. Brennan

Contents

6. Politics, Lived Islam and Muslim Public Discourse in Zanzibar: Reflections on Cultural Identity, Belonging and Governance, 1984–2016 143
   Kjersti Larsen

7. The Inter-religious Dynamics of Muslim Politics: The Zanzibar Case 160
   Hans Olsson

PART II: INSTITUTIONS

8. The Supreme Council of Kenya Muslims (SUPKEM): Jostling for Representativeness among Muslims in Kenya 183
   Hassan Mwakimako

9. Muslim Networks, Public Services and Development Intervention in Post-socialist Tanzania: Between Liberalisation and Alienation 199
   Felicitas Becker

10. *Shehes* and the State: The Role of Muslim Religious Leaders in Public Health Governance in Rural Tanzania 220
    Mohamed Yunus Rafiq

11. Facing Change at the Margins of the Kenyan Nation: The Promise of the Lamu Port 245
    Charlotte Knote

PART III: LAW

12. Beyond an Impasse: Rule of Law and the Kenyan Kadhis' Courts 263
    Susan F. Hirsch

13. The Law of Evidence Applicable in the Kadhis' Courts of Kenya: A Study of Two Decisions by Kadhi Abduljabar, Kadhis' Court Nairobi at Upper Hill 278
    Tito Kunyuk

14. Courts within Courts: Kadhis and their Courts in the Kenyan Judicial System 291
    Abdulkadir Hashim

15. The Case of the Stubborn Heir: State and Non-state Actors in Zanzibar's Kadhis' Courts 306
    Erin E. Stiles

About the Contributors 319
Index 321

Acknowledgements

The idea for this volume has had a dual beginning. It emerged initially at a workshop organised at the Aga Khan University Institute for the Study of Muslim Civilisations (AKU-ISMC) to discuss themes of interest for the series *Exploring Muslim Contexts*. The idea took a more concrete shape after it was discussed in the context of various aspects of Muslim governance, both in Muslim majority and minority countries, under the aegis of the Institute's Governance Programme. The planning of the book accordingly started with a consideration of its structure from a governance perspective. We are grateful to Dr Charlotte Whiting (then Publications Manager and Governance Programme Manager), Professor Gianluca Parolin (Faculty Lead for the Governance Programme), Dr Hassan Mwakimako, Professor Kai Kresse and Professor Erin E Stiles for evolving the three themes discussed in the volume, and for identifying and formulating questions under each theme.

Our thanks to Professor Leif Stenberg, Dean of the AKU-ISMC, for his support for holding the Conference at the Aga Khan University campus in Nairobi in January 2018, and to Dr Alex Awiti, then Director of AKU's East African Institute, for co-hosting it. It was an apt location for the Conference, as colleagues from universities in Kenya and Tanzania were able to join us in presenting papers and discussing issues pertinent to the two countries and the region. Our thanks again to Dr Charlotte Whiting for organising the Conference, and for liaising with colleagues in Nairobi, and subsequently with the contributors to this volume.

I acknowledge with much gratitude the support of the co-editors, Kai Kresse, Hassan Mwakimako and Erin E. Stiles, in editing the sections of this volume, 'Politics', 'Institutions' and 'Law' respectively, and for their assistance in the

Acknowledgements

editorial process. My thanks to Kai especially for our many months of engagement and support.

We are grateful to the AKU-ISMC, and particularly to the Dean, Professor Leif Stenberg, for supporting the publication of this volume, with special thanks to the present and former Publications Managers, Donald Dinwiddie and Charlotte Whiting. It has been a pleasure to work with them.

Farouk Topan, July 2023

Map of eastern Africa. Design by Rainer Lesniewski.

Introduction

FAROUK TOPAN, WITH KAI KRESSE, ERIN E. STILES
AND HASSAN MWAKIMAKO

Kenya and Tanzania possess relatively large Muslim populations (though the figures for their actual demographic percentages are contested), whose relationship with their respective governments is the focus of this volume. In the two countries, the Swahili region – the coastal lands and islands – have had a Muslim presence for many centuries, commencing with the gradual introduction of Islam in the 8th century (Horton and Middleton 2000: 48). Over the years of the *longue durée*, Muslims of the coast have developed and shaped a shared Swahili culture that, though diverse in some respects, nonetheless reflects common beliefs, values, practices and a worldview forged through the confluence of Islam and pre-existing cultural traits.[1]

Kenya and Zanzibar gained their independence from Britain in 1963, and the Union of Tanganyika and Zanzibar was established as Tanzania in 1964.[2] Since the two countries gained independence, the relationship between Muslims and the state has been strained, at times severely. For differing historical reasons, Muslims have felt marginalised to varying degrees in the two nations, attributing the cause of their situation to factors both external and internal to the countries and the region. Scholars in recent decades have examined the Muslim–state relationship mainly through two (not mutually exclusive) approaches. The first

---

[1] This is manifest among the Swahili through the dual concepts of *mila*, custom, and *dini*, religion. See, among others, Kresse 2007: 80–6 and Topan 2009: 57–68.
[2] The United Republic of Tanzania, established on 26 April 1964, consists of the two major islands of Zanzibar (Unguja and Pemba) and the former British-administered Trust Territory of Tanganyika, now referred to as mainland Tanzania. Tanganyika became independent in December 1961; Zanzibar, a Sultanate and a British Protectorate, gained its independence from Britain in December 1963. The Zanzibar Revolution of January 1964 abolished the Sultanate and established a Revolutionary Government.

encompasses security issues, particularly after the bombing of American embassies in Nairobi and Dar es Salaam in 1998, the tragic event of 9/11 and the ensuing 'War on Terror', whose consequences continue to surface in both countries. The second relates to issues of reform or 'development' within Muslim communities and the way these are perceived to have been instigated, or at least influenced, by the state to its advantage. As will be clear below, both approaches are evident in this volume.

A third approach, which also finds resonance with chapters in this volume, is discussed by Soares and Otayek (2007: 17–19) as *islam mondain*: 'Islam in the present world'. This attempts to answer the question: what does it mean to be Muslim in contemporary times? From the viewpoint of this volume, the question applies to Muslims in the two countries who make choices, face challenges and live their lives as citizens, as members of the *umma* (the broad global community of Muslims) and as individuals, each of whom has her or his own way of negotiating through these concentric identities.

Muslims in the colonial period had been part of the administrative infrastructure of both German and British rule, thus continuing (albeit at a lower level) a practice initiated by Omani rule at the coast and the islands whose population was largely Muslim (Iliffe 1979: 208–15; see also Ekemode 1973). In time, as the movement for independence from Britain gained ground in both Kenya and Tanganyika in the late 1950s and early 1960s, as it also did in Zanzibar, Muslims of different backgrounds and orientations actively participated in the struggle, as did social actors belonging to other religions. However, this happened through different pathways and with different attitudes and expectations, as dictated by the circumstances of their respective local and national positions in each of what were at that time three countries.[3]

Kenya had a dual status under British rule. The greater part of the country was designated a British colony and was ruled directly as such. Its coastal territory, a strip ten miles deep into the mainland along the whole of Kenya's coast, belonged to the Sultanate of Zanzibar (it had become a British Protectorate in 1895 under the sovereignty of the Sultan of Zanzibar). As independence approached for Kenya and Zanzibar, the status of the 'Coastal Strip' (Mwambao) became an issue. There were three basic options for its residents: (1) to integrate with the rest of Kenya at independence, an option favoured by Jomo Kenyatta's party, the Kenya African National Union (KANU); (2) to continue to belong to the Sultanate of Zanzibar with some form of political arrangement with the government of Kenya, an option supported by some of the Muslims of the coast, mainly the subjects of the Sultan; and (3) for the coastal strip to

---

[3] Two individuals who may be cited as examples of Muslims active in the struggle for independence are Abdulwahid Sykes in Tanganyika (Said 1998) and Abdilahi Nassir in Kenya. Salim 1970, 1972.

INTRODUCTION

be politically autonomous. Two movements represented the views of most of the coastal Muslim residents, who aspired for the coastal region to be a base of political power. The Mwambao movement campaigned for the autonomy of the coastal strip; its rival, Majimbo, advocated the autonomy of the coastal province, a far wider geographical region than the coast. While most coastal Muslims supported Mwambao, some Muslims, particularly from the northern areas of the coastal strip, allied themselves with Majimbo.[4] Others subscribed to a national vision under KANU, but many coastal residents had increasing apprehensions about ongoing external political dominance from Nairobi, even if under an independent African government.

As the situation on the Kenyan coast became politically heated, the British government appointed a commission in 1961, headed by a former governor of Nigeria, James Robertson, to investigate the legal status of the coastal strip and to make recommendations. The remit of the Robertson Commission was then widened to include the coastal province as a whole, thus expanding the territorial coverage to a 90-mile region inland (and thereby enabling the submission of views of a larger population beyond the coastal boundaries). In its findings, the commission did not consider it feasible for the coastal strip to exist as an independent entity (Brennan 2008: 849). Besides, in its negotiations, KANU made it clear that it would not accept a solution that left Kenya divided. The recommendation from the commission, discussed at the Lancaster House Conference in London between the relevant parties in March and April of 1963, was for the annexation of the ten-mile coastal strip to an independent Kenya. Both the British government and the Sultan of Zanzibar, as relevant signatories of the 1895 Treaty, accepted the recommendation, and the coastal strip duly became an integral part of Kenya upon its independence in December 1963.[5]

When the Sultan of Zanzibar had agreed to the annexation of the coastal strip to mainland Kenya, he could not have foreseen a similar fate for his country, Zanzibar itself, barely five months after its independence, also in December 1963, for in April 1964, Zanzibar and Tanganyika united to become Tanzania. Two events in Zanzibar had propelled the island nation towards the union with Tanganyika: its independence from Britain (when Zanzibar was admitted into the United Nations as a sovereign state), and the revolution in January 1964. The latter was far-reaching and cataclysmic in its socio-political and economic impact within Zanzibar and its relations with its neighbours (primarily Tanganyika). The causes attributed to the revolution are varied and complex.

---

[4] See Brennan 2008 for a salient discussion of the Mwambao movement in the socio-political and religious context of the Kenyan coast. See Nassir 2008 for an internal perspective by a coastal Mwambao representative.
[5] Note that the political representatives of the Mwambao movement present at the negotiations did not agree and refused to sign the treaty.

It is thus not surprising that, among the sources written by those closely related to it, there exist two strikingly different accounts of its origins, representing opposite views of the event, of its *raison d'etre* and outcomes (Barwani 1997; Mapuri 1996).[6] Sources differ, for instance, about the identity of the planners of the revolution, the extent and depth of the violence and atrocities committed, and the involvement and support from individuals and countries, especially Western ones (Wilson 1989).[7] It falls outside the scope of this introduction to rehearse their respective narratives and arguments, but the starkest political outcome was the end of the Bu Said Sultanate, the overthrow of the coalition government, and its replacement by the Revolutionary Council of the Afro-Shirazi Party (ASP), later incorporated into Tanzania's long-term ruling party CCM (Chama Cha Mapinduzi), the 'party of the revolution'.

In the immediate aftermath of the revolution, the attitudes of revolutionary leaders towards religious practices seem to have been mixed. While race and class were the primary factors in the grievance and sense of injustice against 'Arabs' and the Sultanate, aspects of religion too featured as 'unwelcome things' (Loimeier 2009: 463) that were not conducive to the steadiness of the regime in its new milieu or to its image as a politically 'leftist' undertaking. Public celebrations of *maulid* (the anniversary of the birth of the Prophet) were banned, along with the Sufi practice of chanting God's name (*dhikiri*); visits to venerated scholars' graves were also forbidden. Qur'an classes in schools were suspended, the teaching of Arabic was removed from government school syllabuses, and the same applied to religion as a subject, at least between 1965 and 1972 (Loimeier 2009: 464; Purpura 1997: 138–41). More significantly, the Muslim Academy, a college in Zanzibar that had attracted students and scholars not only from the island itself (notably the cosmopolitan Sufi leader Sayyid Omar Abdallah; see Bakari 2018) but from other East African countries as well, was closed in 1965. It was reopened in 1972 as the Islamic College (*Chuo cha Kiislamu*, CCK), by when its international standing as a leading Islamic institution had dissipated following the departure from post-revolution Zanzibar of almost all the renowned scholars and intellectuals whose families had for decades contributed to the development of the island as a centre of Islamic knowledge in the region. To Loimeier, the transition from the Muslim Academy to its newer iteration as the Islamic College 'represented a conscious break with the pre-revolutionary past and was never intended to recreate old traditions of Islamic learning'

---

[6] Mapuri's book has an interesting 'boxed' disclaimer on page viii: 'All views and opinions expressed in this book are those of the author on [sic] his individual capacity and do not necessarily reflect government or any political party's position or policy.' See also Nathaniel Mathews' recent research and forthcoming monograph on Zanzibari–Omani relations.

[7] Besides Barwani and Mapuri, there is extensive literature on the background, causes and aftermath of the Zanzibar Revolution, commencing with an earlier account by Lofchie (1965); see also Clayton (1981), Myers 2000 and Petterson 2002, among others.

INTRODUCTION

(2009: 440). The main aim of the Islamic College was to train a new generation of government scholars 'who would be able to provide some notions of Islamic legitimacy to the post-revolutionary education system of Zanzibar' (ibid.). While this might have been the government's aim for the future, the vacuum left by the older, traditional scholars was filled in the meantime by a cadre of younger ones who had trained at universities in Sudan and the Middle East (mainly in Egypt and Saudi Arabia). These younger scholars tended to propagate the teachings and implement the strictures derived from those particular schools of Islam – especially the Wahhabi – that were often at odds with the generally more accommodating approach of local practitioners. Some of the younger graduates applied a stricter and more literal interpretation of Islam, viewing as 'innovations' the *bida'a* – practices that had not been endorsed specifically by the Qur'an or attributed to the Prophet himself through the hadith, his sayings. That said, it is also interesting to note that some scholars from the older generation of Swahili Muslims, such as Abdulla Saleh al-Farsy and Muhammad Kassim Mazrui, made a distinction between different levels of *bida'a*, qualifying some as acceptable and good for the individual and the *umma* (Kresse 2006).[8]

As with the revolution, so too with the Tanzanian Union, a number of questions and views have been advanced regarding its planning, its swift execution by the presidents of Zanzibar and Tanganyika, its aims, and even its legality. These have been debated over the decades. A detailed account and analysis of the formation of the Union and the issues that emerged in its aftermath are provided by Shivji (2008).[9]

Zanzibar's union with Tanganyika has faced varied forms of opposition and has generated various manifestations of dissatisfaction since its infancy. Both the Union and the Zanzibar governments have acknowledged the existence of such views and have developed platforms to deal with what have been termed *kero za Muungano* – literally, irritations or vexing concerns about the Union. Religion has featured at times as a major factor in the political discourse and protest against the Union.

As Hans Olsson points out in his chapter, whatever the reality of the situation, some Muslims in Zanzibar perceived Islam and Christianity as opposing each other on either side of the Channel, with a 'Muslim Zanzibar' against a 'Christian mainland'. Similar perceptions existed on the Tanzanian mainland

---

[8] See Purpura 1997: 126–44, 349–98 for an insightful analysis of the activities of the anti-*bida'a* scholars, or 'essentialists', as she calls them. Young graduate scholars with similar backgrounds were also active in Kenya, opposing what they perceived as *bida'a* practices; see Bakari 1995: 168–93 and Kresse 2006: 209–28; 2007: 94, 101–2.

[9] Shivji 2008: 1–68 also provides a rich and valuable account of the background and aftermath of the Zanzibar Revolution as a necessary precursor to understanding Zanzibar's Union with Tanganyika; earlier sources on the Revolution are referenced in his bibliography. See also Olsson's chapter in this volume and Brennan 2012.

and coastal Kenya among some Muslims who considered the Christian government as not only ignoring their grievances but also of being prone to acting against them (Njozi 2000, 2003; Kresse 2018; Cruise O'Brien 1995).

James R. Brennan's chapter provides a valuable backdrop to such sentiments in Tanzania as part of its broader analysis of Muslim–state relations during the colonial and the immediate post-colonial periods. It explores the connection between the Muslim population and urban Islamic institutions, on the one hand, and the rise of African nationalism and the establishment of a secular socialist regime between 1966 and 1968, on the other. Brennan notes in his chapter that African Muslims were frustrated by their marginalisation: 'This dynamic had originated under the policies of British rule, but Muslims feared that it would continue under a Christian-dominated TANU government.' Brennan references the state of Muslim education as one factor (among others) that most concerned Muslim leaders. Muslim children lagged behind the mission-educated Christian children in the acquisition of Western education, which was the requisite for good employment, positions of influence and political power. Some Muslim leaders had even suggested that independence for Tanganyika be delayed to allow time for the educational imbalance to be redressed. But, as Brennan points out after exploring this and other factors, the authority of the nation-state ultimately prevailed over a deeply rooted urban Muslim establishment. In the process, there emerged a secularisation of political authority itself vis-à-vis major Islamic institutions whose leaders either chose to side with Tanzania's party-state government or to oppose and attempt to subvert its influence and control over those institutions.

The chapters in this volume discuss the Muslim–state relationship under three broad but interlinked themes: politics, institutions and law, as introduced in the following sections. The chapters relating to each theme are contextualised in relation to the overall aim of the book.

Politics

The field of 'politics' as an area pertaining to the relationship between Muslims and the state over the last decades is covered in this section, in terms both of the ways in which the nominally secular governments of Kenya and Tanzania have dealt with their Muslim populations and of the ways in which 'Muslim politics' (Eickelmann and Piscatori 1996) were shaped and internally contested among East African Muslims as agents.

In this section of the book, Jeremy Prestholdt and James R. Brennan present historical accounts of longer periods of the post-colonial history of Kenya (Prestholdt) and Tanzania (Brennan). Kjersti Larsen and Hans Olsson, meanwhile, focus on Zanzibar, offering case studies on lived Islam and the tensions between religious practice and politics in that area. Mark LeVine examines the recent challenges and successes of community building among the Muslim minority in Kenya's neglected northern Turkana region. Halkano Abdi Wario focuses on initiatives for creating and cultivating popular and peaceful Muslim counter-discourses on 'jihad', while Kai Kresse outlines the relevance of certain Muslim publics as accessible discursive spaces that are used and shaped assertively in different ways by Muslim groups locally and across Kenya.

LeVine's chapter on the Turkana case opens this section, providing lucid and refreshing entry points for thinking about the state, and Muslim–state relations in East Africa that have rarely been brought into play for regional studies on politics and religion. He uses Timothy Mitchell's conception of the 'effects of the state' as a starting point for research on these relations, on the one hand, and draws on his rich knowledge of Islamic Studies and Islamic history on the other, to bring welcome stimulation for the study of Muslim–state relations in East Africa. Both these aspects function for him not just as entry points for research but also as foci for conversations with interlocutors.

A wealth of research literature has been published over the last twenty years or so, on Muslims, Islam, the state, and politics in Africa in general (following earlier volumes such as Brenner 1993 and Westerlund and Rosander 1997), and on Kenya and Tanzania specifically, illustrating some shared general contours and features as well as national and regional differences. While we cannot provide a comprehensive account or a review of these titles here, we are building on these works as a basis and background for orientation.[10]

Other chapters in this section illustrate, in differing ways and by means of various case studies, a characteristic fundamental tension embedded within both the Kenyan and the Tanzanian Muslim community – and between Muslims and the state in each country. A strong sense of internal difference and the diversity of Muslim sub-groups and their doctrinal and ideological orientations is visible vis-à-vis an overarching sense of solidarity and an invocation of unity vis-à-vis the post-colonial state, despite their internal frictions, rivalries and oppositions. The post-colonial state – or the post-colony, as Mbembe (2001) called it – has long been seen and experienced by Muslims in Kenya as a rather external dominating force – indeed, the phrase 'Christian government' is often invoked by them – that imposes demands, restrictions and pressures upon the Muslim community.

---

[10] On Kenya, see e.g. Oded 2000; Seesemann 2007; Brennan 2008; MacIntosh 2009; Prestholdt 2010; Prestholdt 2014; Willis and Gona 2013; Anderson and McNight 2014; Willis and Chome 2014; Ndzovu 2014; Mwakimako and Willis 2016; Weitzberg 2017; Kresse 2018; Hillewaert 2020; Meinema 2021. On Tanzania (incl. Zanzibar), see e.g. Westerlund 1980; Becker 2006; Becker 2008; Brennan 2012; Loimeier 2007; Loimeier 2009; Gilsaa 2012; Fouere 2015; Bissel and Fourere 2018; Nieber 2020. For accounts by Muslims, see Said 1998; Njozi 2001; for the build-up to and context of the Zanzibar Revolution, see Glassman 2011.

Jeremy Prestholdt's chapter for this section lays out, for Kenya in particular, how the post-colonial present, and the social and political experiences of the Muslim community connected to it, still is (and needs to be) understood in relation to the foregoing colonial experience and political structures and features connected to it, in a nominally secular state. Readers may keep related regional or national histories in mind, from Tanzania and elsewhere. Prestholdt discusses in particular the alienation of coastal Muslims from mainstream Kenyan politics. External rule has at times been likened to 'colonial rule' (*ukoloni*) by coastal Muslims in Kenya, for instance, publicly visible in pamphlet literature and public speeches (Kresse 2018: 5–10). An emphasis on distance from the state was visible particularly during phases when Muslims became assertive about their rights. This happened when, during the beginnings of multi-party democracy in the early 1990s, the Islamic Party of Kenya (IPK), which had wide-ranging popular support but was never registered as a political party, emphasised the need for equal rights for all Muslims as citizens; and also more recently, when renewed calls for secession and coastal independence from Kenya re-emerged and gained momentum, as a trope for the newly founded Mombasa Republican Council (MRC) in 2010, following the initial Mwambao independence movement (c. 1959–63). '*Pwani si Kenya*' (the coast is not Kenya) became their motto, referring to the historical belonging of the Kenyan coast to the Sultanate of Zanzibar on the one hand as much as a factual sense of difference and division between coast (*pwani*) and mainland (*bara*), and coastal and up-country people – the latter largely Christians, whose interests were, as Muslims saw it, in any case covered and represented by the state. For Zanzibar, as a political sub-unit of Tanzania, very similar tensions existed between Muslims 'on the islands' (in Swahili '*visiwani*', meaning Zanzibar and Pemba) and the majority of other (Christian) citizens and the national government based on the mainland (*bara*). Indeed, in communal discourse the argument re-occurs that, just as European colonial powers had imposed external interests upon the political, economic and social realities of subjected societies and communities, the post-colonial African states imposed their interests upon citizens. On Kenya, a Muslim scholar commented in a public lecture in Mombasa during Ramadan in December 1998 that the state was indeed promoting Christianity where it could, so that the supposedly 'secular' state was actually 'Christian'. As he put it, 'Kenya is secular but it is Christian' (Kresse 2007: 199).

Meanwhile, James R. Brennan's chapter focuses on the situation in Tanzania. Independent Tanzania became, and long stayed, a socialist country, with Nyerere's *ujamaa* politics of an African socialism led by the ruling TANU (later CCM) party in a one-party state. Since at least the 1990s and with the beginnings of multi-party politics, such a sense has increasingly been building up among Muslims in Tanzania too – visible, for instance, in weekly publications of the national *An-Nuur* pamphlet published in Swahili. In both countries there has been little sense of a trusted relationship between Muslims and the state over the past three decades, nor is Muslim representation within the state regarded as organic or appropriate by Muslim citizens. In fact, the two respective representative bodies BAKWATA (for Tanzania) and SUPKEM (for Kenya) have been regarded with suspicion and as potential instruments of the state by Muslims. Brennan's chapter addresses 'how Islam served multiple political roles in what is today mainland Tanzania', looking at the early post-colonial decades and its colonial beginnings. His account covers how public Muslim festivals, particularly *maulid*, were seen as important events that could involve and raise aspects and issues of governmental authority and control. It also conveys a sense of the government's initiation of the Muslim representative body, BAKWATA, which has remained internally contested by Muslims ever since.

In their various chapters, Brennan, Olsson and Larsen all explore the fundamental tension between the actually existing internal difference and diversity and an envisaged unity and solidarity of Muslims – which is often invoked when it comes to national politics for the reasons just described. This plays out in different ways, in scenarios of everyday life as well as during special festive and ritual occasions, in Zanzibar and mainland Tanzania as well as in Kenya. Demands for reform and 'purification' of religious practice, which increased during the second half of the 20th century, stimulated by global debates and developments in the Muslim *umma*, have long put pressure upon those Muslim groups and actors for whom participation in public *maulid* performances (and less public ones, like *dhikiri*) had long been part of their religious identity. The long and ongoing relevance of such public events, also symbolising and highlighting a co-operation between the state and Muslim leaders, for Tanzanian politics is put in view and commented upon in Brennan's chapter, while Olsson's and Larsen's chapters treat related matters for Zanzibar.

As we know from historical sources and recent research (also from other parts of the Muslim world), these kinds of internal critical contestations and public controversies have been present in Muslim societies over decades and centuries. For East Africa, they are partly documented over the course of the 20th century, yet more research is needed for a more complex picture, also of the centuries before. For many Muslim believers, individually and as local groups, a sense of uncertainty and insecurity emerging out of such internal Islamic critique among Muslims, about the adequacy and propriety of one's actions and public self-presentation, has become a challenging task to deal with.

Larsen's chapter on Zanzibar points to such reformist pressures within the Muslim community – pressures that are increased by local returnees and also by funded missionaries from Ibadhi (Omani) or Salafi-oriented institutions of higher education in the Muslim world (e.g. Saudi Arabia, Egypt, Sudan or

Pakistan). Being subjected to such internal doctrinal and ideological pressures about faith, piety and being a 'good Muslim' in everyday practice, as well as to the external political demands and pressures of the respective secular states and governments, increases insecurity and uncertainty for East African Muslims, fundamentally questioning their belonging to the political national entity within which their existence is framed.[11]

The fragility and the prospective danger arising out of such a situation, turning from the religious to the political realm, when a significant minority of citizens are alienated by the politically dominant, is being addressed. Abdi Wario's chapter, for example, focuses on national publications that seek to create and cultivate a sense of unity and balance within the Muslim communication – as with *The Friday Bulletin* in Kenya – and also through joint initiatives of Muslim NGOs, the post-colonial state and international donors (from the Muslim world and beyond). These initiatives engage in the important struggle to re-appropriate and redefine the meaning of, for instance, 'jihad', as a renewed, positive and constructive connotation of the term is presented and sought to be established, overcoming its common associations with violence and terrorism. In this sense, a different kind of engaged missionary-like activity is being shaped in response to what we mentioned above. In Kenya, these developments have been happening within the context of an ongoing period (since around 2013) of extra-judicial killings and 'disappearances' that, as many Muslim sources say, seem to point to government involvement.

Both Abdi Wario and Kai Kresse address the pressing issues of how overcoming the sense of fundamental insecurity, including mutual distrust, might be achieved by collaborative active discursive and practical engagements and initiatives within the Muslim community itself. Counter-narratives and -initiatives to combative ideologies and understandings of Islam are covered (Abdi Wario), and so are sample projects of the dynamic use of public discursive spaces (Islamic print media and radio stations) for addressing and negotiating such troubles and pressures directly, openly and up front (Kresse). Inclusive efforts at frank talk and open exchange such as these show us also how certain forces and qualities of intellectual creativity and mediating critique, concerned with (re)shaping the community, are in play, and samples of this kind can also be found in Tanzania and in East Africa more widely.

Along similar lines, the sensitive portrayal of an active and engaged Turkana Muslim minority that we see in LeVine's chapter conveys a sense of the dynamic and changing features of communal life of even more peripheral Muslim communities. Despite political neglect and historical marginalisation, they are able to create 'conditions for self-governance in order to grow and provide services

---

[11] See also Goodman 2017 for cases in Mombasa, particularly of South Asian Muslims.

Introduction

that the state is unwilling and/or unable to do for them' (LeVine). LeVine provides a fascinating account of how a community is built and bound as community members take and shape an initiative that itself becomes possible within changing economic circumstances and potentials. In conceptual terms, LeVine pushes us to think more critically about the 'effects' of the state and, more comparatively, also along the lines of long-established Islamic traditions of political thought and scholarship; these also provide basic reference points for orientation by local sheikhs and Muslim leaders in East Africa, as they address and negotiate challenges and political tensions.

As mentioned already, the relationship between colonial past and postcolonial present – especially in the way that structural and experiential features persist from colonial times – remains a central reference point for the Muslim community's sense of self. For Zanzibar, William Bissell has covered important aspects of this under the term 'colonial nostalgia' (Bissell 2010); for coastal Kenya, Kai Kresse has described the dynamics of a 'past present continuous' mode of experience that seems to envelop many Muslims (Kresse 2018). These are dynamics that recent initiatives such as those described by Wario (this volume) seek to overcome, with an emphasis on local Muslim agency and positively defined political empowerment, particularly for the youth.

The Tanzanian case studies are complemented by Larsen's and Olsson's accounts of religious and political dynamics on Zanzibar Island, where on the one hand the sense of a dominant Muslim majority being challenged by increasingly vocal and visible Christian groups in public (Olsson), and on the other the tensions and contestations raised within the Muslim community in everyday life through challenges brought forward by reformist groups (of different kinds), are illustrated and discussed (Larsen). Thus the different case studies presented on 'politics' in this volume complement each other, in ways that widen and deepen, and also complexify, the range of perspectives on Muslims (of diverse kinds and groups) and the state in East Africa.

Institutions

The focus of this section is mainly on Muslim leadership within and through institutions, exploring its dynamism, its leeway for negotiation within and outside the communities, its perception by other actors, and the cultural and religious environment within which Muslim leadership functions. Muslims have attempted to further their causes and interests through various institutions during the colonial and post-independence periods, sometimes in unity and at times in factional and politically divisive environments.

An institution of major significance for Muslims during the colonial period was the East African Muslim Welfare Society (EAMWS). It was established in

Kenya in 1945 on the initiative of Aga Khan III, Sir Sultan Mahomed Shah (d. 1957). He and the Sultan of Zanzibar at the time, Sayyid Khalifa bin Haroub (d. 1960), became its patrons. It was recognised that Muslims, like their compatriots in the region, faced socio-economic challenges after the Second World War. The main aim of the society was therefore 'to secure the social welfare and the economic wellbeing of the Muslim communities in the region' (Juma and Islam 2017: 2). It functioned from its headquarters in Mombasa until 1961, the year Tanganyika became independent, when it shifted its base to Dar es Salaam.

The locations represent two phases of the status and activities of the EAMWS in its relations with the respective governments of these periods. During the Mombasa phase (1945–61), which was within the colonial period, EAMWS focused on its mandate of building mosques, opening schools, operating socio-economic welfare schemes and setting up branches in various parts of the East African region (and also forming links with allied organisations).[12] While EAMWS continued performing some of these activities from its new base in Dar es Salaam, it also became increasingly involved in the politics of the newly independent nation of Tanganyika. The EAMWS was led into the political arena, where powerful rival personalities vied for its control. Once the organisation was politicised, the government viewed it as a threat – not to its existence, but to its authority over particular segments of the Muslim population. The two-pronged clash, internally within the EAMWS and externally with the government, eventually led the government to ban and disband the EAMWS in 1968 while aiding the establishment of a newer national organisation for Muslims, 'Baraza Kuu la Waislamu Tanzania' (BAKWATA, a Swahili acronym whose official English equivalent is given on its website as 'The National Muslim Council of Tanzania'). This link between the demise of the former and the birth of the latter, made all the more tangible by the direct transfer of EAMWS property and assets to BAKWATA, sparked strong opposition from some Muslims who considered BAKWATA an organisation whose main concern was to ensure that Muslim activities resonated with the expectations of the government.[13] Felicitas Becker (in this volume) finds similar attitudes towards the organisation vis-à-vis its activities related to AIDS. Also, according to a recent survey, such perceptions of the organisation have remained unchanged among some Muslims decades later.[14] The government view is that, through BAKWATA, 'the Tanzanian government tries to foster unity (*umoja*) and peace (*amani*).

---

[12] It was during this period that the patrons of the EAMWS – the Sultan of Zanzibar and the Aga Khan – participated in the establishment of the Mombasa Institute of Muslim Education (MIOME), the forerunner of the current Technical University of Mombasa (TUM).

[13] See Said 1998: 282–315 for a narrative critical of the government's role in the abolition of the East African Muslim Welfare Society (EAMWS).

[14] See Wijsen and Mosha 2020.

Repeatedly, the government voices that it has no religion (*serikali haina dini*) and no preference (*serikali haina ubaguzi*) for any existing religion'.[15]

Muslim representation within the community and externally vis-à-vis the government – its legitimacy, platform and personnel – was an issue much debated in Kenya. As in Tanzania, Muslims in Kenya operated within the framework of a one-party state in the post-independence period up to 1992. Hassan Mwakimoko's chapter explores the establishment and role of the Supreme Council of Kenya Muslims (SUPKEM) within this context, highlighting its three main facets as a Muslim organisation: its role as a forum for the articulation of Muslim identity 'in a secular state dominated by a Christian elite'; its role as an umbrella organisation meant to accommodate varied local interests and dynamics; and its role as a conduit for Muslim grievances against policies and acts of the state. In many ways, BAKWATA and SUPKEM leaders in Tanzania and Kenya respectively have faced similar challenges internally within the organisations (rivalry and strong disagreements) and in interactions with their Muslim constituencies, both during the one-party phase (independence until 1992) and beyond.

Felicitas Becker's chapter posits the argument that 'the impression of pervasive alienation between Muslims and the state' needs to be qualified in terms of Muslim leaders' perception of the interests of their communities, the projects and activities of the state institutions or donor authorities, and, perhaps more significantly, the discourse employed in the interaction and negotiation between the parties. Thus, alienation and interaction are relative to expectations and contexts. Where Muslims do engage with state institutions or donor authorities in developmental projects – as shown in the case study of HIV/AIDS activism given in Becker's chapter – they do so from a vantage point of their perceptions and expectations. They are aided in this in the way they interpret the discourse employed by the authorities. There occur, in such situations, what Becker terms 'working misunderstandings': 'situations where representatives of Muslim constituencies on one hand, and those of state and/or donor authorities on the other, cooperate on aims that they use the same terms to define, while *interpreting* these shared terms very differently'. Such interpretations enable representatives of Muslim congregations 'to position themselves very carefully to both retain moral authority with their communities, who are often mistrustful of state institutions and Western donors, and appear as plausible "intermediaries" to donors concerned about efficiency, corruption and "value for money"'.

Mohamed Yunus Rafiq's chapter discusses a similar occurrence in health projects sponsored by NGOs in villages in the Morogoro and Tanga districts

---

[15] Ibid. 227.

of Tanzania. The term *shehe* (a rendering of *sheikh*) carries in the local Tanzanian context the meaning of being 'a madrasa teacher, a marriage counsellor, a popular and religious person, an elder, a leader, a dear friend, a healer, a politician, and/or an imam'. The family planning projects of the NGOs, however, focused on a single meaning of *shehe* as 'a religious leader'; whatever the background of the personnel recruited to fill these positions, they were known as *shehe*. Rafiq explores the roles and outcomes of such *shehe* who assume the title for the purpose of fulfilling the expectations of the NGOs; he also examines their position and efficacy in the rural Muslim societies in which they function as family planning officials.

State interventions for development are discussed by Charlotte Knote in relation to the construction of a new mega-port on the mainland near the small island of Lamu in Northwest Kenya; she examines the project as a case study for exploring processes of marginalisation and local discourses of social change among coastal Muslims. Opinions are divided among the local people: some, especially the youth, view the coming of the port near them as an opportunity for jobs (a 'new Dubai'), while others fear cultural and social setbacks as part of a continuing phenomenon of the marginalisation of the coastal people since independence. Through questioning as to how the port discourse elicits concepts of coastal Muslim identity vis-à-vis Kenyan citizenship, Lamu is conceptualised as an entity not only in a geographical sense but also as located on the cultural and political periphery of the Kenyan nation.

Law

An important question in the relationship between Muslims and the state concerns the status of Islamic law. The four chapters in this section address the issue of law, Islam and governance by focusing on the role of kadhis and kadhis' courts in Kenya and in Zanzibar. Throughout East Africa, Islamic courts are generally referred to as 'kadhis' courts'; Islamic judges are called 'kadhi' in Swahili, derived from the Arabic term *qadi*. In Kenya and Zanzibar, kadhis' courts are worked into the state legal system in similar ways. They have jurisdiction over personal status matters for Kenyan and Zanzibari Muslims; this includes issues of marriage, divorce, inheritance and, in some cases, child custody. The legal system of Zanzibar differs significantly from that of mainland Tanzania – most specifically, for the purposes of this volume, by the fact that the semi-autonomous state of Zanzibar incorporates kadhis' courts into its legal system. Thus, with respect to accommodations of the Muslim population, the legal system in Zanzibar resembles that of Kenya more than it does that of mainland Tanzania. Indeed, we find nearly identical language in the Kenya and Zanzibari constitutional provisions for kadhis' courts and in the Kadhis' Acts. In both contexts, the legal

INTRODUCTION

system is a holdover from the colonial era, in that it is based on British common law with the incorporation of Islamic personal status law for Muslims; both the constitutions of Kenya and Zanzibar establish the Islamic courts.

The chapters by Susan Hirsch, Tito Kunyuk and Abdulkadir Hashim address the changing role of the courts in Kenya. Although the Muslim population in Kenya is, at around 15 per cent of the total population, not large, Kenya is a fruitful place in which to study the intersections of Islam, law and governance, as there has been much public debate in recent years about the constitutional status of the kadhis' courts. The chapter by Susan Hirsch, a legal anthropologist, considers these debates in the context of discussing the commonly perceived 'impasse' between rule of law and Islamic law and how discourses of incompatibility entered recent debates in Kenya on the constitutional status of Islamic courts. Hirsch has been a pioneer in studying the everyday proceedings of Islamic courts, and is well-known for her work on language and gender with regard to Mombasa and Malindi's courts (1998, 2010) and beyond. In his chapter, Tito Kunyuk, who is a senior resident kadhi in Kenya's judiciary and a broadly trained scholar in religion and law, reflects his particular interests in the practical application of law in Kenya. The chapter also evidences his role as a public intellectual; Kunyuk publishes and presents in varied academic media outlets on matters of law and Kenya's kadhis' courts (2018). In his chapter, Abdulkadir Hashim, both a lawyer and a senior lecturer in Islamic studies at the University of Nairobi, examines areas of dispute and collaboration between kadhis and judges. Hashim has published widely on Islamic personal law in Kenya (2012, 2021), and offers an important voice in matters of Islam and law in Kenyan public discourse. We move to Zanzibar in the chapter by Erin Stiles, an anthropologist, who considers Zanzibar's kadhis' courts and various modes of authority as part of the multifaceted disputing process concerning inheritance in Zanzibar. Stiles has published on marital disputes on Islamic courts in Zanzibar (2005, 2009, 2015, 2019), and this chapter is the first step in new research on inheritance.

A key area of convergence in the chapters is the consideration of 'the relationships between religious and secular normative orders', to use a phrase from Hirsch's chapter. The levels of analysis, however, are quite different. The chapter by Stiles is a micro-level look at how Muslims in rural Unguja – the larger island and administrative capital of the Zanzibar archipelago – navigate different modes of authority: religious, state, community and family. Hashim and Kunyuk adopt a mid-level analysis in their chapters. Hashim examines areas of dispute and collaboration between kadhis and judges, while Kunyuk considers the impact of ambiguities in the rules of evidence applicable in Kenya's kadhis' courts. Hirsch's more macro-level analysis shows how the greater integration of Islamic courts into the Kenyan state may enhance the rule of law, posing the question 'What does Rule of Law look like when multiple, seemingly divergent, systems operate in the same space?'

All the chapters engage with this idea of 'seemingly divergent' legal orders, and in doing so emphasise the 'seemingly'. In practice, how divergent are these orders? One of the key points Stiles raises in her chapter is that Zanzibari Muslims in rural Unguja do not tend to consider state and non-state, religious and non-religious, actors and authorities as alternatives or divergent systems, but rather as sequential steps in dispute processing that takes them in and out of the state. Stiles has found this to be the case in her previous work on marriage disputes (2018), and this chapter looks at an inheritance dispute that was eventually taken to a rural kadhi's court. In this case, Stiles finds that the claimant, who was trying to get his older brother to divide property after their father's death, approached the kadhi in an effort to encourage his brother to engage in the normal process of property division, which is typically done extra-judicially within the family.

In his chapter, Hashim shows the promise of an emerging comparative jurisprudence where the reasonings of kadhis and secular magistrates inform one another and influence decision-making. This is evident in a few key areas, particularly child custody, matrimonial property and succession. In child custody cases, for example, Hashim shows that although there is disagreement in the legal community as to whether child custody cases are 'personal status' matters that should be heard in Islamic courts, Kenyan kadhis today show flexibility, and have 'adopted the criteria of best interests to safeguard the welfare of children' rather than basing their reasoning solely on classical Islamic jurisprudence.

Kunyuk's chapter raises the question of how kadhis in Kenya might be engaging with state-mandated rules of evidence that limit or even contradict Islamic rules of evidence. He is particularly interested in how this engagement plays in court practice, and he examines two cases from the Nairobi kadhis' court to illustrate this. In one case, the kadhi involved referenced two provisions of Kenya's Evidence Act to determine that a contested marriage was actually legal and valid. Kunyuk writes that the kadhi 'has expanded the scope of evidence law applicable in the kadhis' courts to include specific provisions of the Evidence Act and any other law that is, in the opinion of the kadhi, relevant to meeting the ends of justice'.

Hirsch's analysis of the changes in Kenya's kadhis' courts allows us to rethink the 'impasse' in academic and public discourse that has characterised Islamic and secular state law as incompatible. Hirsch describes how the integration of the kadhis' courts into the Kenyan legal system has enhanced aspects of the rule of law; for example, in relation to the passing of a new Kadhis' Courts Act and Marriage Act in 2012, she observes that the 'crafting of procedural and

Introduction

evidentiary rules specifically for the kadhis' courts has the combined effect of enhancing rule of law and embracing Islamic legal practice'.

Together, the chapters suggest that in the realm of law, stark boundary lines between secular and religious, and even state and non-state, are more difficult to draw than might be expected. The chapters reflect on this to some extent in light of the attitudes and activities of Muslims, and this seems a promising area for discussion and future research. In Kenya, how do Muslims in various parts of the country think about increased legal integration efforts? How does that affect court usage and litigation strategies? Is the intriguing 'submission clause' actually resulting in forum shopping by Muslim disputants and advocates, as some of the chapters suggest? In Zanzibar, it would be useful to take a more careful look at whether political attitudes and affiliations shape perceptions of the theoretically apolitical kadhis, and how this resonates with debates about the relationships between mainland Tanzania and Zanzibar.

Going forward, it is clear that we need more research comparing the role and function of today's kadhis' courts in Kenya and Zanzibar. The similarities in the structure and make-up of the courts are intriguing, and it would be useful to look more closely for similarities and differences in jurisprudence, court usage and Muslim perceptions of and attitudes towards the court. Deliberately comparative scholarship of this nature is not common, but is a promising avenue for future research. A model might be the recent volume edited by Erin Stiles and Ayang Utriza Yakin, *Islamic Divorce in the 21st Century: A Global Perspective* (2022), which takes such an approach with respect to Islamic divorce law and Muslim divorce practice in nine countries.

The three themes set out above provide a framework for exploring the main issues discussed in the chapters which follow. The relationship between Muslims and the state emerges as a complex phenomenon forged through history, particularly in the recent colonial and post-colonial periods. Issues of identity, power, self-interest, and the coexistence of state and Muslim law are fundamental to any understanding of Muslim status in Kenya and Tanzania and Muslim engagement with the state in the two countries.

Bibliography

Anderson, D. and McKnight, J. (2014), 'Kenya at War: Al-Shabaab and its Enemies in Eastern Africa', *African Affairs* 114(454), pp. 1–27.

Bakari, Mohamed (1995), 'The New "Ulama in Kenya"', in Mohamed Bakari and Saad S. Yahya (eds), *Islam in Kenya*, Nairobi: MEWA, pp. 168–93.

Bakari, Mohamed (2018), *The Sage of Moroni: The Intellectual Biography of Sayyid Omar Abdallah, a Forgotten Muslim Public Intellectual*. Nairobi: Kenya Literature Bureau.

Barwani, Ali Muhsin (1997), *Conflicts and Harmony in Zanzibar* (Memoirs). Dubai.

Becker, Felicitas (2008), *Becoming Muslim in Mainland Tanzania, 1890–2000*, Oxford: Oxford University Press.

Becker, Felicitas (2006), 'Rural Islamism during the "War on Terror": A Tanzanian Case Study', *African Affairs* 105(421), pp. 583–603.

Bissel, William C. and M.-A. Fouere (eds) (2018), *Social Memory, Silenced Voices, and Political Struggle*, Dar es Salaam: Mkuki na Nyota.

Brennan, James (2012), *Taifa: Making Nation and Race in Urban Tanzania*, Athens: Ohio University Press.

Brennan, James (2008), 'Lowering the Sultan's Flag: Sovereignty and Decolonization in Coastal Kenya', *Comparative Studies in Society and History* 50(4), pp. 831–61.

Brenner, Louis (1993), *Muslim Identity and Social Change in Africa*, London: Hurst.

Clayton, Anthony (1981), *The Zanzibar Revolution and its Aftermath*, London: Hurst.

Cruse O'Brien, Donal B. (1995), 'Coping with the Christians: The Muslim Predicament in Kenya', in Holger Bernt Hansen and Michael Twaddle (eds), *Religion and Politics in East Africa: The Period since Independence*, London: James Currey.

Eickelman, Dale F. and James P. Piscatori (eds) (1996), *Muslim Politics*, Princeton, NJ: Princeton University Press.

Ekemode, Gabriel Ogunniyi (1973), 'German Rule in North-East Tanzania, 1885–1914', PhD thesis, School of Oriental & African Studies, University of London.

Fouere, Marie Aude (ed.) (2015), *Remembering Julius Nyerere in Tanzania: History, Memory, Legacy*, Dar es Salaam: Mkuki na Nyota.

Gilsaa, Soren (2012), 'Muslim Politics in Tanzania: Muslim and National Identities before and after the Collapse of Ujamaa', PhD thesis, Centre of African Studies and Department of Political Science, University of Copenhagen.

Glassman, Jonathon (2011), *War of Words, War of Stones: Racial Thought and Violence in Colonial Zanzibar*, Bloomington: Indiana University Press.

Goodman, Zoe (2017), 'Tales of the Everyday City: Geography and Chronology in Postcolonial Mombasa', PhD thesis, School of Oriental & African Studies, University of London.

Hashim, Abdulkadir (2012), 'Shaping of the Sharia Courts: British Policies on Transforming the *Kadhi* Courts In Colonial Zanzibar', *Social Dynamics* 38(3), pp. 381–97.

Hashim, Abdulkadir (2021), 'Application of Muslim Personal Law in the Kenyan Courts: Problems and Prospects', *Islamic Africa* 11(2), pp. 208–31.

Hillewaert, Sarah (2020), *Morality at the Margins: Youth, Language, and Islam in Coastal Kenya*, New York: Fordham University Press.

Hirsch, Susan F. (1998), *Pronouncing & Persevering: Gender and the Discourses of Disputing in an African Islamic Court*, Language and Legal Discourse series, ed. William M. O'Barr and John M. Conley, Chicago: University of Chicago Press.

Hirsch, Susan F. (2010), 'State Intervention in Muslim Family in Kenya and Tanzania: Applications of the Gender Concept', in Shamil Jeppie, Ebrahim Moose and Richard Roberts (eds), *Muslim Family Law in Sub-Saharan Africa: Colonial Legacies and Post-Colonial Challenges*, Amsterdam: Amsterdam University Press, pp. 305–29.

Horton, Mark and John Middleton (2000), *The Swahili: The Social Landscape of a Mercantile Society*, Oxford: Blackwell.

Iliffe, John (1979), *A Modern History of Tanganyika*, Cambridge: Cambridge University Press.

Kresse, Kai (2007), *Philosophising in Mombasa. Knowledge, Islam and Intellectual Practice on the Swahili Coast*, Edinburgh: Edinburgh University Press (for the International African Institute, London).

Kresse, Kai (2018), *Swahili Muslim Publics and Postcolonial Experience*, Bloomington: Indiana University Press.

Kresse, Kai (2006), 'Debating *maulidi*: Ambiguities and Transformations of Muslim Identity along the Kenyan Swahili Coast', in Roman Loimeier and Rüdiger Seesemann (eds), *The Global Worlds of the Swahili: Interfaces of Islam, Identity and Space in 19th and 20th-Century East Africa*, Berlin: Lit Verlag, pp. 209–28.

Kresse, Kai (2009), 'Muslim Politics in Postcolonial Kenya: Negotiating Knowledge on the Double-Periphery', *Journal of the Royal Anthropological Institute*, n.s., 15, pp. 76–94.

Kunyuk, Tito (2018), 'The Need for a Substantive Fatwa Institution in Countering Violent Extremism in Kenya', in M. Christian Green, T. Jeremy Gunn and Mark Hill (eds), *Religion, Law, and Security in Africa* 5, pp. 147–61, https://www.jstor.org/stable/j.ctv21ptz2w.14

Lofchie, Michael F. (1965), *Zanzibar: Background to Revolution*, Princeton, NJ: Princeton University Press.

Loimeier, Roman (2009), *Between Social Skills and Marketable Skills: The Politics of Islamic Education in 20th Century Zanzibar*, Leiden: Brill.

Loimeier, Roman (2007), 'Perceptions of Marginalization: Muslims in Contemporary Tanzania', in B. F. Soares and R. Otayek (eds), *Islam and Muslim Politics in Africa*, New York: Palgrave Macmillan, pp. 137–56.

Mapuri, Omar R. (1996), *Zanzibar: The 1964 Revolution: Achievements and Prospects*, Dar es Salaam: Tema.

Mbembe, Achille (2001), *On the Postcolony*, Berkeley: University of California Press.

McIntosh, Janet (2009), *The Edge of Islam: Power, Personhood, and Ethnoreligious Boundaries on the Kenya Coast*, Durham, NC: Duke University Press.

Meinema, Erik (2021), 'Regulating Religious Coexistence: The Intricacies of "Interfaith" Cooperation in Coastal Kenya', PhD thesis, Utrecht University, The Netherlands.

Mwakimako, H. and Willis, J. (2016), 'Islam and Democracy: Debating Electoral Involvement on the Kenya Coast', *Islamic Africa* 7(1), pp. 19–43.

Myers, Garth A. (2000), 'Narrative Representations of Revolutionary Zanzibar', *Journal of Historical Geography* 26(3), pp. 429–48.

Nassir, Abdilahi (2008), 'Kenyan Muslims and the Righting of Historical Injustices: The Case of Mwambao', lecture given at ZMO, Berlin, July 2008, forthcoming as ZMO online publication, https://www.zmo.de/en/publications

Ndzovu, Hassan (2014), *Muslims in Kenyan Politics: Political Involvement, Marginalization, and Minority Status*, Evanston, IL: Northwestern University Press.

Nieber, Hanna (2020), 'Drinking the Written Qur'an: Healing with Kombe in Zanzibar Town', PhD thesis, Utrecht University, The Netherlands.

Njozi, Hamza M. (2001), *The Mwembechai Killings and the Political Future of Tanzania*, Ottawa: Globalink Communications.

Njozi, Hamza M. (2003), *Muslims and the State in Tanzania*, Dar es Salaam: Dar es Salaam University Muslim Trusteeship.

Oded, Arye (2000), *Islam and Politics in Kenya*, London: Lynne Rienner.

Petterson, Don (2002), *Revolution in Zanzibar: An American's Cold War Tale*, Boulder, CO: Westview Press.

Prestholdt, Jeremy (2011), 'Kenya, the United States, and Counterterrorism', *Africa Today* 57(4), pp. 2–27.

Prestholdt, Jeremy (2014), 'Politics of the Soil: Separatism, Autochtony, and Decolonization at the Kenyan Coast', *Journal of African History* 55, pp. 249–70.

Purpura, Allyson (1997), 'Knowledge and Agency. The Social Relations of Islamic Expertise in Zanzibar Town', PhD thesis, City University of New York.

Said, Mohamed (1998), *The Life and Times of Abdulwahid Sykes*, London: Minerva.

Salim, Ahmed I. (1970), 'The Movement for "Mwambao" or Coast Autonomy in Kenya, 1956–1963', in B. A. Ogot (ed.), *Hadith 2*, Nairobi: East African Publishing House, pp. 212–28.

Salim, Ahmed I. (1972), 'Early Arab-Swahili Political Protest in Colonial Kenya', in B. A. Ogot (ed.), *Politics and Nationalism in Colonial Kenya*, Nairobi: East African Publishing House, pp. 71–84.

Seesemann, Rüdiger (2007), 'Kenyan Muslims, the Aftermath of 9/11, and the "War on Terror"', in B. F. Soares and R. Otayek (eds), *Islam and Muslim Politics in Africa*, New York: Palgrave Macmillan, pp. 156–76.

Shivji, Issa G. (2008), *Pan-Africanism or Pragmatism? Lessons of Tanganyika–Zanzibar Union*, Dar es Salaam: Mkuki na Nyota (in association with Organisation for Social Science Research in Eastern and Southern Africa).

Stiles, Erin E. (2009), *An Islamic Court in Context: An Ethnographic Study of Judicial Reasoning*, New York: Palgrave Macmillan.

Stiles, Erin E. (2014), 'The Right to Marry: Daughters and Elders in the Islamic Courts of Zanzibar', *Islamic Law and Society* 21(3), pp. 252–75.

Stiles, Erin E. (2015), 'An Unsuitable Husband: Allegations of Impotence in Zanzibar', in E. E. Stiles and K. D. Thompson (eds), *Gendered Lives in the Western Indian Ocean: Islam, Marriage, and Sexuality on the Swahili Coast*, Athens: Ohio University Press, pp. 245–68.

Stiles, Erin E. (2018), 'How to Manage a Marital Dispute: Legal Pluralism from the Ground Up', University of California, *Irvine Law Review* 8, pp. 101–22.

Stiles, Erin E. and Ayang Utriza Yakin (eds) (2022), *Islamic Divorce in the Twenty-first Century: A Global Perspective*, New Brunswick, NJ: Rutgers University Press.

Topan, Farouk (2009), 'Towards a Paradigm of Swahili Religious Knowledge. Some Observations', in Kjersti Larsen (ed.), *Knowledge, Renewal and Religion: Repositioning and Changing Ideological and Material Circumstances among the Swahili on the East African Coast*, Uppsala: Nordiska Afrikainstitutet, pp. 57–68.

Weitzberg, Keren (2017), *We Do Not Have Borders: Greater Somalia and the Predicaments of Belonging in Kenya*, Athens: Ohio University Press.

Westerlund, David (1980), *Ujamaa Na Dini: Study of Some Aspects of Society and Religion in Tanzania, 1961–77*, Stockholm Studies in Comparative Religion, Stockholm: Almquist & Wiksell.

Westerlund, D. and E. E. Rosander (eds) (1997), *African Islam and Islam in Africa*. London: Hurst.

Wijsen, F. and P.T. Mosha (2020), 'BAKWATA Is Like a Dead Spirit to Oppress Muslims', *Utafiti* 14(2), pp. 223–41. doi: https://doi.org/10.1163/26836408-14010013

Willis, J. and N. Chome (2014), 'Marginalization and Political Participation on the Kenya Coast: The 2013 Elections', *Journal of Eastern African Studies* 8(1), pp. 115–34.

Willis, J. and G. Gona (2013), 'Pwani si Kenya? Memory, Documents and Secessionist Politics in Coastal Kenya', *African Affairs* 112(446), pp. 48–71. doi:10.1093/afraf/ads064.

Wilson, Amrit (1989), *US Foreign Policy and Revolution: The Creation of Tanzania*, London: Pluto Press.

Part I

Politics

I

An Islamic Interpretive Strategy for Exploring Grassroots Governance in Northern Kenya

Mark LeVine

When I was first invited to the workshop that gave rise to this volume, it was hard for me to find a narrative that could adequately address the numerous complexities involved in governance in the public interest in Muslim societies. This applies particularly to those in East Africa, where Islam coexists in an uneasy balancing act with other religions and sects within it, and various forms and practices of governance converge that routinely violate not only core Islamic precepts of good governance and ethics, but universal human, civil and social rights as well. The inherent difficulty in engaging this narrative becomes clear when we disaggregate the title into its constituent terms: 'governance', 'Islam', 'East Africa', 'Muslims' and, last but certainly not least troublesome, the 'State'.

All these terms have histories and connotations that remain under often intense debate. Even if we put aside centuries of religious polemics, Orientalism, and now Islamophobic attacks against Islam, what 'Islam' means to those within the community of faith – who is a 'Muslim', what constitutes proper Islamic belief, behaviour, values and culture – are questions that continue to occupy Muslims at all levels, from Detroit to Dakar, Malmö to Mombasa, from religious scholars to lay women and men. Indeed, who is a 'Muslim' is a question that still too often produces violent and tragic consequences within and between Muslim societies.

East Africa, home to some seventy million Muslims for well over half a millennium if not longer, is, like all 'areas studies' regions, a product of imperial and Cold War histories, cartographies, wars and epistemologies that can often overwhelm the actual shared histories and cultures of this part of Africa. In fact, Islam's history in East Africa dates from well before the 14th century (it first appeared along the coast around 800 CE, within years of the rise of the Ummayad caliphate), by which point travellers such as Ibn Battuta painted vivid portraits of an almost entirely Muslim East African coastline, with Arabic as a lingua franca of the region. Yet rather than Arabise East African cultures and politics, it is more accurate to say that the large Arab populations that migrated through and came to live across the region were 'swahilised', as Islam became an indigenous East African religion and culture (Lodhi 1994).

As for 'governance', the term has become one of the centrepieces of contemporary development and donor discourses. Defining which of the myriad regulatory, legal, discursive and communal structures through which social norms, institutions and power are produced and distributed throughout a society properly fall under the rubric of 'governance' is a far from objective task, depending on what larger religion, culture, society or type of government is under consideration (or imagined by those writing about them). No element of this larger matrix of factors is more charged than 'religion' itself, which has long been a contributing factor to larger structures of governance in either negative and/or positive ways depending on the issues(s) and broader political system within which it exists.

Particularly with an orthopraxic religion like Islam in which, unlike in Judaism, creed and dogma have been deeply imbricated by political and even imperial power for most of the last millennium and a half, the religious and political spheres are not really separable even if, as we will see in northern Kenya, there is no official connection between them. The 'captivating picture' (Asad 2015, quoting Wittgenstein) of religion as a separate sphere of social life, removed from the domain of 'secular' political and economic power, cannot account for the far messier realities on the ground. A phenomenological view of religion that is at the same time performative and praxic is necessary for any meaningful understanding of social Islam to emerge. If 'we live in a society that is very fluid', as Azim Nanji, Special Advisor to the Aga Khan University Provost, mentioned in the January 2018 Nairobi workshop where contributions to this volume were first discussed (Aga Khan University 2018), describes it, then almost all aspects of Islamic life and institutions are going to be fluid, changing and sometimes chaotic as well.

This brings us to perhaps the most fraught term in this discussion: the state. Just how to define and analyse the communities of people whose exercise of political power and monopoly on violence enable them to mould people into an ordered 'polis' (as Aristotle put it in his *Politics*) remains intensely debated within and across different disciplines, political affiliations and societies more broadly. Even Islam's earliest political document, the 'Constitution of Medina' that united the various communities of Medina under Muhammad's leadership soon after the Hijra in 622 CE, was born out of a difference over who should govern and how governance should proceed.

Far closer to the present era, the diversity of East African political structures before 19th-century European colonisation resists any attempts to generalise them. Chieftaincies, matrilineal clans, feudal aristocracies, slave states and other configurations were all characterised by a general lack of boundaries between the natural and spiritual worlds. The British attempted to impose more uniform, colonial forms of governance, which saw the resulting (post- or neo-) colonial states cycling through various forms of political power – what Foucault has described as 'pastoral', 'sovereign', 'disciplinary' and 'bio' – which, while emerging over the course of half a millennium in Europe, were concentrated in the course of a few decades in colonial East Africa as in the rest of the colonised world. When independence in equatorial East Africa was achieved in the early 1960s after almost three quarters of a century of (mostly) British rule, the post-colonial states were handicapped and stunted from the start by the willing adoption by their leaders of the same divide, rule and extract policies of the former imperial powers, who did everything possible to ensure that their post-colonial relations remained similarly exploitative and undemocratic.

Indeed – and this is crucial for the larger analysis I will present – even after independence and well into post-colonial attempts to modernise society through more or less socialist political-economic systems, and through the neoliberal transitions since the 1980s, East African states, like their counterparts across the Global South, remained inherently colonial in their modes of operation and the manner in which power has been displayed and deployed, with citizens more often than not treated as little better than colonised subjects (cf. wa Th'iong'o 2018). This dynamic has been well explored within the field of Latin American decoloniality/modernity studies (cf. Dussel, Garcia-Canclini, Mignolo, Grosfoguel), as well as, to a lesser extent, in the Middle East (cf. LeVine 2005a, b); yet its application to Africa has remained the exception rather than rule. Even African scholars such as Mamdani (1996), Hountondji (1983, 2002) and Wiredu (1980, 1998), in their deep analyses of colonial and post-colonial states, did not apply such a methodology, focusing more on the literal 'decolonisation' process and its aftermath rather than on the ongoing discourses of coloniality. I argue that such a perspective is crucial to understanding why governance remains such a problematic endeavour to map and attempt to improve; why the nature of state power is so fluid and hard to pin down even in the most 'stable' states; and why the very sectors of society that are supposed to both rein in the state and help implement 'good governance' – civil society, the public sphere, and so on – are so prey to the kinds of ideologies, narratives and manipulation that render attempts at good governance moot.

One's particular methodological and theoretical orientation is important here. If one works through one of the various Marxist understandings of the state and state power, as organising and enforcing bourgeois supremacy and hegemony, or Weber's (1946) ideal-type of a state as 'a human community that (successfully) claims the monopoly of the legitimate use of physical force within a given territory' and inscribes that monopoly in law, or, drawing on Weberian concepts of legitimacy and domination, focuses on neo-patrimonial and neo-patriarchal discourses of state power (Eisenstadt 1973; Sharabi 1992), or, finally, focuses on the criminal nature of 'deep' and 'mafia' states (Horkheimer 1930; Tilly 1985), all of these approaches both help to elucidate and limit our ability to obtain a full picture of how state power translates into policy and impacts and shapes citizens in the act of governance. Finally, whether one subscribes either to the assumption in the 1970s and 1980s that the power and coherence of the state had been 'over-stated' or to the more recent drive in development discourses to 'bring the state back in' will profoundly impact where one assumes the locus of governance is and who the primary agents of the process are.

If Joel Migdal's (1989) differentiation of state/society types into 'strong' and 'weak' remains a foundational organising tool for analysing state power in the Global South, Africa in particular suffers from a predilection towards considering the Continent rife with both weak and, even, 'failing' or 'failed' states and societies. One way of addressing such characterisations is by developing more nuanced understandings of the nature of the state and the networks of power that flow through and from it. The work of Timothy Mitchell remains the foundation for such an effort. Building on the seminal work of Michel Foucault in *Discipline and Punish* and his 1970s lectures at the Collège de France, Mitchell (1991) argued for understanding the state not merely as a set of concrete institutions and actors but, equally and in some ways more importantly, as an 'effect of power': that is, the discursive product of relations of power and knowledge in which the boundaries between political authority and the polities such political authorities govern are both opaque and porous, permeable yet powerfully creative of the social relations that surround them. Rather than try to 'sharpen' the definition, Mitchell argues for seeing its elusive qualities as clues to its nature. The internally erected state–society boundaries become locations in which Mitchell can investigate the nature of modern forms of sovereign and disciplinary power, and are reflective of the broader dynamics of modern social order. In short, rather than seeing the state as a set of institutions or a 'human community' that acts with some coherence and mandate, Mitchell sees the state as a culmination of multifarious processes, as an 'effect' of a wider spectrum of power relations across society.

Viewed thus, what we understand to be a 'state' has coherence as long as it fulfils its strategic function of gathering, augmenting, redirecting and distributing power. Although Mitchell does not spend any time on it, Foucault's discussions of the raison d'état and coup d'état are quite important for understanding the nature and functioning of state systems and apparatuses. Specifically, in his *Psychiatric Power: Lectures at the Collège de France, 1973–74*, he argues that the coup d'état is central to the core rationality of the state, rather than being an aberration as it is normally viewed. Let us recall here that Foucault takes resistance to power as the starting point for any interrogation of its functioning, in which case we need to look at the more complex negotiations of power as it is being discharged by various locations and conglomerations of power holders. As I explain in detail below, the contest today becomes more clearly over who literally are the members of the community with the power to 'bind and loose' – *ahl al-hall wa-l-'aqd*: that is, who is qualified to appoint or depose a ruler on behalf of the Muslim community. For most patrimonial/authoritarian/praetorian/sultanic/ totalitarian regimes, that would be the army or security services of some sort. However, for those risking everything in the streets of Cairo, Tunis, Sanaa, Manama or other locations, it is no one but *ash-sha'ab* – the people.

This more sophisticated and accurate view requires, however, the re-imagining of the boundaries between state and society, political and civil societies, political and public spheres. Like the state, the borders or limits of these arenas are effects of the types and specificities of the power relations, truth regimes and disciplinary apparatuses behind them. In that regard, Mitchell's analysis proved far more nuanced, and possessed far greater explanatory power, than either theories attempting to get rid of the state altogether as a useful analytical concept or the subsequent attempts to 'bring the state back in' to scholarly analysis of political processes.

Yet despite the clear utility of Mitchell's analysis for Africa or the Middle East, few scholars have taken up his analysis as a starting point for exploring the nature and dynamics of the state in the region. The state in all its messiness, complexity and elusiveness, power and weakness, presence and absence, remains woefully under-theorised. This continues to be the case despite a decade of political upheaval that has challenged the very foundations of political and state power across the Arab world. From street protests to uprisings, revolutions to civil wars, changes of government to dissolution of polities, governance has been shaken and reformatted more or less inadequately across the MENA region since late 2010. These events are rooted in long-standing neoliberal transformations going back nearly half a century. Neoliberalism is only one way in which power has been transformed during this period, forging new networks, conduits, subjects and discourses along the way. Many other dynamics, from new technologies to older patterns of public religiosity, have also played an important role. Pastoral, sovereign and disciplinary power, analytically disaggregated by Foucault, have often seemed to be squeezed together as if in a fusion reaction, with large swathes of citizens falling into precisely the states of exception, as Agamben describes it, that modern governmentality normally renders inefficient. Moreover, space and the spatial dynamics of power and its circulation have become more important analytically at the very moment space and time have been ever more compressed experientially.

As Angela Joya demonstrates (2020), concomitant with the focus on authoritarianism is the focus on democratisation, or the lack thereof in the region (the so-called 'democracy deficit'). The reasons attributed to the broad failures of democratisation include 'authoritarianism' in its many variations, in particular its perceived qualities of 'resilience', 'persistence' 'rebound' and 'upgrading'. More sophisticated and less ideologically biased analysis has moved away from asking why the states have not succeeded in becoming democratic to ask why they remain unable even to initiate such a process in any meaningful sense. The 'uniquely robust coercive apparatuses' (as Bellin 2004 describes them) have become so strong that even the act of change itself becomes 'change for stability'.

What happens when the 'state effect' essentially 'wears off' or at least thins out and loses its holding power as some sort of political 'earthquake' shakes loose the ties that bind most members of the society to it? Similarly, what happens when processes, such as those of neoliberalism, powerfully disrupt existing political as well as economic networks? When do new conglomerations of power start to take on attributes of the state, especially when they explicitly reject existing notions of political responsibility? When we also consider Tilly's understanding of states as essentially mafias or other criminal organisations, the implications of Mitchell's more amorphous and deliberately hazy narratives of the state become clear.

I would like to end this discussion of terminology by pointing out the potential role of the author in any attempt to analyse governance. In my case, that has happened to me as a foreign researcher with access to significant funds to come to East Africa, and especially Northern Turkana, and study the role of artistic production, distribution and consumption in the effectiveness of governance programmes. My own presence, and discussions with local arts producers as well as community and even government officials, becomes part of the broader local discussions on governance, and helps re-shape, however subtly, the local dynamics and debates.

People 'Power': Those who Loose and Bind

In late 2019, an unprecedented wave of protests in Sudan removed not only the long-ruling dictator, Omar Bachir, but, only one day later, the head of the armed forces who led the coup against him. Suddenly, after over half a decade in which we were told that large-scale non-violent protests, people power, could not succeed in toppling long-entrenched states or 'systems' of rule, the Sudanese 'people' did just that, and in so doing were joined by that of Africa's largest country, Algeria, whose people also forced its long-serving dictator from power in 2019. These events bring back memories of the two great African revolutionary upheavals that began the last decade – Tunisia beginning in late 2010 and Egypt in early 2011 – where chants of 'the people want the downfall of the regime' actually produced a revolutionary transformation in state power in both countries. Experiencing the Egyptian uprising first-hand and attempting to analyse it in the context of Mitchell's and Foucault's understanding of the state at the time helped me to understand how states function as political capacitors or transformers, or like hubs in a many-spoked wheel, as power flows in, through and out of the central hubs – the core of the 'state' – as directed by both the individuals at the leadership level of the state and the institutions – parties, bureaucracies, military, intelligence and/or security services, and seemingly 'privatised' companies controlled by state military and/or political elites.

And yet, just as occurred in every other Arab country, including Tunisia, the move toward greater democracy was soon thwarted by the imposition of military rule, and in Sudan's case, a return to civil war in 2023. Until quite recently the production of knowledge about African politics and societies has been dominated by European scholars working within Eurocentred if not Eurocentric epistemology and methodological groundings. Yet however problematic scholarship on Africa has been, the reality of African politics has been little better, as the continent has long known some of the weakest types of state system precisely because of centralising elites' inability to redistribute power in a way that maintains the hegemony of the state across the national territory and the distribution of power and wealth and loyalty across it in a sustainable manner that incorporates the widest cross-section of often ethnically, religiously and otherwise divided societies. In this regard, the 'effect' of state power is strong when it can maintain coherence and legitimacy/hegemony, and encourage a widespread level of both common identity and development without high levels of violence against various sections of the populations living within its borders.

This understanding of state power led me directly to one of the most fundamental but least discussed notions about the state and state power in Islamic political discourse: the concept of *ahl al-hall wa-l-'aqd*, known in English as 'those who loosen and bind' (literal meaning: 'the people of solving problems and making contracts'). Although the concept is rooted in Jewish and then Christian ideology concerning the authority to determine what is permissible or not (cf. Psalm XX, Matthew 6:19, Acts 2: 14–40), it was more immediately drawn from one of the most important verses in the Qur'an (4:59). Specifically, *ahl al-hall wa-l-'aqd* is a term that was fairly well used in medieval Islamic political discourse by jurists such as ibn Taymiyya and al-Juwayni to refer to members of the religious and the political elite in a society who were tasked with selecting and, when necessary, deposing a ruler. Also known as *ahl al-ikhtiyar* (the people who choose, or electors – i.e. of the next imam or leader), the *ahl al-hall wa-l-'aqd* were those who possessed the 'might' – that is, the *shawka*, power and authority – to ensure that their choices would be accepted most widely by the whole community and in so doing ensure stability as well as effective rule.

There is a historical arc to the understanding of who constitutes the *ahl al-hall wa-l-'aqd* and the nature and extent of their power and responsibility. As the great Muslim empires were consolidated, the dominant view among Sunni ulama (scholars) was that, rather than a fairly large and representative body of the elite, as few as one qualified person (such as a *mujtahid*, or senior jurist, or the present imam himself) could legitimately choose a new imam or leader (cf. al-Mawardi). However, ibn Taymiyya thought that there needed to be a larger group of people, the *al-shawka* – that is, people without whom he would lack the authority, but also the power, necessary for effective governance – involved in choosing and advising a ruler (see his Minhāj, 1:365–6).

The question remains, whether in the classical era or today, as to who has the power to 'bind and loose' the highest level of political authority. Not surprisingly, women, ordinary people, non-Muslims and slaves were rarely counted among the *al-shawka* and thus the *ahl al-ḥall wa-l-'aqd* (cf. al-Juwaynī, 62, no. 73). But in the modern era, the *ahl al-ḥall wa-l-'aqd* came to take on particular significance, related to the expanded meaning of shura or consultation, related in turn to the spread of the idea of democracy in Islamic thought. This begins with the Tunisian jurist Khayr al-Din al-Tunisi, who likened the concept to that of a European-style parliamentary assembly. The great Egyptian moderniser Muhammad Abduh and his disciple Rashid Rida furthered this notion, and expanded the kinds of people who possessed the *shawka* to be part of the *ahl al-hal wa-l-'aqd*, to include businessmen and others, such as journalists, to whom the mass of people would turn when considering what was in the common interest (*maslaha al-'am*). Similarly, the *ahl*'s power increased to the point where the ruler would be bound by its members' decisions even when he opposed them and where, for all practical purposes, the concept itself demanded some sort of democratic form of governance based on the sovereignty of the people (cf. Crone 2001; Bowering 2015).

The *Ahl al-hall wa-l-'aqd* and Local Governance: The Case of Turkana

My interest in bringing the concept of the *ahl al-hall wa-l-'aqd* into this discussion is not to lay the groundwork for an analysis of governance at the level of the state in a country like Kenya or even Nigeria, where Muslims constitute 10 and 50 per cent of the population respectively. Rather, my goal is to understand how this concept can be deployed by scholars to understand governance at the local level in Muslim communities in these countries, and, at the same time, to explore how local community leaders themselves understand and potentially utilise the concept. For my case study I will explore the local Muslim community in the city of Lodwar, the capital of Turkana State, which is home to around 20,000 Muslims, the vast majority of whom migrated into the area (many from Uganda and other neighbouring countries) in the last thirty years. I focus particularly on the Islamic Centre of Lodwar, a local organisation that is the primary Muslim community organisation in Lodwar and for the Turkana region, and both offers both traditional religious services and sponsors broader projects and initiatives that benefit the local Muslim and wider Turkana communities. My information is drawn from two fieldwork trips to Turkana, in 2018 and 2019.

Islam has been present in East Africa for well over a millennium in some form, beginning with the coastal regions and moving towards the interior. Although coastal rulers did not send missionaries to the interior, trade and other mechanisms made Islam a known commodity throughout the region long before it had a well-established foothold, including a steady stream of converts over the centuries. But it was the conquest and consolidation of European power and rule in East Africa that broke open previously strong traditional religious bonds and networks, which in turn opened space not just for Christianity but also for Islam, which was already seen as a local religion. Throughout Kenya specifically (beyond the coastal and northern regions), Islam took strong root in the last decades of the 19th century through the first three decades of the 20th.

As Trimingham described it, this was the period when not just social structures but the larger worldview of local peoples were 'shattered', which opened space for a new, all-encompassing religious system to become attractive (Trimingham 1964). However, as in other parts of Africa, there were competing forms of Arab(ised) Islam – as part of networks linked to the Hadramaut, Oman, Sudan and so on – that became dominant rather than forms of the religion already indigenised in other parts of the continent. This would impact the way local ideas of governance evolved in more recent years. In particular, as revivalist movements and political Islam spread across Africa and the Middle East and the number of Muslims in Kenya began to rise, there was what Esposito terms an 'Islamic reassertion in public life', including more schools, religious courts and equality with Christians in terms of allocations of budgets (Esposito 1999).

In the last decade, this dynamic has become more acute as the Muslim population has both surged and done so in the context of growing violence and terrorism. Even though Christians make up approximately 80 per cent of the country's population, Muslim Kenyans are becoming far more active in both politics and civil society, with the number of mosques and schools mushrooming across the country. This growth has led many Christians, including faith leaders, to worry about the 'menace' of Islam, a sentiment that obviously strengthened with mass terrorist attacks like that at the Westgate Mall in 2013 (Zirulnick 2013). But the attack only highlighted the broader inter-religious tensions, which have included tit-for-tat killings of religious leaders on each side in the last decade.

Not surprisingly, such tensions have been a major focus of the main umbrella organisation of Kenyan Muslims: the Supreme Council of Kenya Muslims. Known by the acronym SUPKEM and founded in 1973, its goal from the start was to 'improv[e] the welfare of Kenya Muslims [through] a clear vision of uniting and therefore strengthening the Muslim Community in the country'. Even as SUPKEM has sought both to define a moderate Kenyan Islam and point out the lack of development and resources available to the Muslim community (particularly outside the main cities in 'low-potential' areas), its activities have not reached all the way north; in discussions with local Muslim organisations and networks in Turkana, it is clear that they do not have significant regular contact with SUPKEM – or the Kenyan central government, for that matter (Naado 2015).

Devolution and Local Muslim Governance in Turkana

Governance in Kenya in the decades after independence in 1963 had long been heavily centralised, which added to the level of corruption and mismanagement that has always characterised the local political system. In part to address these concerns, a process of 'devolution' was begun in 2010 that moved power to the country's forty-seven counties, giving them more control over their budgets, resources and development. As the Danish Refugee Council defined it in a 2015 study, devolution 'involves the creation of two or more levels of government that are co-ordinated, but not subordinate to each other. Each is protected by the Constitution, with the functions and resources set out and defined by the Constitution. The system combines self-governance and shared governance at the local and national levels, respectively' (Hall 2015: 9).

At least officially, devolution brought a lot more money to the poorest regions in the country, or at least to county governments. The Governor of Turkana put it this way: 'In Turkana County, devolution is viewed as a blessing for the forgotten people of Turkana. Devolution has been received in the sub-counties with much appreciation due to its direct benefits to the citizens. The current administration shares out these benefits equally to all sub-counties in addition to enhancing citizen participation in development activities' (Turkana County Government 2017).

According to the United Nations Development Programme (UNDP), Turkana County was particularly empowered because of its high budget-to-population ratio, which made it the third 'wealthiest' county in terms of funds allocated per capita. That money was supposed to go to things like water, irrigation and agriculture, holistic development focused in part on gender, developing energy, resources and tourism, developing governance in areas from sanitation and health to finance, and similar priorities (UNDP Kenya n.d.). However, several factors militated against a successful implementation of the programme. First, devolution also led to an upsurge in ethnic tension as the various counties were dominated by certain tribal, ethnic or religious communities that now saw themselves pitted in a potentially zero-sum game for resources. Second, in the Lodwar region of Turkana and the arid pastoral areas that surround it, corruption and the rise of the oil sector have meant that wealth has been concentrated locally rather than dispersed and disbursed in a representative manner.

Indeed, even as the region was by 2018 awash in money, a years-long drought and the corruption and incompetence of the county government meant that hunger was at extremely high levels, with local residents actually dying of hunger and hunger-related health complications on the rise across Turkana in 2019; so much so that the government, supposedly flush with money, had to ask aid agencies for help (Gulleid 2019). In the south of the country, these levels of poverty and marginalisation clearly contributed to a rise in sympathy for jihadi violence by Muslim youth. That has yet to happen in Turkana, but it certainly could, and it will take significant efforts from local leaders to prevent it (BBC 2012).

In southern Kenya, groups like the Coast Interfaith Council of Clerics, or CICC, comprising 2,000 religious leaders, became something of a firewall against an explosion of inter-communal hostilities even after major terrorist attacks. As with SUPKEM, these kinds of groups are not so publicly present in the north, yet they have not been as needed in the region, given the lack of attacks. Similarly, Christian leaders have not had to play the role of moderators between the Muslim community and the government as they have in the south. Rather, in Turkana, the overall population – and the Muslim percentage within it – is still too small and the needs of residents more broadly too great for such concerns to dominate the public sphere.

Ungovernable Life

Indeed, such are the social and economic conditions of life in Turkana that the region has long been, at best, barely governable. Like Morocco's *blad as-siba*, or 'land of dissidences', or Pakistan's Northwest Frontier Province and tribal areas (and, more or less, the whole of Afghanistan), Kenya's tribal north has rarely been governed in any meaningful way by the central government. One statistic demonstrates the reality and impact of this lack of governance: poverty in Turkana affects well above 90 per cent of the population, more than double the 45 per cent poverty level for the country as a whole, and this in one of the country's most sparsely populated areas with plentiful natural resources.

Devolution offered a chance, finally, for the region's citizens officially to govern themselves. Instead, however, during the last decade the level of ungovernability has only increased, even as more money has entered the local economy through devolution and the beginning of the oil industry, as Kenya continued to experience 'multiple, overlapping conflicts, which sometimes coincide with electoral cycles that act as triggers for politically motivated violence' (Rohwerder 2015: 3).

Years of drought, along with the widespread availability of automatic weapons, have meant that cattle-raiding, which has always been part of the traditional ecosystem, has become much more violent and indeed has reached an 'industrial' scale, as hundreds of cattle are sometimes take in one raid. Second, oil has severely disrupted the local political economy, not at all positively thus far, and the promises of large riches being widely distributed among some of Africa's poorest communities have remained largely undelivered (which is not surprising). Moreover, the devolution that did occur was from a corrupt centralised system to a corrupt regional and local one. Accountability, never mind governance, did not improve; the people continue to have to fend, largely, for themselves. These dynamics occurred in a time of increasing environmental and in turn social stress. This has inevitably produced increased conflict and violence, as has occurred in so many other resource-rich 'developing' countries without the promised jobs and investment (Agade 2014). Indeed, in mid-2019 the government of Turkana County sued the national government, claiming it had entered into secret contracts with Tullow Oil without community or local government approval or any involvement at all. As the backroom dealing continued, Lake Turkana was put on the World Heritage danger list – where it remains.

In sum, Turkana, and Lodwar in particular, exist in a strange and contradictory space. There is more power and wealth locally than ever before, but most of it is siphoned off by corrupt local officials after the national ones have taken their share. There is not the level of inter-religious hostility and suspicion as in the southern and eastern part of the country; nor is there a desire for 'separate but equal' accommodations for Muslims as has occurred in more heavily populated regions, and there is more of a general sensibility that the two communities will get along fine as long as there is no outside interference. However, because of the smaller and sparser population and its attendant lack of a thick civil society, there is also more of a need and opportunity for self-governance by various communities.

In this situation, the actions of the major Muslim organisations such as SUPKEM did little to change the dynamics in Turkana or the country more broadly. 'We have been engaging the government of Kenya from different levels, trying to encourage and change … policies', was how Hassan Ole Naado put it in a 2015 discussion at the Berkley Center (Naado 2015). But how could they engage a government that was so corrupt and against which they had so little power to mobilise support? More relevant was the desire to 'use the media or ... human relations at the community level' to build trust and a working relationship at the level of local and even self-governance (ibid.). However, the idea of focusing on long-ignored areas of 'low potential' for modernisation and relying on the World Bank and similar organisations to develop them is not a strategy that will enable significant self-governance soon.

Moreover, there is little in their policy goals that demonstrates a realisation of the importance of incorporating culture into planning or of focusing on such grassroots efforts, a problem also faced by larger organisations such as the Kenya Muslims Charitable Society and the more locally rooted Turkana Dawaa Muslims Organisation. Its Facebook page, which is one of the primary ways it would communicate through social media, was not updated between May 2014 and May 2018, while in May 2019 the previous General Secretary of SUPKEM, Adan Wachu, had only forty-six Twitter followers (cf. SUPKUM 2015; also see the website for the Kenya Muslim Charitable Society and of the Facebook page of the Turkana Daawah Muslims).

Building a Community in a New Land: The Islamic Centre in Lodwar

Turkana might be home to some of the earliest humans, but the town of Lodwar was only established in 1933, when a Muslim trader named Shah Mohammed established a trading post in a then remote and roadless part of north-western Kenya. It slowly became the economic as well as the administrative centre for the Turkana region during the colonial era (the country's first president, Jomo Kenyatta, spent two years under house arrest here), and remained so after independence. While mostly catering to the local (and often belligerent) pastoral tribal population, Turkana's economic importance grew as tourism became important within Kenya (Lake Turkana is one of the largest salt lakes in the world and is home to many species of animal life), partly due to the discovery of some of the most ancient proto-human remains yet known.

Over the years, Lodwar's population has grown to about 60,000 people, while the county population rose to 855,000, still leaving it among the most sparsely populated in Kenya. In the 2015 development plan for the county, put forth by the county government, the governor declared, 'It is the policy of my government to enhance the welfare of the people of Turkana County and get them on track in the long, yet worthwhile, journey towards self-reliance by the turn of the decade' (Turkana Community Investment Plan 2015). Yet Turkana remains the poorest county in Kenya. Even after a significant upturn in its government revenue with devolution, and investment from the International

Finance Corporation (the lending arm of the World Bank), and the beginning of the oil industry, it is clear that little of the larger flow of cash into the county is reaching the poorest residents.

In a country wracked by massive long-term and endemic problems with governance at the central, regional and even local levels of the state, it is not surprising that non-state actors within communities would play an important role in shaping and maintaining communities and advocating for their interests. The Muslim community of Lodwar offers a powerful case study in how a local, recently established, minority community creates conditions for self-governance in order to grow and provide services that the state is unwilling and/or unable to do for them. Although Islam has existed in East Africa for centuries, it was never a major presence in Turkana until about forty years ago, when a community gradually formed, comprising traders and forced migrants from neighbouring Uganda, after the overthrow of Idi Amin in 1979 led to a backlash against that country's more established Muslim community (whose long history of trade with nearby areas meant Turkana was not unknown).

Almost as soon as the community was established, the Islamic Centre of Lodwar was created, in 1980, on land owned by a prominent community member. Al-Haj Salim Naida, the current head of the Centre and one of the leaders of the community today who grew up in the then still new environs of the centre, explained during my second fieldwork visit in May 2019 that the community developed relatively rapidly after the Centre's founding, both through increased migration and, even more so, through conversion. Organisationally, the Islamic Centre was funded initially and primarily through the al-Momin Foundation, a Nairobi-based Islamic trust (in its words, a 'locally registered NGO'), whose primary area of operation according to its Facebook page is situated in 'remote parts of Kenya, running orphan homes, schools with integrated madrassa syllabus, *masajid* [mosques]'. Al-Momin has established over half a dozen Islamic Centres across Kenya, most of them either in the Nairobi area or Turkana (al-Momin administers the capital's biggest mosque, the Jamia Mosque).

Despite being a nation-wide NGO, each of the centres established by al-Momin is governed and administered individually by local people who are almost all former students of the schools that are at the core of each Centre's operation and mission. In Lodwar, the Centre fulfils a broad range of functions. The first and most visible function is the mosque, Lodwar's second largest, which for Friday prayers and feast days can see more than two hundred worshippers. With its Moorish architecture, the mosque is one of the most noticeable buildings that catch one's eye when descending into Lodwar by air. But whereas the city's other major mosque, as well as its two other, smaller ones, are used almost exclusively for prayer, the Islamic Centre sees itself as more intrinsic to daily life – a school, after-school and sports centre, food distribution centre for the poorer members of the community during feast days, and so on. 'We are an institution; they are just mosques', explains the Centre's deputy director, Said Erot.

Indeed, the Centre houses an orphanage, two schools, and a rudimentary sports field, as well as some beautiful shade trees that are especially welcome in what remains today Kenya's, and one of the world's, hottest cities (determined by average daily temperature). The orphanage has approximately fifty-five children, more or less evenly divided between boys and girls (the exact number and gender ratio change as older students graduate to boarding schools for high school and new children move in). The orphans, most of whom come from very poor families in the town and its surroundings who cannot provide for their children, attend the Centre's private nursery and primary school that more or less follow the state curriculum. There is also a madrasa, or religious school, on site, that provides an Islamic education on weekends and holidays. Paying students from the community help subsidise the costs for those too poor to pay.

Aside from its religious, custodial and educational missions, the Islamic Centre also runs many activities for young people and the broader community. Its football team is among the strongest in the area and has produced several players good enough to be considered for the national youth team. One of Kenya's major rappers, Ibra, lived at the orphanage as a child. Delegations from Muslim countries as far away as Malaysia also visit the Centre and work with the children and the community.

In talking to members of the staff and looking at its Facebook page and tweets, the most important public activity the Centre routinely engages in is the distribution of food to Lodwar and surrounding Turkana communities, which, thanks to support from al-Momin and other groups can reach more than two hundred and fifty households during Ramadan. The activities are not limited to children and charity, however. There are also adult activities, including training for entrepreneurs and 'women's circles' that include everything from religious study to welfare and business training.

These activities would not sound out of place undertaken by one of the numerous churches (particularly Catholic churches, whose regional diocese is in Lodwar) that have a far longer and deeper presence in Lodwar and the Turkana region as a whole. However, despite its relative youth, the Islamic Centre has developed a sophisticated system of self-management and governance. As Al-Haj Naida tells it, 'Islam is still young here in Turkana. Right now we have about six hundred people in our community, but every day or week we have new people coming, many of them converts. Most of the converts are Catholics; we don't do *dawa*' among the tribespeople who are the most hungry. Most converts are Christian, they want to know about Islam, so we are setting foundations for the future, a moderate (Arabic: *wasatiya*) future. You can find other, more extreme, groups in Kenya, but we are teaching pure Islam and we don't allow them here.'

What is pure Islam? I asked during our third meeting, as we sat in the Centre's main office among student files, administrative flow charts and football trophies. 'That's the five pillars and the *mathahab*, or schools of law. Now, some people don't follow schools, they follow a particular sheikh or sheikhs, from Yemen, Somalia, etc. But they don't count here, because the religion is too new and the people don't have that level of sophistication to make those judgements. We aren't at that level. They're new converts so can't deal with that. If you start at that level of sophistication you confuse them. It's better to start simple.' Of course, even the most simple renditions of Islam – in fact, particularly the more simple renditions of any ideology – can be twisted or used to justify all kinds of beliefs and behaviours that betray its core principles. Al-Haj Naida understands this, and interjected before I could ask the question: 'How do we deal with misconceptions? Most people think violence and Islam are the same thing. In fact, Islam is pure but these violent people have their own agenda. Ash-shabab, Boko Haram and others, they're not fighting for Islam, they're fighting for resources, or they're being used to fight [for] other people's agendas.'

One might imagine that social media is a chief way in which the Islamic Centre of Lodwar spreads its message and informs its members and the broader public about events and goings on, but in reality its impact is somewhat limited. As of late 2023, the Centre's Facebook pages had around 5,700 likes. The Twitter account, @LodwarIslamicC, created in November 2017, had as of late 2023 around 1,600 followers, most of them local to Lodwar. While the Centre tweets regularly as well as posting to Facebook, it seems more locally focused than similar social media platforms would be for larger organisations.

Binding a Community

When I met Haj Amin and his associate at my hotel in Lodwar, our conversation quickly turned to what we had been working on since we last saw each other. I explained to him my research into the contemporary relevance of the *ahl al-hall wa-l-'aqd* and they nodded in agreement at the contemporary relevance of the term. While not ubiquitous in contemporary Muslim discussions on governance or related subjects, it clearly made sense in the context of a minority community trying to administer its own affairs in a situation where any relationship with the state was either fraught or not very relevant for its day-to-day functioning or planning. But we could not recall together in which specific Qur'anic verse the concept was most clearly grounded. As we entered the Centre's mosque, I picked up a Qur'an and skimmed through the first few chapters, remembering that it was most likely a verse, or *aya*, from Surat 4, 'an-Nisa' (The Women). Soon enough we arrived at the verse we both recognised as the most likely origin: The 'authority verse', 4:59: 'Obey Allah, obey the prophet and those charged with authority among you' (*awala'i al-'amri minkum*). Immediately, the question comes to the fore for us both not merely as to who precisely is 'in authority' but, just as important, who determines who is in authority.

This is a crucial question, not just in a larger political context at the level of the state and political system but at the community level as well. Who is in authority and how can communal decisions be made? In this regard, perhaps the most important component of the Islamic Centre's activities is the strong local control it enables and reflects on community activities. I would argue that this autonomy, which constitutes an important kind of 'self-governance', evolved out of necessity. As a relatively small if disproportionately impactful minority in Kenya, the Muslim community does not have the level of wealth, government connections and networks, and international funding to have created the more top-down, foreign-funded and centralised internal governmental structure within the community that exists in Nigeria, or Muslim-majority countries. In the context of the territorially, politically, socially and economically marginalised spaces of Turkana, a more centralised governance would not work.

As another member of the Centre's leadership explained as we drove to the nearby aquifer, which despite being utilised by the local community for generations is now off-limits and declared non-potable (at the time of writing the reality is that the water will likely be either sold to Tullow Oil to pump into its wells to push out the oil, or to other customers who will pay a premium), 'We wrote a letter to the Governor to ask for the budget for water, and to suggest a new [method of] water governance. We demanded more information from the government, but we don't even get a response.' This lack of engagement by the government of the local community extends to issues of land expropriation, in which politicians from outside Turkana came and bought land very cheaply from locals who had no conception of private property. They then sold it on to the government at a huge mark-up. Thus it turns out that politicians at all levels of the government are too riven with corruption to offer any stake or responsibility for governance to the community.

Specifically, while significant funding comes from the al-Momin Foundation and the Muslim community in Nairobi (and to a lesser extent, Mombasa) more broadly, the Islamic Centre of Lodwar more or less administers its own affairs when it comes to the mosque, the orphanage, the schools, activities, and providing food and other *zakat*, or charity, to the community. Here I would like to focus not on the mundane issues of school administration or disbursement of flour and other foodstuffs to the poorest members of the local community, but rather on two areas where, from my discussions with Muslim leaders in Lodwar, and particularly at the Islamic Centre, the community has developed clear policies to ensure its security and development: ensuring a 'moderate' version of Islam is taught to communities, and maintaining independence and distance from other, more mainstream, NGOs.

In that regard, the local Muslim community, like the remainder of the Turkana population, has been forced to collaborate and co-ordinate efforts to resist government and private pilfering of land and resources, placing common interests ahead of sectarian identities as a matter of survival. This stance is epitomised in the participation of the Centre leadership in the local inter-religious council, whose explicit goal is, according to its governing 'ten principles', to have the entire community 'speak with one voice'. Among the principles are no contributions from politicians to the council, to request all politicians come to Lodwar and meet with them in person and listen to their concerns, and, crucially, to act on behalf of the Lodwar community as a whole in fighting against local or national level government policies when necessary.

As Haj Amin argues, the council has taken on added importance 'because we can't always use civil society, since some of the people in civil society are part of the government and thus have divided loyalties'. Here we see the interesting reality of the principle of *ahl al-hall wa-l-'aqd* in a context where those in political 'authority' and 'power' are in fact quite removed from the community and where the community has to join together to 'loose' whatever power it can from corrupt elites and, to the extent possible, 'bind' it in a more grounded fashion. As much as it is successful, the Islamic Centre sees the inter-religious council as simply a platform, and it also goes to the sub-counties and towns in Turkana, and that places it in a position to more forcefully and collectively demand better representation and local governance. As another member of the Centre explained in an interview, 'We have the big problem now, hunger. It doesn't matter what or who you are, we are all one people. We have to come together as one [to fight it].' Haj Amin concurred, adding that 'we can't help or comfort people when they're hungry. But beyond this, Muslims and non-Muslims all have the same idea: to have democracy. All the politicians are compromised or corrupt. But our job is to give the people information. Once we give them information they can speak for themselves.'

What we see here is that in the context of self-governance, terms like 'good governance' and democracy are still buzzwords; the language of NGOs, however problematic the organisations, remains. But they are modified by a realisation that the process of governance cannot proceed when, as Haj Amin continued, you simply 'go there and meet [with officials] and they say nice things and when you leave they ignore everything they promised'. Crucial here is that the funding autonomy of the Centre, relying as it does on no foreign donations, the government or wealthy Kenyans outside of al-Momin, gives it enough independence to push for change 'from below – below even the NGOs, which are supposedly working for change but actually run from it or steal the idea and put their name on it and nothing happens'.

There remains significant political marginalisation of Muslims in Kenya and conflicts in regions like Mombasa and Nairobi that have more significant and long-standing populations. Nevertheless, the smaller size and more recent presence of Turkana's Muslim communities has meant they are not at the heart of inter-communal, ethnic or tribal conflicts in the region, and Islam per se is not such a prominent marker of inter-communal struggle against either government or private/corporate malfeasance and incompetence.

In terms of the portrayal of Islam put forward by the Centre in its public as well as its educational discourse, from discussions over the course of two years of fieldwork it is clear that creating a moderate or *wasatiya* vision of Islam and inculcating that into the community is an important goal of the leadership. The Centre's education and pastoral mandate is at heart at least partially defensive – to 'defend against extremism, both inside and outside' its ranks. To that end, while there is little co-operation with the local and national government on many issues, when it comes to how the government views the Muslim population, the Centre and its leadership work hard to push back against Islamophobic sentiments and prejudice from government and security officials. 'We just had a seminar about this exactly', Al-Haj Salim Naida explained to me during an April 2019 meeting at their office.

As another official told me near the end of our last interview, the Centre's leadership spends a lot of time 'talking about how to best counter extremist ideologies. We point out to them that such extremism is not Islam. The government has asked us not to talk about these briefings as they're confidential, but in general we explain that we don't allow Salafis and *ikhtilaf* people. As a group that is ultimately under the umbrella of the Kenyan government, we will try to fight [the extremists]. So if you bring your own things like extremism, if we see someone preaching radicalisation, they are not allowed to preach here and we throw them out.' Indeed, Haj Amin added, 'If people go outside of Turkana to study and start to become extreme and come back that way, the local people won't like them and in fact reject them. They tell them, "This is not what we want." Two or three people tried to do this, but we told them to get lost and be quiet. Follow what we have or leave, or we'll report you to the government.'

The Environment and Social Justice

During my research visit to Lodwar in April 2019, the first place Al-Haj Naida and his colleagues wanted to take me to was not the Centre, but rather the area outside Lodwar that is nominally the location for the local underground aquifer. We drove several kilometres outside the city into a pastoral area under which lies a large aquifer that is supposed to be used by the community, but whose pipes have been closed off to local use. It is adjacent to a massive aquifer discovered in 2013 that is among the largest in Africa and could provide enough water for all of Kenya for upwards of seventy years (ITV News 2013).

As mentioned above, Al-Haj Naida and other members of the community leadership took turns explaining to me, as we drove past a few poor Turkana tribespeople moving across the land, that rather than being 'discovered', this area was long known as a water source, but was now closed off from use, its water deemed too saline for human consumption or irrigation even though both have been engaged for as long as anyone can remember. The reason for bringing us here was to point out the difficulties and the powerful local, national and international forces that the growing community in Lodwar (whose population has risen dramatically in the last decade) are facing at the very moment when desertification is intensifying across the already fragile Turkana ecosystem.

As we walked around the fenced-off enclosure where the water pump was and observed the few grazing goats and local shepherds, they made clear that there was no point in trying to bind the community together, never mind grow it, if the most basic ingredient for life remains closed off and inaccessible while being 'right where we're sitting, [where] people are suffering', as one senior community member put it. Indeed, when I first tried to discuss how the idea of *ahl al-hall wa-l-'aqd* might function in a place like Lodwar, he remonstrated with me slightly, reminding me that 'we have *the* big problem now, hunger ... because you can't help comfort people when they're hungry. In that regard, it doesn't matter what you are, we are all one people. We come together as one ... to fight for democracy regardless of faith.'

Not surprisingly, the Islamic Centre and community are attempting to work with their neighbours in Lodwar to ensure local access to water before any potential development occurs, a job made all the more difficult by the historic lack of co-ordination between various non-governmental organisations in the area. 'Here all the NGOs were working on their own but were not strong, so we decided to come together and now we're much stronger', is how Naida described the situation in 2019.

The dynamics of this collaboration bear out the importance of the concept of *ahl al-hall wa-l-'aqd*. First, in a traditional society like Turkana's, which is now home to a burgeoning population of communities hailing from outside the region, civil society has had to grapple with the reality that transformation in the nature of land ownership mandated by the Kenyan state enabled politicians and other interests to come from outside and purchase previously communal land very cheaply from locals who did not understand the nature and implication of selling 'their' land. The land was subsequently sold on by the purchasers to the government for huge profits.

Ensuring that people continued to have local access to water meant that groups like the Islamic Centre function as vehicles for 'giving people information [so they] can speak for themselves'. At the same time, and at a more micro-physical and even quantum level of political power (LeVine 2018), in order to accomplish this goal even more profoundly 'grassroots' networks have to be fostered that are not part of, and thus not corruptible by, the existing, increasingly co-opted, local NGO system, in which, as the Islamic Centre official quoted above put it, the NGOs that should be working for change either run away from change or sit on the idea for change, claiming that they are doing something about it when, in fact, they are doing nothing at all.

That is, a truly people-centred and people-powered grassroots governance system that 'moves beyond buzzwords' and actually holds the powerful accountable – first and foremost for constant demands for information from the government on its activities and the data and policies it is creating and pursuing – would have to actively weaken the existing NGO system that is so reliant on donor money. One way is for the Centre to remain completely financially independent and sustained purely by local people, as the Islamic Centre's leaders were at pains to point out it remains. It has become a cornerstone of the Turkana Inter-Religious Council, which also accepts no contributions from the state or politicians, and has become the headspring for what to me has shades of the Zapatista practice in Chiapas, Mexico, of establishing 'good government councils' (*juntas de buen gobierno*) to administer the affairs of local autonomous communities for whom any state-level governance would be disastrous (cf. LeVine and Reynolds 2018). 'We use the council to fight the government because if you use civil society some of the people in civil society organisations are part of the government, and thus corrupt', is how another official explained it.

Conclusion

Ultimately, the 'moderate foundation' of Islam in Lodwar as preached, taught and disseminated by the Lodwar Islamic Centre not only unifies a community that is little interested in Salafi or otherwise harshly conservative views (which would make inter-communal co-operation and solidarity in a harsh environment already riven by tribal and other divisions and violence that much more difficult), but has helped the Centre and the community more broadly when problems do arise with the security forces or central government, who are often suspicious of all Muslim organisations but feel reassured by local officials who work regularly with them. That some high-level local officials, like the County Commissioner, are converts who come from the Centre makes this process that much easier.

Not long after my last visit to the Islamic Centre, I stopped by the Friends of Lake Turkana, a well-known and respected Lodwar-based environmental

NGO that not only works to protect one of Africa's most important lakes from devastation by oil drilling, nuclear power plants on its shores, over-fishing and other highly destructive practices advocated at various points by private or government officials, but more recently has expanded its activities to advocate for the broader Turkana region. Ikal Ang'elei, the founder and Executive Director of Friends of Lake Turkana, is an old friend of Haj Amin and works with him on the inter-religious council.

Despite years of successful and celebrated advocacy for the people and environment of Turkana, the organisation has found it difficult to communicate with the local people, whose extreme poverty and lack of education make them easy targets for government or oil industry promises of jobs, money or contracts. 'I do PowerPoints and show them what is happening and what's at stake, but they don't get it. We don't have the language yet for them. We are talking to them or at them but not with them. We need to talk to them about their stories.' Of course, religiously grounded organisations have an easier time communicating with adherents, who are already invested and believe in the core stories, and who have a built-in narrative to unite the community and, when necessary, help it resist the government.

As Ang'elei explained, 'Sometimes you need enough resistance to force negotiations' that neither the government nor Tullow are inclined to pursue unless they see a united community aligned against them. In a place as poor as Turkana, one beset by marginalisation now coupled with a massive influx of money and attendant corruption, enabling local residents to defend their communal interests will rarely be achieved by top-down methods. The experience of Turkana shows the complexity of self-governance in such conditions, when the mandate to provide education and training for the community as well as material support, spiritual guidance and political leadership led ultimately to a situation where the only authority that can engage in all these areas simultaneously is the community itself.

* * *

The research for this chapter was conducted during four fieldwork visits to Turkana from 2015 through 2019. Interviews were conducted in English and Arabic, with a small amount of Swahili. All research was funded by a FORMAS grant from the Swedish Research Council.

Bibliography

Aga Khan University (2018), 'Governance and Islam in East Africa: Muslims and the State', conference held at the East Africa Institute, University of Nairobi, 17–18 January.

Agade, Kennedy Mkutu (2014), 'Ungoverned Space and the Oil Find in Turkana, Kenya', *The Round Table: The Commonwealth Journal of International Affairs* 103(5), pp. 497–515.

Asad, Talal (2015), 'Genealogies of Religion, Twenty Years On: An Interview with Talal Asad', *Bulletin for the Study of Religion*, 25 November 2015, http://bulletin.equinoxpub.com/2015/11/genealogies-of-religion-twenty-years-on-an-interview-with-talal-asad/

Bowering, Gerhard (2015), *Islamic Political Thought*, Princeton, NJ: Princeton University Press.

Crone, Patricia (2001), 'Shura as an Elective Institution', *Quaderni di Studi Arabi* 19, pp. 3–39.

Gulleid, Mohamed (2019), 'Nearly One Million Drought-Hit Kenyans at Risk of Starvation', *TRTWorld*, 19 March 2019, https://www.trtworld.com/africa/nearly-one-million-drought-hit-kenyans-at-risk-of-starvation-25088

Hall, Samuel (2015), *Devolution in Kenya: Opportunity for Transnational Solutions for Refugees*, Copenhagen, DK: Danish Refugee Council.

Haugbolle, Sune and Mark LeVine, eds (2022), *Altered States: The Remaking of the Political in the Arab World*, London: Routledge.

Horkheimer, Max [1942] (1985), 'Die Rackets und der Geist', in Gunzelin Schmid (ed.), *Gesammelte Schriften, vol. 12, Nachgelassene Schriften 1931–1949*, Frankfurt: Noerr, pp. 287–8.

Hountondji, Paulin J. (1983), *African Philosophy: Myth and Reality* (original title: *Sur la 'philosophie africaine'*), trans. H. Evans and J. Rée, Bloomington: Indiana University Press.

Hountondji, Paulin J. (2002), *The Struggle for Meaning: Reflections on Philosophy, Culture and Democracy in Africa*, Athens: Ohio University Press.

ITV News (2013), 'Exclusive: Huge Water Reserve Discovered in Kenya', 10 September, https://www.itv.com/news/2013-09-10/kenya-water-aquifer-found-in-lotikipi/

Joya, Angela (2020), *The Roots of Revolt: A Political Economy of Egypt from Nasser to Mubarak*, Cambridge: Cambridge University Press.

Kinyua, Omari Hassan (2014), 'Islamic Leadership in Kenya: A Case Study of the Supreme Council of Kenya Muslims (SUPKEM)', PhD thesis, University of Nairobi, C80/83061/2012, November, http://erepository.uonbi.ac.ke/bitstream/handle/11295/78259/Omari_Islamic%20leadership%20in%20Kenya_%20a%20case%20study%20of%20the%20supreme%20council%20of%20Kenya%20muslims%20(Supkem).pdf%3Bsequence=3

LeVine, Mark and Bryan Reynolds (2018), 'Fugitive Pedagogy: Guattari's Ecosophy in the Mural Discourse of the Zapatistas', in David Cole and Joff P. N. Bradley (eds), *Principles of Transversality in Globalisation and Education*, London: Springer, pp. 149–72.

Lodhi, Abdulaziz (1994), 'Muslims in Eastern Africa: Their Past and Present', *Nordic Journal of African Studies* 3(1), pp. 88–98.

Mamdani, Mahmood (1996), *Citizen and Subject: Contemporary Africa and the Legacy of Late Colonialism*, Princeton, NJ: Princeton University Press.

Migdal, Joel (1989), *Strong Societies and Weak States: State–Society Relations and State Capabilities in the Third World*, Princeton, NJ: Princeton University Press.

Naado, Hassan Ole (2015), 'A Discussion with Hassan Ole Naado, Supreme Council of Kenya Muslims', Berkley Center for Religion, Ethics & World Affairs, interview, 15 April 2015, https://berkleycenter.georgetown.edu/interviews/a-discussion-with-hassan-ole-naado-supreme-council-of-kenya-muslims

Tilly, Charles (1985), 'War Making and State Making as Organized Crime', in Peter Evans, Dietrich Rueschemeyer and Theda Skocpol (eds), *Bringing the State Back In*, Cambridge: Cambridge University Press, pp. 169–91.

Trimingham, J. Spencer (1964), *Islam in East Africa*, Oxford: Clarendon Press.

Turkana County, *Turkana County Investment Plan, 2016–2020*, https://www.turkana.go.ke/index.php/documents/county-investment-plan-2016-2020/

Turkana County (n.d.), *Gains of Devolution*, https://www.turkana.go.ke/index.php/benefits-of-devolution/

UNDP, *A New Dawn for Turkana County* (n.d.), https://www.ke.undp.org/content/kenya/en/home/ourwork/democraticgovernance/successstories/A-New-Dawn-for-Turkana-County.html

wa Thiong'o, Ngugi (2018), *Wrestling with the Devil: A Prison Memoir*, New York: The New Press.

Weber, Max (1946 [1918]), 'Politics as a Vocation', in H. H. Gerth and C. Wright Mills (eds), *From Max Weber: Essays in Sociology*, Oxford: Oxford University Press, pp. 77–128.

Wiredu, Kwasi (1980), *Philosophy and an African Culture*, Cambridge: Cambridge University Press.

Wiredu, Kwasi (1998), 'Toward Decolonizing African Philosophy and Religion', *African Studies Quarterly* 1(4), pp. 17–46.

Zaman, Muhammad Qasim (2007), 'Ahl al-ḥall wa-l-'aqd', in Kate Fleet, Gudrun Krämer, Denis Matringe, John Nawas and Everett Rowson (eds), *Encyclopaedia of Islam 3*, Leiden, NL, http://dx.doi.org/10.1163/1573-3912_ei3_COM_0027

Zirulnick, Ariel (2015), 'In Kenya, Religious Coexistence Feels Pressure of Stronger Muslim Identity', *Christian Science Monitor*, 29 March 2015, https://www.csmonitor.com/World/Africa/2015/0329/In-Kenya-religious-coexistence-feels-pressure-of-stronger-Muslim-identity

2

The Kenyan State and Coastal Muslims: The Politics of Alienation and Engagement

JEREMY PRESTHOLDT

Muslims on Kenya's Indian Ocean coast occupy a 'double periphery', as Kai Kresse has suggested, on the periphery of the wider Muslim world and a minority community at the margins of Kenyan national politics.[1] This position, combined with a range of socioeconomic grievances, has contributed to a strong sense of alienation. Since Kenya's independence, the question of how to address this alienation has engendered different, and in some cases competing, sociopolitical agendas shaped by national and international interpretive frames. In Kenya, concerns over political inclusion, economic opportunity and civil rights are not unique to the coast, but these have occasioned a wide range of political action by coastal Muslim communities.

Since the late 1950s, Muslim communities have engaged in concerted political action at the regional and national levels. As Hassan Ndzovu has shown, in the post-colonial era such concerted action has often been in the context of debates over legislation and other issues that affect the Muslim community as a whole. Indeed, the catalytic political power of Muslim identity has in many ways strengthened since the 1990s.[2] The politics of alienation, or the range of political responses to marginality, have had other consequences as well. While Kenya's central government has generally disregarded coastal grievances, its responses to Muslim dissent and political mobilisation have often been severe. Moreover, the varied political tacks taken by coastal political thinkers have evidenced and in some cases exacerbated tensions within coastal Muslim communities.

---

[1] Kresse 2009. My sincere thanks to Justin Willis and researchers with the British Institute in Eastern Africa for assistance in obtaining copies of materials from Kenyan newspaper archives, and special thanks to Dillon Mahoney for sharing other valuable research materials.
[2] Ndzovu 2014, 2009.

Such tensions proceed in part from the unequal rewards of political contests. Unlike legislative debates, political contests return to questions of power and local resource access, which are linked in divisive ways to class, ethnicity, race and age. As a result, concerns about inclusion and civil rights have contributed to political action across a broad spectrum, strategies ranging from separatism in the 1960s to working within the ruling party in the 1970s and 1980s, support for opposition parties in the 1990s and reiterations of separatism in the 2000s. Additionally, in the 2010s coastal grievances intersected with new forms of militancy in the context of increasing state violence, the conflict in neighbouring Somalia and al Shabaab-linked militants' efforts to destabilise Kenya.

I have elsewhere addressed how coastal socioeconomic grievances encouraged alternative socio-geographic imaginings and coastal political thinkers attempted to gain political leverage through claims of autochthony, or 'original' habitation.[3] This chapter outlines the broader spectrum of coastal responses to and engagements with Kenya's national political sphere. I consider how the politics of alienation have been alternatively catalytic and divisive since the era of decolonisation. Specifically, I trace Muslim political thinkers' responses to alienation and the Kenyan government's reactions to dissent at three critical junctures in which political actors utilised Muslim identity as a political catalyst: the era of decolonisation in the 1960s, the demise of the one-party state in the 1990s and the recent era of counter-terrorism. At these junctures, Muslim identity gained significant political value at the coast as a frame for interpreting alienation and collective action.

The chapter also outlines how the politics of alienation engendered concepts and practices that proved divisive among Muslims and between religious communities. And I outline how state and non-state actors exploited these divisions to quell dissent. First, political thinkers evoked religious territoriality, or the notion of the coast as a bounded social entity. Much like autochthony discourse elsewhere in Kenya, concepts of Muslim 'ownership' of the coast resonated in moments of crisis but also magnified socio-political divisions. Second, periods of high political tension such as the 2000s saw an increasing refusal among some at the coast to engage in formal political processes or acknowledge state authority. Lastly, political crises such as in the era of counter-terrorism have amplified debates over the very definition of 'Islamic', increasing frictions within coastal Muslim communities. Thus, not only has the concept of a coastal Muslim political community rarely been sufficient to challenge state policies or overcome socioeconomic divisions within coastal communities, but the ways in which Muslim identity has been mobilised for political action have in some cases also exacerbated ethnic, racial, generational and ideological cleavages.

---

[3] Prestholdt 2023.

Coastal Muslims share many grievances, but heavy-handed responses to Muslim dissent by Kenya's security forces, socioeconomic divisions within the coast region and their exploitation by state as well as non-state actors have frustrated efforts to secure recompense for historical abuses and inequalities.

Mwambao, the Question of a Coastal State and Post-colonial Politics

The history of Kenya's Indian Ocean coast has been shaped by transregional linkages and heterogeneity on the one hand and socioeconomic inequalities and contests over belonging on the other. These in turn have affected and been affected by discordant continental and maritime imaginaries. Specifically, the perception of the coast as either essentially Indian Ocean or continental in orientation has been a core social tension defining citizenship and inclusion since the colonial era. Moreover, British administrators in colonial Kenya implemented race-based legal designations that hinged on the primary categories of 'native' and 'non-native': the former referring to people of African ancestry and the latter to those of Arab and Asian ancestry. Though the boundaries of these categories were imprecise, they were given significant weight through economic and political rights granted to 'non-natives' and the denial of these rights to so-called 'natives'.[4] In the era of decolonisation, this system of racially defined rights engendered significant political friction. The end of colonial rule raised questions about regional political power and socioeconomic privilege, and, by extension, the position of the coastal region in the wider political order.[5]

In the colonial era much of the population of the coast region fell under the jurisdiction of the Protectorate of Kenya, a 10-mile wide coastal administrative region technically leased from the Sultanate of Zanzibar. The symbolic import of the division between the Protectorate and Kenya Colony, including the fact that the Sultanate retained titular sovereignty over the coastal strip, increased as independence approached. Fully incorporating the Protectorate into Kenya was an unspoken desire of the departing British administration. Yet, the perceived possibility of a separate, independent coastal nation became a central political debate at the coast during the waning years of colonial rule. Many political thinkers at the coast believed that conjoining the coast with Kenya and its Christian majority would lead to the erosion of the rights of religious, racial and ethnic minorities. These anxieties led some coastal politicians, including Ronald Ngala of the Kenyan African Democratic Union (KADU), to advance a federalist

---

[4] Salim 1976, 1973; Willis 1993; Chome 2021.
[5] Salim 1979; Ndzovu 2009.

alternative termed 'majimbo'.⁶ A spectrum of other political visions responded to anxieties about the future, with tacks ranging from a union with Zanzibar to a fully independent coast. In this fractured political context, Muslim political leaders of various ethnic backgrounds, including Digo, Swahili, Bajuni, Pokomo and Arab, gravitated to the concept of an autonomous coastal region. And the Swahili word 'Mwambao', or coastline, became shorthand for separatism generally. Critics within and beyond the Protectorate, such as Ronald Ngala and Jomo Kenyatta, leader of the rival party Kenya African National Union (KANU), charged that separatism was an attempt by British imperialists and Arab supremacists to perpetuate the racial privileges of 'non-natives' and deprive Kenya of the region's most valuable port: Mombasa.⁷ Some detractors even suggested that, given their racial backgrounds, Arab, Swahili and other Muslim Mwambao supporters were foreigners in Kenya and had no right to demand an independent coastal state.⁸

Coastal separatism reflected wider political trends in late colonial Kenya. At the end of the 1950s, decolonisation appeared to many to be a contest for the spoils of the post-colonial nation. This perception held that representatives of larger ethnic blocs would position themselves to take the reigns of power and use that power to gain greater political and economic advantages. Such anxieties led representatives of smaller groups to rely on ethnic identity and the notion of exclusive group ownership of subnational territories as catalysts for political cohesion. In regions such as the Rift Valley and the coast Protectorate, what Gabrielle Lynch has termed 'ethnic territoriality' engendered demands for regional rights linked to claims of autochthony.⁹ This would take its most extreme form in Somali irredentism in the northeast and the subsequent Shifta War (1964–8).¹⁰

At the coast, anxiety over the future, combined with new forms of territorial thinking, contributed to multiple separatist visions. While being a subject of the Sultan of Zanzibar had no great significance in coastal Kenya for much of the colonial period, rekindled emotional and political affinities with Zanzibar meant that, for some political thinkers, Zanzibari irredentism seemed an alternative to Kenyan nationalism.¹¹ Additionally, some Arabs and Swahili feared status reversal. However, most separatist thinkers harboured more existential concerns. They argued that 'up-country' groups enjoyed superior economic and educational opportunities during the colonial era, and therefore integration with independent Kenya would both perpetuate such disparities and compromise Muslim advancements. Some additionally believed that integration might

---

⁶ Anderson 2010, 2005.
⁷ National Archives of the United Kingdom and Ireland (hereafter NA) 1961b; Aseka 1993: 8–9; *East African Standard* 1961.
⁸ Prestholdt 2014; Brennan 2008; Ndzovu 2010.
⁹ Lynch 2011: 17; Forrest 2004; Branch 2011.
¹⁰ Weitzberg 2017; Whittaker 2014.
¹¹ Brennan 2015, 2008; Salim 1970.

severely diminish the Islamic culture of the coast. Stressing this perceived existential threat of integration with Kenya, separatists demanded that the colonial administration grant autonomy to the Protectorate at independence.[12]

In the late 1950s and early 1960s, divisions along racial and ethnic lines prevented a single separatist platform.[13] For instance, the conservative, Arab-dominated Coastal League lobbied for reintegration with Zanzibar. The majority-Swahili and -Digo Coast Peoples Party (CPP), on the other hand, argued for complete independence. Led by the Legislative Council member Abdilahi Nassir, the CPP was the most influential coastal separatist group. The CPP rejected the ethnic and racial biases of rival parties such as the Coastal League. Instead, the CPP emphasised both 'multiracialism' and the deep history of Islam at the coast. Spokespeople such as Omar Rashid Bakuli asserted that the coherent sociocultural orientation that resulted from this history defined the coast as distinct from the rest of Kenya, and thus the coast deserved separate statehood.[14] The debate over the future of the Protectorate in this way revealed and amplified conflicting spatial imaginaries bound to social identity. These imaginaries often emphasised either a continental African or a maritime Indian Ocean essence of coastal society, spatial definitions conceptually bound to race, ethnicity and religion. By throwing into question the boundaries of the Kenyan state, debates around decolonisation gave political gravity to divergent sociocultural definitions of the region. This, in turn, further divided Muslims along racial, ethnic and class lines.[15]

British emphasis on the economic interests of post-colonial Kenya led to a quick settlement of the Mwambao question in 1961. The Colonial Office and the Sultan of Zanzibar decided to join the coast Protectorate and Kenya Colony before independence. As part of a negotiated end to British rule, leaders of KANU and KADU agreed to certain safeguards for Muslims, including the protection of the kadhis' courts, Islamic worship and instruction in Arabic.[16] These concessions assuaged some of the concerns of Muslim leaders, but deepening anxieties about Nairobi's potential dominance of the coast's economy and political sphere encouraged a rethinking of the factional divisions that defined the Mwambao debates. Thus, in the year preceding independence former coastal political opponents formed two parties, Mwambao United Front and later the Coast United Front, to demand a separate independence for the coast. Despite this show of regional unity, in 1963 the Protectorate was integrated with Kenya 'at the stroke of a pen'.[17]

---

[12] Kenya National Archives (hereafter KNA) 1958; Salim 1973; Prestholdt 2014.
[13] Stren 1970.
[14] NA 1961a.
[15] Chome 2020; Prestholdt 2014, 2023.
[16] NA 1962.
[17] Prestholdt 2014; KNA 1963a.

In the post-colonial era, questions of inclusion, regional identity and the position of Muslims in the majority-Christian nation lingered and intensified. Coastal leaders registered their dissatisfaction with the implementation of safeguards for Muslims. As petitions to the Kenyan government attest, many claimed that coastal Muslims were targets of discrimination, particularly when applying for government documents and services.[18] Additionally, in 1964 Ronald Ngala, as President of KADU, called for a ban on Arabic and Mombasan Swahili (Kimvita) from the Voice of Kenya radio services on the grounds that programmes in those languages privileged a 'minority community'.[19] Some ethno-nationalist organisations, such as the Coast Muslim Political Union and the Swahili People's Party, continued to operate in the early years of independence. But the post-colonial era ultimately saw a political landscape defined by new questions of power and social identity to which coastal Muslims responded in multiple ways.[20]

Separatism gave way to Muslims' increasing engagement in national politics. Even in areas such as the Lamu Archipelago, where interest in national debates was at first limited, political engagement increased markedly in the early years of the post-colonial era. Many coastal Muslims remained concerned about the centralising interests of KANU's leadership, particularly after the dissolution of the main opposition party, KADU, in 1964. Some of KANU's critics threw their support behind the Kenya People's Union (KPU), the only remaining opposition party of influence by the late 1960s. Moreover, one of the most notable critiques of President Jomo Kenyatta's KANU government, *Kenya: Twendapi?*, was penned in Kimvita by the Mombasan poet Abdilatif Abdalla, brother of former CPP leader Abdilahi Nassir. As KANU employed increasingly authoritarian tactics, the Kenyatta government responded to Abdalla's criticism by jailing him for three years.[21] By the end of the 1960s, KANU neutralised the KPU, making Kenya in effect a one-party state.

Coastal Muslims, the Kenyan Government and the Islamic Party of Kenya

In the 1970s and 1980s, coastal Muslims' engagement with the national political sphere was impacted by an emergent identity as Kenyan and the belief that political engagement could pay dividends. As Thomas P. Wolf argued, Kenyan politics increasingly operated as a 'patronage-based' system in which political elites 'bought' support rather than a 'policy-choice-based' system where

---

[18] Ndzovu 2010; KNA 1964.
[19] KNA 1966; Brennan 2015.
[20] See e.g. KNA 1963b; Kresse 2009, 2018; Waddilove 2020.
[21] Kresse 2016; Beck and Kresse 2016.

candidates 'won' votes.[22] At the same time, many at the coast saw voting as the only means to check the power of KANU at the local and national levels. As a critique of national policies, coastal residents frequently voted against the wishes of the Executive and its regional organs, including the Provincial Administration and KANU local office holders. Through actions that Goran Hyden and Colin Leys termed 'reprisal voting', elections served to rebuke local elites who dominated KANU at the coast. Given the structure of the one-party state, this political engagement virtually ensured that national party politics became enmeshed in local racial, ethnic and class tensions.[23] Parliamentary returns became contingent on local disputes, for instance over settlement schemes that provided land to non-coastal residents.

In the 1970s and 1980s, coastal political engagement contributed to the rise of a small number of high-profile Muslim politicians within KANU, notably Mombasan MP Shariff Nassir, who gained a cabinet position as Minister of Home Affairs. But the influence of coastal elected officials rarely translated into significant national policy gains for coastal Muslims generally. Rather, many charged that the political, and by extension financial, power of leaders more often manifested in assistance to individual constituents.[24] By the 1980s, many at the coast perceived Muslims' socio-economic circumstances to be in appreciable decline, particularly in relation to other groups in Kenya. Many voiced alarm over economic marginality, political underrepresentation, land allocation, employment discrimination, limited educational opportunities and a repressive political environment under President Daniel arap Moi. The president's alliances at the coast lay primarily with the business class, including elites of Arab and South Asian descent as well as expatriates. Thus, by the beginning of the 1990s many coastal Muslims felt that KANU offered few mechanisms for Muslims to secure greater rights.[25]

Frustration with the one-party state defined politics and fuelled calls for reform in the early 1990s. Subsequent multi-party elections in 1992 had strong reverberations at the coast. Indeed, deepening political and socioeconomic grievances, along with the perceived potential for structural change, produced a range of responses. Like elsewhere in Kenya, a primary interest of political thinkers was inclusion. This 'striving for inclusion', to use E. S. Atieno Odhiambo and John Lonsdale's phrase, took multiple forms among Muslims at the coast.[26] One of the most impactful political movements developed in Mombasa, taking loose form in 1992 around the Islamic Party of Kenya (IPK). The IPK was denied official party status, but it became a primary voice for mounting grievances at

---

[22] Wolf 2000: 145; Branch 2011.
[23] Hyden and Leys 1972.
[24] Bakari 2013.
[25] Wolf 2000; Saalfeld and Mwakimako 2023.
[26] Atieno Odhiambo and Lonsdale 2003.

the coast and it electrified young Muslims.[27] The IPK represented something new at the coast, a 'political initiative', in Thomas P. Wolf's words, 'responding to grass-roots issues and [the] needs' of coastal Muslims.[28]

The IPK was inspired by Islamic parties elsewhere on the continent and aimed to show solidarity with a global Muslim political awakening, but it did not develop an Islamist platform. Instead, it emphasised government reform and Muslim political engagement in national politics. In contrast to the coalition model, wherein smaller ethnically defined political parties joined forces to challenge Kenya's ruling party, the IPK mobilised across social divides, simultaneously emphasising youth engagement and Muslim identity. As a result, it became a powerful grassroots movement. While the IPK's leadership structure was diffuse and often opaque, its spokespeople were among the most vocal critics of Daniel arap Moi's government and became known across Kenya for their blunt verbal attacks on KANU. This approach alienated many religious and political elites, but it resonated strongly with young, urban Muslims.[29] The IPK became particularly adept at mobilising its rank and file. Thus, their activities in Mombasa, including rallies and demonstrations, often paralysed the urban core.[30] Additionally, the IPK gained financial support within and beyond Kenya, which offered the party some freedom from Kenya's conventional system of patronage. Just as important, given their desire to influence the national political process, party leaders allied with the national opposition party the Forum for the Restoration of Democracy (FORD)-Kenya.[31]

As the influence of the IPK grew, the Moi government saw the party as a major threat to KANU's power in Coast Province. In the run-up to the 1992 elections, Kenya's attorney general denied the IPK registration, citing a constitutional restriction on religious-oriented parties.[32] Following the ban, authorities in Mombasa began a more intense campaign of intimidation against the IPK, arresting party leaders and forcing many others to seek refuge abroad.[33] Most notably, Kenyan authorities arrested the popular street preacher Khalid Balala, who, though not a formal leader of the IPK, was a figurehead for the party able to draw a large crowd. To neutralise Balala, the authorities tortured him, charged him with treason and later revoked his passport while he was abroad. Given Balala's popularity in Mombasa, his arrest stoked discontent. The aggressive

---

[27] Bakari 1995; Oded 2000; Saalfeld and Mwakimako 2023.
[28] Wolf 2000: 141.
[29] Wolf 2000.
[30] *Daily Nation* 1993a.
[31] Wolf 2000.
[32] *The Weekly Review* 1992a.
[33] US Department of State 1995.

actions of authorities, in addition to historical grievances, drew more young people to the IPK's cause and drove more young Muslims onto the streets.[34]

KANU leaders and non-state actors in Coast Province sought to undermine the IPK's influence within Muslim communities. Since some IPK leaders were of Arab descent, and many activists were Swahili, critics painted the group as a movement of 'Arabs' seeking to regain power.[35] In more extreme cases, detractors spoke of Arab designs to enslave black Kenyans, rhetoric that echoed earlier accusations against Mwambao separatists. Though the IPK's base was both inter-ethnic and inter-racial, a group called the United Muslims of Africa (UMA) drew on this rhetoric and began to harry the IPK's base. UMA denied links with the ruling party, but many sources suggested that UMA's operations received financial backing from a Muslim-nominated KANU MP from the coast.[36] UMA leaders recruited Digo and other Mijikenda young men from Kwale and Mombasa, and in 1993 an UMA leader claimed that a 'bush army' was prepared to attack IPK supporters.[37] UMA subsequently mounted attacks on Mombasan neighbourhoods associated with IPK activism that included 'petrol bombing' and assaults on presumed IPK supporters.[38] Moreover, police harassment of the IPK's base provoked a number of violent clashes in Mombasa that, along with the targeting of the party's leaders, contributed to the collapse of the movement. Though IPK candidates running on the FORD-Kenya ticket succeeded in gaining parliamentary seats in 1992, in the mid-1990s the IPK deteriorated.

The IPK used Muslim identity to rally coastal Muslims, and the Kenyan state cited this emphasis as a rationale to deny it legitimacy. Thus, the catalytic power of Muslim identity contributed to the growth of a political movement, but it also in effect became an impediment to sustaining a robust national political platform. Moreover, state and non-state actors exploited racial and ethnic tensions within the wider coastal Muslim community to neutralise the IPK. Muslim identity, race and ethnicity continued to play a role in coast politics in the late 1990s.[39] At the same time, events of the late 1990s and 2000s would affect the relationship between coastal Muslims and the Kenyan state in dire ways. Specifically, this relationship was profoundly impacted by a complex matrix of counter-terrorism, ideological tension and violence.

---

[34] *The Weekly Review* 1992b; Human Rights Watch 1992; Mazrui 1993; Oded 2000; *The East African Magazine* 2005.
[35] Prestholdt 2023.
[36] Ndzovu 2009: 7.
[37] *Daily Nation* 1993a; *Daily Nation* 1993b.
[38] Human Rights Watch 2002; Awori 1993; Akiwumi 1999; *Daily Nation* 2012b.
[39] Ndzovu 2012; MacIntosh 2009; Mghangha 2010.

Alienation and Communal Division in the Era of Counter-terrorism

After the dissolution of the IPK, authorities at the coast and in Nairobi continued to view young Muslims in Coast Province with suspicion. State attitudes towards young Muslims had immediate and long-term repercussions after Kenya became the target of international terrorism. Specifically, al Qaeda's 1998 bombing of the US Embassy in Nairobi, an attack that killed hundreds of people, reshaped Kenya's domestic politics and foreign relations.[40] Most of the operatives who carried out the attack were not Kenyan. Nevertheless, in the aftermath of the embassy bombing investigators focused on coastal Kenyan communities. Policy-makers saw the long history of Muslim dissent in Kenya as a justification for communal indictment. Kenyan authorities thus relied on ethnic profiling and the use of force rather than subtler investigative techniques.[41] In the 2000s, and particularly after the Kenyan invasion of Somalia in 2011, counter-terrorism took more extreme forms. Disappearances, extra-judicial killings and other violence against civilians deepened the grievances of coastal Muslims and spurred greater radicalism. In the most extreme cases, this resulted in the rejection of the political process altogether, the rise of militant groups linked to al-Shabaab insurgents in Somalia, such as al Hijra and Jaysh Ayman, and violence against those perceived to be aligned with the Kenyan state.

In the years immediately following the 1998 embassy bombings, authorities employed measures against terrorist suspects that included ethnic profiling, harassment and prolonged detention. Yet, since the target had been the US Embassy, Kenyan policy-makers initially saw terrorism as a largely external concern. That changed in 2002 when al-Qaeda operatives attacked a hotel near Mombasa and attempted to down an Israeli airliner departing Mombasa's Moi International Airport. President Mwai Kibaki's administration soon faced internal and external criticism for failing to adequately address the threat of terrorism. In response, the administration defined the threat of terrorism as emanating primarily from the coast. This was a multi-faceted tack aiming to salvage Kenya's international image, appease foreign critics and suggest that the violence was localised. As a result, expanding counter-terrorism efforts focused on specific Muslim communities, notably Swahili, Somali and Arab Kenyans. As one young Muslim man in Mombasan explained in 2003, 'You can be arrested just for wearing a bushy beard or a *kanzu* [long shirt]'. Another man similarly

---

[40] Harmony Project 2007.
[41] Prestholdt 2019; *Independent Online* 2000; Salmon 2003.

reported that the authorities questioned him simply because his mobile screen featured an image of the Kaaba.[42]

Coastal Muslim political leaders and human rights activists were widely critical of intensifying yet counterproductive counter-terrorism measures. They also strongly opposed the 2003 Suppression of Terrorism Bill, draconian legislation that ultimately failed to receive parliamentary approval.[43] Muslim engagement with national elections, including support for the Orange Democratic Movement, remained high in the 2000s, and the 2010 constitutional referendum saw national support for the maintenance of the kadhi court system.[44] Nonetheless, political successes and demands for the reform of counter-terrorist praxis did not improve circumstances for most coastal Muslims. Continued state suspicion of coastal Muslims, combined with indifference to enduring historical grievances, stoked resentment of Kenyan civil authorities. This contributed to a form of popular rejection of the national political process, particularly among young people.

From 2005, and notably in the years immediately following the contested 2007 national elections, a group called the Mombasa Republican Council (MRC) rearticulated elements of earlier separatism and nativism to develop an inter-faith message rejecting mainstream politics. Specifically, the MRC resurrected the concept of the coast region as a separate state, recalling the late colonial Mwambao movement. Employing the slogan *Pwani si Kenya* (the coast is not Kenya), the MRC's leaders, many of whom were Muslims, stressed exclusive rights to land and other regional resources. The MRC's message, like the IPK's, was resolutely critical of the power of the central government and its influence at the coast, but it was not a wholesale return to 1960s nativism. Instead, it developed a more encompassing autochthony discourse, combining aspects of Mwambao separatism and demands for social justice that transcended racial, ethnic and religious lines. The MRC thus catalysed a larger community of sentiment in the coast region.[45] However, the authorities banned the MRC, charged that it was planning violence and worked to delegitimise the group. Thus, despite support in the coast region, the MRC, much like the IPK, succumbed to state pressure.

In the early 2010s, state policies of counter-terrorism continued to encourage political mobilisation and calls for the recognition of Muslims' human rights. But Kenya's invasion of Somalia in 2011 dramatically affected relations between coastal Muslims and the state while deepening ideological rifts within Muslim communities. In response to security concerns around al Shabaab, including the insurgent group's actions in Kenya and potential impact on

---

[42] Quoted in Maclean 2003; see also Al-Bulushi 2021; Prestholdt 2019, 2011; Mwakimako 2007.
[43] Amnesty International 2003; Kinyanjui 2003; Thoya 2003; Hassan 2003.
[44] Ndzovu 2017.
[45] Mahajan 2023; Willis and Gona 2013; Goldsmith 2011.

the Lamu Port-South Sudan-Ethiopia-Transport Corridor project, the Kenya Defense Forces launched operations in Somalia, the first aggressive international deployment in Kenya's history. Soon after the 2011 invasion, al-Shabaab and its Kenyan affiliates significantly expanded a destabilisation campaign in Kenya that included attacks on shops, restaurants, bars, buses, schools and churches.[46] Within months, the dynamics of terrorism in Kenya changed dramatically. The frequency of attacks in cities such as Nairobi, Mombasa, Mandera and Garissa only increased in 2012–13, with a shocking assault on Nairobi's Westgate shopping mall in September 2013, which drew sustained international attention.[47] Also in an effort to destabilise Kenya, al Shabaab utilised various media platforms to portray itself as a champion of oppressed Kenyan Muslims. This, along with promises of material gain, became a cornerstone of al Shabaab's strategy to recruit Kenyan Muslims. As a result, some Kenyan Muslims, including from the coast region, travelled to Somalia to receive military training.[48] Al-Shabaab's campaign of terror in Kenya posed a multi-dimensional challenge to Kenyan security and the state's relationship with Muslim communities. It likewise elicited calls for greater internal security. The resulting counter-terrorism impetus entailed overlapping domestic and international dimensions, tying events in Kenya closer to those in Somalia.

Counter-terrorism efforts in Kenya expanded throughout the 2010s, and suspicion focused increasingly on Muslim leaders and specific mosques that authorities believed were promoting radicalism, dissent and violence. Government representatives accused outspoken preachers and other radicals of terrorism-related crimes. Human rights organisations, journalists and others suggested that this was followed by a campaign of assassinations targeting Muslim activists.[49] A key example was the murder of Aboud Rogo, a radical preacher and al-Shabaab supporter. In 2012, Rogo was shot while driving in Mombasa. Human rights groups and political leaders condemned the killing, and the presumption that state actors were responsible for Rogo's death sparked riots in Mombasa. The unrest led to the destruction of five churches and the deaths of three police officers. In the months that followed, other preachers were assassinated in what many saw as a thinly veiled state effort to silence radical leaders.[50] Young radicals in Mombasa responded by occupying several mosques.[51] Though outrage over police violence united Muslims at the coast, it was increasingly

---

[46] Anderson 2020; Prestholdt 2019.
[47] Reuters 2012.
[48] Anderson and McKnight 2015; Lowen 2014; Jerejian 2017.
[49] See e.g. Kenya National Commission on Human Rights 2008; United Nations Human Rights Council 2009; Kenya Television Network 2013; Haki Africa 2016; The Open Society Justice Initiative and Muslims for Human Rights 2013.
[50] Horowitz 2012; Nyaundi 2018.
[51] Mwakio 2013.

clear that intergenerational and ideological debates were expanding political cleavages within the Muslim community. For instance, these generational and doctrinal fault lines were evident during 2012 *maulid* celebrations in Mombasa. Celebrations at Old Town's Mlango wa Papa mosque were interrupted by young people who demanded they cease. This led to confrontations inside and later outside the mosque. Ultimately, quelling the hostilities required the intervention of clerics, the Mombasan DC Abdi Hassan and the police.[52]

Radicals met ongoing reprisals with attacks against Muslim leaders who challenged their ideological positions. In the 2010s young radicals targeted moderate Muslim leaders whom they imagined sided with the Kenyan government. As Hassan J. Ndzovu has shown, al-Shabaab and its affiliates in Kenya labelled these leaders 'apostates'. Though radicals remained a small minority, several moderate imams, police officers and police informants were murdered in what many believed was a counteroffensive.[53] This cycle of violence intensified in 2014 when Mombasan police attacked mosques dominated by radicals. Police arrested hundreds of young men, some of whom disappeared.[54] Also in 2014, Jaysh Ayman, a militant group made up primarily of Kenyans dispatched from al-Shabaab training camps in Somalia, launched horrific attacks on towns in Lamu and Tana River counties, murdering Christian men. During the violence, the attackers appropriated earlier discourses of territoriality and claimed to be 'rescuing Muslim lands from Christian invaders'. For several years thereafter, Jaysh Ayman militants continued to operate in the vicinity of Boni Forest, mounting small-scale but deadly attacks in Lamu and Tana River counties, including against transit arteries and local government officials.[55]

Indignation and fear exacerbated fissures within coastal Muslim communities in the years after the 2014 mosque raids in Mombasa and attacks in the Lamu area. Young radicals were of a generation that experienced increased state repression, violence and economic alienation, which they interpreted as religious persecution. Encouraged by international extremist discourses and proponents of militancy within Kenya, some young Muslims rejected both conventional politics and pacifism.[56] Some young people turned to a more extreme and unprecedented ideological position: the militant union of religion, politics and violence that linked domestic grievances with counter-terrorism to the insurgency in Somalia as well as broader extremist currents.[57]

---

[52] *Daily Nation* 2012a. For greater context, see Kresse 2006.
[53] Ndzovu 2017.
[54] Oketch et al. 2014.
[55] Quoted in Chome 2017; Bocha 2017; Harper 2014; Khalid 2014; Mwakimako and Willis 2014.
[56] Anderson 2014; Nzes 2014; Ndzovu 2017. For greater context see Mwakimako 2010.
[57] Chome 2019.

In the early 2010s, al-Shabaab-linked militants attempted to appeal more directly to disaffected Kenyan Muslims through multimedia formats. Their rhetoric was evident in the Swahili- and English-language online magazine *Gaidi Mtaani* ('Terrorist in the Neighbourhood') and recruitment videos such as the *Mujahideen Moments* series. These repackaged Kenyan social, economic and other grievances for a youthful audience and included interviews with militants, combat footage and even Swahili-language poetry. Specifically, they bundled long-term grievances with a host of contemporary concerns about police repression, belonging and the rights of Muslims in Kenya, with an emphasis on Muslim oppression and humiliation. Attempting to capitalise on public outrage around events such as the killing of clerics and mosque raids, as well as the longer history of alienation, these media productions suggested that the most effective response to repression in Kenya was violent resistance and the establishment of a global caliphate. For example, Swahili poetry featured in the first *Mujahideen Moments* (2013) video included verses such as 'I refuse to be humiliated. Give me my own gun', and 'it's time for revenge'.[58] In echoing Kenyan Muslims' grievances, this messaging attempted to exploit social and political frictions as a means to further destabilise Kenya and weaken policymakers' commitment to the ongoing campaign in Somalia.

Post-2011 militant rhetoric revealed a form of political thinking that drew upon and repackaged multiple historic grievances. Repeating other political rhetoric in Kenya, militants attempted to tap into and redirect concerns about political marginality, social identity and belonging. Thus, in these discourses of militancy, familiar references to exclusive territoriality re-emerged. Yet, unlike the interfaith rhetoric of MRC separatists, radicals linked to al-Shabaab claimed the coast as a historically Muslim land to be 'liberated'. In this way, they combined global rhetorics of jihadist thought with a message that was resolutely local.[59]

Conclusion

The history of Muslim alienation outlined in this chapter has engendered fragile and contingent communities of sentiment among Muslims in coastal Kenya. As we have seen, at multiple historical junctures Muslim identity gained political value as a frame for interpreting alienation and collective action. Moreover, some political thinkers embraced religious territoriality as a discursive tool. However, state efforts to subvert Muslim dissent also became increasingly severe over time, notably in the era of counter-terrorism. In part because of this, both disinterest in and outright rejection of the political process grew among young people at multiple junctures, notably in the 2000s. While the strength of

---

[58] *Gaidi Mtaani* 2012; *Mujahideen Moments* 2013.
[59] Chome 2019; Ndzovu 2013–14.

Muslim identity as a political catalyst seems to have increased in recent decades, the mobilisation of Muslim identity, and state responses to this, have at times exacerbated ethnic, racial, ideological and generational cleavages.[60]

It would be a mistake, however, to discern only enduring cleavages in the history of the politics of alienation. The coast has seen moments of concerted action and neither political frictions nor alliances have been static. For instance, while ethnic tensions often limited the power of a concerted Muslim voice in the 1960s and 1990s, political divisions across ethnic lines were somewhat less pronounced in the 2010s. Similarly, the IPK's pan-Kenyan alliances contrasted dramatically with the geographical insularity of the 1960s Mwambao movement, the MRC's coastal nativism and the doctrinal insularity of al-Shabaab-linked militants. Additionally, coastal Muslims across ideological and socioeconomic lines agree that state responses to terrorism have violated Muslims' civil and human rights with impunity. As with earlier junctures, what divides Muslims at the coast is the question of *how* to address these and other grievances.

In more recent years, the tension between engagement with and rejection of the Kenyan state has eased. Nevertheless, the Kenyan state's disregard for coastal demands for social justice and the authorities' heavy-handed responses to the politics of alienation have deepened Muslims' sense of marginality over time. Just as important, since the 1990s, state responses to dissent have often constricted the political space available to address long-held grievances. And, as we have seen, events of the 2000s and early 2010s emboldened more radical voices and encouraged the rejection of the Kenyan state altogether, not only by young militants but also by the MRC, inter-faith separatists with very different interests. These modes of thinking and the alternative political spaces they inhabit may continue to present obstacles to conventional forms of political engagement, or they may dissipate. What is clear, however, is that while coastal Muslims share many grievances, the power of Muslim identity to catalyse political action and seek redress for injustices has been limited by shifting communal divisions, the Kenyan state's habitual indifference to Muslim grievances and Kenyan authorities' often violent responses to dissent.

Bibliography

Akiwumi, A. M. (1999), *Report of the Judicial Commission Appointed to Inquire into Tribal Clashes in Kenya*, Nairobi: Republic of Kenya, pp. 254–5.

---

[60] Ndzovu 2009.

Al-Bulushi, S. (2021), 'Citizen-Suspect: Navigating Surveillance and Policing in Urban Kenya', *American Anthropologist* 123(4), pp. 819–32.

Amnesty International (2003), 'Memorandum to the Kenyan Government on the Suppression of Terrorism Bill 2003', https://www.amnesty.org/en/documents/afr32/003/2004/en/

Anderson, D. (2005), '"Yours in Struggle for Majimbo": Nationalism and the Party Politics of Decolonisation in Kenya, 1955 to 1964', *Journal of Contemporary History* 39, pp. 547–64.

Anderson, D. (2010), 'Majimboism: the Troubled History of an Idea', in D. Branch, N. Cheeseman and L. Gardner (eds), *Our Turn to Eat! Politics in Kenya since 1950*, Berlin: Lit Verlag, pp. 17–43.

Anderson, D. M. (2014), 'Why Mpeketoni Matters: Al Shabaab and Violence in Kenya', Norwegian Peacebuilding Resource Centre, September 2014, http://peacebuilding.no/eng/Regions/Africa/Publications/Why-Mpeketoni-matters-al-Shabaab-and-violence-in-Kenya

Anderson, D. (2020), 'Kenya's War in Somalia', in N. Cheeseman, K. Kanyinga and G. Lynch (eds), *The Oxford Handbook of Kenyan Politics*, Oxford: Oxford University Press, pp. 577–589.

Anderson, D. M. and J. McKnight (2015), 'Understanding al-Shabaab: Clan, Islam and Insurgency in Kenya', *Journal of Eastern African Studies* 9(3), pp. 536–57.

Aseka, E. (1993), *Ronald Ngala*, Nairobi: East African Publishing House.

Atieno Odhiambo, E. S. and J. Lonsdale (2003), 'Introduction', in E. S. Atieno Odhiambo and J. Lonsdale (eds), *Mau Mau and Nationhood: Arms, Authority and Narration*, Athens: Ohio University Press.

Awori, H. (1993), 'Two Killed in "Religious" Riots in Mombasa', Inter Press Service, 10 September 1993.

Bakari, M. (1995), 'Muslims and the Politics of Change in Kenya', in M. Bakari and S. Yahya (eds), *Islam in Kenya: Proceedings of the National Seminar on Contemporary Islam in Kenya*. Nairobi: MEWA, pp. 234–51.

Bakari, M. (2013), 'A Place at the Table: The Political Integration of Muslims in Kenya, 1963–2007', *Islamic Africa* 4(1), pp. 15–48.

Beck, R. M. and K. Kresse (eds) (2016), *Abdilatif Abdalla: Poet in Politics*, Dar es Salaam: Mkuki na Nyota.

Bocha, G. (2017), 'How Boni Forest Became the Warzone It Is Today', *Daily Nation*, 19 July 2017.

Branch, D. (2011), *Kenya: Between Hope and Despair, 1963–2011*, New Haven: Yale University Press.

Brennan, J. R. (2008), 'Lowering the Sultan's Flag: Sovereignty and Decolonization in Coastal Kenya', *Comparative Studies in Society and History* 50(4), pp. 831–61.

Brennan, J. R. (2015), 'A History of Sauti ya Mvita (Voice of Mombasa): Radio, Public Culture, and Islam in Coastal Kenya, 1947–1966', in R. I. J. Hackett, B. F. Soares and F. B. Nyamnjoh (eds), *New Media and Religious Transformations in Africa*, Bloomington: Indiana University Press, pp. 19–38.

Chome, N. (2017), 'Why raids are a cause for worry as Al Shabaab changes face,' *Standard*, 23 July, https://www.standardmedia.co.ke/counties/article/2001248735/why-raids-are-a-cause-for-worry-as-al-shabaab-changes-face.

Chome, N. (2019), 'From Islamic Reform to Muslim Activism: The evolution of an Islamist Ideology in Kenya', *African Affairs* 18 (472), pp. 531–52.
Chome, N. (2020), 'The Political Role of Islam,' in N. Cheeseman, K. Kanyinga, and G. Lynch (eds), *The Oxford Handbook of Kenyan Politics*, Oxford: Oxford University Press, pp. 150–62.
Chome, N. (2021), 'Uses of Race: Moral debate and political action in Mombasa, 1895–1990', PhD dissertation, Durham University.
Daily Nation (1993a), 'Maitha Army "To Attack on Sunday"', 21 May 1993.
Daily Nation (1993b), 'Two Killed as Muslims Riot On', 10 September 1993.
Daily Nation (2012a), 'Four Injured in Clashes at Mosque', 10 February.
Daily Nation (2012b), 'The Radical world of the MRC', 15 October, http://www.nation.co.ke/Features/DN2/The+radical++world+of+the+MRC/-/957860/1532968/-/ek2exvz/-/index.html
East African Standard (1961), 'Coast Not Separate Says Mr. Kenyatta', 5 October.
East African Magazine, The (2005), 'Return of Balala the Fiery Street Preacher', 31 October.
Forrest, J. B. (2004), *Subnationalism in Africa: Ethnicity, Alliances, and Politics*, Boulder, CO: Lynne Rienner.
Gaidi Mtaani (2012), Issue 3, https://jihadology.net/2013/03/03/new-issue-of-the-magazine-gaidi-mtaani-issue-3
Goldsmith, P. (2011), 'The Mombasa Republican Council. Conflict Assessment: Threats and Opportunities for Engagement', Kenya Civil Society Strengthening Programme, November, p. 4.
Haki Africa (2016), *What Do We Tell the Families?: Killings and Disappearances in the Coastal Region of Kenya, 2012–2016*, Haki Africa website, December, hakiafrica.or.ke/wp-content/uploads/2017/02/HakiAfricaWDWTTF_V14.pdf
Harmony Project (2007), *Al-Qaida's (Mis)Adventures in the Horn of Africa*, West Point, NY: Combating Terrorism Center at the US Military Academy.
Harper, M. (2014), 'Kenyan Coastal Region of Lamu Hit by Deadly Attacks', *BBC News*, 6 July, www.bbc.com/news/world-africa-28181246
Hassan, A. I. (2003), 'Pitfalls of the Anti-terrorism Bill', *Daily Nation*, 27 June.
Horowitz J. (2012), 'Assassinations, Disappearances, and Riots: What's Happening in Mombasa?', *Open Society Justice Initiative*, 29 August, www.soros.org/voices/assassinations-disappearances-and-riots-what-s-happening-mombasa
Human Rights Watch (1992), *Kenya: Human Rights Developments, 1992*, www.hrw.org/reports/1993/WR93/Afw-02.htm
Human Rights Watch (2002), 'Playing with Fire: Weapons Proliferation, Political Violence, and Human Rights in Kenya', May.
Hyden, G. and C. Leys (1972), 'Elections and Politics in Single-Party Systems: The Case of Kenya and Tanzania', *British Journal of Political Science* 2(4), pp. 389–420.
Independent Online (South Africa) (2000), 30 May, www.iol.co.za/news/africa/fbi-interrogations-incur-muslim-wrath-39059
Jerejian, T. E. (2017), 'A Helping Hand? Recruitment of Kenyan Youth to al-Shabaab', MA thesis, University of Oslo.
Kenya National Archives (1958), CQ 1/1/100a, G.M. Wilson, 'Mombasa – A Modern Colonial Municipality'.
Kenya National Archives (1963a), PC/Coast/2/1/118 Annual Report Coast Region.

Kenya National Archives (1963b), KA/6/35 Swahili People's Party to Jomo Kenyatta, 29 July.

Kenya National Archives (1964), KA/6/35 Muhammad Hussein, Kenya Protectorate Nationalist Party, to Jomo Kenyatta, 6 January.

Kenya National Archives (1966), ACH 13/2; 'V.O.K. Broadcasts' I. M. Mathenge to the Permanent Secretary, 10 June.

Kenya National Commission on Human Rights (2008), *'The Cry of Blood': Report on Extra-Judicial Killings and Disappearances*, September, file.wikileaks.org/file/kenya-the-cry-of-blood/crimes-against-humanity-extra-judicial-killings-by-kenya-police-exposed.pdf

Kenya Television Network (2013), *Jicho Pevu*, 23 March.

Khalid, H. (2014), *Mpeketoni Killings: Human Rights Fact Finding Report*, Haki Africa, July, http://hakiafrica.or.ke/wp-content/uploads/2017/02/Haki%20Africa%20-%20Mpeketoni%20Booklet%20FINAL.pdf

Kinyanjui, H. (2003), 'Opinion: Anti-Terror Law Will Roll Back Kenya's Civil Liberties', *The East African*, 30 June.

Kresse, K. (2006), 'Debating *maulidi*: Ambiguities and Transformations of Muslim Identity along the Kenyan Swahili Coast', in Roman Loimeier and Rüdiger Seesemann (eds), *The Global Worlds of the Swahili: Interfaces of Islam, Identity and Space in 19th- and 20th-Century East Africa*, Berlin: Lit Verlag, pp. 209–28.

Kresse, K. (2009), 'Muslim Politics in Postcolonial Kenya: Negotiating Knowledge on the Double-Periphery', *Journal of the Royal Anthropological Institute* 15(1), pp. 76–94.

Kresse, K. (2016), '*Kenya Twendapi?*: Re-reading Abdilatif Abdalla's Pamphlet Fifty Years after Independence', *Africa* 86(1), pp. 1–32.

Kresse, K. (2018), *Swahili Muslim Publics and Postcolonial Experience*. Bloomington: Indiana University Press.

Lowen, M. (2014), 'Kenya al-Shabaab Terror Recruits "In It for the Money"', *BBC News*, 29 January.

Lynch, G. (2011), *I Say to You: Ethnic Politics and the Kalenjin in Kenya*, Chicago: University of Chicago Press.

MacIntosh, J. (2009), *The Edge of Islam: Power, Personhood, and Ethnoreligious Boundaries on the Kenya Coast*, Durham, NC: Duke University Press.

Maclean, W. (2003), 'Kenya Arabs Say Anti-Terror Probe Hurts Muslims', *Reuters*, 2 August.

Mahajan, N. (2023), 'The Coast is not Kenya: Mwambao in a Moment of Danger in Lamu', *Monsoon* 1(1), pp.92–106.

Mazrui, A. (1993), 'The Black Intifadah? Religion and Rage at the Kenyan coast', *Journal of Asian and African Affairs* 4, pp. 87–93.

Mazrui, A. (1997), *Kayas of Deprivation, Kayas of Blood: Violence, Ethnicity and the State in Coastal Kenya*, Nairobi: Kenya Human Rights Commission.

Mghangha, M. (2010), *Usipoziba Ufa Utajenga Ukuta: Land, Elections, and Conflicts in Kenya's Coast Province*, Nairobi: Heinrich Böll Stiftung.

Mujahideen Moments (2013), https://jihadology.net/2013/02/26/al-kataib-media-presents-a-new-video-message-from-%e1%b8%a5arakat-al-shabab-al-mujahidin-mujahidin-moments/

Mutonya, N. (1993), *Daily Nation* 'Strike Paralyzes Mombasa Town', 29 May.

Mwakio, P. (2013), 'Muslim Youth Extremism Out of Hand, Warn Leaders', *Standard*, 24 December, http://www.standardmedia.co.ke/thecounties/article/2000100745/muslim-youth-extremism-out-of-hand-warn-leaders

Mwakimako, H. (2007), 'Christian–Muslim Relations in Kenya: A Catalogue of Events and Meanings', *Islam and Christian–Muslim Relations* 18(2), pp. 287–307.
Mwakimako, H. (2010), 'Risk Assessment: Violent Religious Extremism and the Muslim Population in Kenya', Washington, DC: Management Systems International.
Mwakimako, H. and J. Willis (2014), 'Islam, Politics, and Violence on the Kenyan Coast, Observatoire des Enjeux Politiques et Sécuritaires dans la Corne de l'Afrique', note 4, July, www.lam.sciencespobordeaux.fr/sites/lam/files/note4_observatoire.pdf
National Archives of the United Kingdom and Ireland (1961a), CO894/13/2 Maalim Omar Rashid Bakuli, Memorandum on Coastal Strip Autonomy, 20 October.
National Archives of the United Kingdom and Ireland (1961b), CO894/10, Memorandum by the President of KADU on the Coastal Strip, 26 October.
National Archives of the United Kingdom and Ireland (1962), NA CO 822/2159/4, Record of a Second Meeting, Kenya Coastal Strip Conference, 9 March.
Ndzovu, H. J. (2009), 'Muslims and Party Politics and Electoral Campaigns in Kenya', *Institute for the Study of Islamic Thought in Africa*, Northwestern University, Working Paper Series, n.09-001.
Ndzovu, H. J. (2010), 'Muslim Relations in the Politics of Nationalism and Secession in Kenya', Program of African Studies Working Papers, no. 18.
Ndzovu, H. J. (2012), 'The Politicization of Muslim Organizations and the Future of Islamic-Oriented Politics in Kenya', *Islamic Africa* 3(1), pp. 25–53.
Ndzovu, H. J. (2013–14), 'The Prospects of Islamism in Kenya as Epitomized by Shaykh Aboud Rogo's Sermons', *The Annual Review of Islam in Africa* 12(2), pp. 7–12.
Ndzovu, H. J. (2014), *Muslims in Kenyan Politics: Political Involvement, Marginalization, and Minority Status*, Evanston: Northwestern University Press.
Ndzovu, H. J. (2017), 'The Rise of Jihad, Killing of "Apostate Imams" and Non-Combatant Christian Civilians in Kenya: Al-Shabaab's Re-definition of the Enemy on Religious Lines', *Journal for the Study of the Religions of Africa and its Diaspora* 3(1), pp. 4–20.
Ndzovu, H. J. (2017), 'Muslim and Christian Contestation over the Entrenchment of the Kadhi Courts in the Constitution of Kenya: Challenging the Principle of a Secular State', in M. C. Green, et al. (eds) *Religious Pluralism, Heritage and Social Development in Africa*, Stellenbosch: Conf-RAP.
Nyaundi K. (2018), 'Kenya: Fighting Terrorism Within and Without the Law', in M. Ruteere and P. Muthahi (eds), *Confronting Violent Extremism in Kenya*, Nairobi: Centre for Human Rights and Policy Studies, pp. 43–70.
Nzes, F. (2014), 'Al-Hijra: Al-Shabaab's affiliate in Kenya', *CTC Sentinel* 7(5), pp. 24–6.
Oded, A. (2000), *Islam and Politics in Kenya*, Boulder, CO: Lynne Rienner.
Oketch, W., N. Kithi and P. Mwakio (2014), 'Foreigners among Mombasa Mosque Chaos Suspects', *Standard*, 6 February, http://www.standardmedia.co.ke/?articleID=2000104030&story_title=foreigners-among-mombasa-mosque-chaos-suspects&pageNo=2
Open Society Justice Initiative and Muslims for Human Rights, The (2013), *'We're Tired of Taking You to the Court': Human Rights Abuses by Kenya's Anti-Terrorism Police Unit*, New York: Open Society Foundations.
Prestholdt, J. (2011), 'Kenya, the United States, and Counterterrorism', *Africa Today* 57(4), pp. 3–27.
Prestholdt, J. (2014), 'Politics of the Soil: Separatism, Autochthony, and Decolonization at the Kenyan Coast', *Journal of African History* 55(2), pp. 249–70.

Prestholdt, J. (2019), 'Counterterrorism in Kenya: Security Aid, Impunity and Muslim Alienation', in M. J. Boyle (ed.), *Non-Western Approaches to Counterterrorism*, Manchester: Manchester University Press, pp. 386–409.

Prestholdt, J. (2023), 'Kenyan Muslims and the Political Imagination of Space on the Indian Ocean Rim', in D. S. Powers and E. Tagliacozzo (eds.), *Islamic Ecumene: Comparing Global Muslim Societies*, Ithaca: Cornell University Press, pp. 62–81.

Reuters (2012), 'Islamists Blamed for Nairobi Church Killing', 30 April.

Saalfeld, J. and H. A. Mwakimako (2023), 'Integrationism vs. rejectionism: revisiting the history of Islamist activism in coastal Kenya', *Journal of Eastern African Studies* 17(1–2), pp. 40–56.

Salim, A. I. (1970), 'The Movement for "Mwambao" or Coast Autonomy in Kenya, 1956–63', B. A. Ogot (ed.), *Hadith 2*, Nairobi: East African Publishing House, pp. 212–28.

Salim, A. I. (1973), *The Swahili-Speaking Peoples of Kenya's Coast*, Nairobi: East African Publishing House.

Salim, A. I. (1976), 'Native or Non-Native?: The Problem of Identity and the Social Stratification of the Arab-Swahili of Kenya', *Hadith 6*, Nairobi: East African Publishing House, pp. 65–85.

Salim, A. I. (1979), 'The Impact of Colonialism upon Muslim Life in Kenya', *Journal – The Institute of Muslim Minority Affairs* 1(1), pp. 60–6.

Salmon, K. (2003), 'Muslims Say FBI Targets Them', *Inter Press Service*, 6 March.

Stren, R. (1970), 'Factional Politics and Central Control in Mombasa, 1960–1969', *Canadian Journal of African Studies/Revue Canadienne des Études Africaines* 4(1), pp. 33–56.

Thoya, F. (2003), 'Imam's Fury Over New Anti-Terror Bill', *Coast Express*, 20 June.

United Nations Human Rights Council (2009), 'Report of the Special Rapporteur on Extrajudicial, Summary or Arbitrary Executions, Philip Alston: Addendum: Mission to Kenya', 26 May, reliefweb.int/sites/reliefweb.int/files/resources/15D4D9 C184ADDBAA492575C90024524F-Full_Report.pdf

US Department of State (1995), 'Kenya Human Rights Practices, 1994', February.

Waddilove, H. (2020), 'The Coast: an elusive political bloc', N. Cheeseman, K. Kanyinga, and G. Lynch (eds), *The Oxford Handbook of Kenyan Politics*, Oxford: Oxford University Press, pp. 715–28.

Weekly Review (1992a), 'Muslims Question Ban Decision', 5 June, pp. 22–3.

Weekly Review (1992b), 'Second Wave of Coast Violence', 24 July, pp. 20–1.

Weitzberg, K. (2017), *We Do Not Have Borders: Greater Somalia and the Predicaments of Belonging in Kenya*, Athens: Ohio University Press.

Whittaker, H. (2014), *Insurgency and Counter-insurgency in Kenya: A Social History of the Shifta Conflict, c. 1963–1968*, Leiden: Brill.

Willis, J. (1993), *Mombasa, the Swahili and the Making of the Mijikenda*, Oxford: Clarendon Press.

Willis, J. and G. Gona (2013), '*Pwani si Kenya?*: Memory, Documents and Secessionist Politics in Coastal Kenya', *African Affairs* 112 (446), pp. 48–71.

Wolf, T. P. (2000), 'Contemporary Politics', in J. Hoorweg, D. Foeken and R. A. Obudho (eds), *Kenya Coast Handbook: Culture, Resources and Development in the East African Littoral*, New Brunswick, NJ: Transaction, pp. 129–55.

3

Counter-narrativity as Peace, Love and Unity: Citizenship and Belonging in a Kenyan Muslim Counter-radicalisation Programme

HALKANO ABDI WARIO

INTRODUCTION

'*Jihad* is not killing the innocent ... Islam is peace, love and unity' proclaims a poster on a Facebook page called *Jihad for All*.[1] The page is affiliated to an initiative called Building Resilience Against Violent Extremism (BRAVE), which was formed in mid-2015. This is no ordinary civil society engaged in preventing and countering violent extremism (P/CVE) in Kenya. It aspires to inspire hundreds of thousands of Muslims within the country to join its course in producing alternative narratives to those of jihadists and to delegitimise these groups as un-Islamic, a threat to national unity and inter-religious relations, and a danger to the lives and properties of its citizens. To support this goal, BRAVE runs a series of radio, print and television advertisements, produces manuals, trains dozens of religious leaders and civil society activists, and maintains a presence online and offline for various audiences so as to engage potential stakeholders and recipients with its activities. By engaging with militants on the interpretation of core Islamic concepts that form the bulk of their recruitment props, BRAVE and similar organisations fall back on century-old Muslim intellectual traditions that reaffirm the plurality of jurisprudential positions. Coming back to the poster, it is striking for BRAVE to call its affiliate Facebook page on counter-narrativity campaigns *Jihad for All*. It is an attempt to democratise the often-monopolised discourses about jihad beyond what militants want it to be. By stretching the meanings of jihad from the 'military expedition against unbelievers and their associates' to more mundane concerns about everyday

---

[1] https://web.facebook.com/jihadforall/photos/a.667782010019922.1073741826.66

struggles and charity to self and others, the producers wish to turn the tables on the jihadists in their own field.

However, this poster is intriguing not for stating that jihad is not killing innocent people, but for labelling Islam as meaning peace, love and unity. The three qualities associated with Islam here are long-standing national values as espoused in the *Nyayo* philosophy of the country's second president, Daniel arap Moi.[2] The three virtues still invoke patriotism, inter-faith and inter-ethnic cohesion, tolerance and even belonging in multi-religious and cultural society. One need only read the country's Loyalty Pledge.[3] This poster, as the chapter will explore, hints at strong tendencies within some Muslim faith-based counter-radicalisation initiatives that attempt to reconcile Muslim citizenship and belonging within the Kenyan state amid alluring meta-narratives levelled against vulnerable youth by violent extremists. I use the word 'attempt' because this task has been dauntingly difficult. BRAVE also distances the heterogeneous Muslim communities from the brutal acts committed by violent extremists within the country as neither representative of their faith traditions nor congruent with their membership in the peaceful multi-religious nation-state of Kenya. For better comprehension of the nuances within these P/CVE programmes, let me quote verbatim another advertisement that ran on national television and radio stations:

> Violent extremists have tried to divide the country on religious lines.
> We the Muslims in Kenya have said no more divisions.
> Let's reclaim and take charge of the narratives used by the extremists.
> How? By speaking the truth …
> Islam does not condone the killings of innocent lives … Never.
> As Muslims, Christians and other denominations.
> Let's unite in the fight against radicalisation and violent extremism.

---

[2] This appropriation of triune national values in such campaigns may be akin to the French Muslim attempt to reconcile *Laïcité, Egalité, Fraternité* despite long-standing exclusion and marginalisation for decades in the secular French Republic. Daniel arap Moi came to power in 1978 following the death of the first president, Jomo Kenyatta. His rule followed the developmentalist agenda set in place by Kenyatta. He called his national philosophy *kufuata nyayo*, which means 'trending along established footsteps' (Adar and Munyae 2001; Ahluwalia 1996). Nyayoism was best espoused through and epitomised by its cherished national values of peace, love and unity (Musila 2009). Despite the fact that his one-party rule was despotic, oppressive and devoid of freedom and official opposition, Kenyans largely remember him for reigning over a relatively peaceful state. As people gradually forget the tribulations of his regime, people still reminiscence about this era of relative tranquillity and national cohesion.

[3] Loyalty pledge: 'I pledge my loyalty to the President and the nation of Kenya, my readiness and duty to defend the flag of our republic, my devotion to the words of our national anthem, my life and strength in the task of our nation's building, in the living spirit of embodied in our national motto – *Harambee*! And perpetuated in the *Nyayo* Philosophy of Peace, Love and Unity.' This pledge was recited every Friday in all secondary and primary schools across the country, and still is in some schools, despite it not being part of the current constitution. *Harambee* was both a rallying call and a philosophy of collective co-operation and resources during Kenyatta's regime.

Counter-narrativity as Peace, Love and Unity

By fostering peaceful coexistence built on friendship and development.
We can influence the narratives and counter-narratives by countering the narratives of violent extremists.
We are Kenyans, brought together by our national values.
We must not be divided by violent extremists.
Be a part of the BRAVE Movement.[4]

Now more than at any moment in its history, Kenyan Muslims of all persuasions face tremendous social challenges as a result of heightened radicalisation and youth recruitment into violent extremist groups in the Horn of Africa and their local variants in Kenya. They bore the brunt of ruthless state machinery that often engaged in extra-judicial killings and other forms of gross human rights violations. Due to the myriad alleged and real marginalisation and historical injustices meted out against their co-religionists by successive regimes in the coastal and northern regions of Kenya, propagandist ideologies often depict the Kenyan state to its potential recruits as a hostile territory for believers, warranting *hijra* (migration) to Somalia and other parts of 'jihadist'-controlled utopias as a commendable solution. Muslim faith-based organisations have of late been crucial in countering radicalisation and recruitment into such groups. This places a considerable burden on ulama (scholars) and Muslim civil society activists as producers of counter-narrativity to re-appropriate the Kenyan state as a multi-religious and hospitable secular state, condemn selective targeting of members of non-Muslim communities in terrorist attacks, and re-interpret and contextualise appropriate religious knowledge as the basis of this agenda. This chapter relies an ongoing research using oral interviews and in-depth analysis of performative aesthetics and contents of selected audio-visual and written materials by one Muslim civil society organisation (the BRAVE Movement) that is at the forefront of the production of counter-narrativity as part of its de-radicalisation programmes, and interrogates citizenship, belonging and pan-Kenyan-ness as core drivers of Muslim–state, Muslim–non-Muslim and Muslim–Muslim relations.

This chapter is divided into three sections. In the first section, I examine the historical basis for strained Muslim–state relations during the colonial and post-colonial periods that immensely exacerbated discourses of inequality, marginalisation, neglect and historical injustices, and that subsequently fuelled the feelings of second-class citizenship that have often been exploited by militant groups for radicalisation and recruitment. The second section is a case study in how BRAVE constructs counter-narrative campaigns as legitimate ideological responses to jihadist propaganda, and how it attempts

---

[4] See https://www.youtube.com/watch?v=t2py6BcvsJI

to weave convincing strategies that interrogate citizenship, relations between Muslims and the state, and membership in a global community of believers. The last section highlights the promises and perils of BRAVE and other faith-based counter-narrativity initiatives that are engaged in countering violent extremism. It also proposes measures that inform the best interventions to counter violent extremism.

A note on methodology: the primary data for this chapter were collected between August 2015 and January 2018 in Nairobi, Mombasa and Isiolo through individual and group interviews, expert interviews, participant observations and documentary reviews of materials produced by those involved in P/CVE programmes. In-depth discussions were held with officials of the BRAVE Movement, select members of the Muslim religious cadre, civil society activists drawn from other P/CVE programmes, and recipients of counter-radicalisation programmes in specific urban quarters in Nairobi and Mombasa. Secondary data were sources from books, journals and other written literature on the subject.

Ambivalent Decades of (Mis)rule: Muslims and Colonial and Post-colonial Kenya

Prior to colonialism, the coastal region in East Africa had a number of semi-autonomous city-states that existed either autonomously or in alliance or were under the rule of external administrative regimes for centuries. City-states including Mombasa, Malindi, Lamu, Mogadishu, Zanzibar and Kilwa dotted the Indian Ocean coastline all the way to Sofala. The coastal stretch of what is today Kenya came under Portuguese (16th–17th century) and then Omani Arab rule (17th–19th century). Immediate coastal and hinterland communities had ambivalent relations with settled Swahili and Arab populations that, among other exchanges, included trade and intermarriages (Insoll 2003; Loimeier and Seesemann 2006; Bakari 1995).

The terms of the 1884 Berlin Conference set the pace for declarations of sphere of influence and subsequent colonial occupations of different parts of Africa. Germany and Britain expressed interest in East Africa (present-day Kenya, Somalia, Uganda, Tanganyika and Zanzibar). Both of these European colonial powers signed dozens of treaties with East African chiefs, sultans and other community representatives. Through the Helgoland–Zanzibar Treaty, Germany and the United Kingdom settled numerous territorial possessions in Witu, Zanzibar, Tanganyika, Namibia, Togo and Heligoland (Gillard 1960; Pyeatt 1988). Signing this in 1895, the British declared a protectorate over Zanzibar and areas under the rule of its Sultan, including a ten-mile strip on the Kenyan coast, the so-called 'Mwambao' (Singh 1965; Brennan 2008; Mwaruvie 2011).

The building of the Kenya–Uganda Railways and related colonial infrastructure set the pace for the full integration of the coastal region into the colonial project. Hundreds migrated inland via the road and railway networks, establishing small coastal Muslim communities in emerging towns and urban centres as small-scale traders and lower-cadre colonial functionaries (Mwakimako 2008).

During the colonial period, due to the racial nature of the colonial project, Africans (including those in the Protectorate) were merely subjects while Europeans, as proper citizens, enjoyed exclusive rights, including the highest opportunities and privileges such as land ownership and representation in colonial legislative assemblies. Arabs and Asians were given some limited rights and privileges that included representation in legislative assemblies and recognition of their socio-cultural, educational, economic and political institutions after their heightened advocacy and protests (Aiyar 2015; Salvadori and Feddders 1989).

These differential treatments and attendant privileges formed the basis for suspicion and mistrust between indigenous African communities, the Swahili and Arabs and others in the period leading to independence over whether the coastal strip should be autonomous, rejoin Zanzibar or be a semi-autonomous province in the newly emerging post-colonial Kenya. The repercussions of this era are still felt today through emergent discourses of secession by Mombasa and Kwale County Governors and by the Mombasa Republican Council, a group whose rallying call was *'Pwani si Kenya'* (the coast is not Kenya).[5]

Present-day northern Kenya – the home area for Kenyan Somalis and other Cushitic speakers – was a closed district during the colonial period, with entry and exit from the region policed by the colonial administration. It was aptly called Northern Frontier District and included a swathe of areas all the way from the Tana Basin through the present-day counties of Garissa, Wajir, Mandera, Marsabit and Turkana (Castagno 1964). Just like the protectorate, the region was predominantly Muslim and also had very limited investments from the colonial regime in terms of educational and health institutions, or infrastructural development (Lewis 1963), a trend that continued in the decades after independence. Given the low levels of pan-Kenyan political consciousness prior to the granting of independence, the people overwhelmingly rejected the union with the new Kenyan republic in a 'referendum' conducted in the region, opting instead to join the Somalian state. A brutal six-year civil war (*shifta*) was fought in the region (Whittaker 2015; Weitzberg 2016; Oba and Khalif 2013). One author summarises the state of affairs in the region as follows:

---

[5] The Mombasa Republican Council is a proscribed group. Its main form of agitation is for separation of the coastal region from greater Kenya. Its rallying call has been *'Pwani si Kenya'* (the coast is not Kenya). Its leaders and sympathisers have been subjected to arrests, detention and countless court trials (Willis and Gona 2012).

> In 1962, the British held a series of meetings in the NFD which was attended by 40,000 Muslim Somalis, Boran, and Sakuye, who expressed their desire to join Somalia rather than remain in Kenya under a Christian and Bantu-speaking government. However, in March 1963, without consulting the Somalia government as agreed, the British announced their decision to make the Northern Frontier District a seventh province in Kenya. Political opposition was swift. Somalis and their Muslim Boran and Sakuye allies boycotted the Kenyan national elections and called for secession. They began an armed insurrection which included the mining of roads and attacking government officials and missionaries in Marsabit, Wajir, and Garissa Districts; they also raided livestock from non-Muslim Boran, Rendille, Ariaal, Samburu, and Gabra pastoralists who had remained loyal to the Kenya government ... The Kenya government responded by forcing Somali, Sakuye, and Waso Boran into enclosed 'strategic villages' (or *daba*). Camel herds were shot as 'supporting the enemy', and residents found a mile outside the villages were considered *shifta* and arrested or shot. (Fratkin and Roth 2015: 41–2)

In the coastal region, the dissolution of KADU and its absorption into KANU did not compel the Kenyatta regime to grant a form of Majimbo-style federal state, for which coastal political elites agitated (Ndzovu 2014; Anderson 2005). Dissatisfaction persisted over the following decades. Many issues were raised as urgent for redress: issuance of land ownership documents, problems of absentee land owners and decades of squatting on their own ancestral lands, redress of inequality and lack of economic opportunities for the youth, few health and educational institutions, inadequate political representation, the need for greater autonomy and a share of the billions generated from East Africa's main port of Mombasa, inadequate economic opportunities and 'land-grabbing' of prime beach-front properties by up-country political elites, strained inter-faith relations, and stringent requirements in issuance of citizenship documents, among many others (Mwakimako 2007).

The impotence of coastal political elites to go beyond self- and ethnic interests to wage a united platform for resolving the region's problems has heightened the sense of loss of hope and of belonging to the Kenyan state. It is little wonder that groups such as the Mombasa Republican Council (MRC) proclaim that the coast is not part of Kenya and that they are/were/will be alone (Willis and Gona 2012; Goldsmith 2011).

In the Upper Eastern and North Eastern regions, similar discourses of marginalisation and neglect have been expressed over the years. Subsequent regimes since independence have treated the residents with suspicion since *Shifta* insurgencies and have not shied away from using force to subdue politically instigated violence or even simple protests. The region has extensive porous borders with

Somalia and Ethiopia. The pastoralist communities in the region are found across international boundaries. They move freely across the borders in search of pastures and water, trade, kinship visits and cultural events. The Truth, Justice and Reconciliation Commission investigated years of state repression in the region, including the 1984 Wagalla Massacre and military and police excesses during the war against Somali insurgents in the 1960s and 1970s (Anderson 2014). It is not uncommon for residents to be subjected to the most stringent requirements of proof of citizenship before they are granted national identity cards or passports. Massive unemployment, low levels of investment by the state and the private sector, poor transport infrastructure, rampant droughts and famines, and controlled mobility through numerous police barriers on the roads in the region make the residents feel subjected to a repressive colonial-like security regime (Mahmoud 2008; Salvadori 2000). Due to the civil war in Somalia and problems of violent extremism, profiling and controlled mobility and surveillance of travellers in and out of the region have increased since 2011. The militant group al-Shabaab has recruited hundreds of disenfranchised Kenyan youth since its rise, peaking perhaps between 2009 and 2013 (Hansen 2012).

Selective co-option into post-colonial regimes has not necessarily resulted in amicable resolution of discourses of neglect and historical injustices in the coastal and northern regions. Political processes such as the introduction of multi-party politics indeed made the regional elites align themselves with emerging power bases. Attempts at forming region-specific political outfits have often failed or were fought by the state for fear of its destabilising ramifications (Kresse 2009; Oded 2000). The negotiations over constitutional change shook relations between Muslims and non-Muslims (mostly over the status of kadhis' courts), but were finally retained within the new constitutional dispensation that came into force in 2010 (Wario 2014).

So pervasive were the discourses of marginalisation and state neglect that in October 2007 the third president of Kenya, Mwai Kibaki, constituted a special commission entitled 'Presidential Special Action Committee to Address Specific Concerns of the Muslim Community in Regard to Alleged Harassment and/or Discrimination in the Application/Enforcement of the Law', led by A. M. H. Sharawe, himself an ethnic Somali. The report was handed over in 2008, though its contents were never made public or implemented to restore confidence and integrate the faith community into mainstream development in the country.[6] Violent extremist groups hence found a large repertoire of existing grievances against the state, grinding poverty and unemployment through which to craft convincing meta-narratives for radicalisation and massive recruitment of youths from Muslim-majority regions into their cause.

---

[6] Lynch 2014.

Turning CVE into Nation-building: Politics of Counter-narrativity in the BRAVE Movement's Intervention

Prior to October 2011, when the Kenya Defence Forces made a unilateral incursion into Somalia to oust al-Shabaab militants from towns close to its borders and from the main maritime ports that they controlled, terrorist attacks, though growing in frequency, were few and far between and were limited to cross-border raids and sporadic attacks against security apparatus. Much earlier, attacks associated with al-Qaeda and other transnational terrorist organisations largely targeted so-called foreign establishments, especially American and Israeli enterprises and embassies. However, terrorism has become truly localised in these first decades of the 21st century and feeds off local contextual discourses of disenfranchisement to radicalise and recruit foot soldiers, especially at the coast, and in Nairobi and northern Kenya. The KDF presence in Somalia is often evoked by al-Shabaab for its continued attacks against Kenya.

While, on a regional scale, Somalia is the epicentre of al-Shabaab terror attacks and resultant instability, the second most affected country is Kenya (Maruf and Joseph 2018). The country remains attractive to the terror operatives for a number of reasons (Marchal 2019). It shares more than 1,000 kilometres of a porous and poorly guarded border with southern Somalia, with the other side controlled with limited success by Somalia's Jubaland Federal Member State. The country is also a regional hub that hosts a vast number of international organisations, foreign embassies, multinational financial investments and key critical infrastructure that are ready targets for terrorist attacks. In October 2011, Kenya Defence Forces made unilateral incursions into Somalia, displacing al-Shabaab from key maritime ports and hinterland territories (Lind et al. 2015). The group has since waged a series of low- and high-priority attacks within Kenya and KDF camps in Somalia. The following are the sites of some of the most devastating attacks on Kenya: the Westgate Shopping Complex in Nairobi (2013), with 67 fatalities; Garissa University College (2015), with 148 fatalities; Mpeketoni, with 57 fatalities (2014); waylaying of buses plying the Mandera–Nairobi route; numerous attacks against Mandera quarry workers (2014); El Adde (2016), with 180 Kenya Defence Forces killed; Dusit D2 Complex, with 21 fatalities (2019), and Camp Simba (2020), with three United States personnel dead. Countless civilians, non-local teachers and civil servants in North Eastern region and security officers have been maimed and killed in dozens of small-scale attacks in Kenya.[7] The use of Improvised Explosive Devices (IEDs), the kidnapping of government functionaries

---

[7] According to an observatory on terrorism attacks at the Centre for Human Rights and Policy Studies, Nairobi, between 2017 and 2020, as of May 2020 there were 110 terror-related attacks, with 251 fatalities. https://www.cve-kenya.org/

and cross-border raids by small terror operative units are increasingly common (Pkalya and Cannon 2019; Ombati 2015; Hansen 2012).

Until recently, the state's counter-terrorism strategies have been largely counter-productive and punitive to suspect communities. This has heightened suspicion, community profiling and the feeling of persecution due to the rampant abuse of suspects' human rights; there are many unresolved cases of enforced disappearances, extra-judicial killings, security swoops on Muslim-majority areas, endless months of security curfews and treatment of those often targeted by militants as suspects rather than potential collaborators (UNDP Report 2017; Botha 2014; Khalil and Zeuthen 2015).

A donor-driven paradigmatic approach has led to the gradual preference for (and complementarity of) so-called softer community-based and community-led counter-radicalisation strategies, called Preventing and Countering Violent Extremism, over the hard military ones of counter-terrorism (Lind and Howell 2010; Bachmann and Honke 2009). These new initiatives have seen the emergence of dozens of international and national organisations, including Muslim-led groups that undertake diverse intervention measures to reduce youth radicalisation and recruitment into militant groups, among other issues. These interventions, though uncoordinated, aspire to address so-called push-and-pull factors that make youth join or want to join these groups in the first place.[8]

Despite the complexities of why individuals join militant groups, the underlying unresolved marginalisation discourses related to community/citizen–state relations provide an overarching rationalisation for potential recruits and terrorism groups.[9] The UNDP Report *Journey to Extremism* argues that militarised responses to violent extremism have only served to deepen long-standing mistrust and alienation, with governments and counter-terrorism strategies often explicitly identified as a source of grievance.[10]

Do Muslims in Kenya feel that they belong? As argued above, the narratives of recruitment feed on existing discourses of disenfranchisement, of contested citizenship, of lack of representation in matters of national politics and economy, of systemic regional underdevelopment and neglect by various regimes since independence, of stringent requirements upon application and acquisition of national identity documents; growing communal identification with and

---

[8] Push factors are context-specific and much more complex, and include, among others, social marginalisation, endemic corruption, ungoverned areas, police harassment and state repression, poverty and unemployment, unattended historical injustices and racial and cultural profiling. Pull factors include access to material resources, belonging, adventure, the prospect of glory and fame, the personal appeal of radical preachers, and radicalised religious environments, among others. https://www.stabilityjournal.org/articles/10.5334/sta.ee/
[9] The quality of state–citizen relationships across a range of indicators is increasingly recognised as an important factor driving the spread of violent extremism. UNDP Report.
[10] Ibid.

suspicion of support for foreign militant groups or their local affiliations; and subsequent tough repressive state security actions against terrorism suspects, communities, educational and/religious institutions, among others.

Prior to the establishment of the 'Building Resilience Against Violent Extremism' (BRAVE) initiative, ideological responses to violent extremists by Muslim leaders were often individualised, and few and far between. These efforts were associated with so-called moderate sheikhs in urban settings, especially in Mombasa. They became the target for sympathisers with radical preachers and violent extremist groups, and some were even murdered.[11] Whenever terrorist attacks were carried out within the country, it had been a routine response for Muslim religious leaders to issue declarative statements that the Muslim community unequivocally condemns such attacks carried out by people who purportedly represent their faith community. BRAVE rose out of the frustration of the religious cadre in Kenya and its impotence to provide alternative ideological narratives to those of the militants in an institutionalised manner, and to equip vulnerable youth, madrasa teachers, mosque prayer leaders and officials, civil society activists involved in P/CVE programmes and government officials with legitimate counter-narratives to use.

The programme was born in the aftermath of the brutal Garissa University College attack in April 2015. It rose to occupy the national limelight when, from mid-2015, it ran a series of fascinating paid advertisements on all broadcast media during prime viewing time. The BRAVE officials straddle multiple civil society organisations and have several responsibilities geared towards their visibility, while addressing diverse conflicts in the region. Eventually, they rose to the status of authorities in the field of addressing violent extremism and other insecurities (Wario 2017).

BRAVE has described itself as a systematic programme to prevent and counter violent extremism in Kenya. Its strategy is centred on ideological elements related to violent extremism and terrorism, including the narratives and counter-narratives. It also focuses on returnees, young persons (including children and youths) and adults in areas considered hot spots.[12]

In comparison with other initiatives in the United Kingdom (PREVENT, CONSENT, etc.), France, Saudi Arabia and the UAE, BRAVE is largely

---

[11] Sheikh Mohammed Idris, chairperson of the Council of Imams and Preachers of Kenya and a staunch opponent of radical youth who support militancy, was shot dead by unknown gunmen on 10 June 2014. He was eulogised by President Uhuru Kenyatta as a great loss to the country's war against religious extremism as he was at the forefront in the fight against radicalisation of the youth. Sheikh Idris was the fourth moderate religious leader killed by suspected violent extremism operatives between 2012 and 2014. https://www.bbc.com/news/world-africa-27776743

[12] The BRAVE programme 'is anticipated to trigger, initiate and sustain a momentum for actions on counter-violent extremism, counter-radicalization and de-radicalization. Momentum built is expected to continuously undermine information asymmetries that favour violent extremist groups gained and used by the violent extremists and militant groups' (Ali and Bwana 2015: viii).

intra-faith, Muslim-led and free from state control; hence it enjoys relative legitimacy and authority in this field. In terms of organisational structure, the Movement has zones of operation in five regions – Nairobi, Coast, North Eastern, Upper Eastern, WE or rest of Kenya – based on the demographic distribution of Muslims in Kenya and the prominence of violent extremism in an area. Each of the zones is further divided into BRAVE County, BRAVE Youth, BRAVE Professionals, BRAVE SAVE and BRAVE WAVE. The Movement has a steering committee (steering committee against violent extremism, or SCARVE) and a reference group upon which its bureaucratic organisational structure is based. The Movement instituted a reference committee composed of Muslim religious leaders to validate (read and certify) the materials it produces in light of Islamic religious knowledge. The Movement also initially roped in communities through the use of particular individuals accepted and recognised as reliable and competent leaders. There is an advisory committee comprising prominent elderly Muslim leaders (mostly men and a few women). The Movement closely collaborates and partners with almost all national Muslim organisations, including the Kenya Council of Imams and Ulamaa, the Council of Islamic Preachers of Kenya and *Majlis Ulama*.[13]

The BRAVE initiative contextualises its campaign, basing it on a comprehensive understanding of how violent extremist groups propagate their ideologies, recruit potential fighters through rampantly self-serving misinterpretation of the scriptures for violent ends and increasingly otherise (*kuffar, murtad, dar al islam, dar al harb/kufr*,[14] etc.) opposing religious and political elites and the general non-Muslim populace. The Movement identifies the following as misleading narratives associated with al-Shabaab and other groups that wish to recruit Kenyans to their causes: that there is a 'war against Muslims' going on in the country; that Kenya is part of the war against Islam; that there are planned and calculated efforts to marginalise and exclude Muslims from all aspects of Kenyan society in order to weaken Islam; that Muslims in Kenya have a duty to wage 'holy war' against non-Muslims, especially against the government of the Republic of Kenya; that a *shaheed*'s (martyr's) desirable and ultimate honour is to attain martyrdom in this cause and earn the greatest reward from Allah; that making *hijra* from Kenya is not *dar al islam*, that jihad is mandatory, or that receiving training for jihad back home is necessary; that the only way to address and achieve victory against the 'war on Islam' is through armed struggle,

---

[13] Interviews with Sheikh R. Aula, September 2018.
[14] For comprehensive analysis of classical and contemporary discussions on Islam and territoriality, see Albrecht 2018: 150. Albrecht aptly observes that the categorisation of the world into a 'territory of Islam' and a 'territory of unbelief' also plays a crucial role in the worldview promulgated by Islamic State and various other jihadist propagandists and endorses a dichotomous understanding of territoriality, distinguishing between *dār al-islām* on the one hand and *dār al-kufr* or *dār al-ḥarb* on the other.

self-sacrifice and/or active support for their version of the 'jihadist' cause, and ultimately that there is an urgent need to restore *khilafa*.[15]

So critical is recruitment of Kenyans into their ranks that al-Shabaab leaders even constituted an elite military unit called Jaysh al-Ayman to engage in asymmetrical war in Kenya, placing Ahmed Iman Kimanthi, a Kenyan, as one of its leaders. The unit has relentlessly targeted civilian and military installations in the Boni Forest in Lamu. Recruits from the country are seen as pivotal in furthering their agenda and are often cited and praised among other foreign fighters as people who sacrificed more to solve problems of Muslim marginalisation in their country. Below is an excerpt from such a speech, attributed to Sheikh Ali Mahmoud Rage, al-Shabaab spokesman and senior leader, during a pass-out parade in May 2017:

> You have to be the army that will conquer Kenya so that we may return to our families and relatives in a state of honor and glory, and uplift them from the humiliation, by the permission of Allah, the Exalted.[16] *Muhajireen* brothers have endured the intense training sessions and exerted a great effort to learn the different ways of combating the enemies of Allah …You, my dear brothers, have made *Hijra* from faraway lands and have completed intense training courses and have endured great hardships …You are well aware of the situation of the Muslim *Ummah* in general, and particularly, the Muslims of East Africa, and the humiliation and suffering they are faced with …We have to eliminate all other systems of governance and laws of Kufr such as democracy, communism and secularism enforced upon us by the pagans and govern the land according to the Qur'an and Sunnah of the Prophet …We have to wage war until we either elevate the banner of *Tawheed* [monotheism] or meet Allah …We know and the Kenyan crusaders also know the oppression and immense atrocities they have perpetrated against the Muslims who live under the occupations of the Christians.[17]

Similar themes of reconstitution of governance structures based on some ambiguous Islamic principles and the urgency of waging war against the state have often been used by radical preachers and radicalisers, including the well-known cases of the late Aboud Rogo and the late Abubakar Shariff (also known as Makaburi) (Ndzovu 2017). These fiery religious scholars called for a total overhaul of the system of governance. Emigration to Somalia, incorporation into al-Shabaab and eventual return having undergone combat training were seen

---

[15] Ali and Bwana 2015: 8.
[16] https://www.longwarjournal.org/archives/2017/05/shabaab-spokesman-calls-on-kenyan-jihadists-to-form-an-army.php
[17] Ibid.

as urgent and necessary. Their thesis was: as Kenya does not accept us, let us emigrate, learn insurgency skills and establish an Islamic form of government upon return.

In countering narratives of violent extremists, the Movement reinterprets key concepts and issues that often form the jihadist groups' meta-narratives: varied and legitimate meanings of jihad, hijra (emigration), permissibility of war (*qital*) and promotion of peace between diverse multi-religious communities, classical ideological positions on *Dar ul Islam* and *Dar ul Harb* (Muslim territory and territory of war), *Istish'had* (martyrdom), *walaa wal baraa* (loyalty and disavowal to the faith) and *Qisas* (retaliation). The classical compartmentalisation of the major and minor jihad is expounded upon: the former being an inward effort to be good and right and to avoid sins and wrong, and the latter concerning militarised engagement. BRAVE even broadcast fascinating clips where individual Muslims demonstrated that their quotidian struggle for livelihood, assistance to others and work was their jihad.[18] The underlying jurisprudential position that the Movement pushes is best captured by similar lines of thought held by Muslim jurists and scholars on belonging in Europe (Albrecht 2018):

> With the exception of some of those authors who classify the West as *dār al-kufr* or *dār al-ḥarb*, all of the scholars, intellectuals, and activists urge Muslims in the West to respect the laws of their countries of residence – regardless of whether they conceptualize them as *dār al-'ahd*, *dār al-islām*, *ghayr dār al-islām*, *dār al-da'wa*, or *dār al-shahāda*, or whether they do not use such terms at all. In their view, there is no fundamental contradiction between obeying Western laws and living a virtuous life in line with Islamic norms. Proceeding on the assumption that Muslims are, qua believers, religiously obliged to respect contracts, they argue that abiding by the law is part of a binding social contract between Muslims and the non-Muslim states in which they reside. (Albrecht 2018: 342)

The BRAVE Movement's manuals attempt to reconcile Muslims with belonging to the Kenyan state and being protected by the country's new progressive constitution (from 2010). They suggest that Kenya can be and is an abode of peace and security despite the existence of perceived or real discourses of disenfranchisement and call for obedience to its laws and regulations within the confines of the laws.

BRAVE posits that violent extremists urge youths to migrate to Somalia, leaving behind their families and communities to wage 'a holy war' (jihad) against infidels in their home countries. However, the Movement questions

---
[18] Ali and Bwana 2015: 8.

such moves as un-Islamic as it neglects care and concern for one's family and relatives, and maintains that 'in an ideal situation a physical migration should only be considered in a dire situation when one fears for one's religious freedom, personal rights, dignity and wealth'. The counter-argument offered by BRAVE is that Kenyan Muslims should be able to prosper in their birthplace, as a sign of thankfulness to God. It is further argued that it is even compulsory for Kenyan Muslims to remain in their country and work towards the enhancement and progress of their community. Classifying emigration into two categories, physical and metaphorical, BRAVE emphasises that Kenyan Muslims should see the need for emigration in terms of more introspective and inward mobility. This symbolic emigration into one's soul from numerous temptations, sins and challenges points to the spiritualisation of *hijra*.[19]

The BRAVE manual lists classical conditionalities for the permissibility of war as valid in prevention of imminent attack; in defence of oneself or others; when all options for arriving at peaceful resolution have been exhausted. In addition, declarations must only be made by the head of an Islamic state or commander of the armed forces; war must be against oppression and tyranny (only); and finally, war must be waged only to remove oppressive barriers to freedom of conscience, freedom of association, freedom of expression, and freedom to practise and share Islam with others through kindness and good character.[20] A closer look at this text-based jurisprudential position leads one to clearly decry any blatant decontextualisation of Kenya's security dilemma. Muslims are citizens in a secular, multi-religious nation-state. They are not migrants from distant lands but are accidental residents of a post-colonial state based on arbitrary borders, just like other communities are. The prerogative of waging war or peace lies with state organs headed by a president and based on a pluralistic secular constitution. The head of state is elected through universal adult suffrage by all citizens including Muslims and there are legitimate laid-down mechanisms to oppose state tyranny and oppression and to fight for community and individual rights and freedoms through civil society, political representation and processes, protests and picketing and other pillars of secular democracy.

BRAVE acknowledges that the concept of *Dar ul Islam*, 'land of Islamic governance', is a constant theme within violent extremist groups' narratives. It adds that in order for the militant groups to establish the religion, it is necessary to establish an Islamic state, which in turn will lead to the re-establishment of the caliphate (*khalifat al-Islamiyyah*) – a project for which they recruit foot soldiers and ideologues to wage war. BRAVE hypothetically argues that, in today's world, Muslim scholars believe *Dar ul Islam* to be a relative term that may not

---

[19] Ibid. 35.
[20] Ibid. 26–40.

have a precise meaning. As there are no clear injunctions in core Islamic texts concerning the establishment of such a state, the Movement questions the justification for killing or spilling blood to achieve this vague notion, calling it derogative and licentious. However, it optimistically points out that 'even if Muslims desire an Islamic state, a reasonable approach should be applied to realise it'.[21] In its manuals, the conveners of the Movement provide their audiences with historical roots and contemporary readings of some controversial verses (e.g. the 'sword verses') and demonstrate that these verses are not the kind of jihadi 'blank cheques' that they seem now to have become.[22]

Citizenship is based on belonging to and recognising the multi-religious and multi-cultural nature of the state. It comes with rights and duties. In Kenya, it is obtained by birth and registration. Acquisition and possession of a national identity card or a passport for adults over the age of eighteen affords access to political participation processes and state and non-state social services and travel out of the country. As noted earlier, it is often not easy for individuals in the predominantly Muslim north and the coastal region to obtain these documents.[23]

In a capacity-building session for civil society activists at their office, one of the BRAVE trainers brought up fascinating comparative discussions on an often quoted or misquoted classical edict on emigration and military action against 'non-Muslim states'. This edict, called the Mardin *fatwa*, is attributed to Ibn Taymiyya (d. 1328), the ideological figurehead whom militant groups love to quote and legitimise their actions with (Michot 2011; Mavani 2011). Mardin was the sheikh of his home region before the family fled from a Mongol invasion when he was seven years old. He was asked about the people of Mardin: should the Muslims who remained behind be considered hypocrites? Is it obligatory for the Muslims there to emigrate? Is Mardin still to be considered part of the Muslim world?

---

[21] Ibid. p. 34.
[22] The so-called sword verses refer to Surah at Tawba verses 1–7. They are often evoked by jihadist groups as a justification for waging war against non-Muslims on the basis of a misinterpretation of similar precedents during Prophet Muhammad's time. The verse often used is 9:5: '5When the [four] forbidden months are over, wherever^b you encounter the idolaters,^{c} kill them, seize them, besiege them, wait for them at every lookout post; but if they turn [to God], maintain the prayer, and pay the prescribed alms, let them go on their way, for God is most forgiving and merciful' (Abdelhaleem 2004).
[23] This difficulty in obtaining citizenship documents emanates from the marginality and proximity to porous international borders of Muslim-majority regions. Due to the ease of movement of people across international boundaries, coupled with the cultural and ethnic similarities between persons across these borders, the state often subjects locals to further stringent vetting to reduce the chances of non-Kenyans gaining such documents. Individuals with Muslim names applying for national IDs or passports often wait for longer periods than other Kenyans before obtaining such documents. In addition, the police subject locals travelling to and from northern Kenya to numerous security checkpoints as part of counter-terrorism measures.

The following are said to be his answers:

1. The lives and properties of the people of Mardin are inviolable. Their living under the subjugation of the Mongols does not compromise any of their rights nor can they be maligned verbally or accused of hypocrisy.
2. As long as the inhabitants of Mardin are able to practise their religion, they are not obliged to emigrate.
3. They should not give assistance to those who are fighting against the Muslims, even if they are forced to flatter them, be evasive or absent themselves.
4. The territory is neither wholly a part of the Muslim world, since it is under the domination of the Mongols, nor part of the non-Muslim world, since its population is Muslim. It is in fact a composite of the two.

There has been great debate about the last part of the *fatwa*. One version argues that Muslims be treated according to their rights, and non-Muslims according to theirs. A second version states that Muslims should be treated according to their rights and non-Muslims should be fought (*yu'amal/yuqatal*). The latter is invoked by militant groups against the non-Muslim populace or Muslims who do not ascribe to their ideologies. A major conference was convened on 27–8 March 2010 in Mardin, Turkey, by, among other prominent Muslim religious leaders, Sheikh Abdullahi bin Bayyah[24] and the Global Center for Renewal and Guidance (GCRG) in co-operation with Mardin's Artuklu University, Turkey. The purpose of the conference was to debate and correct the words of the famous sheikh along the former lines and deny militants their favourite edict for violence and takfirism (the casting of others as non-believers). Uproar from jihadi ideologues followed this corrective move.

Retrospectively, it would have been useful for the BRAVE sheikhs to debate the *fatwa* within local contemporary and historical contexts. This *fatwa* has implications for Muslim minorities in predominantly non-Muslim states.

One of the core themes that neither the Movement nor the debates on Muslim faith-based counter-narratives attempt to raise is the nature of the Kenyan state with respect to Islamic jurisprudence. How should Muslims perceive their citizenship in a country that is demographically predominantly Christian? Should being numerically a minority also necessitate a redefinition of how to do jurisprudence, for instance, in the application of *fiqh al aqalliyat*? Jasser Auda (2017), reviewing classical Sunni, Shia and Ibadi sources, classifies the definition of 'land of Islam' as including any of the following criteria: a land where Islamic rules (*ahkam al Islam*) apply; a land where a Muslim ruler has control (*isteela'*) over its affairs; a land of security (*amn*); a land where the practising of public acts

---

[24] https://muslimmatters.org/2010/06/29/the-mardin-conference---a-detailed-account/

of worship (*sha'a'ir al-islam*) is allowed; and finally, a 'land of justice' (*dar al-'adl*). As per this list, almost all the criteria are applicable to Kenya's Muslim situation except perhaps two, as the head of state has so far hailed only from various Christian denominations. As per the first criteria, some aspect of Islamic law (especially Muslim family law) is even enshrined in the country's constitution. Certain concessions have been granted to the Muslim community, such as the enshrinement of personal law courts. The country has a secular constitution that does not privilege any religious community. Kenya is also, to a great extent, a land of security for all its citizens in comparison with most of its neighbours, although, as in any developing country, incidences of violence – whether by private individuals, jihadi groups or state-affiliated agencies – are common. It is evidently a land where the practising of Muslim public acts of worship is allowed and cherished. To this end, the state designates Muslim festivals as national holidays and allows Muslims to build places of worship across the country, and leaders have historically sent messages of solidarity and good wishes to members of other faiths at the beginning and end of the Muslim fasting month (among other occasions), thus showing recognition for and acknowledging Muslims as citizens of the country. One could also argue that Kenya is a land of *adl* (justice), as the country has a robust and independent judiciary, though there are instances of executive interference.[25] However, such positions have not so far been articulated by the prime movers of counter-narrative productions such as those of the BRAVE Movement.

The Promises and Perils of Faith-based Prevention/Counter Violent Extremism Programmes

One of the fundamental differences between other interventions and those fronted by a Muslim faith-based organisation such as BRAVE is its strength to take on and publicly confront the core driving ideologies of militant groups. These organisations not only offer counter-narrativity that delegitimises jihadist narratives, but also offer alternative conceptualisations of belonging to a multi-religious and multi-cultural state. Their strategy tries to make Muslims come to terms with the secular modern state and negotiate for their rightful place within it, despite numerous challenges to the contrary.

By engaging in discussion with militants about the interpretation of core Islamic concepts that form the bulk of their recruitment props, BRAVE and similar organisations fall back on centuries-old Muslim discursive intellectual traditions that reaffirm the plurality of jurisprudential positions. One can even argue, further, that this desecuritises these kinds of P/CVE and may open possibilities

---

[25] Conversations with Sheikh Mahmednur, Isiolo, 2017.

of winning back not only potential recruits but also their ideologues in future in a peaceful manner. In fact, it is the opinion of some religious leaders that they should be allowed to engage in open debates over concepts such as jihad, *hijra* and the like with ideologues drawn from violent extremist groups. Such direct endeavours are dangerous for the religious leaders and are discouraged by state security agencies.

Since the launch of the Kenya National Strategy on Countering Violent Extremism by the National Counter-Terrorism Centre, a number of coastal counties have also launched their own county action plans to address P/CVE. Most of these counties are at the stage of plan implementation. Devolved governments also receive millions of shillings annually for their counties. These funds, if well utilised, may alleviate the poverty of thousands of residents and put in place infrastructures that have been neglected by the centralised state for many decades, thereby solving problems of neglect and marginality.

It is important for BRAVE and other similar civil society organisations to go beyond theological readings of the texts and interpretation to contextualise their outreach materials to address particular Kenyan Muslim circumstances in jurisprudential and citizenship issues. In circumstances in which state security agencies still engage in approaches that are insensitive to human rights to address violent extremism, it is an uphill task for BRAVE and other organisations to keep winning the hearts and minds of potential recruits, or to facilitate the rehabilitation of those who return from Somalia and other jihadi theatres of war. In addition, structural inequalities, underdevelopment and unemployment should be addressed to better the lives of locals who may fall prey to easy recruitment money from militant groups. BRAVE and similar initiatives should not shy away from addressing or presenting alternative ways of solving existing grievances instead of pushing them under the carpet.

The provision of amnesty and the management of returnees is an acid test for the state agencies, donor communities and civil society organisations – particularly because of the role of Muslim faith-based organisations such as BRAVE in critical de-radicalisation processes. These processes are yet to take shape as the country still lacks a viable policy framework for them. One of the teething challenges of Countering Violent Extremism programming, including faith-based counter-narrative production, is its exclusive focus on Muslim communities as at-risk, suspect or vulnerable groups. Moreover, their youth are subjected to subtle or even outright surveillance practices. The excessive focus on the communities robs them of the agency to make rational decisions to choose not to be enticed by VE groups and hence become subjected to dozens of customised interventions from state, non-state and fellow Muslim groups. It has been noted that a Countering Violent Extremism framework assumes that any Muslim, at any moment, may be 'radicalised' to engage in acts of non-state violence, and the logics of counter-terrorism draw on older epistemic traditions of Orientalism, in which Muslims are seen as irrational, enraged and unpredictable simply because they are Muslim.[26] As observed in the United States, schools (by extension other spaces that Muslims frequent) are particularly poignant sites where CVE programmes and the carceral imagination of surveilling Muslim bodies come into direct contact with the liberal democratic vision of the school or university as a liberal and liberalising space (through the notion of governance rather than political affiliation).

One of the most challenging tasks in CVE interventions is evaluating the success and failure rates over a given project timeline for initiatives such as those undertaken by the BRAVE Movement. At the core of this monitoring and evaluation activity is the phenomenon of attribution. It is difficult to ascertain fully what (for instance) accounts for a reduction or an increment in radicalisation, recruitment into violent extremism, community resilience or vulnerability to violent extremism, co-relations between economic empowerment and propensity to join VE groups, or being attracted to radical teachings – and the list goes on to include all the various interventions.

There are numerous structural challenges facing CVE interventions in Kenya, including the BRAVE programme. They include the reliance on external funding sources for programme/project implementations; short funding project timelines that can only achieve short- and medium-term goals; duplication of interventions by competing civil society actors and funding agencies; poorly designed monitoring and evaluation frameworks that cannot measure results over given time schedules; strong tendencies by mandated state CVE agencies to control instead of co-ordinate project activities; corruption in the security sector; growing incidences of extra-judicial killings; enforced disappearances and other human rights violations that erode CVE gains; poor community–security agency relations; the lack of clear implementation plans in County Action Plans for CVE; rivalries between national and county governments on the CVE agenda; the reinforcement of community profiling and stereotyping due to a repetitive focus on a few 'hot spots' of radicalisation and VE; and the lack of clear policy frameworks to deal with returnees, or an amnesty to attract defection from VE groups, among others (Saghal 2018; Marsh, White and Chalghaf 2018; Baruch, Ling and Warnes 2018).

Conclusion

The BRAVE Movement represents a pioneering intra-faith initiative for addressing the problems of radicalisation and recruitment into violent extremism through the use of religious texts. It attempts to delegitimise jihadist

---

[26] See Ali 2017.

narratives that denounce the Kenyan state, glorify the use of religious ideologies for political ends, inculcate sectarianism and hi-jack decades of grievances that Muslim citizens have against the state for the purposes of radicalisation and recruitment into their cause. In doing so, BRAVE spurred what it means to be a Muslim and a Kenyan in a country that has a history of injustice, discrimination and marginalisation of its religious constituencies. By launching this interactive movement that at its peak had a national outlook bringing on board religious leaders, women, youth, politicians and general Muslim publics, BRAVE opened up a space for the critique of hitherto feared jihadist ideologues and ideologies in the public sphere and allowed Muslims to discuss issues such as jihad, *takfir*, *dar ul Islam* and *hijra*, among many contentious political concepts and imaginations. However, as with most other civil-society-driven development agendas, it faced challenges such as long-term sustainability and a short project timeline. It implicitly called for a reconciliation between being a member of the faith community and a fuller and more hopeful imagination as a proper citizen of the republic of Kenya. True to its name, BRAVE's attempts to wrestle with jihadists over the meaning of jihad and the right to war and peace in Kenya demonstrate the extent of the engagement of religious scholars and activists in contemporary jurisprudential debates in the Muslim world. As a home-grown initiative formed to address growing trends of youth recruitment to jihadism in Kenya, the programme resonates with the similar dilemmas that faith-based organisations and Muslim scholars contend with in many jihadi theatres across the continent.

Bibliography

Abdelhaleem, M. A. S. (2004), *The Quran: A New Translation*, Oxford: Oxford University Press.

Adar, K. G. and I. M. Munyae (2001), 'Human Rights Abuse in Kenya under Daniel Arap Moi, 1978–2001', *African Studies Quarterly* 5(1), pp. 1–17.

Ahluwalia, P. (1996), 'Founding Fathers, Presidencies and the Rise of Authoritarianism in Kenya: A Case Study', *Africa Quarterly* 36(4), pp. 45–72.

Aiyar, S. (2015), *Indians in Kenya: the Politics of Diaspora*, Cambridge, MA: Harvard University Press.

Albrecht, S. (2018), *Dār al-Islām Revisited: Territoriality in Contemporary Islamic Legal Discourse on Muslims in the West*, Leiden, Boston: Brill.

Ali, Arshad Imtiaz (2017), 'The Impossibility of Muslim Citizenship, Diaspora, Indigenous, and Minority Education', *Studies of Migration, Integration, Equity, and Cultural Survival* 11(3), pp. 110–16.

Ali, M. Y. and O. M. Bwana (2015), *Building Resilience against Violent Extremism (BRAVE) Training Manual and Resource Guide*, Nairobi: CSCR.

Anderson, D. M. (2005), '"Yours in Struggle for Majimbo". Nationalism and the Party Politics of Decolonization in Kenya, 1955–64', *Journal of Contemporary History* 40(3), pp. 547–64.

Auda, Jasser (2017), 'Introduction', in Jasser Auda (ed.), *Rethinking Islamic Law for Minorities: Towards a Western-Muslim Identity*, http://www.jasserauda.net/new/pdf/kamil_fiqh_alaqalliyaat.pdf 3–16

Bachmann, J. and J. Honke (2009), 'Peace and Security as Counterterrorism? The Political Effects of Liberal Interventions in Kenya', *African Affairs* 109(434), pp. 97–114.

Bakari, M. and S. Yahya (1995), *Islam in Kenya: Proceedings of the National Seminar on Contemporary Islam in Kenya*, Nairobi: Mewa.

Baruch, B., T. Ling and R. Warnes (2018), 'Evaluation in an Emerging Field: Developing a Measurement Framework for the Field of Counter-Violent-Extremism', *European Evaluation Society* 24(4), https://doi.org/10.1177/1356389018803218

Botha, A. (2014), 'Political Socialization and Terrorist Radicalization Among Individuals Who Joined al-Shabaab in Kenya', *Studies in Conflict & Terrorism* 37(11), pp. 895–919.

Brennan, J. R. (2008), 'Lowering the Sultan's Flag: Sovereignty and Decolonization in Coastal Kenya', *Comparative Studies in Society and History*, 50(04), pp. 831–61.

Castagno, A. A. (1964), 'The Somali–Kenyan Controversy: Implications for the Future', *The Journal of Modern African Studies* 2(02), p. 165.

Fratkin, E. and E. A. Roth (2005), *As Pastoralists Settle*, New York: Kluwer Academic/Plenum, New York.

Gillard, D. R. (1960), 'Salisbury's African Policy and the Heligoland Offer of 1890', *The English Historical Review* 75(297), pp. 631–53.

Goldsmith, P. (2011), *Mombasa Republican Council: Conflict Assessment Threats and Opportunities for Engagement*, MRC Conflict Assessment Report, Nairobi: USAID.

Hansen, S. J. (2012), *Al-Shabaab in Somalia: The History and Ideology of a Militant Islamist Group, 2005–2012*, Oxford: Oxford University Press.

Insoll, T. (2003), *The Archaeology of Islam in Sub-Saharan Africa*, Cambridge: Cambridge University Press.

Khalil, J. and M. Zeuthen (2014), 'A Case Study of Counter Violent Extremism (CVE) Programming: Lessons from OTI's Kenya Transition Initiative', *Stability: International Journal of Security & Development* 3(1). doi: 10.5334/sta.ee.

Kresse, K. (2009), 'Muslim Politics in Postcolonial Kenya: Negotiating Knowledge on the Double-periphery', *Journal of the Royal Anthropological Institute* 15, pp. S76–S94.

Lewis, I. (1963), 'The Problem of the Northern Frontier District of Kenya', *Race*, 5(1), pp. 48–60.

Lind, J. and J. Howell (2010), 'Counter-terrorism and the Politics of Aid: Civil Society Responses in Kenya', *Development and Change* 41(2), pp. 335–53.

Lind, J., P. Mutahi and M. Oosterom (2015), *Tangled Ties: Al-Shabaab and Political Volatility in Kenya*, Brighton: Institute of Development Studies.

Loimeier, R. and R. Seesemann (2006), *The Global Worlds of the Swahili: Interfaces of Islam, Identity and Space in 19th and 20th-century East Africa*, Berlin: Lit.

Lynch, Gabriel (2014), 'So Many Questions, So Many Fears: The Dilemma of Muslims in Kenya', *Nation* (updated 2020), https://mobile.nation.co.ke/blogs/1949942-2355996-format-xhtml-14kh1h7z/index.html

Mahmoud, H. (2008), *Seeking Citizenship on the Border: Kenya Somalis, the Uncertainty of Belongingness and Public Sphere Interactions*, Dakar: CODERIA.

Marchal, R. (2019), 'Motivations and Drivers of Al-Shabaab', *War and Peace in Somalia*, pp. 309–17.

Marsh, S., K. White and B. Chalghaf (2018), 'Emerging Best Practices and Lessons Learnt', in S. Zeiger (ed.), *Expanding the Evidence for PCVE: Research Solutions*, Abu Dhabi: Hedaya, pp. 95–116.

Maruf, H. and D. Joseph (2018), *Inside al-Shabaab: The Secret History of al-Qaeda's Most Powerful Ally*, Bloomington: Indiana University Press.

Mavani, H. (2011), 'Tension between the Quran and the Hadith: The Case of Offensive Jihad', *Journal of Shi'a Islamic Studies* 4(4), pp. 397–414.

Michot, Y. (2011), 'Ibn Taymiyya's "New Mardin Fatwa". Is Genetically Modified Islam (GMI) Carcinogenic?', *The Muslim World* 101(2), pp. 130–81.

Musila, G. (2009), 'Phallocracies and Gynocratic Transgressions: Gender, State Power and Kenyan Public Life', *Africa Insight* 39(1), pp. 39–57.

Mwakimako, H. (2007), 'Christian–Muslim Relations in Kenya: A Catalogue of Events and Meanings', *Islam and Christian–Muslim Relations* 18(2), pp. 287–307.

Mwakimako, H. (2008), 'Kadhi Court and Appointment of Kadhi in Kenya Colony', *Religion Compass* 2(4), pp. 424–43.

Mwaruvie, John (2011), 'The Ten Miles Coastal strip: An Examination of the Intricate Nature of Land Question at Kenyan Coast', *International Journal of Humanities and Social Science* 1(2), pp. 176–82.

Ndzovu, H. (2014), *Muslims in Kenyan Politics: Political Involvement, Marginalization, and Minority Status*. doi:10.26530/oapen_628770.

Ndzovu, H. (2017), 'The Rise of Jihad, Killing of "Apostate Imams" and Non-Combatant Christian Civilians in Kenya: Al-Shabaab's Re-Definition of the Enemy on Religious Lines', *Journal of Religion in Africa and its Diaspora* 3(1), pp. 4–20.

Oba, G. and Z. Khalif (2013), '"Gaafa dhaabaa – the Period of Stop": Narrating Impacts of Shifta Insurgency on Pastoral Economy in Northern Kenya, c. 1963 to 2007', *Pastoralism: Research, Policy and Practice* 3(1), https://doi.org/10.1186/2041-7136-3-14

Oded, A. (2000), *Islam and Politics in Kenya*, Boulder, CO: Lynne Rienner.

Ombati, M. (2015), 'Crossing Gender Boundaries or Challenging Masculinities? Female Combatants in the Kenya Defence Forces' (KDF) War against Al-Shabaab Militants', *Masculinities & Social Change* 4(2), pp. 163–85.

Pkalya, D. and B. Cannon (2019), 'Why Al-Shabaab Attacks Kenya: Questioning the Narrative Paradigm', *SSRN Electronic Journal*. pp. 836–52.

Pyeatt, D. N. (1988), 'Heligoland and the Making of Anglo-German Colonial Agreement in 1890', MA thesis, Texas Tech University.

Saghal, G. (2018), 'Monitoring and Evaluation of CVE: Lessons Learnt from STRIVE II', in S. Zeiger (ed.), *Expanding the Evidence Base for P/CVE: Research Solutions*, Abu Dhabi: Hedaya, pp. 71–94.

Salvadori, C. (2000), *The Forgotten People Revisited: Human Rights Abuses in Marsabit and Moyale Districts*, Nairobi, Kenya: Kenya Human Rights Commission.

Salvadori, C. and A. Fedders (1989), *Through Open Doors: A View of Asian Cultures in Kenya*, Nairobi: Kenway.

Singh, C. (1965), 'The Republican Constitution of Kenya: Historical Background and Analysis', *International and Comparative Law Quarterly* 14(3), pp. 878–949.

UNDP (2017), *Journey to Extremism in Africa: Drivers, Incentives and the Tipping Point for Recruitment*, Nairobi: UNDP.

Wario, H. A. (2014), 'Debates on Kadhi's Courts and Christian–Muslim Relations in Isiolo Town: Thematic Issues and Emergent Trends', in Franz Kogelmann and John Chesworth (eds), *Sharī'a in Africa Today: Reactions and Responses*, Leiden: Brill, pp. 147–67.

Wario, H. A. (2017), 'Reading from a Muslim Perspective: Forging the Way Ahead', in David Tarus and Gordon Heath (eds), *Christian Responses to Terrorism: The Kenyan Experience*, Eugene: Wipf & Stock, pp. 205–14.

Weitzberg, K. (2016), 'Rethinking the Shifta War Fifty Years after Independence: Myth, Memory, and Marginalization', in Michael Mwenda Kithinji, Mickie Mwanzia Koster and Jerono P. Rotich (eds), *Kenya After 50: Reconfiguring Historical, Political, and Policy Matters*. London: Palgrave Macmillan, pp. 65–81.

Whittaker, Hannah (2015), *Insurgency and Counterinsurgency in Kenya: A Social History of the Shifta Conflict, c. 1963–1968*, Leiden: Brill.

Willis, J. and Gona, G. (2012), 'Pwani si Kenya? Memory, Documents and Secessionist Politics in Coastal Kenya', *African Affairs* 112(446), pp. 48–71.

4

Beyond Vicious Circles in the Kenyan Post-colony? On the Value of Discursive Space

KAI KRESSE

In post-colonial Kenya, the relationships between Muslims and the state, run by Christian and up-country governments ranked around the respective presidents (Jomo Kenyatta, Daniel arap Moi, Mwai Kibaki and Uhuru Kenyatta), have for the most part been fraught with tension since independence. The indigenous Kenyan Somalis, Swahilis and Arabs (of Omani and Hadrami descent) were from early on viewed as peripheral to the newly independent nation, as Kenyan troops fought Somali rebels in the North Eastern region, and Swahili and Arab Muslims (as former rulers and slave-holders) were threatened with being sent 'back to the sea' or 'back to Arabia' in the sharp political rhetoric of early post-independence Africanisation.[1] For the longest period of Moi's rule, from the late 1970s till the early 2000s, coastal Muslims were seen as docile, timid and accommodating to government demands imparted to them by the president's coastal right-hand, Shariff Nassir (Nassir 2008). As second-class citizens of sorts, Muslims had to arrange themselves with adverse conditions; a sense of being at the margins of the state – sometimes with more influence and political positions, sometimes with less – has been at the centre of post-colonial experience for Muslims in Kenya (Kresse 2009, 2018a). Internal discussions and public debates among Kenyan Muslims in the contemporary period are being studied more and more (e.g. Mwakimako and Willis 2013; Deacon et al. 2017; Alidou 2013); for earlier decades, this was hardly possible, partly due to the repressive character of the first Kenyatta and Moi regimes, which left no open, unregulated spaces for discussion or critique.

---

[1] On the political history, see Hornsby 2012, Branch 2011 and, in particular, Prestholdt in this volume. On the ideological politics of the soil, see Prestholdt 2014.

In this chapter, I focus in on two discursive media spaces that became relevant from the late 1990s and early 2000s: a weekly pamphlet and an Islamic radio programme. Both were developed by Kenyan Muslims as platforms for public discussion, largely for internal debate. I seek to show how these media constitute important and much-needed discursive spaces that Muslims make use of for a more assertive public self-positioning.

First, the dynamics of the political tensions between Muslims and the state, over the last two decades or so, need to be laid out. An ascending dynamic of mutual suspicion and an ambiguous resource involving the potential use of power vis-à-vis each other characterises the scenario, and it seems in the hand of the government to determine how the balancing of mutual opposition can work. As Susan Hirsch has observed in the concluding reflections of her book that works through issues of loss and grief through terrorism in East Africa, in the aftermath of the bombings of the US embassies in Dar es Salaam and Nairobi in August 1998,

> state control cuts both ways. Depending on the tactics used, governmental power can contain or eliminate those voices advocating violence, and yet the use of tactics that disregard human rights can fuel the oppositional logic that leads disaffected individuals to join groups promising a new regime. (Hirsch 2006: 260)

This statement encapsulates the dynamics of a vicious circle of mutual suspicions and accelerating oppositions between the Kenyan government and Kenyan Muslims.[2] These mutual tensions have been in place in Kenya for well over two decades now, underpinned by long and complex historical antagonism between coastal and up-country people, Muslims and Christians, from the pre-colonial through to the post-colonial period. Over the past two decades that were dominated by the war-on-terror rhetoric shaped and enforced by the United States, these tensions have created new dimensions of mutual distrust. It is with a view to these that I seek to discuss the importance of the existence of publicly accessible discursive spaces in which concerns about the state of affairs can be raised, and related challenges be addressed and negotiated, within an internally diverse and often divided Muslim community that asserts and expresses unity and solidarity vis-à-vis a state that continues to view and treat its Muslim citizens with general suspicion. For the purposes of this chapter, I take the leitmotif of a vicious circle of worsening mutual relations, accelerated by

---

[2] In her admirable book, Hirsch, an American legal anthropologist who lost her Kenyan Swahili husband in the Dar es Salaam bombing, has worked through personal and social as well as moral and legal dimensions in the political context that the 'war-on-terror' scenario has created for East African states and citizens.

mutual suspicion and distrust, as an entry point for discussion. While, as Hirsch says, the state could contain and diminish the voices of violent protest (if it did so with sensitivity and understanding), it has so far mostly increased discontent and resentment among Muslims by largely disregarding their concerns.

A public space in which these dynamics have been documented and reflected, building a representative platform for the perspectives and opinions of Kenyan Muslims, is *The Friday Bulletin* pamphlet. This was established after a longer struggle to establish such a shared public space, drawing inspiration also from comparable projects in place in other Muslim minority countries (e.g. South Africa's *Muslim News*).[3] It is a weekly publication (of 8–12 pages) prepared and circulated (in pdf format, for a number of years now) by the Nairobi Jamia Mosque as the central national institution for Sunni Muslims in Kenya. By virtue of its status as a representative public voice of Kenyan Muslims, *The Friday Bulletin*'s editorial articles usually employ a language that aims at consensus and points to common convictions and shared sentiments among the majority of Muslims. Over the past years, the articles have regularly voiced concerns about human rights abuses and the mistreatment of Muslims in Kenya, admonishing and criticising the government (though not in confrontational or inciting language).

An example can be found in the issue of 1 November 2018, which featured a commentary on the governmental amnesty for suspected 'supporters' of al-Shabaab, the Somali-based terrorist group.[4] This had been granted in February 2016, with the goal that many would renounce violent opposition and could then pursue social rehabilitation programmes and become reintegrated into the community. This initiative, however, failed, it is stated (referring to the assessment of a US-based thinktank), due to a mistaken approach by the government. While approximately 1,500 men originating from the coastal districts of Kwale, Kilifi, Lamu and Mombasa had surrendered in response to the announcement, the government did not follow through with its promise of providing opportunities for them to be rehabilitated. In fact, many 'disappearances' or killings occurred of the men who had been granted amnesty, at the hands of security forces. The article criticised this, quoting also a policy advisor concerned with the process. He identified this as another instance of the government accelerating Muslims' resentment and strengthening their resolve to oppose the state (rather than building rapport and gaining support for its rehabilitating measures from the affected Muslim community, as it should have). Over recent years, many accounts and commentaries of this kind have filled the pages of *The Friday Bulletin*. I discuss a small selection of representative comments below.

---

[3] I am grateful to Hassan Mwakimako for pointing this out.
[4] *The Friday Bulletin*, no. 808 (1 November 2018): pp. 1–2.

Over a period of two decades, since the bomb attacks on the US embassy of August 1998, all Kenyans, and Kenyan Muslims in particular, have been living in a state of ongoing fundamental insecurity, of fear and anxiety facing possible sudden violent attacks in the midst of everyday life. The Kenyan government's decision in 2011 to send its army across the border into Somalia, in order ostensibly to 'protect the country' (i.e. via *linda nchi*, the Swahili name of the military operation), is seen to have backfired, as terror attacks on Kenyan ground multiplied in response (Anderson et al. 2014): highly publicised terror attacks aimed at non-Muslims with many deaths that were linked to the al-Shabaab group occurred in 2013 (in a Westlands shopping mall in Nairobi), 2014 (in Mpeketoni, on the mainland near Lamu Island) and 2015 (in a university in Garissa, in the North Eastern Kenyan Somali region). Earlier major 'Islamic' terrorist attacks on Kenyan soil were al-Qaeda attacks on a tourist hotel and an aeroplane in Mombasa in 2002, and initially (as mentioned), in 1998, on the US embassy in Nairobi (parallel to the one in Dar es Salaam).

In a country in which Muslims have long felt politically marginalised, the mutual suspicions that have haunted the country have in turn been accelerated, as Muslims were generally suspected to be supporters of such deeds, by a government that closely collaborated with the United States and its 'war on terror'. A range of restrictive controlling measures on Muslims by the state was put in place (e.g. increased observations, massive and regular ID controls and curfews for whole communities).[5] Being subjected to an increasing number of such measures, in turn, has fuelled frustration and discontent among Muslims, many of whom regard this as the perpetuation of historical injustices by the state, of them being denied common rights as citizens. It is in these terms that we can witness a kind of vicious circle of mutual suspicion at work, and some of the backfiring effects of the state's so-called 'counter-terrorism' initiatives have been well-documented (Prestholdt 2011).[6]

However, these matters are more complex than this summary has thus far been able to suggest. 'Kenyan Muslims' are an internally diverse and highly heterogeneous group, spanning not only different (and often competing) denominations, and different interpretations and ideologies of Islam, but also different basic approaches and personal preferences regarding engaging in politics. Their perspectives are also shaped by a wide variety of specific transregional connections and affiliations. On the ground, the lived realities also cut across the dual opposition invoked thus far, as a significant proportion of Muslims have variable kinds of allegiance to the state, and some strongly identify as Kenyans while

---

[5] For vivid and close descriptions and discussions of these contexts, see Chome 2016a and 2016b. See also Seesemann 2007; Anderson et al. 2014; Mwakimako and Willis 2014.
[6] See e.g. Nassir 2008. Susan Hirsch also conveys a remarkable sense of such dynamics, partly in anticipation of future circumstances, in her sensitive and admirable study (Hirsch 2008, esp. pp. 261–2).

others do not. Indeed, before the elections in 2013, the slogans that 'democracy is unbelief' (*demokrasi ni ukafiri*) and 'the coast is not Kenya' (*Pwani si Kenya*) were popular among some coastal Muslims.[7] Still, despite their differences, all Muslims seek to be able to claim the legal rights that many of them feel they are being denied. Thus, the state of uncertainty and vulnerability that all Kenyans have been living in has been paired for Muslims with increasing political pressures. These include not only arbitrary (and often unjustified) arrests from in their midst, but also 'disappearances' of those arrested, and extra-judicial killings of suspected sympathisers or supporters of al-Shabaab, notably Muslim clerics who had spoken up in public against the government and seemed to support armed resistance and attacks against it.

This has been well documented and commented upon over the years, and it is particularly instructive to consult Muslim media and public debates to see how these politically sensitive tensions have been addressed and handled in internal debates among Muslims. It is helpful, for instance, to look at *The Friday Bulletin* as a representative mainstream publication that seeks to address the majority of Muslims in the country, inform them on relevant issues, and disseminate relevant debates and opinions among the wider public.[8] As a national publication for Kenyan Muslims (with at times a detectable Sunni stance), it is circulated widely throughout the country, and its electronic copies are distributed by email and WhatsApp groups and are also downloadable from the website of Jamia Mosque in Nairobi, where it is edited and published, exclusively in English. This constitutes an attempt to shape a balanced representation of voices that reflect a sense of national solidarity and mutual concern among Muslims. It also reflects their internal diversity and international connections. We now turn to its illustrative accounts and commentaries on the tense and vulnerable relations between Kenyan Muslims and the state.

THE FRIDAY BULLETIN: ILLUSTRATIVE READINGS BY/FOR KENYAN MUSLIMS

As this pamphlet constitutes a national forum for mediating and disseminating relevant news and developments among all Muslims in Kenya, the editors of the Anglophone[9] *Friday Bulletin* needed to aim for representative and balanced statements in its publications. Concerning the issue of 'terror' and living in a

---

[7] Mwakimako and Willis 2016.
[8] This has been pursued in a research project by Halkano Abdi Wario. An alternative way would be to look more closely at the existing accounts of investigative journalism; see e.g. Mohamed Ali's 'Jicho Pevu' documentaries and Aljazeera's related report on extra-judicial killings.
[9] English would have been chosen as the best compromise for a main mediating language so as not to privilege or exclude a particular linguistic segment of the national Muslim community and thereby accentuate divisions between the coastal Swahili speakers (including the Mijikenda) and the North

fundamentally insecure state of being, this means voicing the concerns and grievances of Kenyan Muslims, while at the same time consistently condemning terror and violence in the name of Islam. This is indeed what we can see in the pamphlets.

In 2014, after several violent attacks and killings happened in the mainland area of Lamu District that were attributed to al-Shabaab, a string of 'extra-judicial killings' of Muslim suspects took place. As the lead article of *The Friday Bulletin* said, such killings were 'widening [the] rift between Muslims and State' (14 November 2014, pp. 1–2). The article was relying not on Muslim sources, but quoted the well-known critic and former 'watchdog' over government corruption John Githongo, who had famously been in charge of anti-corruption campaigns on behalf of former President Mwai Kibaki and had then fled the country in order to save his life when he had found out too much; he then became based at Oxford University as a fellow (Wrong 2009). The article said, 'Githongo accused state agents of being behind the extra judicial killings and disappearances of Imams and preachers which he said are now being seen as a normal feature of life', and quoted Githongo saying that 'the war against terror feeds on the basic rights of citizens'.

A reader's letter from 30 May 2014 addressed to President Uhuru Kenyatta reports alarm over the ongoing discrimination that Muslims suffer, pointing to incidents in everyday life. I quote it in full to convey a good sense of the common anxieties:

> Dear President Uhuru Kenyatta, I hope this letter finds you in the best of Health. I am saddened by the continuous harassment of Muslims in the country. *We are not second class citizens* and it is never our fault that we are born Muslims in Kenya. The profiling that is going on especially in Eastleigh and Mombasa is hurting Muslims so much. I am calling upon you to stop this profiling and start fighting terrorism and not Muslims.
>
> I am no longer comfortable walking while dressed in a *kanzu* as everyone looks at me like a terrorist. Even boarding a *matatu* to and from my work station is becoming a problem. I have to carry my identity card even while going to the mosque which was not the case before.
>
> My Muslim sisters in their respectful *buibui* and *niqab* feel intimidated wherever they are. They don't know what will happen to them especially when night falls. Recently, some were not allowed to board matatus going to Kariobangi and South C on the basis of their dressing.

Eastern Somali speakers, the two largest historical groups of indigenous Muslims in Kenya. For more historical context and details on post-colonial Kenya, see Hornsby 2012 and Branch 2011.

It is becoming too much for us to bear. We are Kenyans and we are NOT terrorists. Please we need our security and freedom back as it was before. Mr. President and your deputy William Ruto you should stand by the constitution you swore to protect and give us Muslims our rights in our country.
(from Kaloleni, Kisumu)

Letters and statements such as these bear witness that harassment, profiling and being suspected as terrorists have become common everyday experiences for Kenyan Muslims, and that they demand recognition of their full rights as Kenyan citizens in response. The appeal to 'start fighting terrorism and not Muslims!' expresses a shared sentiment of anger and irritation about being targeted because of their faith, and it demands that public safety and security be re-established by the government. This letter also expresses a fundamental worry about dress, as wearing even the most common markers of religious identity, a white *kanzu* for men and a black *buibui* for women, is seen to lead to fear of discrimination and intimidation.[10] Finally, the letter demands that quality and respect must be granted and assured by the government for *all* its people, and that a differentiation between better and lesser citizens is unacceptable.

Along these lines, a strong sense of justice and legal entitlement comes across in many commentaries and texts featured in *The Friday Bulletin* editions. Keeping our attention focused on the summer of 2014 only, we can look at a few further examples: an editorial ending with a demand that the government fulfil its obligation to *all* – otherwise it would not be worthy of its name: 'The government has a cardinal responsibility of protecting the lives and property of its people. Failing to discharge this innate responsibility is tantamount to abdicating the obligation the State has to its people' (13 June). The same issue mourns the death of Sheikh Muhammad Idris, a leading figure within the coastal Muslim community, who had recently been shot dead when going for morning prayers. As a moderate reformist who had engaged in mediating tensions within a heavily divided community, he had been very popular and left many mourners behind. In the article reporting on this, representatives from national Muslim bodies, the Council of Imams and Preachers in Kenya (CIPK), the Supreme Council for Kenyan Muslims (SUPKEM) and the Muslims for Human Rights initiative (MUHURI), were quoted, praising Idris and scolding the government for failing to protect Muslim lives and not bringing any perpetrators to account.

---

[10] The remarks on distinct Muslim dress here deserve some explanatory comment for readers unfamiliar with the region. A *kanzu* is the common proper white attire for men, worn for Friday prayers and on festive occasions (though people seeking to make a point about their status or standing may wear it on any day). The respective female equivalent forms of Muslim dress are the black veil (in different forms and fashions) covering the shoulders and head, generically called *buibui*, or covering the face, then called *niqab*. Both constitute immediately recognisable material forms of Muslim identity for men and women across East Africa.

On this point, the former Kenyan Chief Kadhi, Sheikh Hammad Muhammad Kasim Mazrui, reiterated a sharp critique: 'We have had several Sheikhs killed before and many times these scholars have reported receiving direct threats … but we have not seen the government take very decisive measures to protect them or find the killers.'

There was a sense of deep frustration about the government in the air, then, in the pages of *The Friday Bulletin*, over the months of 2014, with headlines and articles asking 'Till when will these senseless killings continue?' (13 June 2014),[11] or showing why police must be blamed for lax security (27 June 2014)[12] and how the practice of profiling Muslims as a standard security procedure was wrong (1 August 2014).[13] While a clear stance is taken against violence and terrorism, the government's actions are themselves implicitly cast as violations of the law and basic human rights, to be condemned and rejected. 'We condemn terrorism in no uncertain terms but we equally condemn the discrimination, profiling, persecution, torture and killing of Muslims at the pretext of and under the guise

---

[11] Here is the full text of this brief editorial, for purposes of fuller illustration: 'A clear pattern in these killings is that while the government has been firm that investigations will be carried out to unearth the killers and their motives, to date this has remained empty rhetoric and it is this unfulfilled pledge which continue to heighten concerns in the Muslim community. Questions which are now being asked is who is next on the firing line of these apparent trigger happy criminals? The government has a cardinal responsibility of protecting the lives and property of its people. Failing to discharge this innate responsibility is tantamount to abdicating the obligation the State has to its people.'

[12] Here for illustration is another extensive quotation, from 'Police Blamed Over Security Laxity' (27 June 2014): 'In a press release, the executive director, Hussein Khalid, raised concerns over the state of security faulting the manner in which the police have handled operations. "Whatever the reasons, the killings point to laxity in and failure of authorities to guarantee Kenyans their right to security as enshrined in the constitution. The police are sleeping on their job and as a result more Kenyans are losing their lives," said Hussein. The lobby group called for urgent action to address the deteriorating security situation in the country, adding that the situation is causing alarm and consternation among Kenyans. "With these fresh killings, it is a clear indication that the situation has not been arrested and what the security authorities were assuring Kenyans of improved security in the area was mere lip service," he said.'

[13] Here for illustration is the quotation from 'Profiling of Muslims Counterproductive to Terror War' (1 August 2014): '"We condemn terrorism in no uncertain terms but we equally condemn the discrimination, profiling, persecution, torture and killing of Muslims at the pretext of and under the guise of fighting terrorism," he [Abdullatif Essajee] said last week at Jamia mosque while addressing worshippers who turned up for the last Friday of the month of Ramadhan. He explained that the socio-economic marginalization of Muslims was further alienating the community, particularly the youth who lacked opportunities to make their lives better … the lecturer reiterated his concerns about the extra judicial killings of Muslims saying that despite the pledges from the government to investigation and bring to book the perpetrators, the State is yet to demonstrate its resolve to live up to its pledge to identify and apprehend the attackers. The latest killings involved the murder of a prominent Mombasa businessman Shahid Butt who was gunned down in Changamwe area. Like most of the previous killings, he had been linked by security services to so-called radical elements. Sheikh Muhammad Idris, a prominent scholar in Mombasa who spoke against extremist teachings also met his death while heading for dawn prayers from his Likoni home. His killers also remain unknown … Abdullatif urged the government to live up to its promise to bring back Kenyans who were renditioned to Uganda. "Government after government has turned a blind eye and a deaf ear to their plea, the plea of their families and Kenyans to have them brought back and properly charged in our courts in Kenya," he asked.'

of fighting terrorism', the speaker during the *hotuba* for the final Friday prayers of Ramadhan, Abdullatif Essajee, a lecturer at the University of Nairobi, is quoted as having said publicly. Seeing that a moderate representative was on record as issuing such a damning public criticism of the government, the situation must be regarded as dire. Question marks remained about the possible involvement of the government in the disappearances of unsuspecting Muslim citizens, while the government itself did not follow up on its earlier public pronouncements of resolve: 'despite the pledges from the government to investigation [sic] and bring to book the perpetrators, the State is yet to demonstrate its resolve to live up to its pledge to identify and apprehend the attackers', while, the article says, on the other hand 'government after government has turned a blind eye and a deaf ear to … the plea of their families' to have all abducted Muslims brought back from security camps in Uganda, to be properly charged in court according to Kenyan law (1 August 2014).[14] Such disappearances and killings of suspects and radical preachers were also documented by investigative journalism, in which the Kenyan Somali journalist Mohamed Ali took a central role (he was later elected as Member of Parliament for Nyali constituency, north of Mombasa).[15]

In public commentaries and popular debates about these developments, an assumption of a general 'radicalisation' of Kenyan Muslims is often expressed in the face of these experiences: an assumption that over the course of these developments Muslims on the whole may have become more likely, and indeed more willing, to be supportive of armed resistance in response.[16] While there is an understandable logic to such claims, we have to be cautious and suspend any urge to identify (and by doing so judge) such links and relations swiftly, not least because such assumptive thinking plays into the hands of an increasing climate of general mutual suspicion, pushing the vicious circle yet further. While some may indeed have become more radicalised, due to their sense of being seen as opponents of the state – a state that has continuously rejected them and denied them equal rights as citizens (and in turn indeed disallowed them from identifying as such) – other Muslim groups may have invested in strategies of countering calls for violence, and in emphasising their affinity with and contribution to the Kenyan nation.[17]

Here, I give attention to how Kenyan Muslims in their internal (yet public) debates are dealing with the kind of 'double confrontation' they experience (internally and externally, as Muslims and as Kenyans) under these

---

[14] Further *Friday Bulletin* texts in which these kinds of concerns and criticisms of the government are raised have since appeared frequently, in response to similar occurrences of disappearances, killings or contested charges over the last years.
[15] Al-Jazeera English. 'Africa Investigates: Inside Kenya's Death Squads', 7 December 2014 (film).
[16] See also e.g. KMYA [Kenya Muslim Youth Alliance] 2016.
[17] See e.g. Goodman 2017 for Khoja Muslim groups in Mombasa.

circumstances – echoing a kind of 'double periphery' situation (Kresse 2009). As part of the Kenyan populace, they have been potential victims here (just like other Kenyan citizens), but also a targeted community of potential suspects (which Kenyan Muslims of Somali descent, especially, have been identified as being). Within these developments of increasing pressures, restrictions and threats of violence (by terrorist groups on the one hand and the state on the other), they have needed to prove themselves publicly not only as being against such violence and the killings of innocent people, but emphatically also as *being seen to be active against* the possible spread of support or acceptance of such violence, insofar as it is proclaimed to be perpetrated in the name of Islam. As we can see not only from the samples of *Friday Bulletin* articles above, but also from observations in the conduct of everyday conversations and discussions in such a situation, the topic of 'terror' (*ugaidi*) and its variable effects upon the Muslim community needs to be openly, frankly and critically addressed within the community itself.

Especially in a situation like the one currently under discussion, of heightened tensions and confrontations between Muslims and the state, with thus an increased likelihood of frustrated and discontented male youth (especially) becoming tempted to turn to an armed response and joining the likes of al-Shabaab, much effort and energy needs to be invested into keeping these potential aberrants in check, and on the right path of peaceful/non-violent engagement. Thus, internal counter-discourses to a commonly (and often all too easily) assumed 'radicalisation' of Muslims, including the condemnation of violent retaliation or revenge, have also been developed in a variety of ways, by individual actors from within the community itself, employing different voices and rhetorical strategies, and drawing from a variety of locally available (and contested) interpretations of Islam. Indeed, as Susan Hirsch (2006) has observed, the cultivation of pluralism can counter the dynamics of radicalisation.[18] Calls for moderation, or for verbal confrontation and civil disobedience (only), and for measured outspoken political critique in Kenya and international solidarity beyond, are part of the wider complex scenario within which Kenyan Muslims negotiate the challenges they are confronted with. To reiterate, a simple assumption of 'radicalisation' among Muslims (in terms of assuming a general tendency towards increasing support for terrorism or armed struggle) is counter-productive as regards the goal of understanding what is actually going on within the Muslim community. This community is heterogeneous and marked not by unity but by internal frictions, tensions and oppositions

---

[18] In her account, Susan Hirsch also emphasises the relevance of pluralism as a condition for countering 'radicalism' and the use of violence (see esp. 2006: 244, 264; on the variable contextual factors feeding into decision-making processes, see 2006: 260).

between diverse sub-groups, as much as diverse and differing standpoints, positions and strategies for dealing with the ongoing crisis it is facing, from within as well as from the outside. However, the dynamics of political tensions between state apparatus and Muslims play into the creation of increased resilience (and even resistance) by Muslims against the state.

Within such an established situation of fundamental mutual mistrust between Muslims and the state, *listening in* to the internal and pressing debates among Kenyan Muslims is a valuable and necessary exercise for an adequate understanding of what is going on. Such an exercise of paying close attention to the discursive dynamics in Muslim publics provides us with a better idea of what the most salient and most contested topics are (in the respective discussions), and how they are raised and argued about. In the next section, I re-visit an earlier ethnographic 'listening in' exercise of mine, focusing on a broadcast discussion programme that ran on Radio Rahma, an Islamic radio station based in Mombasa, between 2005 and 2007.[19] While my account of these radio debates cannot clarify the exact nature of people's current sentiments about the situation today, it can shed light on how internal debates on topics that matter to the Muslim community have been initiated, moderated and conducted.

Listening in on Islamic Talk Radio

Building on my earlier work, I now discuss some key aspects of the radio programme *Elimika na Stambuli!* ('Get Educated with Stambuli!') that was initiated in 2005 by Stambuli A. Nassir (whom I have known since 1998).[20] Stambuli came from a historically established Mombasan Swahili family belonging to the so-called Twelve Tribes, with a number of healers, scholars and poets on one side and a Kutchi captain from Western India as an ancestor on the other; his father was Sheikh Abdilahi Nassir (1932–2022), a prominent Swahili Muslim scholar, Shii convert, and former leader of the Mwambao coastal independence movement that was campaigning for its aspirations in the early 1960s when Kenyan independence was being negotiated with the British Crown (Brennan 2008; Salim 1970). Having travelled and worked in other parts of Kenya and neighbouring countries, Stambuli had returned to Mombasa and begun to give public speeches as a self-educated independent activist, seeking in the late 1990s to raise coastal Muslims' political consciousness (Kresse 2007: 214–18).

---

[19] During visits to Mombasa in that period, I was able to observe and listen to some of these programmes live and discuss them with friends. I also received a set of recordings directly from Stambuli A. Nassir, the initiator.

[20] This section builds on and develops further reflections I presented first and at length in Kresse 2018a, Ch. 5. It also builds on and extends my reflections on discursive agency in relation to this programme (Kresse 2018b).

Discontent with the coastal Muslim elite and its neglect of the concerns of ordinary Muslims had led Stambuli to the idea of an openly accessible call-in discussion programme. This was supposed to pick up on these concerns and provide a platform for the community to discuss them openly and seriously, in public and live on air. All kinds of topics were welcome and listeners' wishes and suggestions were taken on board to be focused upon for specific shows, from practical matters of the city council's waste management and water supply to concerns about adequate dress in mosques and public spaces, appropriate ways or people to address each other and refer to others, and more. Given the situation of strained political tensions, Stambuli also decided to dedicate a double session of the programme to the discussion of 'terror' (*ugaidi*), and whether terrorism in the name of Islam was justifiable as jihad. My discussion of that below will re-connect us to the situation outlined above. The point here is to acknowledge and convey the significance of the possibility (indeed the reality) of such a frank and internally contested discussion of a sensitive topic that concerns everyone fundamentally, then as much as now.[21]

Elimika na Stambuli! was a popular show that aired every Saturday morning on Radio Rahma, the first Islamic radio station in coastal Kenya in the post-colonial period.[22] People of all backgrounds and ages were invited to call in with their opinions, or ask questions live on air, and engage in a wider conversation about current concerns affecting coastal Muslims in Kenya. The discussions were moderated by Stambuli and his co-host, Abubakar Amin, a well-educated, like-minded professional moderator, and a full-time employee of the radio station.[23] Both conceived of this radio show as adopting a bottom-up approach to mutual education about social, political and religious matters, giving voice to ordinary people. With its innovative conception of live call-in debates, this programme invited all listeners to participate actively, raising their own concerns.

The show attracted a wide audience, among them women, the elderly and even children – for instance, a young boy called in to remind everyone about the need for proper neighbourhood solidarity (*ujirani*). The moderators used their first show as a brainstorming session, asking listeners for topics and issues to be addressed and discussed in future. They announced they would discuss such

---

[21] For a similar point in the Arabic Gulf context, see Eickelman 2005.
[22] Previously, between 1947 and 1966, Islamic broadcasts in Swahili (with Qur'anic recitations and music also in Arabic) had been popular on the coastal national radio programme *Sauti ya Mvita* (Voice of Mombasa). But that was abolished due to growing popular pressure and demands for 'Africanisation', and against Arabic and Islamic sounds on the airwaves, by the demographic majority (Brennan 2015).
[23] Stambuli Abdilahi Nassir and Abubakar Amin are their full names. Having read a draft of this chapter, both indicated that they wanted their full real names to be used in this publication. I already knew Stambuli well before becoming interested in covering this radio broadcast as part of my research, and I got to know Abubakar during my visits to Mombasa since 2005. I had a string of conversations with each of them, while also talking to other interlocutors in Mombasa about the programme.

concerns in topical programmes to which people could contribute by calling in or texting. Any relevant matters, they declared, could be raised for discussion, but callers were admonished to stick to the rules of respectful dialogue. Among the initial suggestions for discussion by listeners were: the problem of drugs, the neglect of rules of proper address and behaviour in public, and how the coastal economy was exploited by up-country interests (e.g. how the income generated by Kilindini Harbour was channelled there). The *Elimika* programme became a common reference point for Swahili-speaking Muslim residents, across gender lines and generations in Mombasa, with many tuning in to its live discussions.

Debating Terrorism

As mentioned above, one of the programme's sessions hosted a discussion of 'terrorism' (*ugaidi*), over two consecutive days in July 2005. This addressed and countered claims that acts of terror could be justified as jihad (struggle) and thus as acceptable acts of revenge. Stambuli and Abubakar made clear from the outset that in their understanding there was no way in which killing innocent and defenceless people could be acceptable. A small minority of callers, however, expressed approval of violent acts as a defensive reaction to the aggressive anti-Muslim politics led by the United States and its 'war on terror'.[24] The existence of conflicting voices and opinions on this matter could not be ignored, or taken lightly. An internal discussion was needed, but this presented a dilemma as it would bring conflict and confrontation to the fore. By opting to organise a broadcast on 'terror', Stambuli decided, as he told me, to facilitate a frank and painful discussion that he felt was much needed. He found it important for all who were affected (as members of the Muslim community), by the claim that violence could be exercised also in their name, to pay attention, build their own judgement, and engage in discussion. Initiating such a discussion can itself be seen as an exercise of the general Islamic ethical obligation of 'forbidding wrong' by Stambuli (see Cook 2000). As he argued on air, throughout the discussion, such violence was forbidden by Islam; and as he told me, during subsequent informal conversations, his efforts were aimed at making sure that there would be a public discussion of such a fundamentally contentious and divisive matter, within his own community.

On the whole, Stambuli was aware of the vulnerability of his own position in such a loaded discussion. He cautioned the audience that even if some disliked

---

[24] See also Hirsch's account of the defendant K.K. in the court of law during his trial, testifying along similar lines (Hirsch 2008: 223–4). For contextual literature, see Mamdani 2005 (esp. 45–62, 249–60); for philosophical perspectives on the 'war-on-terror', see Presbey 2007. For specific studies of political tensions in East African contexts, see e.g. Becker 2006; Prestholdt 2011; Mwakimako and Willis 2014, 2016; Loimeier 2007; Seesemann 2007; Ndzovu 2014, 2018.

him or what he said, they had no right to simply dismiss him or insult him as an unbeliever (*mkafiri*). He made a point of expressing that he too considered himself a faithful believer, who had the right to speak and to be listened to with respect, just like he listened to others and heard them out. Tolerance for other opinions and the recognition of the existence of multiple interpretations of Islam were aspects that people, as human beings and as believers, needed to grant each other.

On the Need for Open Discursive Space

At the end of this programme on terrorism, Stambuli invited the senior invited guest on the show, Professor Mohamed Hyder, a retired university professor in biology and a long-term activist for social and religious reform,[25] to comment. Hyder, who had been live on air with the others throughout the show, and who had, earlier on in the programme, introduced the audience to the American linguist and philosopher Noam Chomsky as a recommendable role model for a political critic and activist global citizen, now summarised the relevance of Stambuli's programme for the Muslim community in his concluding vote of thanks. Thereby, he also invoked early Islamic history and the role model of unity, solidarity and mutual care that the Prophet Muhammad had built with his companions, on the basis of *zakat*, the obligation to donate a set proportion of one's wealth – rather than using bombs and violence, as he said.[26] Turning to his listeners in the here and now, he emphasised, in conclusion, that 'Radio Rahma has given us [i.e. the people, ordinary Muslims] a chance to be able to exchange (and possibly change each other's) thoughts about such matters', and he congratulated the programme makers on this important achievement.[27]

Prof. Hyder's closing advice bears thinking about. Making sure that people are communicatively connected provides opportunity for mutual engagement, listening to each other's points while also seeking to convince each other, by means of arguments and reasoning, as competing positions within a discursive tradition (Asad 1986). An open exchange among all those using this space who had called in and voiced their concerns helped to lay out the actual features

---

[25] He was then still running the Muslim Civic Educational Trust (MCET) that was funded by US and other development organisations and produced weekly pamphlets, on 'Kenya as the Muslims want it' (*Kenya Waislamu waitakavyo*); he was also one of the main local campaigners seeking to raise funds (through Muslim networks) to realise the dream of a coastal Mombasa-based university.

[26] He said: 'perhaps we could use such ways too instead of strapping bombs to our bodies and going to blow ourselves up in order to attack others. That is terrorism – and it is not terrorism about which we can say it is Islamic.' (Original: *Je sisi tunaweza kutumia njia zile badala ya kujifungua mabomu, na kwenda kujipasua na kwenda kuwapigana: ule ni ugaidi – na si ugaidi ambao tuaweza kusema ni ya kiislamu.*)

[27] *Na sisi inshallah katika kujadiliana, na kujadiliana zaidi, kuhusu mambo kama haya, Radio Rahma imewapa watu nafasi ya kuweza kubadilishana fikra kwa mambo kama haya. Na napenda kuwapa pongezi, nafurahi sana kuweza kuwa pamoja na nanyi siku ya leo.*

of internal conflict and divisions, so that they could be better understood and addressed by all. Stambuli's radio programme enabled an outspoken exchange within the community, providing all listeners (as potential participants to the live debate) with the opportunity to publicly voice their concerns and sentiments in response to others. This was remarkable and much-needed, especially with regard to such a sensitive and potentially divisive topic as 'terror'. Radio debates such as this one emphasise an egalitarian character within public discursive space, challenging existent social hierarchies and prevailing assumptions. Indeed, here everyone was able to call in and raise their own concerns about common well-being with a view to their peers, thus following the general moral obligation of 'reminding each other' (*kumbushana*) and 'forbidding each other wrong' (*katazana*).[28]

Another crucial position for the discussion was flagged up by Prof. Hyder, namely an alternative interpretation of 'jihad' to that of armed fight, one that is not uncommon in local discussions, whether in scholarly or everyday settings.[29] Prof. Hyder argued that the term here is to be understood as 'struggle' and not 'holy war', that is, the armed fight for the cause of Islam that both Muslims and non-Muslims often commonly understand (or invoke) it as. The struggle that matters most, the so-called 'greater jihad' – which is also commonly linked to the Prophet Muhammad, the major role model for all Muslims – is the *inner struggle* by every person to strive and dedicate him-/herself to living life as it should be lived. The next relevant aspect of 'jihad' is laid out as the obligation to take care of one's peers, that is, one's family and community members (possibly including religious peers).[30] Thus, overall, the interpretation presented here also conveys an implicit appeal not to engage in violent acts that could potentially harm the lives of one's own group, but instead to guard their well-being. Terrorist acts consciously run the risk of killing or hurting innocent people, or even aim

---

[28] See Michael Cook (2000: 584) on the everyday, egalitarian (and even 'democratic') character of command that he sees in play here, in the context of the general Islamic principle of the mutual obligation of commanding right and forbidding wrong – here seen in its Swahili idiom.

[29] Susan Hirsch (2006: 223) also points to the *plurality of interpretations of 'jihad'* in Islam (which is also invoked by one of the defendants, a Swahili man from Pemba, during the trial). She also addresses the fact that those participating in acts of terror did so as part of a series of *choices* they made – while others (living in the same environments) had made different choices (2006: 235).

[30] 'If we talk about the topic of *jihad*, we should remember that the *big jihad* is the one that you fight against yourself (your own will), to compare yourself with God (his demands) so that you orientate yourself with a view to God in everything that you do. If you take that (*jihad*) on then you know that the *second jihad* is about taking care of your own people, so that we can make sure, in a joint effort, that we are all Muslims; so that we can enable them to reach that level.' (Original: *tukisema mada ya jihadi, tukumbuke kwamba jihadi kubwa ni ile ya wewe upigania na nafsi yako, kujilinganisha na Mwenyezi Mungu ili wewe umwelekee Mwenyezi Mungu katika mambo yako yote*. U[30]) He said: 'perhaps we could use such ways too instead of strapping bombs to our bodies and going to blow ourselves up in order to attack others. That is terrorism – and it is not terrorism about which we can say it is Islamic.' (Original: *Je sisi tunaweza kutumia njia zile badala ya kujifungua mabomu, na kwenda kujipasua na kwenda kuwapigana: ule ni ugaidi – na si ugaidi ambao tuaweza kusema ni ya kiislamu.*)

for just that. According to the brief commentary here, this is in fundamental contradiction to a sound understanding of Islam. If this position also stands for the attitude with which the moderators here enacted their stance as facilitators of a necessary debate, similar readings of 'jihad' are cited in internal debates among Muslims, in Kenya and elsewhere.[31] Such invocations, motivated by considerations of care, humane conviction and moral discipline, can be found in the pages of *The Friday Bulletin* as well as in other Muslim media and everyday discussions, in *baraza* (public) meetings and elsewhere.

Stambuli's show was removed from Radio Rahma in late 2007 after his funders, who had been providing the amount of money the station had asked for, discontinued their support. This may have had to do with pressure by those who disagreed with Stambuli's critical stance, and who preferred to avoid or suppress this kind of public discussion; or it could have been linked to the perceived Shii orientation of Abubakar and Stambuli, Stambuli's father being a prominent Shii proponent within the Swahili community. In any case, Stambuli had criticised the Muslim elite along such lines before, saying that they should long since have represented common Muslim concerns and grievances in public – rather than participating in the ongoing political disempowerment of Muslims in Kenya and discouragement of their civic engagement. Stambuli's *Elimika* show itself had been motivated and defined by a critical counter-agenda, of creating and maintaining discursive space for public questioning and debate.

Over the following years, Stambuli continued his mission as best as he could, as an independent consultant, making himself available at accessible meeting points in public, for those who sought his advice and opinion. All the while, he continued making use of historical and contemporary materials on coastal history and politics that could be used as evidence for the kind of purposes that his radio show had provided. In 2018, over ten years later, he was called upon to make radio broadcasts again, now with a proper position and in a full capacity. The newly founded Islamic radio station Pwani FM (Coast FM) made him Productions Manager of its programme. As I myself was able to witness during a visit to the studio for a live show he was moderating (and as I continue to witness while listening in online from afar), the defining features of his *Elimika* show were here taken over, and now Stambuli himself was able to recruit promising young moderators who were able to engage their listeners in the kind of meaningful conversations and debates that matter to people and that can, potentially, make a difference.

The day I was listening in on my visit, Stambuli, in tandem with a young moderator who had just joined Pwani FM from a rival radio station, was leading a discussion on proper parenting and inter-generational relationships. This was

---

[31] E.g. Euben 2002; Asad 2007.

a sensitive and difficult topic for many families on the coast, since for many (particularly male) youths the tension between their material desires and the economic hardships they faced was difficult to handle, and many parents were worried about their sons being tempted to sway from the right path. The discussion itself, following the lead of a reflexive monologue offered by Stambuli, focused in on the domestic sphere more generally (*unyumba*), and specifically the relationship between spouses (a topic that was too rarely talked about, he said). Stambuli maintained that people commonly still married very young (or were pressured to do so), without really knowing their future spouses, and they often did not know how to interact with each other openly and properly. It was important, he pointed out, that partners learned to communicate with each other with sensitivity, understanding and mutual concern. Many young couples had not chosen their partners and did not try enough to get to know each other after marriage, he said. This often resulted in them leading separate lives, largely in communicative isolation from each other (and possibly their families), and loneliness, depression and drug-taking were possible outcomes. As callers engaged in discussion and noted their appreciation that this topic was covered, it was obvious that Stambuli's powerful way of connecting with his audience had lost none of its force. As before, he spoke in an accessible and engaging manner on issues that were relevant to people's lives – including the private sphere and politics.

Conclusion

The previous section, with its focus on specific interrelationships between callers, moderators and the wider public, may seem to have little to do with the bigger issues initially addressed in this chapter concerning the relationship between Muslims and the state. But this is not really so. For what a focus on the use of public discursive space (the radio, or the bulletin) can make clear is that the effort to help build and cultivate an active, politically sensitised and conscious community can make a fundamental difference both to the sense of internal cohesion of that community and to the relationship between the community and the state (the government, and the organisation of national political structures). An alert and well-informed, sensitive and self-confident community of the kind that both *The Friday Bulletin* and the *Elimika* broadcast envisaged helping to create, strengthened by internal communications and an awareness of the most pressing issues, may ultimately overcome its fears, and in consequence resist being pushed or pressured into accepting or doing things that are, in the end, contrary to its interests.

In this sense, the kind of work pursued in the vivid, aurally transmitted and participatory live debates (on radio, television or possibly the internet), as well as in the written commentaries and discussions contained in nationally circulating pamphlets, by using flexible and accessible discursive spaces among Swahili Muslim publics and Islamic media in the way described here, can be understood as constituting a significant and powerful (even an empowering) kind of political work. The resultant discursive sensitisation and a communal sense of empowerment engage Muslims as ordinary citizens. By offering them the opportunity to participate in the re-shaping (and potential strengthening) of the community itself, through public critical engagement, such work points to the possible potential. This may help to build and shape more conscious and alert political actors, and to re-adjust the dynamics and boundaries of political relationships, at the local, communal and national levels.[32]

Bibliography

Alidou, Ousseina (2013), *Muslim Women in Postcolonial Kenya*, University of Wisconsin Press.

Al-Jazeera English (2014), 'Africa Investigates: Inside Kenya's Death Squads', 7 December (film), https://www.youtube.com/watch?v=lUjOdjdH8Uk

Anderson, David M. and Jacob McKnight (2014), 'Kenya at War: al-Shabaab and its Enemies in Eastern Africa', *African Affairs* 114(454), pp. 1–27.

Asad, Talal (1986), *The Idea of an Anthropology of Islam*. Occasional papers series. Washington, DC. Center for Contemporary Arab Studies, Georgetown University.

Asad, Talal (2007), *On Suicide Bombing*, New York: Columbia University Press.

Becker, Felicitas (2006), 'Rural Islamism during the "War on Terror": A Tanzanian Case Study', *African Affairs* 105(421), pp. 583–603.

Branch, Daniel (2011), *Kenya: Between Hope and Despair, 1963–2011*, New Haven: Yale University Press.

Brennan, James R. (2008), 'Lowering the Sultan's Flag: Sovereignty and Decolonization in Coastal Kenya', *Comparative Studies in Society and History* 50(4), pp. 831–61.

Brennan, James R. (2015), 'A History of *Sauti ya Mvita* ("Voice of Mombasa"): Radio, Public Culture, and Islam in Coastal Kenya, 1947–1966', in Rosalind I. J. Hackett and Benjamin F. Soares (eds), *New Media and Religious Transformations in Africa*, Bloomington: Indiana University Press, pp. 19–38.

Chome, N. (2016a), 'Violent Extremism and Clan Dynamics in Kenya'. Washington, DC: Peaceworks no. 123.

Chome, N. (2016b), *'We Don't Trust Anyone!': Strengthening Relationships as the Key to Reducing Violent Extremism in Kenya*, London/Nairobi: International Alert/KMYA.

---

[32] Research on this chapter builds on many conversations with Kenyan Muslim interlocutors inside and outside of Kenya, during regular visits to Kenya between 2005 and 2018; on reading, viewing and listening to Muslim media over these years. Specifically, the argument about the value of discursive space presented here builds on and takes further reflections from Chapter 5 of my recent book (Kresse 2018a). In particular, I thank Stambuli Abdilahi Nassir and Abubakar Amin for their openness to my research interests and for ongoing communication. I thank the participants of the conference in January 2018 for comments and questions, and Farouk Topan and Hassan Mwakimako for comments on a draft.

Cook, Michael (2000), *Commanding Right and Forbidding Wrong in Islamic Thought*, Cambridge/New York: Cambridge University Press.

Deacon, G., G. Gona, H. Mwakimako and J. Willis (2017), 'Preaching Politics: Islam and Christianity on the Kenyan Coast', *Journal of Contemporary African Studies*. 35(2), pp. 1–20.

Eickelman, Dale F. (2005), 'New Media in the Arab Middle East and the Emergence of Open Societies', in R. W. Hefner (ed.), *Remaking Muslim Publics: Pluralism, Contestation, Democratization*, Princeton: Princeton University Press, pp. 37–59.

Euben, Roxanne L. (2002), 'Killing for Politics: *Jihad*, Martyrdom, and Political Action', *Political Theory* 30(1), pp. 4–35.

Friday Bulletin. Nairobi: Jamia Mosque.

Goodman, Zoe (2017), 'Tales of the Everyday City: Geography and Chronology in Postcolonial Mombasa', unpublished doctoral dissertation, University of London.

Hirsch, Susan (2006), *In the Moment of Greatest Calamity: Terrorism, Grief, and a Victim's Quest for Justice*, Princeton: Princeton University Press.

Hornsby, Charles (2012), *Kenya: A History Since Independence*, New York: I. B. Tauris.

KMYA (2016), 'We Don't Trust Anyone: Strengthening Relationships as the Key to Reducing Violent Extremism in Kenya', Working Paper, Kenyan Muslim Youth Alliance. September 2016, pp. 1–37.

Kresse, Kai (2007), *Philosophising in Mombasa: Knowledge, Islam and Intellectual Practice on the Swahili Coast*, Edinburgh: Edinburgh University Press for the International African Institute.

Kresse, Kai (2009), 'Muslim Politics in Postcolonial Kenya: Negotiating Knowledge on the Double-periphery', *Journal of the Royal Anthropological Institute*, S76–S94.

Kresse, Kai (2018a), *Swahili Muslim Publics and Postcolonial Experience*, Bloomington: Indiana University Press.

Kresse, Kai (2018b), 'Dimensions of "Giving Voice": Discursive Agency and Intellectual Practice on Swahili Islamic Radio, in Mombasa 2005–2006', in B. Graef et al. (eds), *Ways of Knowing Muslim Cultures: Essays in Honor of Gudrun Kraemer*, Leiden: Brill, pp. 265–79.

Loimeier, Roman (2007), 'Perceptions of Marginalization: Muslims in Contemporary Tanzania', in B. F. Soares and R. Otayek (eds), *Islam and Muslim Politics in Africa*, London: Palgrave Macmillan, pp. 137–56.

Mamdani, Mahmood (2005), *Good Muslim, Bad Muslim: America, the Cold War, and the Roots of Terror*, New York: Three Leaves Press.

Mwakimako, Hassan and J. Willis (2014), 'Islam, Politics, and Violence on the Kenya Coast'. Observatoire des Enjeux Politiques et Sécuritaires dans la Corne de l'Afrique, note 4.

Mwakimako, Hassan and Justin Willis (2016), 'Islam and Democracy: Debating Electoral Involvement on the Kenyan Coast', *Islamic Africa* 7, pp. 1–25.

Ndzovu, Hassan (2014), *Muslims in Kenyan Politics*, Evanston: Northwestern University Press.

Ndzovu, Hassan (2018), 'Kenya's Jihadi Clerics: Formulation of a Liberation Theology to Muslims' Socio-Political Grievances and the Challenge to Secular Power', *Journal of International Muslim Minority Affairs* (JIMMA), pp. 1–14.

Presbey, Gail M. (ed.) (2007), *Philosophical Perspectives on the 'War on Terrorism*, New York: Rodopi.

Prestholdt, Jeremy (2011), 'Kenya, the United States, and Counterterrorism', *Africa Today* 57(4), pp. 2–27.

Prestholdt, Jeremy (2014), 'Politics of the Soil: Separatism, Autochtony, and Decolonization at the Kenyan Coast', *Journal of African History* 55, pp. 249–70.

Salim, A. I. (1970), 'The Movement for "Mwambao" or Coast Autonomy in Kenya, 1956–63', in B. A. Ogot and A. Brockett (eds), *Hadith 2: Proceedings of the 1968 Conference of the Historical Association of Kenya*, Nairobi: East African Publishing House, pp. 210–28.

Seesemann, Ruediger (2007), 'Kenyan Muslims, the Aftermath of 9/11, and the "War on Terror"', in B. F. Soares and R. Otayek (eds), *Islam and Muslim Politics in Africa*, London: Palgrave Macmillan, pp. 157–76.

Wrong, Michelle (2009), *It's Our Turn to Eat: The Story of a Kenyan Whistleblower*, New York: Harper.

5

Islam, Politics and the Limits of Authority in Mainland Tanzania, 1955–1968

JAMES R. BRENNAN

This chapter examines how Tanganyika's urban Islamic institutions and Muslim population by turns led, negotiated and endured the rise of African nationalism and the establishment of a secular socialist regime between 1955 and 1968. This is explored through four sequential arenas. The first explores how efforts to officialise public elements of Islam, particularly regarding festivals, catalysed fissures that led to a wide-scale reorganisation of Muslim civil society in late colonial Tanganyika. The second arena examines the rise of the All-Muslim National Union of Tanganyika or AMNUT, a short-lived opposition party that challenged the Tanganyika African National Union (TANU)'s control over decolonisation. The third considers the similarly short-lived opposition career of Chief Abdullah Fundikira, who resigned from the ruling TANU party and took up popular laments about Muslim marginalisation following a well-publicised corruption trial. The fourth and final arena concerns the fate of the East African Muslim Welfare Society (EAMWS), which the Tanzanian state banned in 1968. Together, these arenas demonstrate not simply a victory of a nation-state authority over a deeply rooted urban Muslim establishment, but also the secularisation of political authority itself, through which major Islamic institutions and leaders could be either publicly auxiliary to or subversively independent from Tanzania's party-state government. This chapter relies primarily on contemporaneous newspapers and archival evidence from Tanzania and Britain to reconstruct these stories, which are told primarily from the perspective of Dar es Salaam, the country's centre of political authority and official capital during this period.

This story is not about Islamism or 'political Islam', but rather about how Islam served multiple political roles in what is today mainland Tanzania.

Its rituals buttressed the social institutions of ruling patricians while opening doors for parvenus long before European colonial rule. Its calendric observances, festivals and prayers forged long-distance networks of shared practice, characterised by dramatic displays of austere piety and raucous generosity. Yet Islamic authority was often highly localised. This chapter examines key events in the late colonial and early post-colonial period to demonstrate how Muslim politics was effectively domesticated by state actors – on the one hand managing to retain a realm of spiritual autonomy, while on the other acknowledging state control over vital Islamic institutions.

There was little that predestined Muslim communities to act either with or against colonial state structures. Muslim traders, teachers and civil servants played an outsized role in the early organised nationalist politics, and the quick ascent of the Tanganyika African National Union (TANU) owed much to its early support for Muslims in Dar es Salaam and other towns. Yet, Muslims also often proved reliable adjundants of key colonial institutions – playing the role of soldier (*askari*) in the German Schutztruppe and its successor the Kings African Rifles, as well as the role of the 'direct rule' administrator (*akida*), the 'indirect rule' chief (*jumbe*) and the town governor (*liwali*).

Political leadership among Tanganyika's African Muslims was held by older men living in larger towns, many of whom resented the British administration's neglect of their fading status and position. This group, however, equally resented what they perceived as religious conceit by their fellow Arab and Indian Muslims, who had largely benefited from racialised colonial structures. As early as 1934, African Muslims in Dar es Salaam quit the town's primary civic Islamic organisation, the Indian-dominated Anjuman Islamiyyaa, to form the Muslim Association of Tanganyika, or Jamiatul Islamiyya.[1] This and subsequent disputes between African and non-African Muslims centred on educational access or the organisation of Eid and *maulid* celebrations, issues that were ultimately about the distribution of Indian and Arab resources to poorer Africans.[2] Yet shared religious identity and the occasionally generous philanthropy of non-African Muslims – particularly from the Aga Khan's East African Muslim Welfare Society (EAMWS), formed in 1945 – made inter-racial, pan-Islamic organisation as attractive an option for some African Muslims, as secular political opposition to racial inequality formed the core of what became the country's main nationalist movement, TANU. In Dar es Salaam, African political leadership in historically Muslim towns had fluidly crossed secular and

---

[1] For an overview see Brennan 2014.
[2] Among these pan-racial Islamic organisations are the Tanganyika Muslim League (1932), the Muslim Association (1947), the Central Muslim Association and the Muslim Unity Board. *Tanganyika Standard*, 30 April 1932; letter of M. O. Abbasi, *Tanganyika Standard*, 25 February 1955.

Islamic organisations.[3] Accompanying the rise of TANU and its leader Julius Nyerere, however, were programmatic efforts to divorce discussions of religion from TANU's political agenda.[4] This imposed 'divorce' of religion from politics posed a dilemma for African Muslims, which forced a series of fateful political decisions that lie at the core of this chapter.

Public Structures of Late-colonial Islamic Life in Tanganyika: Festivals, Religious Authority and African Nationalism

Perhaps the best arena in which to examine Islamic politics in East Africa is the organisation of and participation in public festivals. Conflicts between such formal figures of collaboration and self-styled nationalists as emerged in the 1950s provides the most useful starting point for tracing the trajectory of Islam and state politics in mainland Tanzania. The framework in which these conflicts occurred concerned the administration of religious public affairs, particularly festivals, control over which formed the backbone of Islamic politics during the late colonial and early post-colonial periods. In Dar es Salaam, *maulid* festivals had previously been organised by the Indian-dominated Anjuman Islamiyya, until a group of African and Arab Muslims broke with the organisation in 1938 to form a separate *maulid* committee.[5] Further factionalism followed until 1942, when the *liwali* or chief Muslim administrator of Dar es Salaam, Hamed bin Salehe al Busaidi, brought in the town's Arab Association to help organise celebrations, which it did through the 1940s and early 1950s.[6]

Key elements of Islamic public life only obtained official status in the final years of British colonial rule. The Central Society of Tanganyika Muslims, established in 1955 to set up an Islamic teacher training college and act as a point of liaison to facilitate state grants for Muslim schools, was invited by the Eid and *maulid* committees in early 1957 to organise Dar es Salaam's first official state holiday Islamic festivals. The Central Society had taken care to enlist nearly all of Tanganyika's influential Muslim figures of all races, including the former president of the Tanganyika African Association (TANU's predecessor) Abdulwahid Sykes as its Assistant Secretary.[7] After years of being lobbied, the government finally recognised Eid al-fitr and Eid al-adha as official

---

[3] Said 1998: 40–9, 80–7, 110–33. Said offers a reasonable account of how a 'Christian outsider' was selected to lead the largely Muslim TAA in Dar es Salaam, but less reasonably and with little evidence argues that Nyerere and the Catholic Church thereafter conspired to marginalise not only Muslim leaders in TANU but Muslims throughout Tanganyika.

[4] Westerlund 1980.

[5] Brennan 2014: 221.

[6] *Tanganyika Herald*, 4 April 1942; ibid., 15 February 1946; note of Maulidi committee meeting, 29 November 1950, TzNA British Colonial Secretariat Minute Papers [hereafter SMP] 38636/f.75D.

[7] A list of management committee members is enclosed in Honorary Secretary, Central Society of Tanganyika Muslims to Chief Secretary [hereafter CS], 7 May 1956, TzNA Acc. 226/ABJ/52/f.1.

holidays in 1957, the same year it cancelled Empire Day. This newly official status, however, also awakened debates about *umma* disunity owing to different calendar reckonings for these holidays. Although the Hamed bin Salehe al Busaidi as *liwali* retained the sole official right to declare moon-sightings upon which Eid festivals could begin, others argued that greater communal unity could be achieved by co-ordinating festivals through the use of astronomy and mathematics, embodied in the published 'Misry' (Egyptian) lunar calendar. Still others insisted that moon-sightings were intensely local matters that could be declared by local Muslim authorities other than the *liwali*.[8]

The newly accorded official status granted to the Central Society of Tanganyika Muslims, combined with the officialisation of Dar es Salaam's most important public holiday, posed a challenge and an opportunity for Africans to express religious authority. The Tanganyika African Muslim Union (TAMU), a new organisation formed in Tabora in early 1956, criticised the Central Society for its failure to represent African Muslims adequately, its annual general meeting in 1957 having included only four Africans out of a total of seventy attendees. Its committee was further attacked for filling African seats without consultation and by secret ballot.[9] The Central Society countered that Africans were free to speak at its meetings.[10] But TAMU itself soon faced serious opposition from TANU, which sought to monopolise questions of public authority over African matters. The TANU publicity secretary E. B. M. Barongo declared that the newly formed Tanganyika African Muslim Union 'plants fences among the people', elaborating as follows:

> This is not to entice a Muslim member of T.A.N.U. from joining the Society, but it is a warning of some sort, if the Muslims will all join this Society socially, educationally, culturally [sic] and economically, what is left for T.A.N.U. to play is only 'politically' which is impossible to achieve without the aforesaid fundamentals in the street of standard civilization. The T.A.N.U. is clearly at stake. The Muslim Society is aiming at strengthening discrimination amongst the African community whereby a non-Muslim will not cooperate with a Muslim ... T.A.N.U. calls for one combined effort as a nation and if these vital aspects are facing interference at this young stage, what do you think shall be the outcome? The Muslim Africans are now being cut off from their Christian and pagan brothers, quite indirectly and very cleverly.[11]

---

[8] Letter of G. H. Hemani, *Tanganyika Standard*, 27 May 1955; letters of 'Hilal' and 'Hilal Sighter', *Tanganyika Standard*, 9 and 22 April 1957. For background to Tanzania's many 'moon-sighting' controversies, see Van de Bruinhorst 2007, Ch. 7.
[9] Abubakar Ulotu 1971: 207; letter of Ali Athmani, *Tanganyika Standard*, 28 February 1957; letter of 'Muslim', ibid., 19 April 1957.
[10] Letter of A. A. Deshukh, *Tanganyika Standard*, 16 May 1957.
[11] Letter of E. B. M. Barongo, *Tanganyika Standard*, 16 February 1956.

The strongest display of public harmony among Tanzania's diverse Muslim communities was the successful organisation of unified Islamic festivals, which remained intact between 1942 and 1956. The festivals were both religiously powerful and wonderfully entertaining. Under the *liwali*'s leadership, Eid al-fitr had also become a spectacle, with hundreds gathering in a ring 'to watch sword dancers swaying, prancing and leaping to the rhythm of a chanting crowd and a thundering drum'.[12] Moments of festival discord – such as when the town's 1952 *maulid* was disrupted by poor attendance, speeches stressing evil and sin rather than celebration, and the premature departure of several participants – were exceptional and not explicitly political.[13] *Ngoma* performances by town groups such as Lelemama Mkwaju, Tokomire, Mganda Gombe Sugu and Legeza entertained audiences around the margins of Mnazi Mmoja, the geographical centre of Dar es Salaam's Islamic public festivals.[14]

While the 1956 Eid celebrations passed 'without any untoward incident', there was a growing unruliness among young children, as well as the official cancellation of 'Crown and Anchor' tables, a dice gambling game whose confiscation provoked stone throwing in retaliation. Officials begged the festival's committee to prevent it from 'degenerating into a four day gambling session'.[15] More political participants began to question the overtly 'official' nature of Dar es Salaam's Islamic festivals, which inevitably featured didactic speeches from either the governor or a high-ranking European official. The religious authority of the *liwali* seemed compromised as a result, particularly on the occasion when, according to Tewa Said Tewa, the governor had the *liwali* flown in a plane over Dar es Salaam, 'trying to cite [sic] the moon so that the following day Iddi Baraza could be held and the Governor could make his policy statement'.[16] Local sheikhs on the town's margins explained in 1957 that Doomsday (*kiama*) would arrive on Saturday immediately following the Eid al-fitr celebration, generating enormous anxiety among their listeners.[17]

A serious rift had formed by the time *maulid* arrived in October 1957. The *maulid* committee had voluntarily affiliated itself with the Central Society, a move that appears to have alienated many African Muslims, who felt sharply underrepresented by the organisation. A new political context had emerged that year with the announcement of elections being held of a 'multi-racial' basis of European, Asian and African candidates. The principle of multi-racialism was

---

[12] 'Dar es Salaam Muslims Celebrate', *Tanganyika Standard*, 18 July 1950.
[13] 'Kwa nini Islam waAfrica wengi hawaji katika Mauli ya Ziara mnazi mmoja?', *Zuhra*, 19 December 1952.
[14] 'Idi Mubarak', *Zuhra*, 22 July 1955.
[15] Ag. Senior Asst. Commissioner of Police [DSM] to Provincial Council, Morogoro, 20 June 1956, TzNA Acc. 540/1/51/II/f.28.
[16] Tewa 1982: 85.
[17] Letter of Chande Rajabu, *Zuhra*, 16 August 1957.

bitterly opposed by TANU, although the party eventually participated in and won the subsequent 1958/9 elections. In contrast, the principle was embraced by the newly founded conservative United Tanganyika Party (UTP), prominent members of which included Central Society leaders like V. M. Nazerali and Hussein bin Juma, the latter a prominent Manyema Sheikh in Dar es Salaam. This made the Central Society a tempting target for TANU.

Like much of Dar es Salaam's ulama, Sheikh Hussein bin Juma established his reputation as a schoolteacher; with his twin brother Hassan he established the El Hassanain School in 1942, which rivalled the Jamiatul Islamiyya school as the town's most prestigious African madrasa. Sheikh Hussein had studied in Yemen and was considered the greatest Arabic grammar (*nahw*) scholar in Tanganyika. He was also the first important personality in Kariakoo to join UTP, and later became its vice-chairman. TANU-supporting parents immediately withdrew their children from his school in protest.[18] Sheikh Hussein loudly and repeatedly lambasted TANU for pursuing 'political irresponsibility' that was impoverishing Tanganyika, and in turn received the most sustained political intimidation of any African figure in Dar es Salaam at the time. His house in Kariakoo was stoned, as, too, was his vehicle when he campaigned for UTP in Kilosa. He and his family were repeatedly threatened with assault – including one near miss by a machete-wielding TANU supporter just days before *maulid*. Sheikh Hussein returned fire by criticising the education levels of his detractors in print.[19] At stake were the loyalties of Dar es Salaam's well-educated African Muslims, some of whom embraced not TANU but TAMU and even the Central Society, and favoured the UTP over TANU because UTP would not pressure non-Africans to emigrate.[20]

TANU's larger conflict with UTP exploded in Dar es Salaam on 6 October 1957, the evening of *maulid*, when UTP member Dr Khan stood up and began speaking in Urdu. Hundreds of TANU supporters immediately stood to leave, turning their backs on the speaker and stating that they could not listen to UTP. *Maulid* stopped shortly thereafter, only midway through the festival. Police were called in to ensure control; untouched food for the 6,000 attendees was transported to Ukonga prison the next day.[21] Zuberi Mtemvu, TANU's organising secretary who himself would break with TANU over participation in the 'multi-racial' election to form the African National Congress three months later, declared that the Central Society had 'made the whole [Maulid]

---

[18] Interview with Ali Abbas, 31 May 2010.
[19] *Tanganyika Standard*, 12 April, 15 August and 16 September 1957; *Zuhra*, 27 September 1957; *Tanganyika Standard*, 8 October 1957; letters of Hussein Juma, ibid., 18 and 26 July 1957.
[20] See e.g. letters of Ali Mohamed and 'African Clerk', *Tanganyika Standard*, 22 March 1956.
[21] Letter of 'Non Politician Muslim', *Tanganyika Standard*, 14 October 1957; letter of I. M. Kiboga, ibid., 11 October 1957.

committee unpopular', and asked that the future festivals be left to 'Sheikhs and Headmasters of Muslim Schools'.[22] It appears that Mtemvu himself had organised the dramatic walk-out, as a protest against the UTP as well as the government's proposed multi-racial election system. A horrified member of the Central Society attending the *maulid* declared the walk-out 'most unpardonable from every point of view', and claimed that it was pre-arranged 'to penetrate the religious field for "political purposes"'. He begged for government protection from this penetration of 'the poison of politics … into purely religious affairs'.[23] Another disconsolate onlooker observed that *maulid* had been 'going on for the last thirty years in peace and happiness', but that this year, 'external agencies have interfered to give a death-blow to its unity and solidarity which may one day widen the gulf between African brethren themselves'.[24] Islamic festivals resumed their unified composure in 1959 following TANU's decisive electoral victories over UTP; they were led by Juma Mwindadi, head of the Jamiatul school, kadhi of Dar es Salaam and an effective legislative council member.[25] For its part, the incoming TANU government managed to avoid similar controversies by leaving Dar es Salaam's *maulid* and Eid committee to determine their own moon-sightings, though it retained the right to intervene if necessary; in a further popular move, it expanded Eid celebrations to become a two-day public holiday.[26]

Festivals also served as sites of conflict over religious authority, which itself became intertwined with nationalist politics. The most intractable disputes date to the inter-war period, and concern ceremonial aspects, specific practices of which were forbidden (*haramu*). The incorporation of drums (in Swahili, *piga duffu*) and the participation of women in the Sufi practice of *zikiri* – most markedly in *askariyya* practices associated with Sheikh Idris and his Lindi-based supporters – formed the most important lines of controversy. After years of participating in the 1920s, women in Tanga were by the early 1930s no longer allowed to take part in *zikiri*.[27] In Bukoba, itself a frequent capital of theological dispute, the town head man and leading Muslim figure, Sharif Salim bin Dossa, strongly protested the use of drums, flags and the participation of young women. The practice, allegedly introduced to the town by a Bugandan named Taibu, had become popular among a large number of younger Muslims.[28]

---

[22] Letter of Zuberi M. M. Mtemvu, *Tanganyika Standard*, 10 October 1957.
[23] Letter of Gulam Mohamed, *Tanganyika Standard*, 15 October 1957. The details and personalities of this conflict remain vague – Abdulwahid Sykes was also a member of the Central Society, and still an important figure in TANU.
[24] Letter of H. S. Alawy, *Tanganyika Standard*, 17 October 1957.
[25] *Tanganyika Standard*, 30 March 1960 and 28 August 1961.
[26] *Tanganyika Standard*, 21 February 1963.
[27] Minute of H.M.K. to Maguire, 21 March 1933, TzNA SMP 21447.
[28] District Officer [hereafter DO] Bukoba to Asst Superintendent of Police, Bukoba, 23 February 1933, enclosed in Provincial Commissioner [hereafter PC] Lake to Chief Secretary [hereafter CS], 10 March 1933, TzNA SMP 21447/f.1; DO Bukoba to PC Lake, 31 May 1933, TzNA SMP 21447/f.6.

The most decisive intervention in the debate occurred in 1948, when Sheikh Hassan bin Ameir, a highly esteemed Shirazi teacher and Qadiriyya *murid* from Zanzibar, sought to purify mainland Islam of its innovations (*bida'a*) by demanding a ban on the use of drums (*duff*) in all Islamic ceremonies. Hassan bin Ameir had moved from Zanzibar to the mainland in the early 1940s and had made a new home in Kariakoo, primarily to carry out *da'wa* on the mainland to stem what he viewed as the tide of Christian missionary successes, as well as to establish his popular Madrasat al-Shirazi in Dar es Salaam's Comorian mosque. Although not a publicly active supporter of nationalist politics, Ameir sat on the TAA political subcommittee in 1951, and was instrumental in selling TANU cards within the mosques of Dar es Salaam.[29] Hassan bin Ameir later became the mufti (jurist) of Tanganyika in the 1950s; his reputation lay not only in his learning and publishing, but also in his reputed success in gaining converts to Islam through a series of trips to Congo, Rwanda, Burundi and various Tanganyikan towns.[30]

Duff disputes often pitted the cosmopolitan learnedness of its opponents against the local authority of *duff* use's supporters. Purging drums was a cause that Qadiriyya sheikhs had similarly been prosecuting in Kilwa and Lindi.[31] In Dar es Salaam, four of the town's most important sheikhs rose to oppose Hassan bin Ameir's position not only by defending *duff*, but also by opposing his proposal to create a town kadhi (Islamic judge). Hassan bin Ameir, however, had gained the critical support of Juma Mwindadi, headmaster of the Jamitaul Islamiyya school and the favoured candidate to become kadhi. For their part, the elders explained that Hassan bin Ameir was a foreigner (*mgeni*) to Dar es Salaam, and that they instead had the right to be consulted about the kadhi appointment.[32] Juma Mwindadi was subsequently appointed kadhi, and Hassan bin Ameir made peace between *duff* advocates by offering a well-received *fatwa* sometime around 1952, which declared that drums were in fact *halal* (permitted), as too was mixed-gender singing among children, but that adult men and women must be separated in *maulid*.[33]

---

[29] Said 1998: 88; interview with Sheikh Ali Bassaleh, 27 May 2010.

[30] *Kaliamatul Hak*, April 1948, in TzNA Acc. 540/27/14; District Commissioner [hereafter DC] Uzaramo to DC Lindi, 28 April 1948, TzNA Acc. 540/27/14/f.7; DC Lindi to DC Uzaramo, 3 May 1948, TzNA Acc. 540/27/14/f.8. On Hassan bin Ameir, see Loimeier 2009: 86–92; Ziddy 2006; Nimtz 1980: 23, 69, 91. Ameir's more enthusiastic supporters claimed that he converted 7 million people to Islam on his up-country journeys; Ziddy 2006: 55.

[31] On *duffu* controversies in Kilwa, see Becker 2008: 186–90, 201–8.

[32] Letter of Sheikhs and Imams, Dar es Salaam to PC Eastern, 20 July 1948, TzNA SMP 10849/1427/f.1A. The four included Sheikh Said Pazi, imam of Manyema mosque; Sheikh Athmani bin Abdallah Muki, imam of Rufiji and Ndengereko mosque; Sheikh Yusuf bin Said, imam of Makonde mosque, and Sheikh Yusuf bin Said, imam of Ilala mosque.

[33] Interview with Ali Abbas, 31 May 2010.

Fully aware of his unmatched ability to resolve contentious religious disputes, TANU organisers recruited Sheikh Hassan bin Ameir in 1955 to help confront their political challenges. His pragmatic approach was characterised by the agreement he made with other leading Muslims in Dar es Salaam (including Sheikhs Mwinyimadi Ali, Nurudin and Abdallah Chaurembo) to support TANU and oppose the 'Bantu Movement', which sought to restore the place of indigenous religion in public and political life. At a fateful 1955 meeting, this group also publicly agreed to avoid mixing religion and politics, and coined the term 'Yuda', after Judas Iscariot, to describe any TANU member who discriminated against another on the basis of faith.[34] For its part, TANU officially adopted the long-standing demand of African Muslims in Dar es Salaam that the town's Arab *liwali* be replaced with an African, and also that an Elders Council be formed within the party, in order to give African Muslims a forum to express their views and to dispel the belief that TANU was exclusively for educated Africans.[35] The Elders Council was an entirely Muslim body initially comprising some 170 members and chaired by Sheikh Suleiman Takadir, an elderly Dar es Salaam auctioneer and Manyema religious leader who 'strongly resent[ed] the Arab claim to superiority in Muslim affairs, asserting that they are in no way superior to the African in the knowledge of the faith'.[36] But there were limits to what Hassan bin Ameir could allow regarding TANU's role in religious life. He drew a firm line when Takadir described Nyerere as a 'prophet' raised by Allah to liberate Africa at a *taarab* concert in Dar es Salaam in August 1957. Hassan bin Ameir warned Sheikh Takadir never to repeat those words again as they were fundamentally *kufr* (blasphemy), as the remark challenged Muhammad's position as the seal of the prophets.[37]

Moreover, a far larger problem loomed on the horizon. TANU's rapid political success from 1955 onwards could only deepen rather than obscure a principal concern of African Muslims, which was their comparative educational marginalisation vis-à-vis African Christians. This dynamic had originated under the policies of British rule, but Muslims feared that it would continue under a Christian-dominated TANU government. At the heart of the debate was the state of Muslim education. African Christians dominated the Tanganyikan civil service because Christian missions provided the best education in the territory

---

[34] 'TANU ilipambana na misukosuko mingi', *Uhuru*, 3 July 1974.
[35] 'Schedule of Resolutions passed at TANU's Annual General Meeting, 1955', Colonial Office, UK National Archives, Kew [hereafter CO] 822/859/f.38; 'Extract from Tanganyika Intelligence Summary for October 1955', CO 822/859/f.39.
[36] 'Tanganyika African National Union', 7, enclosed in Stapledon to Gorell Barnes, 26 November 1955, CO 822/859/f.37. See also Said, 167. The Elders Council, in Kiswahili *Baraza la Wazee*, should not be confused with the generic TANU term 'Elders', often used to describe the upper echelon of TANU's National Executive Committee.
[37] Said 1998: 185–8.

during British rule. Fearing proselytisation, most Muslims avoided these schools, and by the 1950s found themselves significantly behind their Christian countrymen in government employment, status and wealth – in contrast to German rule, when these same Muslims enjoyed greater prestige and received adequate education through secular government schools.[38]

Two events in late 1958 laid the groundwork for a formal political split from TANU over this issue. Suleiman Takadir was the first among the Elders Council to voice concern over growing Christian dominance within the TANU leadership. Following the party's historic Tabora conference earlier that year in which it decided to compete in the government's 'multi-racial' elections, TANU needed to recruit candidates to meet specific educational qualifications for Legislative Council seats – qualifications attainable, for the most part, only by those educated in mission schools. The resulting appointment of a large number of Christians to contest seats moved Takadir to confront the party directly at an executive committee meeting in October 1958, where he pointed his cane at Nyerere and charged that '[t]his man will never come to favour us [Muslims], he would come to favour his brethren!'.[39] Nyerere assured the committee that Muslims would be treated fairly, but would not tolerate Takadir's promotion of religious discord, and expelled him from TANU after he refused to recant – a technically unconstitutional action as only the Elders committee could expel its members.[40] Nyerere argued that people in India 'hated one another because of religious differences. Such a thing should not be allowed to happen here.'[41] One of the few people to come to Takadir's defence was Ramadhan Machado Plantan, a Swahili newspaper editor who had long hung about the fringes of African politics in Dar es Salaam. He observed in his newspaper *Zuhra* that, although he took no side in the dispute, Takadir had been expelled for only wanting Muslims to 'be given large responsibilities [*madaraka makubwa*] equal with Christians', and that he deserved at least some warning and sympathy for having made a mistake. More accusingly, he went on to ask whether TANU was fighting for *uhuru* (freedom) for the rule of democracy or *uhuru* for communist rule, that is, 'of only one voice'.[42] When Nyerere explained his expulsion of Takadir to a TANU rally of some 20,000 in Dar es Salaam, the crowd was, according to one report, 'not altogether with him'. Speaking for half an hour on this most important subject, Nyerere stated, 'in a far more unpleasant tone and with a scowl on his face, what he thought of anyone who mixed up religion and

---

[38] Nimtz 1980: 88.
[39] Said 1998: 246.
[40] 'Extract from Tanganyika Intelligence Summary – October 1958', CO 822/1363/f.236; Listowel 1965: 303.
[41] 'Tanu Sacks Nine Who Disagreed', *Tanganyika Standard*, 10 October 1958.
[42] 'Kisa gani kilicho mfukuzisha Sheikh Suleman Takadiri T.A.N.U.?', *Zuhra*, 14 November 1958.

politics'. He pointed to India's tragic experience, and although 'several white capped old men' grumbled their agreement, Nyerere's final plea for political unity did not receive its usual raucous response.[43] Takadir's expulsion demonstrated the limits of debate within TANU by suppressing religious anxieties beneath the party's stated intents of independence and unity.[44]

The following month, the East Africa Commission held a conference in Dar es Salaam on the subject of Muslim education, but its conservative terms of reference limited discussion to questions about Arabic and Koranic instruction.[45] Sheikh Yahya Hussein, secretary of the Nairobi-based Federation of African Muslim Associations, criticised the conference for ignoring secular education and indulging in 'complicated Islamic theory with its centre in Zanzibar' that would 'appear to be of doubtful value to the African Muslims'. He further argued that the conference only benefited Asian Muslims who, 'having had good educational facilities, now definitely desire religious education and instruction'.[46] Plantan echoed these concerns by stating rather implausibly that in Tanganyika there were 50 million Muslims, compared to two and half million Christians and just over a million pagans. But whereas the government aided no fewer than 1,814 primary, 158 middle and sixteen secondary schools, and thirteen teacher training centres for Christians through grants-in-aid, there were no more than twenty-eight primary schools and not one middle, secondary or training school for Muslims was eligible for the same. Plantan protested the common practice of district and educational officers limiting Muslim schools to Qur'anic instruction, usually under the control of native authorities, and refusing permission for them to teach 'European' (i.e. secular) subjects.[47] By January 1959 Plantan appears to have lost more faith in TANU's ability to represent Muslim interests when he accepted UTP political advertisements in *Zuhra* – a significant breach for a 'nationalist' African newspaper.[48] Just as TANU began to share power with the colonial government in 1959, a small but vocal group of Muslims sought other organisations through which to represent their concerns.

THE RISE AND FALL OF AMNUT, 1959–1963

The All-Muslim National Union of Tanganyika (AMNUT) was formed out of a splinter group within TANU in April 1959. Mohamed Saidi Chamwenyewe and Sheikh Masoud Khatibu, ranking members in TANU's Elders Council,

---

[43] Eccles to Turnbull, 21 October 1958, CO 822/1362/f.230/2.
[44] For a general overview of TANU attitudes towards religion, see Westerlund.
[45] *Proceedings* 1959.
[46] Letter of Sheikh Yahya Hussein Juma, *Tanganyika Standard*, 1 December 1958.
[47] 'Hutba iliyo tokea katika mkutano wa African Muslim Education Conference 20 November 1958 Dar es Salaam', *Zuhra*, 12 December 1958.
[48] 'Mchague Bwana Tyrell', *Zuhra*, 30 January 1959.

complained that most of the senior Muslims in TANU offices had been replaced by younger Christians at higher salaries. They called a group of Muslim TANU members together to petition Nyerere to settle their grievances or, failing action, threaten to start a rival Muslim party to be called the 'African Muslim Union'. The petition appears to have been ignored, and Chamwenyewe – one of TANU's founding members – began campaigning in Central Province, despite calls from TANU and the Swahili press to keep religion separate from politics.[49] Plantan became the party's General Secretary in July 1959 after being dismissed from the editorship of the new TANU weekly, *Mwananchi*, for associating with Chamwenyewe's movement. The party was formally registered as the All-Muslim National Union of Tanganyika (AMNUT) on 8 August 1959. Its core of leadership and support was in Dar es Salaam, but TANU leaders felt concerned enough to tour through Central and Northern Provinces as well as Rufiji District to warn audiences not to join. AMNUT quickly published a broadsheet edited by Plantan, which argued that the granting of self-government should be delayed because the largely illiterate Muslim population would suffer.[50]

As AMNUT's general secretary, Plantan petitioned relevant authorities to make his party's case. He complained to the Secretariat that Tanganyika's first election had ignored Muslims, and attacked the British government for not supporting the higher education of Muslims 'in the Government schools (Muslim religion and English) which should have been done with less school fees, and allow such higher education to their children'.[51] He appealed to the Colonial Secretary, arguing that TANU's demand for self-government by 1960 was too radical because the country's predominantly Muslim population was not educationally prepared for independence. Accepting TANU's demands, he argued, may result in 'unrest, and civil wars between African Muslims and Non-Muslims (including Christians) who lived as good brothers for many years in this country'.[52] Citing violent precedents, AMNUT petitioned the United Nations Trusteeship Committee to intervene:

> The Fact is quite clear that the self Government without education to the African Muslims who are majority in this country, and on the other side, with a higher education to few African christians [sic] who are much overwhelmed by the majority of the African Muslims, such self Government would certainly result disorders [sic], lootings, murders, and civil wars between the two parties, which we request you to kindly reconsider the facts carefully, before

---

[49] 'Extracts from Tanganyika Intelligence Summary Report – May 1959', CO 822/1363/f.267; Said 1999.
[50] 'Extract from Tanganyika Intelligence Report – August 1959', CO 822/1375/f.2. On Plantan's career and his role in AMNUT, see Brennan 2022.
[51] Plantan to Chairman, Post Election Committee, 2 August 1959, CO 822/1375/f.5.
[52] Plantan to Colonial Secretary, 13 November 1959, CO 822/1375/f.5.

such self Government is allowed. We have already learnt a good lesson from India, between India and Pakistani [sic], after the departure of the British Government, and especially, what is happening now in Ruanda-Urundi. We do not want it happen [sic] here where all people of different races are enjoying full freedom as good brothers, which you won't overlook it [sic].[53]

In late 1959, when Governor Turnbull announced that Tanganyika would receive responsible government following general elections set for September 1960, the AMNUT leadership reaffirmed their position that the country was not yet ready for self-government because the population was not well enough educated, and requested, without success, constitutional guarantees of representation in the Legislative Council for all political parties.[54] The party petitioned the colonial government with the same mantra that government had used in response to TANU petitions: 'education first before self-government'.[55]

The structure and tactics of AMNUT were weak. In January 1960, the party leadership finally convened and, in response to rank-and-file opposition to the strategy of delaying independence, abandoned this position and instead demanded independence immediately. The party never formed a youth league or a women's league, and like the ANC appears to have received little if any support from any women. AMNUT revived *Zuhra* as the party mouthpiece at this time, but its irregular publication finally ceased in April for lack of funds.[56] AMNUT also suffered from an uncharismatic and transitory leadership. At the party's annual meeting in June, it announced that it could not produce a single candidate to compete in the 1960 elections, and selected an obscure career civil servant named Abdallah Mohamed to replace Chamwenyewe as president.[57] AMNUT, in fact, appears to have never contested a single election. In August 1960, the party's vice-president, Sheikh Hamisi Said El Alawy, announced the expulsion of the new president after El Alawy himself had been dismissed from office. Mohamed ultimately prevailed, and Plantan resigned as general secretary in the wake of El Alawy's ouster.[58] Inconsistent party propaganda reflected

---

[53] Plantan to Chairman, Trusteeship Committee, United Nations, 22 November 1959, CO 822/1375/f.42. See also Lohrmann 2007: 235.

[54] 'Note of a Meeting Held at Government House, Dar es Salaam, on 18 December 1959 – with W.B.L. Monson, W. Wood, K.S. El Alawi, and R.M. Plantan', CO 822/1375/f.42.

[55] 'Extract from Tanganyika Intelligence Report – November 1959', CO 822/2130/f.5.

[56] 'Extract from Tanganyika Intelligence Report – November 1959', CO 822/2130/f.5; 'Extract from Tanganyika Intelligence Appreciation for January 1960', CO 822/2130/f.6; Nimtz 1980: 89; 'Extract from Tanganyika Intelligence Report – April 1960', CO 822/2130/f.21.

[57] 'AMNUT Confident of Future Power', *Tanganyika Standard*, 10 June 1960. Mohamed Abdallah had joined the African Association in Dodoma in 1944 and the Railways African Association the following year, and had worked for the Public Works Department from 1953 until he resigned to lead AMNUT in 1960.

[58] 'Extract from Tanganyika Intelligence Report – August 1960', CO 822/2130/f.27.

the fundamental ambivalence with which African Muslims had viewed their non-African co-religionists. AMNUT criticised TANU for practising multi-racialism by appointing Asian and European ministers shortly after criticising TANU for practising simple racialism and appealing to non-Africans that '[w]ith Tanu there is no future for Europeans and Asians'.[59] By the end of 1960, the party had established only one office, its headquarters in Dar es Salaam, had applied for another in Rufiji District, and retained only one of its original office bearers from July 1959, its president, Abdallah Mohamed. Governor Turnbull considered AMNUT 'an insignificant political group, unrepresented in the Legislative Council and torn with internal dissension' that had failed 'to obtain the open support of any influential or respected figure, even amongst the large number of Muslims in Tanganyika; it cannot be regarded as a political force'.[60]

Despite these shortcomings, the party had a potentially powerful issue in educational equality, and was consistent in its religious propaganda, which British officials noted had an effect on 'some disgruntled T.A.N.U. Muslims'.[61] AMNUT continuously raised the spectre of Christian domination through education, in one instance warning of the impending wave of mostly Christian overseas students due to take up posts within the already Christian-dominated leadership of TANU.[62] A significant crowd in Mkenda, Rufiji Province, turned out to hear AMNUT's political secretary Shaaban Said Baajun speak on an organising tour, in which he implored Muslims to unite in order to secure their rights.[63] Despite flirting with racialist appeals, AMNUT also emphasised that membership was open to anyone without regard to religion or race.[64] Supporters in rural areas hoped that the opening of an AMNUT branch would be followed by the opening of a school to teach both religious and secular subjects.[65] Strong religious sentiment motivated some party supporters. One sheikh in Dar es Salaam disagreed with the oft-voiced sentiment that religion and politics be kept separate by arguing that 'Islam indeed has politics, even the entire Koran is filled with politics, and no one can quarrel with this'. He continued:

> Why are Muslims told that every fellow Muslim is a brother? Why are Muslims directed to pray Friday in mosques? Why are Muslims directed to join together like a family? Muslims should not make parties of unity and

---

[59] 'Extract from Tanganyika Intelligence Report – October 1960', CO 822/2130/f.30; 'AMNUT Confident of Future Power', *Tanganyika Standard*, 10 June 1960.
[60] Turnbull to Macleod, 12 December 1960, CO 822/2130/f.31.
[61] 'Extract from Tanganyika Intelligence Report – November 1959', CO 822/2130/f.5.
[62] 'Extract from Tanganyika Intelligence Report – October 1960', CO 822/2130/f.30.
[63] 'Mkutano wa AMNUT', *Ngurumo*, 15 December 1960.
[64] 'AMNUT na utawala', *Mwafrika*, 11 June 1960.
[65] Letter from Abdul-Wahyd A. Karim, AMNUT general secretary, *Ngurumo*, 31 December 1960.

speak out for their rights, are these not words at the market intent on pleasing those ignorant of the laws of Islam?[66]

But the majority of AMNUT's followers were primarily impressed with the argument that Muslims as a group were destined to fall behind their Christian countrymen because of systematic educational neglect.

AMNUT failed either to impress the colonial government or to attract support from abroad. The nature of the party's claims left the party more dependent on a positive reception by the Colonial Office than TANU or ANC had been. AMNUT may well have succeeded had the party been formed a few years earlier, when the Colonial Office and East African governments were casting about for conservative, 'patriotic' movements to combat radical, anti-British groups in the shadow of Mau Mau.[67] But the Aga Khan had instructed his followers to withdraw from Tanganyikan politics in 1952, and his grandson and successor accepted the colonial government's advice in early 1959 to make peace with and cautiously support TANU.[68] By that time the Colonial Office, impressed with Julius Nyerere in particular, had effectively chosen TANU to succeed the colonial administration and no longer had a use for political opposition movements, however conservative and pro-British they might be. Colonial Secretary Iain Macleod refused to receive deputations from AMNUT and ANC when he arrived in Dar es Salaam in March 1961 to negotiate with Nyerere on the details of Tanganyika's independence.[69] A young Afro-Arab named Abdul Wayhd Karim succeeded Plantan as AMNUT secretary in 1960 and, on the invitation of Ali Muhsin, appeared before the Central Committee of the Zanzibar Nationalist Party, a logical ally. However, Muhsin opted not to support AMNUT even as ZNP (Zanzibar Nationalist Party) relations with TANU deteriorated, because he thought its policies divisive, and personally did not believe Christianity posed a threat to Tanganyika's Muslims.[70]

TANU greeted AMNUT with profound hostility, and pressed Muslim leaders across the country to condemn the new party. TANU's organising secretary told an Elders Council assembly that mischievous people with no wish to build the nation were using 'the foreigners' newspapers' as their weapon and 'fooling the people for money'.[71] TANU mobilised some forty sheikhs in Dar es Salaam

---

[66] Letter from Sheikh Alli Yusuf, *Zuhra*, 29 January 1960.
[67] See minute of E. L. Scott, 2 October 1953, CO 822/428; Aga Khan to Mitchell, 15 April 1952, CO 822/427/f.E1; and Mitchell to Lennox-Boyd, 19 April 1952, CO 822/427/f.1.
[68] 'Extract from a Minute by the Secretary of State to Mr. Gorrell Barnes, 19th December, 1958', CO 822/1363/f.243; Secretary of State to Aga Khan, 2 January 1959, CO 822/1363/f.248.
[69] 'Macleod Awatupa nje Congress na akina Amnut', *Mwafrika*, 22 March 1961.
[70] Said 1998: 251.
[71] 'Extracts from Tanganyika Intelligence Report – May 1959', CO 822/1363/f.267.

to sign a letter, published in Swahili newspapers, denouncing AMNUT.[72] At one stop in his TANU-sponsored trip through Rufiji Province, Sheikh Yakob Mtnguumwa implored his audience of 500 to avoid listening to or following AMNUT, for its leaders sought only to raise religious discord for 'their own profit and not for the profit of this country'. He stated that he and forty-two sheikhs in Dar es Salaam, eighty sheikhs in Tanga, and 100 sheikhs in Lake Province had already separated from the AMNUT leadership. Sheikh Yakob concluded by asking his audience to raise their hands in the air to reject AMNUT, which they did together in prayer.[73] Fifty-one sheikhs in Kondoa issued a statement rejecting AMNUT, stating that, like water and oil, religion and politics are two different things that cannot be mixed.[74] Nyerere himself breezily dismissed the party in answer to a reporter's question: 'at one time I heard that two or three people had joined together and called themselves AMNUT but I don't know anyone more than that, nor do I know what sort of thing AMNUT is'.[75]

The heart of the struggle between the two parties occurred over the TANU Elders section, AMNUT's greatest potential constituency. The influence of older men had been partially displaced by TANU's Youth League, which had taken over informal but important functions such as community policing in Dar es Salaam.[76] AMNUT sought to gain support of Elders section members by invoking religious and racial anxieties. In late 1960, the party accused TANU of practising *mseto* or 'multi-racial' government that protected European and Asian privileges.[77] In AMNUT's first and only large public meeting, held in January 1961, Abdallah Mohamed told a crowd at Arnatouglu Hall that, because Muslims outnumbered all other religions, AMNUT would form a government with TANU that would be led by a Muslim prime minister. 'Elders saw', he stated, 'that the leader who says that politics should not enter religion is today throwing them out' – a clear reference to the expulsions of vocal Muslims from the Elders section.[78] TANU naturally dismissed any possibility of coalition government and responded to AMNUT's accusations with racial fire. The leadership of the Elders Council distributed a circular that posed a series of rhetorical questions to AMNUT:

---

[72] 'Extract from Tanganyika Intelligence Report – September 1959', CO 822/1375/f.4; letter from I. M. M. Mchowera, *Mwafrika*, 19 September 1959.
[73] 'Kitoseni chama cha Amnut', *Mwafrika*, 12 December 1959.
[74] 'Mashekh wa Kondoa hawamtaki AMNUTI', *Mwafrika*, 16 January 1960.
[75] 'Shirikisho letu wenyewe', *Ngurumo*, 25 November 1960.
[76] Brennan 2006.
[77] Letter of Abdul-Wahyd A. Karim, AMNUT general secretary, *Tanganyika Standard*, 23 December 1960.
[78] 'AMNUT iunde Serkali', *Ngurumo*, 24 January 1961.

a. Why is an African Muslim refused permission to pray in the mosques of Omanis, Hadhramis, Bohoras, and Ithnasheris, and are these people Muslims or is there no African Muslim who should know this?
b. Why is the African Muslim refused permission to read in the school of Arabs, Bohoras, and Ithnasheris and the state of these schools where the Koran and secular subjects are taught?
c. Why do the graveyards of Arabs, Bohoras, and Ithnasheris not permit the burial of African Muslims?

The circular concluded, 'It would be very suitable if we first would remove discrimination from these religious matters which disturb every African Muslim who is civilized and religiously observant.'[79]

TANU, however, also had to quell these racial fires to ensure the loyalty of the Elders Council. Following widespread discontent towards Tanganyika's Citizenship Bill in October 1961, Nyerere summoned a special meeting of the Elders Council to explain the reasons for adopting non-racial citizenship.[80] TANU sympathisers observed that elders held the key in this struggle. A branch of the nominally apolitical Tanganyika Society of Muslim Youth explained that it was waiting to see if *wazee* [elders] would be able to end the war between AMNUT and Muslims here in the country', for the youths could only 'condemn AMNUT and recognize TANU alone'.[81] One critical observer asked, 'if this party [AMNUT] is political, then I would rather join hands with the [Tanganyika Society of] Muslim Youth because that letter M should be removed, it shouldn't be in the party's name'.[82] A Dar es Salaam correspondent pointed out that AMNUT undermined its own attacks on TANU's purported multi-racialism by insisting that the prime minister be Muslim. He explained that in this version of democracy, 'Arabs indeed have the right to lead AMNUT', and asserted that 'AMNUT does not hate *mseto* because it is inclined towards Arabs, or are the only foreigners in this country Indians and Europeans?'[83]

Public opinion in the popular press, however, generally condemned AMNUT less for its racial hypocrisies than for its retrograde political vision and for mixing religion and politics that stirred up discord. Shortly after the party's formation, a correspondent warned that AMNUT would only bring *maendeleo ya kufuja* ('development of disorder'), and begged its supporters to quit 'these matters

---

[79] Circular from Baraza la Wazee entitled 'AMNUT ni Maadui wa Uhuru Wetu', n.d. (c. January/February 1961), Chama Cha Mapinduzi archives, Dodoma, Acc. 5/651/14.
[80] Bennett 1963.
[81] 'AMNUT, Moshi, yaleta machafuko', *Ngurumo*, 13 March 1961; 'AMNUT Haiwakilishi Mawaza ya Waislamu', *Mwafrika*, 11 March 1961.
[82] Letter of M. S. Kinega, *Ngurumo*, 17 March 1961.
[83] Letter from W. Mwakitwange, *Ngurumo*, 28 January 1961.

of religion and tribe' and instead to stand together to bring self-government.[84] The party's only public speech in January 1961 brought a flood of disapproving correspondence. The same writer who had chided AMNUT for indulging Arabs also feared that the party would return the country to *umwinyi*, a concept roughly translatable as 'feudalism' but in particular referring to an antique system of chieftaincies held by coastal Muslims.[85] A writer from Tanga questioned AMNUT's demand for a Muslim prime minister by arguing that although Islam had been there for many years, 'we did not see even one sheikh claiming the Arab, German, and Englishman should leave so we can rule our country'.[86] Comparing AMNUT to Muhammad Ali Jinnah's Muslim League, one reader argued that the party's politics would create two countries similar to India and Pakistan, and that therefore 'this party should be ignored, and Government should not permit parties which mix politics and religion'.[87] Another wondered how AMNUT could serve both the interests of religion and politics, declaring that 'one servant cannot serve two masters' and further asking, 'Islam is the first religion in this country, but all these years where were they to claim *uhuru*?'[88] A Muslim reader dismissed Abdallah Mohamed's religious arithmetic by asserting that the numbers of Christians and Muslims were equal and furthermore charged Mohamed for not remembering that Tanganyika is not about religions but about 'Africans whose ancestors are from Tanganyika'.[89] Another observed that AMNUT's president was forgetting that the thing which brings a person to parliament is *uwezo, sio kanzu na kilemba* – 'ability, not a robe and a turban'.[90]

AMNUT failed to reach out to the other major opposition party in this brief multi-party era (1958–64), the Tanganyika African National Congress.[91] Ideological differences played some role. Before splitting from TANU to form the ANC, Zuberi Mtemvu had criticised the Central Society of Tanganyika Muslims as an unpopular organisation and warned that '[p]oliticians are politicians and they ought to confine to politics ... [t]hey must leave religious occasions to Sheikhs and Headmasters of Muslim Schools ... [a]ll we should do is to finance what they organise after we have approved.'[92] Congress supported the

---

[84] Letter from I. M. M. Mchowera, *Mwafrika*, 19 September 1959.
[85] Letter from W. Mwakitwange, *Ngurumo*, 28 January 1961.
[86] Letter from M. Mwinyishani, *Ngurumo*, 5 January 1961.
[87] Letter from P. Mwakibibi, *Ngurumo*, 5 January 1961.
[88] Letter from R. S. Mayao, *Ngurumo*, 27 January 1961.
[89] Letter from Ramadhani Yusufu, *Ngurumo*, 26 January 1961. Mohammed and other AMNUT leaders regularly asserted that Tanganyika was 60 or 70 per cent Muslim, but the actual total was closer to 18–21 per cent. Mohammed to United Nations Visiting Mission, 4 April 1960, CO 822/2130/f.10; Swantz 1965. Swantz comments that this perception was common in coastal town because the towns themselves were predominantly Muslim.
[90] Letter from Ahmed Aloo Onyach, *Ngurumo*, 31 January 1961.
[91] Brennan 2005.
[92] Letter from Zuberi Mtemvu, *Tanganyika Standard*, 10 October 1957.

nationalisation of all education from Standard V upwards in its 1960 electoral platform in order not to prejudice 'the religious teachings of the various denominations under whose control these schools have been'.[93] With neither party wishing to acknowledge its splinter-group origin, Mtemvu dismissed AMNUT as 'a baby of TANU', and AMNUT's vice-president responded by calling ANC 'a small baby of TANU'.[94] But in 1960, an AMNUT committee member assisted in collecting money to pay Mtemvu's creditors for his release from prison, giving his reasons as being 'that Mtemvu was a Muslim and that there was now no difference in the policies of the two parties'.[95] The following year, an AMNUT *taarab* group joined fifteen Congress supporters to welcome Mtemvu at Dar es Salaam airport when he returned from an international fundraising trip.[96] But AMNUT gave no support to Mtemvu's ill-fated presidential campaign, and, in the period's spirit of tortuous political spin, Abdul Wahyd Karim dismissed Mtemvu's post-electoral statement that Tanganyika had rejected political opposition by countering that the electorate had only rejected Mtemvu and ANC, and that results show that more than 3,500,000 voters 'have no confidence either in Tanu or Congress'.[97]

The TANU government's campaign against AMNUT intensified after the November 1962 presidential election in which Nyerere overwhelmingly defeated Mtemvu. Wilbert Klerruu described AMNUT's refusal to accept Nyerere's offer of amnesty for all to rejoin TANU as clear proof that the party's goal was 'to disgrace and ignore countrymen so that they should forget the aim of building the nation'. He continued:

> This nation has one political party; and this is the decision of its citizens. Remember that the votes of citizens buried UTP (1958) and Congress (1952 [*sic*; actually 1962]). Together with this, AMNUT buried itself because it did not dare to contest the past election. Therefore the idle talk of AMNUT has finally been disclosed to the citizens of our great nation.[98]

AMNUT's general secretary, Abdul Wahyd Karim, attacked Nyerere's threefold increase in school fees, contending that 'he knew that the sufferers would be the sons and daughters of the Muslims as they are the ones who depend on government schools'. AMNUT shared Nyerere's concern with the division

---

[93] 'The Party Manifestos', *Tanganyika Standard*, 29 August 1960. TANU at this stage did not support school nationalisation, and AMNUT hoped the government would instead subsidise religious and secular education.
[94] Letter of H. S. El-Alawy, *Tanganyika Standard*, 20 August 1959.
[95] 'Extract from Tanganyika Intelligence Report – October 1960', CO 822/2127/12.
[96] 'Congress na AMNUT zaungana!', *Ngurumo*, 25 April 1961.
[97] 'A.N.C. Still Alive, Claims Official', *Tanganyika Standard*, 20 November 1962.
[98] 'Porojo zao zimeng'amuliwa', *Uhuru*, 1 December 1962.

between rich and poor, but Karim argued that 'the same cannot be said in the bridging of educational division between Muslims and Christians. Particularly as we are now independent.'[99] Karim further elaborated that Muslims were also not sharing other fruits of independence. 'Muslims are many', he wrote; 'therefore their taxes are also large, but not many had received high government positions nor do their children have opportunities to study abroad, and all of this we are told is because Muslims have no education!'[100] Karim responded to Nyerere's proclamation of a one-party state in early 1963 by describing the decision as 'dictatorship, which the people of Tanganyika cannot tolerate very long'.[101] He urged Nyerere to announce that 'everyone, without the imposition of party discipline, including civil servants, should have freedom of speech so that the issue [the one-party system] can be discussed freely through public meetings, the radio and newspapers'.[102] Rumours at this time circulated through Dar es Salaam that a group of sheikhs were planning a coup against the government. Sherif Hussein Badawy, founder of a Muslim school in Dar es Salaam, and his brother Mwinyibaba were declared prohibited immigrants and repatriated to Kenya after Mwinyibaba publicly derided the obsequious praise another leading Muslim gave the government for allowing Friday prayers.[103] AMNUT's president argued that scholarship awards were disproportionately being given to Christians so that 'they will dominate their Muslim brothers' when they returned.[104] One Nyerere supporter responded by begging the government not 'to care about their [AMNUT's] democracy, it should ban parties which make statements like this'. Remembering AMNUT's previous call to delay *uhuru*, the correspondent continued, 'a person who wants slavery should go to Zanzibar into the party of Arabs he will be tended to [*akafugwe*] there, or go to South Africa'.[105]

As AMNUT's criticisms against the government continued to grow despite Nyerere's announcement of a one-party state, TANU struck a forceful blow in the ongoing struggle over the Elders Council. In March 1963, Coast Regional Commissioner Abbas Sykes disbanded an eleven-man TANU Elders committee of Dar es Salaam for soliciting donations from non-African residents. Warning that TANU was a political and not a religious party, Sykes stated that all matters concerning Dar es Salaam's twenty-eight Elders branches would be brought to the notice of the newly appointed district secretary, Ali Mwinyi.[106] Sykes later addressed a meeting of Muslim leaders in Arnautoglu Hall. 'You are

---

[99] Letter of Abdul Wahyd Karim, *Tanganyika Standard*, 17 December 1962.
[100] Letter of Abdul Wahyd Karim, *Uhuru*, 29 December 1962.
[101] *Reporter*, 10 January 1963.
[102] Letter of Abdul Wahyd Karim, *Tanganyika Standard*, 30 January 1963.
[103] Said 1998: 267–8.
[104] *Reporter*, 17 February 1962.
[105] Letter from Stephano Mhina, *Uhuru*, 17 February 1962.
[106] 'Tanu Orders Elders Back to Branches', *Tanganyika Standard*, 12 March 1963.

not concerned with amassing force against any body of people or creed', he exhorted, 'but simply to put the Muslim house in order.' He further instructed:

> You are not concerned with politics in any way. No doubt all present here are members of the party of which we are justly proud and to which we give our loyalty. Anxieties have been aroused by rumours of 'muslim [sic] political action'. No heed should be given to such talk which is mischievous and distorts your endeavours. The Government cannot and will not tolerate a religious party in the country, a party which could only disunite our united people. I positively condemn the careless thought and talk which has given rise to speculation as to all Muslim intentions.[107]

After the dramatic disbanding of the Elders Council committee, AMNUT retreated by restricting itself to unimportant bureaucratic criticisms of the government and hollow challenges to TANU for another national election. Alhough it was never officially banned, by 1965 the party had become silent on both political and religious matters.[108] The struggle between TANU and disaffected Muslims instead shifted away from party politics and into the equally threatening realms of personality politics, religious festivals and private social services.[109]

Searching for a Leader: The Career and Trial of Chief Fundikira

By the time of AMNUT's demise, Abdallah Fundikira had become a major chief of Tanganyika's second largest ethnic group, the Nyamwezi, and, more unexpectedly, a significant symbol for Muslims across the country. Fundikira's aloofness from formal politics in general meant that he never would challenge Julius Nyerere directly, though no one was better positioned than he to criticise the emerging bureaucratic order of the TANU government. He could speak not only for supporters of chiefly rule, but also for Muslims as well as 'conservatives' who disapproved of TANU policies that nationalised land and co-operatives. A classmate of Nyerere at Makerere College and a recipient of a diploma in Agriculture at Cambridge University, Fundikira was one of an extremely small number of Africans in Tanganyika to have a level of education and command of English to match Nyerere's. In 1957, Fundikira became Tanganyika's first African agricultural officer and succeeded his brother Nassoro as Chief of Unyanyembe, a chieftaincy of 150,000 people. Although he had not joined the

---

[107] 'No Politics, Abbas Sykes Warns Muslim Heads', *Tanganyika Standard*, 7 September 1963.
[108] Letter of Abdul Wahyd Karim, *Tanganyika Standard*, 26 April 1963; letter of Abdallah Mohamed, *Tanganyika Standard*, 25 September 1963; Swantz, 28.
[109] See Westerlund 1982: 93–106; Nimtz 1980: 89–91; and, more contentiously, Said 1998: 263–315.

party, TANU supported Fundikira for the Western Province African seat in the 1958 Legislative Council election, on account of his local popularity and exceptional educational qualifications; he was elected unopposed.[110] A man of considerable self-importance – he once said of himself, 'I am tradition'[111] – Fundikira revelled in the role of *Mtemi* or chief, and viewed the British colonial government's deposition and rustication of his father for gross defalcation as the unjust meddling of foreigners. Indeed, conflict with public prosecutors had become a family affair – his brother Nassoro had committed suicide under pressure of prosecution for an array of abuses, including corruption.[112] He explained to a British colonial officer, 'in my position it is important not only to be a great Chief but to seem like one as well', as his subjects expected 'certain things from a Chief. One of them is ... a plurality of women.'[113]

Fundikira demonstrated his aloofness from TANU at a massive party rally held in Dar es Salaam immediately following the 1958 election. Bibi Titi Mohamed sarcastically greeted his late arrival, and, while all the other successful candidates (including Asians) raised their hands in the *uhuru* salute as Nyerere called each of them to the podium, Fundikira said and did nothing.[114] He tried unsuccessfully to convince TANU's parliamentary party to create an advisory council of chiefs, and in May 1960 he publicly criticised Nyerere for inferring that chiefs' justice could be bought with gifts. Fundikira finally joined TANU in July, after TANU resolved to reallocate chiefs' role in local government to bureaucrats, because chiefs no longer enjoyed constitutional protection from politics.[115] As Minister of Lands in 1959–61, Fundikira had promised the continuation of freehold tenure, and he resigned from Nyerere's Cabinet in 1963 after the TANU government abrogated freehold tenure.[116]

Having increasingly fallen out of step with the TANU leadership, Fundikira refashioned for himself a reputation as a regional Muslim leader. As a child, he had received Qur'anic instruction in Bagamoyo from Sheikh Muhammad Ramiya, head of Tanganyika's Qadiriyya movement, although he never affiliated with the *tariqa* Sufi movement.[117] Beginning in 1959, Fundikira regularly made prominent religious addresses to *maulid* and Eid gatherings, and, together with his successor at the Minister of Lands, Tewa Said Tewa, he tried to link African Muslims with Ismailis and Bohoras through the East African Muslim

---

[110] Kurtz 1978: 60; Ofcansky and Yeager 1997: 95–6.
[111] Edgett Smith 1973: 83.
[112] Longford 2001: 226–31.
[113] Bates 1962: 184.
[114] Eccles to Turnbull, 21 October 1958, CO 822/1362/f.E230/2.
[115] Bienen 1967: 60; Iliffe 1979: 569; 'Fundikira Has Decided to Join TANU', *Tanganyika Standard*, 23 July 1960.
[116] Clagett Taylor 1963: 211; Glickman 1964: 12–13.
[117] Nimtz 1980: 164, fn. 29.

Welfare Society (where he was a rising office-holder), proposing that the EAMWS should provide more money for African educational facilities instead of mosques throughout the region.[118] The Ithnasheri community of Zanzibar warmly praised Fundikira's speech at a Hussein Day gathering, and observed that his presence 'clearly indicates his unstinting loyalty to the cause of Islam'.[119] There is no evidence that Fundikira had anything to do with AMNUT, despite obvious ideological affinities, as well as his relationship as brother-in-law to Mohammed Abdullah, the party's president. No figure in AMNUT could ever match Fundikira's stature. By mid-1963, Fundikira was the only nationally respected figure who was publicly criticising the government's attitude towards Muslim education.[120]

A highly public corruption trial rapidly transformed Fundikira from distant aristocrat into a national *cause célèbre*. On 24 June 1963, the TANU government charged the former Minister for Justice with five counts of corrupt transactions as an agent of the National Agricultural Products Board. Prosecutors alleged that Fundikira had corruptly accepted a total of £2,500 'to induce him to do something in relation to granting an agency for purchase of produce to certain merchants', nearly all of whom were Indian.[121] Every day of the trial, Fundikira arrived in Muslim *kanzu* and *kofia* dress and greeted crowds of several hundred well-wishers. For many of Fundikira supporters, the state's case was a cynical attempt to silence Tanganyikan Muslims' most prominent spokesman by exploiting anti-Indian sentiment, as well as to traduce Islamic social mores by dwelling on the expenses Fundikira had to meet to maintain his three wives and twenty children. When the prosecution could not corroborate the testimony of their key witness, Jashbai Patel, the state's case against Fundikira fell apart, and he was acquitted on 5 August. In what was the largest spontaneous demonstration of political support in Dar es Salaam since independence, hundreds of supporters broke through police cordons to cheer Fundikira's acquittal and pushed his car throughout town in a parade.[122]

Fearing the spontaneous and unpredicted enthusiasm unleashed by Fundikira's trial, the government focused its attention on political opposition within coastal Muslim schools. The state declared Sharif Hussein Ahamed, an instructor from Lamu who taught at Dar es Salaam's Badawy Muslim School, a prohibited immigrant in September 1963 for 'inveighing against the inequalities

---

[118] '10,000 Observe Maulid Day', *Tanganyika Standard*, 5 September 1960; Said 1998: 84; 'Muslims Told to Spend More on Schools', *Tanganyika Standard*, 12 October 1960.
[119] 'Husein Day in Zanzibar', *Samachar*, 8 July 1962.
[120] Bourn to Price-Jones, 3 September 1963, DO 168/5/f.78.
[121] 'Fundikira: Corruption Charge', *Tanganyika Standard*, 25 June 1963.
[122] 'Defence Challenges Patel on Payments Statement', *Tanganyika Standard*, 25 July 1963; 'Fundikira Judgment Fixed for Friday', *Tanganyika Standard*, 30 July 1963; 'Fundikira Acquitted by Court', *Tanganyika Standard*, 6 August 1963; 'Fundikira Freed', *Reporter*, 10 August 1963.

of the present educational system and ... spurring on his audience to the extent that there was danger of his incitement leading to a breach of the peace'.[123] The following month, the government rusticated Abdillahy Schneider Plantan and Hamisi Jumanne Hamisi Abedi of the educational organisation Dawat El Islamiyya on the grounds that they were exploiting religious differences for political purposes.[124] Fundikira was dismissed from his position as chairman of the Tanganyika Development Corporation in October 1963, and resigned from TANU in December.

Tewa Said Tewa attempted to defuse the rising tensions by inviting Nyerere to address the EAMWS territory branch in Dar es Salaam, where Nyerere instructed attendees that 'religion must be regarded as distinct from politics'. Tewa himself eagerly distanced EAMWS from Fundikira, explaining to the audience that EAMWS had no intention of meddling in politics, and 'it was their own affairs' for any who did.[125] Other Muslim politicians, however, beseeched Fundikira to oppose Nyerere, most prominently Sheikh Yahya Hussein. Later famous across East Africa as a leading astrologer, dream interpreter and all-round showman, Yahya Hussein was born in Zanzibar and had taught Arabic on the island following an education abroad in Lebanon, and by the late 1950s had become the East African representative of the World Muslim Congress (see above). He had successfully courted the patronage of the Egyptian government and had awarded seventy-one scholarships to East African students by 1962.[126] From his base in Nairobi, he announced that he had formed the Tanganyika African Independence Movement in November 1963, which sought to bring back chiefs and change trade union legislation to permit strikes. When the Registrar refused to register Sheikh Yahya Hussein's party on the grounds that it was 'incompatible with the maintenance of peace, order, and good government', he tried to register another party, the Nationalist Enterprise of Tanganyika.[127]

For his part, Fundikira became an avid supporter of the ZNP (Zanzibar Nationalist Party)/ZPPP (Zanzibar and Pemba People's Party) coalition government, and was made a special guest at the Zanzibar's Uhuru celebrations on 10 December that TANU had boycotted. Immediately upon his return to Dar es

---

[123] Bourn to Price-Jones, 3 September 1963, DO 168/5/f.78.
[124] 'Press Release Issued by Tanganyika Information Services, 11 October 1963', Dominions Office, UK National Archives, Kew [hereafter DO] 168/5/f.92. Schneider Plantan was a brother of Ramadhan Machado Plantan and had been an earlier organiser of TANU in Dar es Salaam.
[125] 'Keep Religion Separate – Nyerere', *Tanganyika Standard*, 15 October 1963.
[126] *Reporter*, 18 August 1962. Shortly before interjecting himself in Tanganyika's politics, Hussein was sentenced to four months' imprisonment in Nairobi for theft of students' scholarships. *Tanganyika Standard*, 8 March 1963. Islamic mission work, particularly by Sunnis from Cairo's Al-Azhar University and Ahmediyyas from Pakistan, was quite active throughout East Africa by the early 1960s. 'Islam Drive', *Reporter*, 13 July 1963; letter from Sheikh Muhammad Munawwar, *Reporter*, 10 August 1963.
[127] *Tanganyika Standard*, 5 November 1963; 'Hussein to Form Another Party', *Tanganyika Standard*, 2 December 1963.

Salaam, Fundikira made a series of highly critical remarks directed at Nyerere.[128] Following Fundikira's resignation from TANU, Sheikh Yahya called on Nyerere either to allow opposition parties in Tanganyika and announce an election date or to resign in favour of Chief Fundikira, urging people to display pictures of Fundikira in their homes; he claimed the support of twenty-one National Assembly members, though he would name no names. Sheikh Yahya was joined by Mwanza-based Samson Masallu of the People's Convention Party, who stated that Tanganyika needed two parties, and AMNUT's general secretary, Abdul Wahyd Karim, issued a statement that AMNUT was happy with Fundikira's resignation and that the 'next step should be for all of us who genuinely disagree with the present Government's policy to come together and ensure the defeat of the common enemy'.[129] Aloof to the end, however, Fundikira denied that he had received any invitation from Hussein, or even considered the Nationalist Enterprise of Tanganyika party to exist because it had not been registered.[130]

Following his resignation from the party, TANU's executive committee demanded that Fundikira resign his Tabora parliamentary seat and face a new election – rejecting his claim that he was not elected by TANU supporters in 1958 and 1960, as he was not then a member of the party. Fundikira stated that he had quit TANU because he disagreed with the principle of a one-party system, and explained to a crowd of 7,000 in Tabora that there was today a 'curtailment of the citizens' right of freedom of political association and freedom of assembly'. He continued: 'TANU leaders failed miserably to make any relevant reply to the very important matters of principle involved ... and indulged in petty personalities, and vituperative language.' Fundikira had agreed to resign from TANU only on the condition that Nyerere would allow the registration of political parties, and further promised that he would never rejoin TANU.[131] On 6 January 1964, Sheikh Yahya formally opened the Nationalist Enterprise of Tanganyika office in Kariakoo, enrolled thirty new members to bring the total to 244, and promised that party members would resort to fasting to gain their political demands.[132] He then, however, had the poor luck to visit Zanzibar the following week, just as a violent revolution broke out that overthrew the ZNP/ZPPP government. Sheikh Yahyha was immediately imprisoned, halting his plans to form yet another party, the Bantu Opposition Movement of Tanganyika.[133] Although Fundikira refused to join an opposition party, he did resign from the National Assembly in February 'in order to give way to the present trend in

---

[128] Leonhart to Department of State, 4 February 1964, Pol 9 Tangan-Zan, RG 59, NARA.
[129] *Reporter*, 4 January 1964; 'Hussein Asks for Elections', *Tanganyika Standard*, 19 December 1963.
[130] 'Fundikira Resigns from Tanu', *Tanganyika Standard*, 18 December 1963.
[131] 'Resign – Call to Fundikira', *Reporter*, 17 January 1964; 'Day Only for My Publicity', *Tanganyika Standard*, 4 January 1964.
[132] 'Party Opens First Office', *Tanganyika Standard*, 7 July 1964.
[133] 'Yahya Held in Zanzibar', *Tanganyika Standard*, 14 February 1964.

the country to establish a one-party state'.¹³⁴ He rejoined TANU the following month with little fanfare, and pursued an unremarkable career as chairman of the board of directors of the East African Airways before retiring from public service in 1973. He would later emerge as a key opposition figure in the early 1990s as a member of the National Convention for Construction and Reform (NCCR), which was formed to demand the legalisation of opposition parties; he then formed his own party, the Union for Multiparty Democracy, before finally rejoining the ruling CCM (Chama Cha Mapinduzi) party in 1999. Perhaps most consequentially, however, Fundikira had distanced himself from the EAMWS by the mid-1960s, despite having briefly served as the organisation's president in 1961. For it was the EAMWS's sprawling, trans-regional civil society network, rich with patronage and religious authority, that posed the greatest potential threat to the secularising, monopolistic ambitions of the TANU government.

EAMWS, *Ujamaa* and Religious Expropriation

The TANU government would ultimately sacrifice the country's pan-Islamic institutions on the altar of anti-Indian racial polemics. Ismailis, the largest and most powerful South Asian group in Tanganyika, had wielded considerable influence among African Muslims primarily through the East African Muslims Welfare Society (EAMWS), which was formed by the Aga Khan in 1945.¹³⁵ More than any other institution, EAMWS had helped to finance the construction of schools and mosques throughout East Africa, earning it the enduring if sometimes ambivalent respect of numerous Tanganyikan Muslims. In 1962, EAMWS convened an All Muslim Congress in Dar es Salaam to address *tabligh*, adult education and the expansion of primary religious and secular education for Muslims, leading to the immediate construction of several schools throughout the country. Tanganyika's ambitious new EAMWS delegation, dominated no longer by South Asians but by Africans, secured the support of Egypt for establishing an Islamic university in Dar es Salaam in 1964; Nyerere later laid its foundation stone in Chang'ombe in 1968.¹³⁶

Such internationally financed autonomy, however, also represented a national threat. The principal actor to exploit this dynamic to ensure TANU control was Abdallah Chaurembo. A prominent Zaramo leader of the town's Shadhiliyya brotherhood and member of the TANU Executive Committee, Chaurembo had badly fallen out with his former teacher and Tanganyika's mufti, Sheikh Hassan bin Ameir, over the autonomy of religion from politics.

---

[134] 'Chief to Resign', *Tanganyika Standard*, 19 February 1964.
[135] For an overview, see Khamis 2017.
[136] Tewa 1982: 27–8, 33–6, 45–6; Hobden to le Tocq, 20 December 1968, Foreign and Commonwealth Office, UK National Archives [hereafter FCO] 31/46/f.4.

Chaurembo had discredited himself in Hassan bin Ameir's eyes in 1963 by thanking the TANU government for allowing Muslims to go to Friday prayers – such gratitude, Sheikh Hassan bin Ameir felt, was owed to Allah alone, not to TANU leaders. According to his critics, Chaurembo thereafter sought to take control of EAMWS and displace Hassan bin Ameir as Tanganyika's mufti.[137]

In 1968, the Dar es Salaam Regional Council concluded that the sheikhs who sat on the Eid and *maulid* prayers committee, a subcommittee of the Council since the *liwali*'s post had been abolished in 1962, had become 'rebellious', as they failed to attend other Regional Council meetings, and thus were accused of having no respect for the Council. To avoid a collision, the Council suggested holding separate *maulid* celebrations that June – the Council's *maulid* at Mnazi Mmoja, and another at a Muslim school in Ilala. The superior organisation and popularity of the Ilala *maulid*, which allegedly attracted over a hundred thousand participants, badly embarrassed organisers of the official *maulid*, which had enjoyed a monopoly over state radio to carry the celebration.[138] The creation of two separate *maulid* celebrations, the first major rupture in Dar es Salaam's central festival since 1957, precipitated a national crisis that led to the defection of regional EAMWS bodies from the national organisation over the latter half of 1968.[139] The withdrawing Tanga delegation declared its lack of confidence in the Aga Khan, still patron of EAMWS. Karume seized the moment to denounce the organisation:

> By giving large sums of money milked out of the resources of the peasants and workers of Tanzania those in actual control of the society hope that they can get us Tanzanians to accept what the so-called local leaders of the society tell us, thereby giving way to the formation of a buffer wall to protect Indian exploitation ... True prophets were not called their Highness. They were not millionaires with properties all over the world. To all intents and purposes they were all workers. Only liars, thieves and hypocrites can misuse religion and the word of God in such a way.[140]

Rashidi Kawawa added that 'Muslims have refused to be used as a tool to oppress their country'.[141]

To forcibly resolve the issue, the TANU government encouraged the establishment of a counter-organisation called BAKWATA, a Swahili acronym for the National Muslim Council of Tanzania, which was formed in Iringa on

---

[137] Loimeier 2009: 91; Nimtz 1980: 91; Ziddy 2006: 58, 67–79; Said 1998: 267–98; Tewa 1982: 37.
[138] Tewa 1982: 49–52; Mayanja 1973: 76; Hobden to le Tocq, 20 December 1968, FCO 31/461/f.4.
[139] Ziddy 2006: 69.
[140] 'Karume Exposes Muslim Society', *Nationalist*, 20 November 1968.
[141] 'Muslims Reject Aga Khan', *Nationalist*, 24 October 1968.

15 December 1968 by a group of pro-government sheikhs, the most prominent being Abdallah Chaurembo. Five days later, the government banned EAMWS, and handed all its assets over to BAKWATA. Tanzania's mufti and most respected Islamic authority, the ninety-year-old Hassan bin Ameir, was taken from his home in the middle of the night and deported to Zanzibar.[142]

It was the post-colonial state's most drastic intervention into religious institutions, done out of both a long-standing principle of separating religion from politics and a growing authoritarian urge, born of vulnerability, to control all institutions that dispensed meaningful patronage. Yet in the wake of the Arusha Declaration, the prohibition on mixing religion and politics sat awkwardly beside a new public conviction that held that religion in Tanzania must not be incompatible with the goals of *ujamaa*. Shortly after its formation, BAKWATA ruled that Friday sermons must no longer be given in Arabic, but only in Swahili.[143] African nationalists continued to target the material excesses of Indian religious festivals – one publicly called for daily inspections of the Ithnasheri mosque during Muharram 'to see how much [food] is being wasted'.[144] Mnazi Mmoja, where *maulid* and Eid festivals had been conducted since 1926, was partially filled just after independence with a *mnara* ('tower', traditionally an Islamic grave pillar or minaret) commemorating *uhuru*, thereby transforming this space into the focal point not just of religious holidays, but also of party and state holidays (Revolution Day, Union Day, Saba Saba, Nane Nane, Heroes Day, Independence Day), which ultimately comprised the majority of events held there. Flags and banners previously inscribed in Arabic now carried Swahili in Roman script. *Maulid* celebrations now sang *qasida* that wished BAKWATA the endurance to triumph over its enemies. 'We Muslims', participants sang at Mnazi Mmoja in 1971, 'say that we are tired of the master's religion (*dini ya Ubwana*), we want a religion that has Guidelines (*Mwongozo*) appropriate for our country.'[145] A shared *ujamaa* aesthetics of asceticism ran counter to the colourful extravagances of earlier Islamic festivals. No less an authority than the *Uhuru* columnist 'Miye' lectured one Muslim mother to abandon plans for dressing her family in expensive new clothing for Eid al-fitr with money she did not have.[146]

---

[142] 'New Muslim Society Formed', *Nationalist*, 16 December 1968; 'EA Muslim Society Banned', *Nationalist*, 20 December 1968. For accounts, see Westerlund 1982: 100–7; Yusuf 1990: 160–79; Liviga and Tumbo-Masabo 2006: 153–9; interview with Sheikh Ali Bassaleh, 27 May 2010. For Tanga, see Chande 1998: 133–40. The fullest account, but also the most contentious, is Said 1998: 282–315. Abdallah Chaurembo and Kassim bin Juma, another BAKWATA supporter, replaced Hassan bin Ameir and the late Idris bin Saad as the town's two most respected ulama during the 1970s and 1980s. Interview with Alhaji Iddi Sungura, 28 September 1998.
[143] *Standard*, 21 December 1970.
[144] Letter of Mamujee, *Daily News*, 11 January 1975.
[145] *Ngurumo*, 8 May 1971.
[146] 'Nguo za Idd zaleta ugomvi', *Uhuru*, 1 November 1972.

Conclusion

The extinguishing of autonomous Islamic institutional life in 1968 marked the apex of Tanzania's statist intervention in civil society, from which a slow but inevitable retreat would unfold. *Ujamaa*-era forms of moral surveillance had often indirectly and sometimes directly attacked features of public Islamic life, in particular sumptuous feasting and transnational patronage networks through which money and ideas flowed. The banning of the EAMWS was certainly a short-term victory – Islamic institutions no longer formed an autonomous basis for political mobilisation or clientage. But the process had been high-handed in the extreme, leaving a bitter memory among many Muslims across Tanzania and, in effect, hobbling BAKWATA with perceptions that it was a 'state stooge' institution for decades to follow. While the nature of public space kept Islamic festivals under the watchful eye of the Tanzanian state, the movement of students, books, pamphlets and media followed increasingly separate and distinct paths that could accurately be described as 'Islamic' rather than as simply involving education and media that concerned Muslims. This ambiguous legacy remains at the heart of public discussion of Islam in Tanzania today – on the one hand, something absorbed into the country's national political culture; on the other, a lingering resentment towards secularist absorption that has inspired generations of outspoken Islamicists ever since.

Bibliography

Abubakar U. (1971), *Historia ya TANU*, Dar es Salaam: East African Literature Bureau.
Bates, D. (1962), *The Mango and the Palm*, London: Rupert Hart-Davis.
Becker, F. (2008), *Becoming Muslim in Mainland Tanzania 1890–2000*, Oxford: Oxford University Press.
Bennett, G. (1963), 'An Outline History of TANU', *Makerere Journal* 7, p. 29.
Bienen, H. (1967), *Tanzania: Party Transformation and Economic Development*, Princeton: Princeton University Press.
Brennan, J. R. (2005), 'The Short History of Political Opposition & Multi-Party Democracy in Tanganyika, 1958–1964', in Gregory H. Maddos and James L. Giblin (eds), *In Search of a Nation: Histories of Authority and Dissidence in Tanzania*, Athens: Ohio University Press, pp. 250–76.
Brennan, J. R. (2006), 'Youth, the TANU Youth League, and Managed Vigilantism in Dar es Salaam, Tanzania, 1925–73', *Africa* 76(2), pp. 221–46.
Brennan, J. R. (2014), 'Constructing Arguments and Institutions of Islamic Belonging: M. O. Abbasi, Colonial Tanzania, and the Western Indian Ocean World, 1925–61', *Journal of African History* 55(2), pp. 211–28.
Brennan, J. R. (2022), 'Print Culture, Islam, and the Politics of Caution in Late Colonial Dar es Salaam: A History of Ramadhan Machado Plantan's *Zuhra*, 1947–1950', *Islamic Africa* 12:1, pp. 92–124.

Chande, A. N. (1998), *Islam, Ulamaa and Community Development in Tanzania: A Case Study of Religious Currents in East Africa*, San Francisco: Austin & Winfield.
Clagett Taylor, J. (1963), *Political Development of Tanganyika*, Palo Alto: Stanford University Press.
Edgett Smith, W. (1973), *Nyerere of Tanzania: The First Decade, 1961–1971*, London: Gollancz.
Glickman, H. (1964), 'Traditional Pluralism and Democratic Processes in Tanganyika', paper delivered at the 1964 annual meeting of the American Political Science Association.
Iliffe, J. (1979), *A Modern History of Tanganyika*, Cambridge: Cambridge University Press.
Khamis, J. (2017), 'The East African Muslim Welfare Society (1945–1968): A Historical Study with Special Reference to its Impact on Tanzania', unpublished PhD thesis, International Islamic University of Malaysia.
Kurtz, L. S. (1978), *Historical Dictionary of Tanzania*, Metuchen, NJ: Scarecrow Press.
Listowel, J. (1965), *The Making of Tanganyika*, London: Chatto & Windus.
Liviga, A. and Tumbo-Masabo, S. (2006), 'Muslims in Tanzania: Quest for an Equal Footing', in Rwekaza Mukandala et al. (eds), *Justice, Rights and Worship: Religion and Politics in Tanzania*, Dar es Salaam: REDET.
Lohrmann, U. (2007), *Voices from Tanganyika: Great Britain, the United Nations and the Decolonization of a Trust Territory, 1946–1961*, Berlin: Lit Verlag.
Loimeier, R. (2009), *Between Social Skills and Marketable Skills: The Politics of Islamic Education in 20th Century Zanzibar*, Leiden: Brill.
Longford, M. (2001), *The Flags Changed at Midnight: Tanganyika's Progress to Independence*, Leominster: Gracewing.
Mayanja, K. (1973), 'The Politics of Islam in Bukoba District', BA thesis, University of Dar es Salaam.
Nimtz, A. (1980), *Islam and Politics in East Africa: The Sufi Order in Tanzania*, Minneapolis: University of Minnesota Press.
Ofcansky, T. P. and R. Yeager (1997), *Historical Dictionary of Tanzania*, 2nd edn, Lanham, MD: Scarecrow Press.
Proceedings of the Conference on Muslim Education Held in Dar es Salaam on 20th–22nd November 1958 (1959), Nairobi: Government Printer.
Said, M. (1998), *The Life and Times of Abdulwahid Sykes: The Untold Story of the Muslim Struggle against British Colonialism in Tanganyika*, London: Minerva.
Said, M. (1999), 'Alhaj Zuberi Mwinshehe Manga Mtemvu', *An-nuur*, 15 October.
Swantz, L. (1965), 'Church, Mission, and State Relations in Pre and Post Independent Tanzania (1955–1964)', Maxwell Graduate School Occasional Paper No. 19, Syracuse University, p. 27.
Tewa, S. (1982), 'A Probe into the History of Islam in Tanzania', unpublished manuscript, [copy in author's possession, shared with the author by Mohamed Said].
Westerlund, D. (1980), *Ujamaa na Dini: Study of Some Aspects of Society and Religion in Tanzania*, Stockholm: Almqvist & Wiksell.

Van de Bruinhorst, G. C. (2007), 'Raise Your Voices and Kill Your Animals': Islamic Discourses on the Idd El-Hajj and Sacrifices in Tanga (Tanzania), Amsterdam: Amsterdam University Press.

Yusuf, I. (1990), 'Islam and African Socialism: A Study of the Interactions between Islam and *Ujamaa* Socialism in Tanzania', PhD thesis, Temple University.

Ziddy, H. I. (2006), *Historia na Maisha ya Sheykh Hassan bin Ameir (Shirazi)*, Zanzibar: Express Printing Services.

6

Politics, Lived Islam and Muslim Public Discourse in Zanzibar: Reflections on Cultural Identity, Belonging and Governance, 1984–2016

KJERSTI LARSEN

In December 2016, when I was returning to Norway via Julius Nyerere International Airport in Dar es Salaam, an airport employee – a young man who made a point of being from mainland Tanzania – asked whether I had been to Zanzibar, 'in that place where all women are veiled to the point of covering their faces'. No matter how I responded to the issue of veiling, he insisted on the scary veiled women. Eventually I suggested that he should visit Zanzibar to see for himself, to which he replied that he would not dare to visit a place containing only Muslims, because in such a place all women would wear the veil.

The brief conversation reverberated with what is an international political discourse on the Muslim 'Other' and its framing, transformation and absorption in different localities. The veil tends to become the symbol of the Other. This phenomenon seems to define the Muslim woman. It includes ascription of a label that reduces all diversity to a single or singular image, which centres on the veil. The idea is that all Muslim women wear the veil (Cooke 2007; Abu-Lughod 2016). Saba Mahmood (2006) argues that, from a modern liberal perspective, the veil has become a symbol of both political and cultural identity. This neglects the fact that women may wear it out of convention, decency or religious devotion. The Muslim veil is in turn associated with authoritarian social structure and tradition, in contrast to choice, aesthetics and progress – facets often connected with notions of modernity and modern governance. Mahmood's research from contemporary Egypt shows the interconnection between religion and modern governance and how state policies regulate when and how religion is practised and expressed in public life. She suggests that secular political orders of governance depend upon the violation of their own principles of religious liberty and minority rights to maintain authority (Mahmood 2016).

The brief conversation described at the outset conveys how an international discourse on global religious politics, targeting Islam, may surface in a local setting. However, in this context, the conversation about the Muslim Other is only one among several elements casting the complex relationship between Zanzibar and the former mainland Tanganyika in what became the United Republic of Tanzania in 1964. Regarding the entanglement of criticism of state politics and Islamic reformist discourse, Felicitas Becker has observed a similar tendency on the Tanzanian mainland (Becker 2009: 416). Currently, on the island, political discord is frequently articulated in terms of religious difference, centrally between Islam and Christianity. The identification of religion as the problem echoes the general predominance of global religious politics. It advocates for the reformation of Islam and an agenda assuming that a reformed Islamic theology and practice, contrary to orthodox Islam, would be adjustable to the modern state (Mahmood 2006).[1] Reductionist and essentialist positions manage to bypass historical, social and cultural difference between and within societies. Within such a framework, most persons whom Zanzibari Muslim publics perceived as learned in matters of religion (*shehe*) would fall within the category of traditionalists defined as uneducated and outdated – representing an approach to Islam incompatible with modern governance and state order.

The analysis concerns how society relates to frictions between governance, belonging and articulation of cultural identity in the wake of recent state engagement in religious practices and forms. Inspired by Mahmood's perspective, I focus on lived Islam (Mandaville 2001; Marsden 2005) and discuss emerging uncertainties regarding moral contestation and socio-cultural convention among women and men in Zanzibar Town. Attention is paid to how recent socio-political transformations, as well as the appearance of reformist Islamic views, affect social relationships and interactions. How do local contestations and negotiations of Muslim practices and conduct interconnect with social uncertainty and recollections of the immediate past? The discussion builds upon ethnographic fieldwork conducted mainly in Zanzibar Town since 1984 up until the present. With a few exceptions, the women and men I have worked with have not been professionals and well-educated; they have not belonged to any urban elite. In this connection, I emphasise a perspective from below, along with local configurations of Muslim devotional and everyday practice and meaning. Ideas about *how to be* and *what it means to be* 'a good Muslim' vary within this group, and their perceptions of *what it means to lead a life as* 'a good Muslim' have also shifted over the course of each of their lives. As a selection, the households included represent a variety of different economic strata and a range of different *kabila*, that is,

---

[1] As a political project, the reformation of Islam 'from the outset was outlined by U.S. security and foreign policy concerns' (Mahmood 2006: 344–5).

identities connected with ancestors' places of origin beyond Zanzibar. The majority of those I have worked with are Sunni Muslims, though a few are Shia, some Christian (Anglican and Roman Catholic) and a few Hindu. During the period leading up to the Tanzanian general election of 2015, I suddenly witnessed how people applied collective memories of the 1964 Revolution and its aftermath as a framework for interpreting current political debates and statements. Then, in the wake of the election, especially from 2016, the government started to place restrictions on the media and civil society organisations. Moreover, public gatherings involving more than five persons were, according to interlocutors, from then on to be considered political meetings.

Local Discourse on Governance and Othering

The stereotypical statement referred to at the beginning of this chapter joins similar kinds of preconceptions from mainland Tanzanians about Zanzibar society: Arabic lifestyle, Arabicised Swahili, (supposedly) 'backward' Muslim practices such as veiling and public observance of Ramadan and thus a reluctance to modernise due to their Muslim faith. Despite their annoyance, these stereotypical claims find no resonance among the Muslim islanders as such, who tend to see themselves as modern and cosmopolitan. Moreover, reformist-oriented Zanzibaris, a different kind of modernisers from those representing the mainland-based stereotypical depictions, also advocate for a reformation of the current society, which they equally see as 'backward', due to its orthodox and locally fashioned Islam. Nonetheless, islanders have their own stereotypical ideas about mainlanders and, in particular, are against what are said to be mainland-driven policies aiming at the eradication of Zanzibar as a Muslim society, ignoring its past.[2] Thus, the conversation at the airport reflected prejudices that are apparent between islanders and mainlanders. In turn, these prejudices refer to the long-term politics facilitated by the 1964 Revolution in Zanzibar and the following Union (Lofchie 1970; Babu 1991; Cameroon 2002). Within the Union, Zanzibar's Afro-Shirazi Party ruled the island state until 1977, when Chama cha Mapinduzi (CCM) was established via a merger between Zanzibar's Afro-Shirazi Party and the Tanzanian mainland party, TANU. Since then, more recent political issues that have surfaced during the period prior to 2016 – that is, national elections, the union issue and the rewriting of the 1977 Constitution of the Union of Tanzania – have further amplified the tension. Mainlanders

---

[2] The two pillars of the governing political party are the 1964 Revolution in Zanzibar and the following Union between Zanzibar and Tanganyika (Cameron 2002: 315). Up until the present, Zanzibar's autonomy as a state within the union has been challenged, 'even if what is in Tanzania named "the Zanzibar problem" was effectively managed into submission during the single party era' (Myers and Muhajir 2013: 663).

emphasise Zanzibar's incapacity to conform within the Union. Islanders argue that the Dodoma-based national government controls Zanzibar politically. They contend that the union between Zanzibar and Tanganyika, and the formation of the United Republic of Tanzania in 1964, have since the beginning threatened their state's autonomy (Cameron 2002: 315; Myers and Muhajir 2013: 663). In everyday political rhetoric, recurrent discussions of the Union include not only the problem of labour migration but also that of religious difference, that is, 'too many Christians from the mainland (*wakristo wa bara*)'. Expanding tourism has resulted in an increase in the number of mainlanders coming to Zanzibar for employment within the wider tourist service sector as well as for settlement. This situation has resulted in the growing presence of Christianity on the island (Keshodkar 2013: 131).[3] Today, the number of newly built churches on the island, financed mostly by missionaries from the mainland or from Western countries, is striking (ibid.). The high visibility of church buildings materialise a shared anxiety concerning Christian and mainland domination. Thus a focus on religion and faith when expressing opposition against what is seen as a mainland political hegemony has entered local discourse in Zanzibar. Women as well as men hold that the political agenda of the state is set by a 'Christian mainland'. It seems that, in social life, culture, religion and politics become interconnected through people's memory and reception of what, for them, has been experienced as decisive events in the aftermath of the 1964 Revolution.

In urban Zanzibar, people expressed apprehension about the ways in which the authorities articulate restrictions on everyday and religio-cultural ritual practices. Restrictions and transformations in how to inhabit the public domain have seemed to evoke both collective and individual memories of post-revolutionary politics. Among my interlocutors, many announced '*Wataiba nchi yetu*': they will steal our country. Others said that, with the current government, they could even return to a one-party state just as before 1992, and if so, that nobody would actually care (*hatujali*) because Zanzibar had no autonomy anyway, or that nobody would vote in the 2020 election. Regulations introduced in the wake of the turbulent 2015 election echoed with memories of the 1964 Revolution and its aftermath – either people's own memories or those mediated by their parents and grandparents' generation (Larsen 2018). 'Remember', I was told, 'most of those who participated in the Revolution were from the mainland.' Some would go further, arguing that many of the newly built churches are meant to be

---

[3] According to Stefan Gössling and Ute Schults, many of the coastal villages have almost doubled their population due to the arrival of hotel owners and migrant labourers. Owners have preferred to employ qualified staff, and most migrant labourers seem either to have previous experience in tourist-related enterprises or to be better educated than Zanzibaris (2005: 43–62). On the presence of Christianity in Zanzibar, and the issues emerging from the Muslim–Christian relationship, see Hans Olsson's chapter in this volume.

harbouring young people from the mainland, and to be warehouses for weapons and *panga* (machetes). Interesting in these stories is how they repeat narratives from the 1964 Revolution, and the way these narratives merge with already existing uncertainties regarding the political situation (Larsen 2018). People's reasoning takes the form of an 'as if expected' repetition of an event of the past. These discourses feed from a growing uncertainty, from 'unease about acting in view of an unpredictable future' (Calkins 2016: 2). People worry about the continuation of social, religious and political institutions and practices combined with what they experience as declining socio-economic well-being. This kind of uncertainty about the future is similar to what Kresse describes, with respect to Kenya, as a 'climate of uncertainty' (Kresse 2007). In Zanzibar Town, people's uncertainty also comprises their current experiences of moral and cultural marginalisation materialised through the ongoing transformations of public space due both to tourism and to what people refer to as an introduction of mainland values and ways of life. They feel annoyed especially regarding the opening of new restaurants and shops advertising pork and alcohol. Still, alcohol has always been legal and publicly available in this secular state. In terms of a moral consensus, the consumption of alcohol has not been promoted, but also has not been condemned. What is new is the over-stated advertisement and presence of alcohol in public places. Moreover, due to a previous commonly shared Zanzibari consensus, pork was, until recently, never openly commercialised. Thus, ongoing transformations of public space create disquiet among the islanders, independently of whether they are Muslim or Christian (Zanzibaris) by faith (Larsen 2017). During Ramadan, these transformations of the public domain are particularly intimidating and are perceived as being yet another sign of the power and influence of the political hegemony of the mainland.

Cultural identity, Africanisation and Islamic reformism

Following the 1964 Revolution, the government launched an ambitious nation-building project moored in an official development discourse on how to rebuild society upon local understandings of what constituted African, Islamic and socialist discipline (Burgess 2002). The main political line was that of Africanisation, aimed at creating national homogeneity – one population, one history, compatible appearance, lifestyle and religious practice.[4] This project rejected the historically configured multi-cultural, cosmopolitan, inter-faith dimensions of the pre-revolutionary society. Again, after more than fifty years,

---

[4] The Revolutionary Government introduced television to the island. TVZ (Television Zanzibar), inaugurated in 1974, was considered a technology that was crucial in promoting universal education and a uniform line of thinking. The government subsidised the purchase of television sets and installed televisions outside party offices to facilitate access for the public.

a recent trend among politicians is to label citizens from particular backgrounds as 'others', alienating them as Tanzanians by calling them *wahindi*, *waarabu*, *wangazija* (Indians, Arabs, Comorians) in public debates and manifestations arguing for African autochthony (Myers and Muhajir 2013). Their use of such labels makes people recall a particular form of social stratification and racism associated with an Africanisation policy that both foretold and followed the Revolution (Glassman 2011). Many express their worries in the same way as Issa, a man in his early forties: 'Why would they use such terms', he said; 'they never used such labels if they refer to *waswahili*, the Africans.' 'Doing this, "they" express their racism', said Abdul, a man in his late thirties. Zanzibaris, for instance, of Asian origin, would often contend that in periods of economic decline or elections, some political voices would always utter the remark that due to their Asian ancestry they do not belong in Zanzibar. Bi Fatima, a woman in her mid-seventies who had experienced the Revolution, explained:

> Somehow, it is true that our place of origin is India [*kwetu India*], but we have never lived there; we have only lived here. This is where we belong. We have nowhere else, and this is where we are born and where we have lived. Still given the unsettled political situation in Zanzibar and being of Indian origin, we can never trust that our government will protect us, whether politically or economically.

After the 1964 Revolution, the ruling revolutionary state redefined the concept of citizenship. It declared that in order to hold citizenship one parent had to be 'African' by origin (Amory 1994: 127, in Keshodkar 2013). Seen in this light, the apprehension expressed in the above quotation seems reasonable. Still, Bi Fatima equally conveys her feeling of belonging despite distrust as to whether future political regimes will acknowledge this designation of affiliation and nationality. Her hesitation regarding governance echoes the way current rumours and their reception evoke social memories of past politics of exclusion formalised through specific regulations introduced, for instance, in 1967, 1970 and 1971. The aim of these policies was to restrict the possibility of people of Asian and Arab descent engaging in private enterprise or holding employment in the public sector, as well as the Forced Marriage Act.[5] These memories, together with actual political and economic circumstances, playing on notions of race and question of autochthony, ensure that the effects of a previous Africanisation policy enacted by the Revolutionary Government of Zanzibar

---

[5] The decree, which lasted from around 1970 to 1972, implied that men of African descent had the right to marry unmarried women of Arab or South Asian descent, even when the women's families protested (Larsen 2018: 258).

continue to resonate in everyday life in Zanzibar, overlapping with dominant discourses in international religious politics (Larsen 2004).

Governance, Religion and Cultural Identity

Today, it seems that the communication of opposition to mainland political and socio-cultural hegemony is often voiced in terms of religious distinction, rather than Africanisation politics. References to religious distinctions rather than difference regarding political aims and ideologies are activated to explain social tensions and conflicts. At the same time, women and men, including the elderly, express apprehension regarding how religious identification and difference are focused, and how this in turn filters open communication on mundane social and political controversy. For them, radical perspectives advocating the need for a reformed Islam create both puzzlement and discontent. In words much the same as the following, they say:

> This is not how it used to be. Today, even among us Muslims, some would claim that they would only be together with those who practise their faith in the same way as they themselves do. These behave 'as if' [*kama*] they were *mashehe* [religious leaders]. Whether people are Muslim, Christian, Hindu, Bohora, this never used to be a problem among the family, within neighbourhoods or in social life. We would be close as family, neighbours and friends, eat together, attend each other's weddings and funerals, and some would even intermarry. Now everybody first asks about religion: she or he is Christian; she or he is Muslim; they are Hindus. Before this was never a problem.

Despite the dismay voiced in the quotation above, coastal East African Muslim communities have for the most part held rather moderate positions, though internal differences, such as between Sufi and anti-Sufi factions and conservative and reform-oriented groups, have always been present. In Tanzania (Becker 2009) as well as in Kenya (Kresse 2009), certain radical groups have even advocated for violence, especially where al-Shabaab has been influential in recent years. However, in Zanzibar, more moderate Muslims, whether Sufi or not, seem to perpetuate a position connecting religious and mundane knowledge, accommodating socio-cultural change. The commonly heard phrase *Dini wal Duniya* (religion and the world) is intrinsic to social life in urban Zanzibar. It encompasses an approach nurturing flexibility and a foundation for how to interweave religious and mundane matters, while emphasising the rectitude of Islam (Saleh 2009: 189–99). Yet in recent years, it seems that the number of Sufi music performances like *maulidi ya homu* and *dufu*, and collective devotional acts like *dhikiri*, remembrance of God performed within the public domain, have decreased in urban Zanzibar, all of them being devotional practices appreciated by women and men. Querying this, women and men, including the elderly, especially contended that the authorities would claim that the performance of such locally moulded, socially inclusive and gratifying practices as those just mentioned would be political gatherings mobilising Muslims along the lines of Salafi doctrine. Next to this, local Salafi-inspired reformist groups would, from their point of view, contend that such devotional practices were incorrect. Recent changes, such as restrictions on the media, civil society organisations and political meetings, have also increased people's uncertainty. Those who had experienced the Revolution and its aftermath especially compared the present situation with previous governance, particularly as it unfolded in the wake of the Revolution, and maintained that the current mainland-dominated governance is continuing to undermine the historical and cultural foundation of Zanzibar society and ways of life. While, previously, people were reluctant to talk about the Revolution, nowadays they spontaneously evoke narratives from that period to use as blueprints for understanding present tensions between mainland-driven and island-driven political agendas, including conflictual issues between Christianity and Islam. Many defined recent regulations concerning public gatherings restricting everyday and religio-cultural ritual practices as censoring their socio-cultural lifestyle. The recent state engagement with religious practices was for them just another way of hampering their Zanzibari-ness, their shared values and cultural identity as Muslims, in coastal East Africa.

Restriction and Revitalisation of Islamic Teaching and Practice

Fearing close ties between Islamic teaching and the Arab world, the revolutionary government abolished religious-learning institutions, dismissed religious scholars and destroyed religious books (Purpura 1997). To discourage any possible incitement of anti-government unrest, the government emphasised the continuation of cultural aesthetics only, such as dress codes, cuisine, and notions of modesty and decency (Burgess 2009: 302; Keshodkar 2013: 45). The Revolution did not uproot Islam, but the politics of the post-revolutionary government discontinued public institutions providing formalised studies in the principles of Islamic doctrine and condemned public aspects of Islamic devotion (Parkin 1995: 205; Larsen 2004: 127). While not instigating an official ban after the Revolution, President Abeid A. Karume, in the earlier period following the Revolution, restricted religious teachings and controlled religious gatherings so as to consolidate his authoritarian regime and prevent any form of anti-government agitation (Keshodkar 2013: 125). However, Islamic institutions perceived to be challenging state authority were closed (ibid.). With time, this policy regarding Islamic teaching engendered a shortage of scholars, which had a severe impact on the standard of education. Only after Karume's death in 1972 was Islamic learning re-introduced, and towards the end of the presidential period of Aboud Jumbe in the early 1980s the Zanzibari revolutionary government initiated a more significant revival of Islamic learning institutions, sending students to study abroad. Drawing on Saudi Arabian assistance and economic support (*msaada*) for the building of schools and mosques, the state-initiated project aimed at restoring the teaching and transmission of morally correct behaviour, and thus in turn revived ritual practices that would be condemned as *bida'a* by Salafi-inspired reformism.[6]

In 1983, the government created a taskforce to provide advice on the employment of male students returning from Islamic studies in Saudi Arabia.[7] In the report, the terms *fanatiki* (fanatics) and *upuuzi* (imprudent, gibberish) are applied to describe the teaching of local religious leaders. At that time, the report was requested by the Chairman of the Revolutionary Council of Zanzibar (*Mwenyekiti wa Baraza la Mapinduzi*), that is, the President of Zanzibar. The committee, including its chair, were all higher officials in Zanzibar, including one member of the kadhis' court (Islamic juridical institution). A main argument of the report was that the teachings of locally educated religious leaders were based on ignorance. The report says that their teachings were built on pure misunderstanding, and that this was due to their ignorance of 'true' Islamic learning; their teachings were said not to be moored in the true foundations of Islam. It further conveys how local religious leaders were 'blindly following ill-conceived learning and become fanatics following nonsense ideas' (Aboud Talib Aboud 1983: 3).[8] According to what I have been told and what seems to be common knowledge among the islanders, this project, initially meant to revive Islamic learning, took place at just that time when President Aboud Jumbe entered into a period of religious rumination. During this period, in the 1980s, my research focused on local knowledge practices among women, including those engaged in Islamic education. In line with Salafi reformist-inspired learning, these young women contended that the practice of local religious leaders should be neutralised in favour of the modern, literal and morally correct version. Women from other milieux argued that the women who were engaged in reformist Islam had 'studied too much' (*soma sana*), insinuating that their studies had made them confused.

---

[6] Among the mosques built was the large one in Kikwajuni that people refer to as *Msikiti ya bidaa*, emphasising how this mosque belongs to those who perceive themselves as the most pious and reverent followers of 'foreign' Muslim teaching and practice. The reference *ya bidaa* should here be read as an ironic label (*ya kinyume*).

[7] *Riporti ya Taskforce ya mafunzo ya kiislam Zanzibar*, 1983. Zanzibar National Archives; BA81/3.

[8] *Watu wengi wanapuuza mambo muhimu ya msingi na kuwa fanatics katika mambo ya upuuzi.*

The government's initiative to restore Islamic scholarship, including the teaching and transmission of morally correct behaviour, and to restrain local innovation in matters of religion (*bida'a*) did not have an immediate effect. Thus, its ambition to reconstruct religious learning and practice in line with Saudi Arabian Islamic scholarship did not find broad resonance among Zanzibar's conventional Muslim public, who tend to be moderate and tolerant with respect to the meaning of a 'good Muslim life'. In general, this indicates that the initiative did not change people's understanding of what it means to be a 'good Muslim'. Moreover, from the late 1980s on, I witnessed an increasing presence of Muslim devotional practices within neighbourhoods, to the contentment of the majority of the population (i.e. *maulid, maulidi ya homu, dhikri, kisomo*). These practices were performed outside the mosques, to form part of a local Sufi-inspired reading of Islam, which incorporates elements of what some research literature refers to as *mila*. Performances including such elements seem to appeal to customary and aesthetic conventions, in contradistinction to performances and forms of aesthetics referred to as purely religious, that is, *dini* (Caplan, 1975, 2009; Larsen 1988; Topan 2004). The government's project to revive Islamic teaching disregarded cultural and social factors that form the foundation of a lived Islam that provides access and affiliation to local cultural and customary practices – precisely those that historically have facilitated people's reception of Islam. Nevertheless, the initiative of President Jumbe's government did over time introduce a reformist Islamic discourse on the island, nourished by global religious politics.

Between Mundane and Religious Governance

The dominant official political line of the revolutionary government was to downplay the role of religion and to disentangle religion from the conceptualisation of identity and way of life. Despite the Africanisation policy and the restraint put on Islamic learning and devotional routine, most Zanzibaris continued to follow local values and practices (Parkin 1995; Nisula 1999; Larsen 2004). The restraints implemented to prevent any kind of anti-government agitation, as already mentioned, involved expulsion of Islamic scholars, destruction of religious books and regulatory control of religious gatherings (Burgess 2009; Purpura 1997; Larsen 2004; Keshodkar 2013). People I have worked with have narrated how any public marking of Islamic devotion and rituals was discouraged, even condemned (Larsen 2004). Since around 2012 up until the present, people have yet again expressed a different kind of apprehension from the one created by the post-revolutionary government, not purely linked with governance. The agitation is especially prevalent among society's youth, who seem to join discourses that feed from reformist ideas. This political and religious rhetoric impacts on social relationships across social strata, cultural identities and generations. The younger generation, contrary to that of their parents, have again had access to religious institutions, teachings, books, pamphlets and discussions through the media in all its various formats, and thus engage with today's international religious politics. Comparatively, they perceive themselves as learned, having had access to informed texts and communication about correct Muslim behaviour. The younger generation question local configurations, claiming that these are old-fashioned (*ya zamani*) or also uninformed – that is, not moored in actual knowledge (*bila maarifa*) – and thus that they should be suppressed in favour of proper Islamic learning compatible with a modern, educated society. Their approach engenders rigid discussions, as when the thirty-year-old son of a woman known as being learned in Islam, *mwalimu*, told his mother:

> The performance of *dhikiri* and *maulidi ya homu* are not prescribed in the Qur'an, not even advised in the hadith. This is only a custom that came about many years ago when people had no access to education, when people were unable to read the Book themselves. Nothing is wrong with performing these rituals, but it is not advisable. They are costly and more for entertainment than for devotion. The arrangement costs a lot of money. It makes people waste their resources, which is not considered good conduct according to Islam.

In this context, the son voiced what he perceived to be a scholarly, informed understanding explaining how devotional completion should take place only in the mosque or in private. The mother challenged her son, saying that he did not understand religion and only listened to the talk of the *fundamentalist* from abroad. In using the term 'fundamentalist', she referred to foreign Muslim missionaries criticising people's conduct and faith. In her view, what they preach is unacceptable and is unrelated to what it means to be 'a good Muslim'. In other settings, similar comments and arguments from younger people who see themselves as modern and educated seem to induce uncertainty regarding locally configured religious learning and practice. Still, what kind of ritual and everyday life practices and aesthetics people hold to be correct Islam is a contextual matter. So far, the rhetorical influence of reformist Islam does not seem convincing to most people. The kind of internal debate among Muslims that I am hinting at here – that is, among both Sufi- and anti-Sufi-oriented groups – have obviously recurred over several generations (Bang 2000, 2003, 2013). The arguments applied by the educated son towards his mother above are prevalent. Dissent among Sufi-oriented and reformist, and also modernist-oriented, Muslims regarding Islamic teachings, ritual practices and forms of transmission is rather conventional. In Zanzibar, the most significant Sufi groups (*tariqas*) are *Qadiriyya*, followed by *Shadhiliyya* and the *Alawiyya*. Anne Bang, who has conducted extensive research on these *tariqas* in Zanzibar, considers how members of the various groups would persist in their transmission of the importance of *dhikiri* including the chanting of poetry and *maulid*, as well as the actuality of miracles, especially of deceased saints (Bang 2000, 2003, 2013). Furthermore, she suggests how, in a non-Arabic-speaking society, locally oriented, orally transmitted traditions have a propensity to enter what is there considered Islamic scholarship (ibid.). In line with my own findings, Bang has stated that interlocutors would clearly express their scepticism towards those they perceive as Salafi-oriented by saying: 'It is not possible to listen to them. We have to continue to practise our religion as we have become used to (*zowea*)' (personal communication, July 2019). Following this attitude, members of the *tariqas* mentioned above would not only refer to religious justifications when discussing the significance of the *tariqas*; they would equally argue their significance with reference to religious unity and involvement in socio-moral issues (Bang 2000, 2003). This is not to deny the intellectual and scholarly basis of the *Qadiriyya*, *Shadiliyya* or *Alawiyya tariqas*, which all belong to scriptural traditions of Sufi and more general Islamic scholarship. To return to the dispute mentioned above, between the educated son and his mother whom the community consider *mwalimu*, this also indicates how modernity favours textual learning, not only for the gaining of historical knowledge, but also for religious comprehension. However, what is commonly questioned both by members of the various *tariqas* and by people in Zanzibar more generally is what they perceive as an attitude and apprehension among the young, educated Salafi- (and possibly Wahhabi-) inspired younger generation. In particular, they worry about the impression left on them by the Islamic missionaries mentioned above, who are from Pakistan (*Tablighi Jama'at*). The missionaries make themselves known by their green turbans and *salwar kameez*, which, according to people I work with, are too-short trousers. Often, Zanzibaris express their irritation regarding their presence by referring to 'those with too-short trousers'. Others with whom I discussed the issue in 2016 said:

The missionaries come from a different country. They are not from here and they have no manners. We do not understand why they are here. It would be better if they return to where they belong.

They are many these days and currently because of the political situation and people's dismay with the Union Government's newly imposed rules and regulations, their presence is bad. You see many of them at the market. People like me [dressed in Western fashion and without any veil] they call *kaffir* [unbeliever]. Our interpretation of Islam and the Qur'an is different from theirs. Zanzibaris do not want to follow their dressing codes. Why do they come here? They should leave us alone to live our lives as we have always done [*kama tumeshazowea*].

The Pakistani missionaries seduce frustrated young people who cannot find any educational or employment opportunities, who see no opening for the future, for a life with a regular income and the possibility to marry and start a family. These *fundamentalist* directions within Islam seem to provide our young Zanzibar women and men [with] a possibility to voice their political discontent. For instance, in contrast to people from the mainland they find themselves increasingly marginalised, without employment opportunities and thus, socially and politically insignificant. Those who follow the fundamentalists have started to make a distinction not only between Muslims and non-Muslims (tourists and other foreigners), but also between good Muslims and bad Muslims. This is very dangerous.[9]

The above quotations disclose people's distress concerning what they see as foreign intrusion into their everyday and religious lives. However, the last quotation simultaneously expresses a fear often heard regarding the socio-political conditions on the island. As discussed, their worry interrelates with what is said to be 'the mainland Christian government's aim to obliterate Zanzibar's political autonomy, to hamper their economy and livelihood, and censor local values and practices anchored in Islam and a Muslim way of life'. It seems that when discussion reaches the question of the union between Zanzibar and what was previously Tanganyika, what comes forward is a unified Zanzibari voice. When discussions turn towards mainland dominance and what in Zanzibar is discussed as being the United Government of Tanzania and its hampering of Zanzibar's economic and social development, internal religious as well as political differences are, for the most, de-emphasised.

Conclusion

Despite what women and men perceive as an ongoing political and social marginalisation within the Union of Tanzania, they continue to emphasise a shared cultural identity moored in their particular Muslim way of life. Still, an ongoing transformation of their habitual environment, which according to them is the result of an increasing number of labour migrants from the

---

[9] The quotation was initially in Swahili. Here I shall not provide the full quotation in Swahili, but only its two last sentences, which I find significant in the context of this argument: *Wale ambayo wanawafuatelia wa fundamentalist, wameanza kugawanya baina ya Waislam safi na Waislam wajinga. Hii ni tabia mbaya sana, ni hatari.*

Tanzanian mainland settling on the island, generates societal apprehension and uncertainty regarding the future. Today in Zanzibar Town and in certain coastal areas, the impact of Christianity is apparent and manifests itself, for instance, in the numbers of new churches built and of choirs performing in public arenas. Not unlike what is happening in Europe in the wake of immigration, the situation engenders a growing tension between the predominantly Muslim society and newly arriving Christian mainlanders, mainly due to different lifestyles and values, but expressed in terms of religious difference (Larsen 2017). Their dismay is further nourished by politico-economic subjugation and domination by mainland Tanzania, together with frustrations due to rising levels of poverty experienced by a majority of the islanders in a context of an affluent tourist industry, mainly operated by foreign and international companies (Keshodkar 2013: 3). In this context, the moral contestation of locally configured socio-cultural conventions in the wake of recent state engagement in religious practices and forms is perceived as yet another condemnation of their society and its autonomy. Zanzibaris feel constrained from at least two sides: from restrictions on ritual practices by representatives of the state, and by reformist ideas voiced from within society itself (for a similar narrative in Kenya see Kresse 2009). Uncertainty and a feeling of unpredictability, of fear and unease, impair people's readiness to cope and their capacity to act. Some recommend performing *dhikiri*, *maulidi ya hom* or *dufu* not in public but in private, because performances could be misunderstood as political gatherings by the authorities, especially by mainland-based governing bodies. Others advise that the practices are seen as customs, incorrect ones according to Islamic teachings and not to be pursued. Saying this, they add that the reason why up until now nobody has questioned these practices is the illiteracy of previous generations. Thus, what commonly used to be considered good Muslim practice and socio-cultural convention is now attacked by two otherwise contradictory voices: one from the governing political system that has evolved from the 1964 Revolution and the Union, and the other that reverberates with revisionist Islamic ideas. The conversation about Muslim women and the veil recounted in the beginning reflects, precisely, the present overlapping of political and moral tensions and a political justification through a discursive practice of othering. In this setting, the idea of the Muslim Other becomes equated with a political and stereotyped socio-cultural incompatibility between the island and the mainland. It encompasses what Myers and Muhajir (2013) denote 'the Zanzibar problem' within the Union. In this context, the phenomenon of Muslim woman can be read from both sides, each representing Islam in an equally singular image, neglecting the potency of lived Islam. Authorities requiring regulation according with state policies of suppressing traditional Muslim devotion see Islam as a political threat. Islamic revisionists condemning locally configured Muslim practices instruct people to reform their Islamic knowledge. In the firing line, women and men living their Muslim faith while coping with matters of the everyday are left in disarray, with growing uncertainty regarding cultural identity and an appropriate way of life.

Bibliography

Aboud, A. T. (1983), *Ripoti ya Taskforce ya Mafunzo ya Kiislam Zanzibar*, National Archives of Zanzibar (BA81/3).
Abu-Lughod, Lila (2016), 'The Cross-Publics of Ethnography: The Case of the "Muslimwoman"', *American Ethnologist* 43(4), pp. 598–608.
Babu, Abdulrahman (1991), 'The 1964 Revolution: Lumpen or Vanguard?', in A. Sheriff (ed.), *Zanzibar under Colonial Rule*, London: James Currey, pp. 220–49.
Bang, Anne (2000), 'Islamic Reform in East Africa, ca. 1870–1925: The Alawi Case', paper presented to the workshop *Reasserting Connections, Commonalities, and Cosmopolitanism: The Western Indian Ocean since 1800*, Yale University, 3–5 November.
Bang, Anne (2003), *Sufis and Scholars of the Sea: Family Networks in East Africa, 1860–1925*, London: Routledge.
Bang, Anne (2012), 'Zanzibari Islamic Knowledge Transmission Revisited: Loss, Lament, Legacy, Transmission – and Transformation', *Social Dynamics*, 38(3), pp. 419–34.
Becker, Felicitas (2009), 'Islamic Reform and Historical Change in the Care of the Dead: Conflicts over Funerary Practice among Tanzanian Muslims', *Africa: Journal of the International African Institute*, 79(3), pp. 416–34.
Burgess, G. Thomas (2009), *Race, Revolution and the Struggle for Human Rights in Zanzibar: The Memories of Ali Sultan Essa and Seif Sharif Hamad*. Athens: Ohio University Press.
Burgess, G. Thomas (2002), 'Cinema, Bell Bottoms and Miniskirts: Struggles over Youth and Citizenship in Revolutionary Zanzibar', *International Journal of African Historical Studies* 35(2/3), pp. 287–313.
Calkins, Sandra (2016), *Who Knows Tomorrow? Uncertainty in North-Eastern Sudan*, New York: Berghahn.
Cameron, Greg (2004), 'Political Violence, Ethnicity and the Agrarian Question in Zanzibar', in P. Caplan and F. Topan (eds), *Swahili Modernities: Culture, Politics, and Identity on the East Coast of Africa*, Trenton, NJ: Africa World Press, pp. 103–17.
Cameron, Greg (2009), 'Narratives of Democracy and Dominance in Zanzibar', in K. Larsen (ed.), *Knowledge, Renewal and Religion: Repositioning and Changing Ideological and Material Circumstances among the Swahili on the East African Coast*, Uppsala: Nordic Africa Institute, pp. 151–76.
Cameron, Greg (2002), 'Zanzibar Turbulent Transition', *Review of African Political Economy* No. 92. ROAPE, pp. 313–30.
Caplan, Pat (1975), *Choice and Constraint in a Swahili Community*, London: Oxford University Press for the International African Institute.
Caplan, Pat (2009), 'Understanding Modernity/ies: The Idea of a Moral Community on Mafia Island, Tanzania', in K. Larsen (ed.), *Knowledge, Renewal and Religion: Repositioning and Changing Ideological and Material Circumstances among the Swahili on the East African Coast*, Uppsala: Nordic Africa Institute, pp. 213–36.

Cooke, Miriam (2007), 'The Muslimwoman', *Contemporary Islam* 1(2), pp. 139–54.
Glassman, Jonathon (2011), *War of Words, War of Stones: Racial Thought and Violence in Colonial Zanzibar*, Indianapolis: Indiana University Press.
Gössling, Stefan and Ute Schutz (2005), 'Tourism-Related Migration in Zanzibar, Tanzania', *Tourism Geographies* 7(1), pp. 43–62.
Keshodkar, Akbar (2013), *Tourism and Socialist Change in Post-Socialist Zanzibar: Struggles for Identity, Movement, and Civilization*, Lanham, MD: Lexington.
Keshodkar, Akbar (2010), 'Marriage as the Means to Preserve "Asian-ness": The Post-Revolutionary Experience of the Asians of Zanzibar', *Journal of Asian and African Studies* 45, pp. 226–40.
Kresse, Kai (2007), *Philosophising in Mombasa: Knowledge, Islam and Intellectual Practice on the Swahili Coast*, Edinburgh: Edinburgh University Press.
Kresse, Kai (2009), 'Muslim Politics in Postcolonial Kenya: Negotiating Knowledge on the Double-Periphery', *Journal of the Royal Anthropological Institute*, pp. 76–94.
Larsen, Kjersti (1988), *Unyago – Fra jente til kvinne. Utformingen av kvinnelig kjønnsidentitet i lys av initiasjonsritualer religiøsitet og moderniseringsprosesser.* (Unyago – From Girl to Woman: The Formation of Female Gender Identity in the Light of Initiation Rituals, Religiosity and Processes of Modernisation), Occasional Papers in Social Anthropology, no. 22, University of Oslo.
Larsen, Kjersti (2004), 'Change, Continuity and Contestation: the Politics of Modern Identities in Zanzibar', in P. Caplan and F. Topan (eds), *Swahili Modernities: Culture, Politics, and Identity on the East Coast of Africa*, Trenton, NJ: Africa World Press, pp. 121–43.
Larsen, Kjersti (2017), 'Multifaceted Identities, Multiple Dwellings: Connectivity and Flexible Household-configurations in Zanzibar Town', in B. Schnepel and E. Alpers (eds), *Connectivity in Motion: Small Island Hubs in the Indian Ocean World*, Cham: Palgrave McMillan, pp. 181–209.
Larsen, Kjersti (2018), 'Silenced Voices, Recaptured Memories: Historical Imprints within a Zanzibari Life-world', in M.A. Fouéré, B. Bissell and M. Walsh (eds), *Memories of the Revolution*, Dar es Salaam: Mkuki na Nyota, pp. 251–79.
Lofchie, M. Y. (1970), 'African Protest in a Racially Plural Society', in R. Rothberg and A. Mazrui (eds), *Protest and Power in Black Africa*, New York: Oxford University Press, pp. 924–7.
Mahmood, Saba (2016), *Religious Difference in a Secular Age: A Minority Report*, Princeton: Princeton University Press.
Mahmood, Saba (2006), 'Secularism, Hermeneutics, and Empire: The Politics of Islamic Reformation', *Public Culture* 18(2), pp. 323–47.
Mandaville, Peter (2001), *Transnational Muslim Politics: Reimagining the Umma*. London: Routledge.
Marsden, Magnus (2005), *Living Islam: Muslim Religious Experience in Pakistan's North-West Frontier*, Cambridge: Cambridge University Press.
Myers, Garth A. and Makame M. Muhajir (2013), '"Wiped from the Map of the World"? Zanzibar, Critical Geopolitics and Language', *Geopolitics*, 18(3), pp. 662–81.
Nisula, Tapio (1999), *Everyday Spirits and Medical Interventions: Ethnographic and Historical Notes on Therapeutic Conventions in Zanzibar Town*, Saarijärvi: Gummerus Kirjapaino Oy.

Parkin, David (1995), 'Blank Banners and Islamic Consciousness in Zanzibar', in A. P. Cohen and N. Rapport (eds), *Questions of Consciousness*, London: Routledge, pp. 198–216.

Purpura, Allyson (1997), 'Knowledge and Agency: The Social Relation of Islamic Expertise in Zanzibar Town', PhD dissertation, City University of New York.

Saleh, Mohamed A. (2009), 'The Impact of Religious Knowledge and the Concept of *Dini Wal Duniya* in Urban Zanzibari Life-Style', in K. Larsen (ed.), *Knowledge, Renewal and Religion: Repositioning and Changing Ideological and Material Circumstances among the Swahili on the East-African Coast*, Uppsala: The Nordic Africa Institute, pp. 198–213.

Topan, Farouk (2004), 'From Mwana Kupona to Mawita: Representations of Female Status in Swahili Literature', in P. Caplan and F. Topan (eds), *Swahili Modernities: Culture, Politics, and Identity on the East Coast of Africa*, Trenton, NJ: Africa World Press, pp. 213–29.

7

The Inter-religious Dynamics of Muslim Politics: The Zanzibar Case

HANS OLSSON

Across the African continent, where nations since the 1990s have undergone economic and political liberalisation, polity reforms and shifts into multi-party politics, religion and religious agents are increasingly visible and audible features of the landscape. Opportunities for new forms of organisations, networks and outreach have diversified already religiously plural societies. In this context, Muslim, Christian and African traditional religious expressions have to varying degrees 'gone public' and entered politics (Otayek and Soares 2007: 12; Englund 2011; Kresse 2018). As Otayek and Soares (2007) have stressed, the religiously plural settings across the continent provide opportunities for exploring the diverse ways in which Islam and Muslim politics today are enacted: something that has brought attention not only to Muslim reform movements and new ways of being Muslim, but also to Muslim relationships with democracy, secularism and Islamic law (Becker 2006; Brenner 1993; Chesworth and Kogelmann 2014; Soares and Otayek 2007). Yet, approaches that use religious pluralism in general and Muslim–Christian interactions in particular to assess the production of religious identities have remained limited (Soares 2006, 2016; but see Cooper 2006, Shankar 2014). How religious diversity and inter-religious encounters shape religious ways of being have therefore been foregrounded as a new comparative framework for approaching religious configurations across Africa (Soares 2016). Such approaches open up means for addressing Muslim–Christian encounters beyond paradigms of 'peace' and 'conflict' by instead exploring how religious practices are borrowed, copied and influenced by encounters across religious traditions (Meyer and Larkin 2006; Janson and Meyer 2016; Peel 2016).

The way in which the religious field has developed in the religiously plural context of the United Republic of Tanzania highlights the importance of

Inter-religious Dynamics of Muslim Politics

looking at manifestations of religious politics through a paradigm of religious diversity. In the spotlight have been Muslim and Christian reform groups and the ways in which emerging religious discourses for change have created social tensions (Mukandala et al. 2006; Heilman and Kaiser 2002). Muslims calling for political change in Tanzania have also raised concerns over Muslims' lack of influence in state matters (Njozi 2000; Gilsaa 2012). For parts of the Muslim community, the state is increasingly seen as connected to Christian interests, with occasional assaults on Christian institutions interpreted as an attack on the state (Loimeier 2007: 138).

Similar trends are present in Zanzibar, the semi-autonomous archipelago with a large Muslim majority (95–8 per cent). Since the revolution in 1964 and the subsequent merger between Zanzibar and Tanganyika into the United Republic of Tanzania (henceforth, the Union) (Shivji 2008), Islam's role in the national identity of the islands has been a returning point of controversy and subject for political contestations (Killian 2008). In this complex political context, with internal strife over Zanzibar's place and future role within the Union, religion has informed politicised discourses of belonging where a Muslim Zanzibar is increasingly put up against a Christian mainland (Glassman 2011: 297–8; Gilsaa 2012: 428; Loimeier 2011). Tracing the contemporary role of religion in Zanzibar, the growing impacts of Muslim reform groups and Muslim publics have been assessed in their relation to history (Fouéré 2012a; Glassman 2011), politics (Gilsaa 2015; Turner 2009), education (Loimeier 2009), the Union (Poncian 2014) and terrorism (Brents and Mshigeni 2004; Mshigeni 2016; Saalfeld 2019). In different ways, the body of literature highlights how the political dynamics of Muslim discourses construct the Union structure as a proxy for Christian interests that are seen to restrict Muslim ways of life in Zanzibar. However, the ways in which Christian practices influence ways of being Muslim in Zanzibar remain largely under-studied.

This chapter therefore approaches the configuration of Muslim ways of being in Zanzibar through the lens of religious pluralism, and argues that the study of Muslim belonging in Zanzibar needs to take the framework of inter-religious encounters (imagined or real) into account when assessing how Muslim political configurations and enactments are manifested among the public. It places a focus on how Muslim identities are constructed relationally, and how religious identities take place through how religious pluralism is, and should be, governed. It takes a broad approach to politics, and views how Muslim ways of being constitute Muslim publics (Kresse 2018). This perspective also embraces the way in which diversity (religious, ethnic, social, cultural, etc.) is, and has been, conveyed in relation to trajectories of negotiating belonging in Zanzibar between what today are officially referred to as the Island Tanzania (*Tanzania Visiwani*) and Mainland Tanzania (*Tanzania Bara*). This means addressing

Muslim–Christian encounters beyond theologies of religion, co-operation and peace (Langås 2019), and instead assessing religious pluralism through a comparative lens of competition that situates religious belonging as relationally constituted despite promoting dualistic and exclusive discourses (Soares 2016).

By looking at public tensions in Zanzibar in 2012, a time when anti-Union protests connected with the Muslim propagation organisation Uamsho ('the Awakening')[1] generated turmoil and attacks on churches, political offices and private property, I will underline how Muslim belonging played a part in (re-)emerging nationalist sentiments that distinguished islanders (*wazanzibari*) from mainlanders (*wabara*) and also, to a large degree, Muslims from Christians. In these politics of belonging, Islam served as a unifying component for discursively (re-)creating Zanzibar along what Kai Kresse (2018: 4) has referred to as 'past present continuous' politics for creating a better and more just Zanzibar society. Christians, and especially a growing number of Charismatic churches, were, on the other hand, seen to erode the image of Zanzibar as a Muslim society. Christianity was, in other words, increasingly a social factor that influenced how Muslim politics, Muslim–state relationships and Muslim public engagements were enacted.

The assessment is based on research conducted in Tanzania and Zanzibar since 2009 that has focused on inter-religious institutions (Olsson 2011) and religious reform movements. A caveat in relation to my methodological approach to how inter-religious encounters influence Muslim ways of being is fitting here. My research in Zanzibar has largely focused on the emerging presence of Pentecostal-Charismatic Christianity and not primarily on Islam (Olsson 2015, 2018, 2019, 2020). However, Christianity has been situated *in relation to* the Muslim majority and Muslim ways of life. Over periods of fieldwork in Zanzibar, I have had countless informal conversations with Zanzibari Muslims. I also conducted interviews with people supporting Uamsho's cause. Muslim responses and the elaboration of the small presence of Christians in Zanzibar reflected the scepticism and suspicions I encountered in day-to-day interactions with Zanzibari Muslims (see also Nieber 2019). The religious diversity connected with mainland origins, an expanding, and morally disputed, tourist economy and the political secularism of the Union shaped the way in which Muslims assessed their ability to live as Muslims. Even though the case presented here reflects attitudes situated in a particular space and time, I would stress that the challenge posed by the presence of religious diversity over the last decades is rooted in historical trajectories through which ideas

---

[1] Jumuiya ya Uamsho na Mihadhara ya Kiislamu Zanzibar (the Association of Islamic Awareness and Public Discourse in Zanzibar), known by its Swahili acronym Jumiki, but more commonly referred to as Uamsho (Awakening).

and configurations of belonging, identity and social inclusion/exclusion have been pondered and accommodated in Zanzibar. The case serves to underline the reality that encounters between Muslim and non-Muslim communities will be a returning point of contestation in the future.

In what follows, I will briefly contextualise the inter-religious dynamics over time in Zanzibar before presenting how Christianity and Christian practices are viewed, pondered and valued in relation to Muslim ways of life. Inter-religious encounters are then situated in relation to different approaches to how to govern religious pluralism at play in Zanzibar, and the at times competing legal frameworks and mediations of secularism in Zanzibar that guide Muslims' perceptions of the Union. This highlights how Muslim ways of being in Zanzibar are situated in between the shifting minority–majority positions connected to Zanzibar's position as a state, yet enclosed by the Union. I conclude by placing this in relation to recent political developments since the 2015 elections.

Islam, Belonging and Christianity

Religious and cultural diversity has been an essential part of Zanzibar's position at the crossroads between the African mainland, the Arab Peninsula and India. Islam and ideas of Muslim unity have, however, played a unifying role in the historical unfolding of what has been known as the Swahili world(s) (Middleton 1992; Loimeier and Seesemann 2006) and the consolidation of cultural values and ideas of civilisation (*uungwana/ustaarabu*) (Bromber 2006). While island identities have remained flexible and negotiable over time (Glassman 1995), issues of belonging (and non-belonging) have remained central in the governance of Muslim ways of being, and distinctions between Muslim (civilised, urban, mercantile) and non-Muslim (barbaric, rural, African mainland interior) beliefs and behaviours (Pouwels 1987; Glassman 2011). These distinctions are today reproduced through discursive practices differentiating between Zanzibaris (*wazanzibari*) and mainlanders (*wabara*).

The hegemony of Muslim ways of life has historically contributed to the fact that Christianity has remained limited on the archipelago. The first Christians to arrive in Zanzibar were connected to Portuguese traders in the early 1500s. While the Portuguese remained in control of the islands until Omani Muslims (with the help of the English) seized power in the 1600s, the Portuguese influence only resulted in a small Roman Catholic community of traders and migrants from Goa, India residing on the islands. With Zanzibar developing into the commercial and cultural centre along the Swahili coast under Omani colonial rule, the 1800s marked a time of increased mobility and a diversified religious field. New religious movements included Christian missions from France, Germany and the British islands. Backed by the British Empire, which in 1890 incorporated Zanzibar into a British protectorate, Christian missions and individuals played their part in officially ending Zanzibar's trade with slaves. However, Zanzibar served mainly as a port of entry for a Christian expansion into the African hinterlands (Allen 2008; Sundkler and Steed 2000: 519–26). The long-standing and still present Roman Catholic and Anglican communities in Zanzibar are a part of the Zanzabari conception of *ustaraabu* (civilisation) and are seen as being among the locally-rooted expressions of Zanzibar's culture. Their continued presence forms part of a story of peace and coexistence between Muslims and Christians that re-affirms a cosmopolitan narrative of Zanzibar as a place of tolerance that prevails to this day (Langås 2019).[2]

Despite growing religious diversity, Islam remained the source through which religious pluralism, inclusion and exclusion were negotiated (Bang 2008: 177). However, in the early 1900s, the hegemonic status of Islam as a unified notion of belonging in Zanzibar started to decline. These changes coincided with the mobilisation of ethnically defined political organisations (Arab, Indian, African) (Sheriff 2001). New subversive sections of society started to reclaim their mainland origins rather than adapting to the hegemony of *ustaarabu*. This undermined Islam's unifying role and increasingly linked assertions of mainland origins to labour migration and Christian belonging (Glassman 2011: 56–7). The construction of two forms of ethno-nationalism in the first half of the 1900s – one maintaining the idea of civilisation (and Islam), the other centred on race[3] – in many ways still reflects two main national imaginaries in Zanzibar today: Zanzibari Nationalism and African Nationalism (Fouéré 2014: 481).

Political differentiation along ethno-national lines constructed the history of accommodating belonging through Islam's contested and politicised ground. Tensions turned to violence up until Zanzibar's independence in 1963, with developments culminating in the Zanzibar revolution, which saw the Afro-Shirazi Party (ASP) seize power (Glassman 2011). With the establishment of a union with Tanganyika in April 1964, the events turned Zanzibar on its head.[4] In its promotion of a new social vision, the Revolutionary Government dismantled important Muslim institutions and the previous public role held by prominent Islamic scholars seen as loyal to the Sultan (Loimeier 2009: 117).

---

[2] An explicit example of this narrative ethos is the 'Religious Tolerance' stamp produced upon independence from British rule in 1963, which displays Muslim mosques, Christian churches and Hindu temples alongside each other.

[3] One was made up by Arab elites asserting Islam so as to restore Zanzibar as a 'beacon of *ustaaraabu*' (Glassman 2011: 62) in the region. The other consisted of a group of intellectuals who, under the influence of pan-African ideals, saw the Sultanate (who was in power under the British protectorate) and 'Arab' rule as an ongoing colonisation of African subjects.

[4] The Zanzibar outlook since the revolution has increasingly been directed towards the African mainland – a development that was further consolidated through the merging of ASP and the Tanzania African National Union as the CCM in 1977.

At the same time, new Christian missions started to make inroads, primarily through mainlanders moving to the islands for work. The Evangelical Lutheran Church of Tanzania, for instance, established its first mission in Kwa Hani, Zanzibar Town, shortly after the revolution (von Sicard 1970: 73).

While Islam regained its public role during the presidency of Aboud Jumbe, Muslim education and Islamic jurisdiction were now in the hands of a new group of Muslim scholars affiliated or seen as loyal to the state. For parts of the Muslim community faithful to the old Muslim establishment, the relationship between Muslims and the state was a growing concern (Loimeier 2009: 117–18). When Zanzibar opened up in the 1980s, alternative Muslim groups therefore started to engage in *da'wa* (Islamic mission) to revive what they saw as an increasingly immoral society (Gilsaa 2015: 46). Yet, Muslims were not alone in such efforts. At the same time, Pentecostal-Charismatic Christian missions from inside and outside Africa made inroads into the island (Olsson 2019: 57–8). It is important to note that these two trajectories – (1) the increasing number of Christian agents in Zanzibar, and (2) the rise of Muslim reform movements – both served, in their respective ways, as a critique of the social status quo. They wanted change, even though their discourses differed between an emphasis on restoration and transformation respectively. While both forms of religious revival initially focused on individuals' behaviour, Muslim reformists, under the umbrella of the Salafi-inspired Ansâr Sunna, gradually engaged in a political critique of the Chama Cha Mapinduzi (CCM) regime's failure to develop the islands economically. Attention was also focused on how increasingly closer ties to the mainland would affect Muslim ways of life and Zanzibar culture – triggering opposition to those closer ties to the mainland would affect these (Turner 2009; Loimeier 2011).

When Zanzibar introduced multi-party democracy in 1992, Zanzibar was divided into two equally large political camps: CCM-Zanzibar and the Civic United Front (CUF). Muslim revival and reform groups connected to the Ansâr Sunna quickly gave their support to the opposition CUF. While much has been written about the politicisation of race, ethnicity and religion in the discursive practices of the two parties (Cameron 2004, 2009, 2019; Larsen 2004; Poncian 2014; Brents and Mshigeni 2004), it is worth repeating that the exclusive national imaginaries of the two respective parties centred around Zanzibar's past, present and future position within the Union. On the one hand, Zanzibar holds a special status in the Union with its own president and semi-secular legislation that includes Islamic family law. For many Zanzibaris, this means that Zanzibar is understood as a territory of defined boundaries, a sovereign polity and common culture that is in line with Anderson's 'imagined community' (Anderson 1983; Fouéré 2014: 481). On the other hand, Zanzibar is also part of a nation that (at least officially) remains equally divided between Christians,

Muslims and African traditional religious practitioners.[5] Here a form of political secularism governs religious pluralism and state–religious relations. With the government of Mainland Tanzania also serving as the Union government, this implies that Zanzibar's ability to act independently at times is constrained by its extensively larger mainland partner. The Union (and a Christian lobby group), for instance, unilaterally prevented Zanzibar from joining the Organisation of the Islamic Conference (OIC) in 1993 (Ludwig 1999: 213). This stirred up public protests in Zanzibar and fed into many Zanzibari Muslims' perception of the islands' autonomy and Muslim rights being restricted by a Christian hegemony (*mfumo kristo*) on the mainland.

With mainland migrations of many Christian workers increasing in connection with an expanding tourist industry in Zanzibar since the 1980s, mainland Christians were increasingly visible on the islands. New Christian inroads were also visible in the organisation of open-air revival meetings and public preaching as a form of evangelising. Such outreach activities, however, also prompted Muslims in Zanzibar to organise themselves along similar lines. During the 1990s, Muslims increasingly used public preaching, so called *mihadhara*, in order to voice their view of Zanzibar's condition while attacking the state and criticising Pentecostal missionary activities (Loimeier 2009: 116). They also set up alternative Muslim structures to promote their cause politically. The establishment of Uamsho in the late 1990s (and an NGO registered in 2001) that aimed at promoting Muslim unity and Muslim rights through public preaching was, according to the organisation, a direct response to Christians' ability to hold public preaching events in the 1990s (Turner 2009: 241–2; see also Bakari and Ndumbaro 2006). Christian practices influenced the production of, as well as the perceived need for, new ways of being Muslim in the public arena.

Religion, Governance and Tensions in 2012

While political turmoil and occasional violence have accompanied Zanzibar's development into multi-party politics, the context surrounding public tensions in 2012 captured new trends. Public outbursts were not manifested through the political antagonists CCM and CUF, which after a round of peaceful elections in 2010 shared power in a political agreement for unity.[6] Unrest was funnelled through public protests for a more autonomous Zanzibar, and, especially, the

---

[5] With the last official census including religious affiliation being conducted in the 1960s, religious demographics in Tanzania remains a tense political issue. While the government upholds its view that there are equal proportions of the population, especially of Christians and Muslims, there are indications that Christians are now in the majority. See e.g. Pew (2010: 23).

[6] After several tense and violent elections in Zanzibar, the construction of what became the Government of National Unity was an attempt to broker peace between the ruling party of CCM-Zanzibar and the opposition party of CUF that had split the Zanzibar electorate in two. For more on the context

increasingly vocal and visible feature of Uamsho.[7] Uamsho had been part of the mobilisation of civil society to promote national unity (and a sense of a unified Zanzibar identity) prior to the 2010 elections (Bakari and Makulilo 2012; Matheson 2012). The movement for a unified Zanzibar, however, also served to push calls in public for a more independent Zanzibar vis-à-vis the Union, sentiments strengthened in Zanzibar after the Union government launched a constitutional review act that left the Union structure out of the discussion in 2011 (Myers and Muhajir 2013). With the Union critical of CUF sharing power with CCM, Uamsho succeeded in building broad alliances with Union-critical politicians and civil society agents through seminars and large-scale *mihadhara*, public talks and events (Fouéré 2012b). In filling the political vacuum left by CUF, Uamsho successfully connected calls for Muslim unity and Muslim rights with how the Union (and the presence of tourism, mainland migrants and Christianity) eroded Zanzibar's sociocultural norms and values (Saalfeld 2019: 219; Loimeier 2011). In the moral critique of external influences, Uamsho was able to reconceptualise the meaning of *ustaarabu* (civilisation) as something happening in the past into something happening in the present continuous. It restated ideas of Zanzibari identity and Muslim ways of life in connection with local moral standards such as *heshima* (honour, respect) and *haya* (modesty, humility). Uamsho also drew on historical discourses that stressed the islands' dislocation from mainland Africa to endorse a political discourse that put 'Zanzibar first' as a means of distinguishing between 'true' Zanzibaris (*wazanzibari*), Zanzibaris in support of the Union (*wazanzibara*) and foreign 'mainlanders' (*wabara*) (Keshodkar 2013: 198). The discourse also asked people and politicians in Zanzibar to decide: were they committed to the Zanzibari people, or were they loyal to the external interests of the Mainland?

When, in May 2012, Uamsho took the agenda of 'Zanzibar first' to the streets after a government-imposed ban on religious gatherings, this resulted in violent confrontations. Violence was directed at Union-supporting individuals and institutions and included both CCM offices and Christian churches (Olsson 2019: 48–51; Mshigeni 2016: 108). It was not until after large-scale riots re-emerged in October the same year (connected with the disappearance of the Uamsho leader Shaykh Ahmed Farid and Muslim protests in Dar es Salaam after a Christian boy had urinated on a Qur'an) and the arrest of all the main Uamsho leaders that the organisation's presence faded.[8] While Uamsho denied

---

leading up to the establishment of the Government of National Unity, see Matheson 2012; Bakari and Makulilo 2012; Myers and Muhajir 2013; Uki 2010.

[7] Due to limited space, the details concerning Uamsho's salience as a political voice in Zanzibar up to 2012 cannot be unfolded here. For a thorough outline of Uamsho's rise see Olsson 2019: 38–51.

[8] See 'Police Tackle Rioters in Dar, Isles', *Daily News*, 18 October 2012; 'Chaos in Dar, Zanzibar', *The Guardian*, 18 October 2012.

any involvement in the attacks on Christians, its movement *for* Zanzibar questioned the presence of a growing number of mainland Christians, many openly opposing Muslim ways of life in Zanzibar. The presence of Christians served as a reminder of Islam, something that influenced how Muslims regarded their place living in, and increasingly in between, two states.

During a focus group interview conducted with eight Zanzibari Muslims from Unguja and Pemba,[9] Zanzibar's complex position within the Union was reflected in how the participants viewed the role of Christianity and Christians in Zanzibar. While none of the interlocutors (three women and five men) stated an affiliation with Uamsho, all expressed support for Uamsho's cause.[10] Uamsho was seen as a defender (*mtetezi*) against corrupt politicians, using Islamic principles to protect society as a whole. The position reflects common Muslim practices of 'commanding right and forbidding wrong' (Cook 2000) that Kresse also stresses as an important dimension in the constitution of Swahili Muslim Publics in nearby coastal Kenya (2018: 48). That Muslim principles should guide society as a whole was also reflected in how Muslim Zanzibaris view their relationship with Christianity: Muslim–Christian relationships needed to be addressed in the context of Islam's past, present and future significance on the islands, and, especially, Islam's role in maintaining norms and moral practices. Implicit in this dwells a moral responsibility to accommodate difference that recaptures the ideas of civility (*ustaarabu*) mentioned above. Representatives of the Muslim majority are obliged to welcome newly arriving guests (one participant gave the example of Omani rulers' hospitable reception of Christian missionaries in the 1800s). But there is reciprocity in this. Guests also have a duty to conform and behave according to the norms of the host. In other words, the minority should respect the culture (*utamaduni*) of the majority. This framework served to categorise Christians in Zanzibar into two different groups: *wakristo wa asili* (original Christians) and *wakristo waliokuja* (arriving Christians).

The former group (mainly consisting of Anglican and Roman Catholic Christian communities present in Zanzibar over the last 100 years) was viewed positively and implied that these Christians had integrated into society by adopting the Muslim majority norms. The latter group was viewed negatively and consisted of newly arriving groups of (primarily mainland) Christians, who were perceived as having little interest in adapting to the moral practices of the local Muslim culture. Newly arriving Christians were therefore often seen to stir up social tensions. Examples of such practices included how new Christian groups used loudspeakers and amplified music to transmit their Christian message

---

[9] Focus group interview, 17 November 2012.
[10] The interview was conducted in November 2012 after the Zanzibar government, with the help of Union military forces, went in hard against leaders and supporters of the organisation.

into Muslim neighbourhoods during their Sunday, and how Christians engaged in door-to-door evangelising during the Muslim month of fasting (Ramadan). Both these examples were seen as provocative in relation to the norms and social rhythms of the Muslim-majority society.

One participant further highlighted new Christian inroads as a form of invasion of land (*uvamizi wa ardhi*), with Christian institutions grabbing land at the cost of the local Zanzibar population. While affirming Christians' greed for land (*uroho wa ardhi*), another participant highlighted Christian movements between Mainland Tanzania and Zanzibar as a deliberate act to add to the numbers of Sunday worshippers in Christian churches and so also distort the image of Zanzibar as a Muslim land (*nchi ya Kiislamu*). While these statements exaggerate the extent to which Christians are actually able to buy land – the prospect for Christians not born in Zanzibar to buy land is notoriously difficult owing to legislation in Zanzibar, and an obstacle causing frustration among Christians themselves – they both point to how arriving Christians are experienced and discursively constructed as a growing threat. New Christian inroads, the construction of new church buildings and the display of Christian public worship challenge Muslim ways of life and the hegemonic role of Islam (Olsson 2019: 171–5).

The growth of Christian churches highlights how new voices enter the Muslim soundscape of prayer calls, distorting everyday rhythms by competing for public space. Christian ignorance regarding the society as a whole, its social norms and behaviours, thus makes it increasingly difficult for Muslims to accommodate religious diversity. Instead, Zanzibari Muslims have started to question why Christians are coming to Zanzibar. What do Christians want? Why are they coming in large numbers? Are they trying to erode Zanzibar's culture? Such questions point to how the host–guest dynamic has been ruined, and so influences how the presence of religious diversity is currently being (re-)interpreted and (re)valued. In other words, newly arriving Christians' presence, behaviour and evangelical methods alter inclusive paradigms of accommodation and, thus, possible ways of being Muslim. All these issues point to how the increasingly visual and audible feature of Christianity in the Zanzibar public since the 1980s onwards is, as already mentioned, a factor behind the emergence of new ways of Muslim preaching as well as the organisation of Muslim publics in the late 1990s.

To be a Muslim hence entails being a custodian of the society (Kresse 2018). The presence of new Christian counter-publics hence helps Muslims to criticise other Muslims in Zanzibar (and especially Muslim politicians) who do not publicly oppose such practices. Muslim critique thus entails processes of (re-)claiming Muslim Zanzibar as a distinct political and sovereign entity, and so also restores the ability to govern the society along Muslim principles.

Against this, the secular structure of the Union and its influence on the Zanzibar polity becomes a point of concern. In this discourse, Christians turn into a publicly visible manifestation of what the Union is trying to accomplish: to dictate the lives of the Zanzibari populace for the Union's own interests. For people giving support to Uamsho, to be a 'true' Zanzibari hence blurs the lines between Muslim ways of life, nationalism and anti-Union sentiments. It is a protest against developments that regulate Muslims' ability to govern each other. What the encounter with Charismatic Christian public performances entails is a reminder that Muslim ways of upholding Islamic principles in the society are eroding. This also connects Christian inroads with wider contestations over lack of economic development, political regulations and cultural erosion seen as connected to the Union (Nieber 2019; Mshigeni 2016). Yet, Christians' public presence point to how ideas of Zanzibari ways of life and Muslim belonging are increasingly enacted in relation to religious diversity in Zanzibar's post-liberalisation era. The Union's structure provides space for mobility, mainland migration and new forms of Christian belonging. This highlights, in the eyes of Uamsho-supporting Muslims, the decreasing ability for Zanzibar as a whole to accommodate (and regulate) difference. As such, religious pluralism reflects how minority–majority dynamics currently are contested and altered in relation to Zanzibar's current place and future role within the Union as a whole.

Shifting Power, Negotiating States and the Issue of Religious Pluralism

The inter-religious dynamics influencing Muslim political publics outlined above situate Muslim–Christian encounters and competition over public space in wider contestations over modes of governance and regulation of religious affairs in Zanzibar. For Zanzibari Muslims considered in this chapter, Christians' ability to roam free – somehow hijacking the pious Muslim soundscape, grabbing land to expand and not respecting codes of conduct – highlights Muslim inability to govern the society. The government's inability to intervene is a sign of (Muslim) leaders' moral decay and forms part of the problem (Loimeier 2011).

What incoming Christians thus reveal is the presence of dual legal structures and different standards of secularity that govern the relationship between the religious and the political sphere, a semi-secular framework for Zanzibar, and the political secularism of the Union. While the Union (at least officially) separates the religious from the political (and the state), the Zanzibar state incorporates leading Muslim institutions into the state structure – including the government-deployed mufti's office dealing with Muslim affairs as well as Islamic courts that adjudicate family law.[11] In Zanzibar, this means that the political secularism of the United Republic of Tanzania exists alongside a local secular mediation that includes religious tenets. However, on legal issues, the Court of Appeal of Tanzania serves as the final Union judiciary, which implies that, despite Zanzibar having its own legal system, Zanzibari court cases (Islamic court cases included) could be appealed on a Union level.[12] While Christians are not included in the jurisdiction of Islamic family law in Zanzibar, the way the Union could supersede Zanzibar legislation nonetheless influences religious agents' ability to move between different modes of governance. This is particularly visible when conversion and inter-religious marriages are at play.

A former Muslim in one of Zanzibar's Pentecostal congregations, and his conversion to Christianity, serve to exemplify some of the issues at play. Originally from Tanga, the man had been living in Zanzibar for nearly thirty years as a Muslim when he became a 'born-again'[13] Christian. His conversion created tensions within his family when his wife and children remained Muslims. Fuming over his turn to Christianity, and the social disgrace this brought to the family, the wife tried to convince him to return to Islam. Meeting with no success, after consulting traditional healers (*waganga*) for help, the wife finally approached the Islamic court, urging the kadhi (Islamic judge) to force through a divorce. The kadhi summoned the man and instructed him to divorce his wife if he intended to remain a Christian. Retelling the story, the man explained how he refused the kadhi's request by stating that the kadhi had no jurisdiction over him as a Christian and thereby could not demand that he divorce his wife (Olsson 2019: 213–14).

While this example should be read primarily as a discursive practising of (and witness to) how born-again Christian belonging is performed in relation to Islam in Zanzibar – emphasising the ability to withstand pressure from the Muslim majority – it nonetheless highlights the limits of Muslim forms of authority. The wife went through the legal institution handling family law certain that this would finally settle the matter. By refusing to abide by the authority of the kadhi, her Christian husband rejected such forms of governance. In relation to experiences, and pressure to conform from the Muslim majority, born-again Christians often turned to the Union and its secular framework to restate their religious freedom. The political secularism of the Union served to enforce

---

[11] Muslim institutions also include the Waqf and Trust commission and educational institutions (primary, secondary and university levels). See also chapter in this volume by Erin E. Stiles.
[12] For an outline of the legal framework of the Union and Zanzibar see http://www.nyulawglobal.org/globalex/Tanzania.html
[13] 'Born-again' here refers to second birth in the Spirit, found in the biblical passage John 3:3ff, and is a commonly used term to distinguish Pentecostal/Charismatic Christians from mainline Christian churches (Roman Catholic, Anglican, Lutheran, etc.). Among Pentecostal and Charismatic churches in Tanzania, the 'born again' experience is discussed in terms of being saved, *kuokoka*.

Christians' ability to practise their faith on the islands. Christian critique of Uamsho followed the same logic. Christians did not oppose the fact that the organisation promoted Islam among the public (that being freedom of religion), but centred on how Uamsho's activities mingled with politics in a way that could regulate Christians' ability to act in the future.

But the 'mixing' of religion and politics in the semi-secular Zanzibar framework was not only an issue among Christians. Muslim counter-publics like Uamsho used the secular framework in their own way to criticise the involvement of the Zanzibar state (and the CCM in particular) in Muslim affairs. For example, the government-employed mufti's office was seen to regulate Muslims' right to elect their own representatives (Bakari 2012: 20; Loimeier 2011: 14–16). Hence, while both Christian and Muslim groups were critical of the state–religious dynamics in Zanzibar, the Christian mediation of religious rights centred on how Islam had too much influence over individuals' lives, while the Muslim reformists' position stressed the lack of proper Muslim governance in the society. These dynamics are even more prominent when lifted to the Union level, where the political secularism of the Union is seen as protecting the rights of Christian (and so religious pluralism) while regulating Muslim ways of life (in a Muslim majority setting).

These different religious approaches to secular frameworks at play in Zanzibar reveal how the governance of religious practices is highly contested. This captures what Saba Mahmood (2015: 4) calls a '*generative* contradiction' within political secularism more generally: namely, the at times unclear yet enforced separation between religion and the state in Zanzibar underlines the presence of a governmentality that regulates religious life in favour of religious freedom. The comparative approach used here shows that views of religious freedom are contextually produced, and are related to locally embedded views on governance in which Muslim belonging is the foundation for, and thus is inseparable from, ideas of Zanzibari nationalism and sovereignty. As Mshigeni (2016: 112) highlights in his work on Uamsho, the activism for Muslim rights and identity as a 'true' Zanzibari also meant the liberation of Zanzibar and break from the colonial oppression of a mainland-run Union, currently in the hands of Christian interests. Uamsho's mediation and use of the secular frameworks available in many ways structure the production of religious identities.

What the comparative focus on religious pluralism helps reveal is that Muslim politics are not 'anti-Christian' or directed against the presence of religious diversity as such, but are deeply embedded in Muslim principles regarding how religious diversity should be governed in a Muslim-majority context. The political secularism of the Union, aiming at providing rights to all religious groups, is hence at odds with views where the (Muslim) community and not the secular state should regulate religious diversity. The Union framework, manifested in

Inter-religious Dynamics of Muslim Politics

the way groups of Christians go public, thus signifies a threat to Muslim ways of governing life more generally. Muslim politics in opposition to the state need to consider how forms of governance regulate religious life, and how this is manifested in encounters, interactions and conflicts with new Christian communities.

The emergence of Muslim politics in Zanzibar has often been seen as both linked and confined to the highly politicised Zanzibar context, and a history of more or less exclusionary political imaginaries that now stretch over a century (Saalfeld 2019; Glassman 2011). This chapter has by no means downplayed these historical dynamics. However, assessments of the relationship between religion and politics have tended to focus on religious belonging for political ends (Cameron 2019). Adding an inter-religious perspective highlights tensions and conflicts between Muslim and Christians as well as the legal framework that structures such encounters. By doing so it also takes religious configurations of faith, belief and practices as part of a complex matrix of social, economic and political circumstances that produce religious sites of belonging.

Discussion and Concluding Remarks

This chapter has highlighted the way in which religious pluralism in general and Muslim–Christian encounters in particular influence and challenge Muslim ways of life. I have argued that these inter-religious dynamics inform the way Muslim politics and Muslims' relationship to the state are enacted. However, the religious reform and revival I have focused on here should by no means be seen as representative of all Muslims (or Christians) in Zanzibar. There are many Muslims who have grown tired of the moral war pondered by Muslim reform groups such as Ansâr Sunna (Loimeier 2011: 16, 27; see also Turner 2009). What Uamsho in 2012 nonetheless managed to do, and gain substantial support for, was to use Muslim principles of unity while revitalising Zanzibari identity against Mainland Tanzania (the Union). Muslim–Christian encounters were a part of this, when new Christian publics talked of experiences many Zanzibaris felt uneasy with: namely, that (mainland) Christian inroads had started to undermine, mix with as well as destroy, the culture (*utamaduni*) of Zanzibar.[14]

This suggests that religious pluralism has moved from being seen as something that defines Zanzibar's cosmopolitan outlook to something that challenges Muslim ways of life. New Christian inroads highlight how the secular framework of the Union is increasingly at odds with deep-seated values that include Muslim ethics of accommodation and respect vis-à-vis the sociocultural embedded norms and customs connected to the Muslim majority. The framework of religious freedom and religious rights thus not only regulates but also shapes religious

---

[14] Male interlocutor, focus group interview, 17 November 2012.

formations in the Zanzibar public sphere. With both Muslim and Christian publics expressed through this paradigm, the governance of religious diversity seems only to contribute to increased tensions.

Muslim public protests in 2012 were in many ways a culmination of contested forms of state–religious regulations and calls for religious and political freedom. However, since the detention of Uamsho leaders in October 2012 – who, after an initial appearance in court in Tanzania Mainland, still remain in jail without any official trial – the space for all political forms of opposition has been severely restricted. The landslide victory for CCM Zanzibar after CUF boycotted a controversial round of re-elections in Zanzibar 2016, in combination with what was perceived as the rigid stance of the Union government, led to a crackdown on all forms of opposition. Yet, CCM's consolidation of power and control of the public arena have not meant that Union-critical sentiments have disappeared in Zanzibar. Rather, forms of political opposition and anti-Union sentiments are boiling under the surface (Cameron 2019; Crisis Group International 2019). Reports suggest that the regulation of Muslim publics into private religious spheres rather feeds into perceptions of Muslim discrimination under a Christian-dominated leadership and bureaucracy in Tanzania Mainland. Growing concerns point to how this could trigger new forms of political radicalisation among Muslim youths on the islands (Crisis Group International 2019: 11). While the lack of 'Islamist' politics in Zanzibar has been seen as related to the presence of a large political opposition party (Saalfeld 2019), CUF's inability to serve as a proper oppositional force has not only led to prominent CUF politicians moving to ACT-Wazalendo (Alliance for Change and Transparency) party, but could also signify a future of more radical forms of Muslim politics.

At the same time, religious groups that support the Union framework and the political secularism of not mixing religion with politics are growing. The Zanzibar International Christian Center (ZICC), Zanzibar's largest Pentecostal congregation and Tanzania Assemblies of God's major outreach on the islands, serve as an example of how current regulations imposed on Muslim ways of life (and especially Muslim politics critical to the Union) at the same time provide avenues for expanding Christian publics on the archipelago. ZICC previously went under the name of City Christian Center (CCC), and was one of the churches attacked in the Zanzibar Town riots following Uamsho's protests in 2012. Instead of repairing the damage to the property, the congregation decided to expand the structure into a larger building that would extend capacity from around 1,000 attendees to at least double that. With a new two-storey church built in 2018, the church is a visible symbol of Christian growth.[15]

---

[15] See the current church building at https://www.facebook.com/ZanzibarInternationalChristianCenter/ For a comparison with the old church structure, see Olsson (2019: 63).

The expansion of the church since its foundation in 1995 (Olsson 2019: 62) was also reflected in the changing of the name to 'Zanzibar International', thus removing the urban connotation of 'City'. The modification first of all signifies a growing international outlook and global aspirations common within Pentecostal-Charismatic churches across Africa (Asamoah-Gyadu 2017). However, adding 'Zanzibar' to the name consolidates the local anchoring for the congregation primarily made up of labour migrants from mainland Tanzania. It is a statement that Christians are there to stay and will form an intrinsic part of the religious landscape on the archipelago.

While Christians make up less than 2 per cent of Zanzibar's population, the ZICC is part of a growing body of new Christian churches spreading across the islands. I have argued elsewhere that the Muslim 'other' in many ways serves to strengthen narratives of Christian commitment, practice and belonging in Zanzibar (Olsson 2019). Christians seem to influence Muslim ways of life in Zanzibar in similar yet different ways. Situated in a wider geopolitical context where the imaginaries of the past present continuous remain important, inter-religious dynamics shape the way religious politics become enacted. Muslim–Christian encounters, religious expansion and the competition over publics become not just a matter of a mainland invasion: they also reveal the ongoing contextual configuration of religion and religious ways of life as deeply relational processes.

Bibliography

Allen, Julia (2008), 'Slavery, Colonialism and the Pursuit of Community Life: Anglican Mission Education in Zanzibar and Northern Rhodesia 1864–1940', *History of Education* 37(2), pp. 207–26.

Anderson, Benedict (1983), *Imagined Communities: Reflections on the Origin and Spread of Nationalism*, London: Verso.

Asamoah-Gyadu, J. Kwabena (2017), 'Symbolising Charismatic Influence: Contemporary African Pentecostalism and Its Global Aspirations', in Joel Cabrita, David Maxwell and Emma Wild-Wood (eds), *Relocating World Christianity: Interdiciplinary Studies in Universal and Local Expressions of the Christian Faith*, Leiden: Brill, pp. 302–23.

Bakari, M. A. and Alexander Makulilo (2012), 'Beyond Polarity in Zanzibar? The "Silent" Referendum and the Government of National Unity', *Journal of Contemporary African Studies* 30(2), pp. 195–218.

Bakari, M. A. and L. Ndumbaro (2006), 'Religion and Politics in Tanzania: The Post-Liberalisation Era', in Rwekaza S. Mukandala, S. Yahya-Othman, S. S. Mushi and L. Ndumbaro (eds), *Justice, Rights and Worship: Religion and Politics in Tanzania*, Dar es Salaam: E & D, pp. 334–59.

Bang, Anne K. (2008), 'Cosmopolitanism Colonised? Three Cases from Zanzibar, 1890–1920', in Edward Simpson and Kai Kresse (eds), *Struggling with History: Islam and Cosmopolitanism in the Western Indian Ocean*, New York: Columbia University Press, pp. 167–88.

Becker, Felicitas (2006), 'Rural Islamism during the "War on Terror": A Tanzanian Case Study', *African Affairs* 105(421), pp. 583–603. doi: 10.1093/afraf/adl003.

Brenner, Louis (ed.) (1993), *Muslim Identity and Social Change in Sub-Saharan Africa*, London: Hurst.

Brents, Barbara and Deo Mshigeni (2004), 'Terrorism in Context: Race, Religion, Party and Violent Conflict in Zanzibar', *The American Sociologist* 35(2), pp. 60–74. doi: 10.1007/bf02692397.

Bromber, Katrin (2006), 'Ustaarabu: A Conceptual Change in Tanganyikan Newspaper Discourse in the 1920s', in Roman Loimeier and Rüdiger Seesemann (eds), *The Global Worlds of the Swahili: Interfaces of Islam, Identity and Space in 19th and 20th-Century East Africa*, Berlin: Lit Verlag, pp. 67–82.

Cameron, Greg (2004), 'Political Violence, Ethnicity and the Agrarian Question in Zanzibar', in Pat Caplan and Farouk Topan (eds), *Swahili Modernities: Culture, Politics, and Identity on the East Coast of Africa*, Trenton, NJ: Africa World Press, pp. 103–19.

Cameron, Greg (2009), 'Narrative of Democracy and Dominance in Zanzibar', in Kjersti Larsen (ed.), *Knowledge, Renewal and Religion: Repositioning and Changing Ideological and Material Circumstances among the Swahili on the East African Coast*, Uppsala: Nordiska Afrikainstitutet, pp. 151–76.

Cameron, Greg (2019), 'Zanzibar in the Tanzania Union', in Lotje de Vries, Pierre Englebert and Mareike Schomerus (eds), *Secessionism in African Politics: Aspiration, Grievance, Performance, Disenchantment*, London: Palgrave Macmillan, pp. 179–205.

Chesworth, John, A. and Franz Kogelmann (eds) (2014), *Sharī'a in Africa Today: Reactions and Responses, Islam in Africa; volume 15*. Leiden: Brill.

Cook, M. A. (2000) *Commanding Right and Forbidding Wrong in Islamic Thought*, Cambridge: Cambridge University Press.

Cooper, Barbara MacGowen (2006), *Evangelical Christians in the Muslim Sahel*, Bloomington: Indiana University Press.

Crisis Group International (2019), Averting Violence in Zanzibar's Knife-edge Election: Crisis Group Africa briefing no 144. Nairobi/Brussels: Crisis Group, https://www.crisisgroup.org/africa/horn-africa/tanzania/b144-averting-violence-zanzibars-knife-edge-election

Englund, Harri (ed.) (2011), *Christianity and Public Culture in Africa, Cambridge Centre of African Studies Series*, Athens: Ohio University Press.

Fouéré, Marie-Aude (2012a), 'Reinterpreting Revolutionary Zanzibar in the Media Today: The Case of Dira Newspaper', *Journal of Eastern African Studies* 6(4), pp. 672–89.

Fouéré, Marie-Aude (2012b), 'Zanzibar Independent in 2015? Constitutional Reform, Politicized Islam and Separatist Claims', *Mambo! Recent Research Findings in Eastern Africa-French Institute for Reseach in Africa* 10(2), pp. 1–4.

Fouéré, Marie-Aude (2014), 'Recasting Julius Nyerere in Zanzibar: the Revolution, the Union and the Enemy of the Nation', *Journal of Eastern African Studies* 8(3), pp. 478–96.

Gilsaa, Søren (2012), 'Muslim Politics in Tanzania. Muslim and National Identities Before and After the Collapse of Ujamaa', PhD thesis, University of Copenhagen.

Gilsaa, Søren (2015), 'Salafism(s) in Tanzania: Theological Roots and Political Subtext of the Ansār Sunna', *Islamic Africa* 6(1–2), pp. 30–59.

Glassman, Jonathon (1995), *Feasts and Riot: Revelry and Rebellion on the Swahili Coast, 1856–88*, Oxford: James Currey.

Glassman, Jonathon (2011), *War of Words, War of Stones: Racial Thought and Violence in Colonial Zanzibar*, Bloomington: Indiana University Press.

Heilman, Bruce E. and Paul J. Kaiser (2002), 'Religion, Identity and Politics in Tanzania', *Third World Quarterly* 23(4), pp. 691–709.

Janson, Marloes, and Birgit Meyer (2016), 'Introduction: Towards a Framework for the Study of Christian–Muslim Encounters in Africa', *Africa* 86(4), pp. 615–19. doi: 10.1017/S0001972016000553.

Keshodkar, Akbar (2013), *Tourism and Social Change in Post-Socialist Zanzibar: Struggles for Identity, Movement and Civilization*, Lanham MD: Lexington Books.

Killian, Bernadeta (2008), 'The State and Identity Politics in Zanzibar: Challenges to Democratic Consolidation in Tanzania', *African Identities* 6(2), pp. 99–125.

Kresse, Kai (2018), *Swahili Muslim Publics and Postcolonial Experience*, African Expressive Cultures, Bloomington: Indiana University Press.

Langås, Arngeir (2019), *Peace in Zanzibar*, Bern: Peter Lang.

Larsen, Kjersti (2004), 'Change, Continuity and Contestation: The Politics of Modern Identities in Zanzibar', in Pat Caplan and Farouk Topan (eds), *Swahili Modernities: Culture, Politics, and Identity on the East Coast of Africa*, Trenton, NJ: Africa World Press, pp. 121–43.

Loimeier, Roman (2009), *Between Social Skills and Marketable Skills: The Politics of Islamic Education in 20th Century Zanzibar*, Leiden: Brill.

Loimeier, Roman (2011), 'Zanzibar's Geography of Evil: The Moral Discourse of the Anṣār al-sunna in Contemporary Zanzibar', *Journal for Islamic Studies* 31, pp. 4–28.

Loimeier, Roman and Rüdiger Seesemann (2006), *The Global Worlds of the Swahili: Interfaces of Islam, Identity and Space in 19th and 20th-Century East Africa*, Beiträge zur Afrikaforschung, Berlin: Lit Verlag.

Ludwig, Frieder (1999), *Church and State in Tanzania: Aspects of Changing Relationships, 1961–1994*, Leiden; Boston: Brill.

Mahmood, Saba (2015), *Religious Difference in a Secular Age: A Minority Report*, Princeton: Princeton University Press.

Matheson, Archie (2012), 'Maridhiano: Zanzibar's Remarkable Reconciliation and Government of National Unity', *Journal of Eastern African Studies* 6(4), pp. 591–612.

Meyer, Birgit and Brian Larkin (2006), 'Pentecostalism, Islam & Culture: New Religious Movements in West Africa', in Emmanuel Kwakue Akyeampong (ed.), *Themes in West Africa's History*, Athens: Ohio University Press, pp. 286–312.

Middleton, John (1992), *The World of the Swahili: An African Mercantile Civilization*, New Haven, CT: Yale University Press.

Mshigeni, Deogratius (2016), 'Globalization and the Rise of Militant Islamic Social Movement Organizations: The Case of UAMSHO (Awakening) Group in Zanzibar', UNLV Theses, Dissertations, Professional Papers, and Capstones 2884, https://digitalscholarship.unlv.edu/thesesdissertations/2884

Mukandala, Rwekaza S., S. Yahya-Othman, S. S. Mushi and L. Ndumbaro (eds) (2006), *Justice, Rights and Worship: Religion and Politics in Tanzania*, Dar es Salaam: E & D.

Myers, Garth Andrew and Makame A. Muhajir (2013), '"Wiped from the Map of the World"? Zanzibar, Critical Geopolitics and Language', *Geopolitics* 18(3), pp. 662–81. doi: 10.1080/14650045.2013.769962.

Nieber, Hanna (2019), 'Islamic Zanzibar: Between the Indian Ocean and the African Mainland', *Journal of Africana Religions* 7(1), pp. 131–7.

Njozi, Hamza Mustafa (2000), *Mwembechai Killings and the Political Future of Tanzania*, Ottawa: Global Link Communications.

Olsson, Hans (2011), *The Politics of Interfaith Institutions in Contemporary Tanzania*, Studies of Inter-Religious Relations vol. 51, Uppsala: Swedish Science Press.

Olsson, Hans (2019), *Jesus for Zanzibar: Narratives of Pentecostal (Non-)Belonging, Islam and Nation*, Leiden: Brill.

Olsson, Hans (2015), 'With Jesus in Paradise? Pentecostal Migrants in Contemporary Zanzibar', *Pneuma* 37(1), pp. 21–40. doi:10.1163/15700747-03701025.

Olsson, Hans (2018), 'Narratives of Change: Healing and Pentecostal Belonging in Zanzibar', *Mission Studies* 35(2), pp. 225–44. doi: 10.1163/15733831-12341568.

Olsson, Hans (2020), 'Chasing Money: Tourist-Induced Labor Migration and Pentecostal Teachings of Success in Zanzibar', *Exchange* 49(1), pp. 3–30. doi: 10.1163/1572543X-12341547.

Otayek, René and Benjamin F. Soares (2007), 'Introduction: Islam and Muslim Politics in Africa', in Benjamin F. Soares and René Otayek (eds), *Islam and Muslim Politics in Africa*, New York: Palgrave Macmillan, pp. 1–24.

Peel, J. D. Y. (2016), 'Similarity and Difference, Context and Tradition, in Contemporary Religious Movements in West Africa', *Africa* 86(4), pp. 620–7. doi: 10.1017/S000197 2016000565.

Pew (2010), 'Tolerance and Tension: Islam and Christianity in Sub-Saharan Africa', *Pew Forum on Religion & Public Life*. www.pewforum.org.

Poncian, Japhace (2014), 'Fifty Years of the Union: The Relevance of Religion in the Union and Zanzibar Statehood Debate', *African Review* 41(1), pp. 161–81. doi: 10.2139/ssrn.2623919.

Pouwels, Randall L. (1987), *Horn and Crescent: Cultural Change and Traditional Islam on the East African coast, 800–1900*, Cambridge: Cambridge University Press.

Saalfeld, Jannis (2019), 'On the Divergent Trajectories of African Islamism: Explaining Salafi Non-Radicalisation in Zanzibar', *Africa Spectrum* 54(3), pp. 201–21. doi: 10.1177/0002039719887825.

Shankar, Shobana (2014), *Who Shall Enter Paradise?: Christian Origins in Muslim Northern Nigeria, ca. 1890–1975*, New African Histories, Athens: Ohio University Press.

Sheriff, Abdul (2001), 'Race and Class in the Politics of Zanzibar', *Africa Spectrum* 36(3), pp. 301–18.

Shivji, Issa G. (2008), *Pan-Africanism or Pragmatism?: Lessons of the Tanganyika–Zanzibar Union*, Dar es Salaam: Mkuki Na Nyoka.

Soares, Benjamin F. (ed.) (2006), *Muslim–Christian Encounters in Africa*, Leiden; Boston: Brill.

Soares, Benjamin F. (2016), 'Reflections on Muslim–Christian Encounters in West Africa', *Africa* 86(4), pp. 673–97. doi: 10.1017/S0001972016000619.

Soares, Benjamin F. and Rene Otayek (eds) (2007), *Islam and Muslim Politics in Africa*, 1st edn, Basingstoke: Palgrave Macmillan.

Sundkler, Bengt and Christopher Steed (2000), *A History of the Church in Africa*, Cambridge: Cambridge University Press.

Turner, Simon (2009), '"These Young Men Show No Respect for Local Customs": Globalisation and Islamic Revival in Zanzibar', *Journal of Religion in Africa* 39(3), pp. 237–61.

von Sicard, Sigvard (1970), *The Lutheran Church on the Coast of Tanzania 1887–1914: With Special Reference to the Evangelical Lutheran Church of Tanzania, Synod of Uzaramo-Uluguru*, Lund: Gleerup.

Uki, A. (2010), *Maridhiano and the Government of National Unity, its Impact on Elections and Constitutionalism in Tanzania*, http://www.kituochakatiba.org/publications/workshopsconferences/maridhiano-and-government-national-unity-its-impact-elections-and

Part II

Institutions

8

The Supreme Council of Kenya Muslims (SUPKEM): Jostling for Representativeness among Muslims in Kenya

HASSAN MWAKIMAKO

INTRODUCTION

The post-independence, one-party state of Kenya forbade religious-based political parties. Instead, the state allowed the establishment of Muslim associations to perform the role of representing Muslims. The task of these associations was to improve the welfare of Muslims in education, religious and social matters. They also acted as a conduit between Muslims and the state, leading them to be termed the 'mouthpiece' of Muslims and respective government policies. Not allowed to get involved in politics, they controlled Muslim constituencies and checked any possible subversive tendencies. They were not entirely led by the ulama (scholars), but were dominated by a powerful secular-oriented Muslim elite, usually in formal state positions and receiving salaries from the state. The goal of these elites was not to seek reform of Muslim spirituality but to ensure the acquiescence and loyalty of the local Muslim population to the state, in return for a degree of access to state resources for possible redistribution to their constituencies in order to maintain allegiance and legitimacy. This chapter takes an overall view of the genesis of one such organisation, the Supreme Council of Kenya Muslims (SUPKEM), and its evolution from the 1970s to the 1990s and beyond. It focuses on the establishment of SUPKEM, and on its aims and structure and the composition of the organisation; it also offers a discussion of the 1990s and the emergence of 'leadership margins' and their efforts to challenge the dominance of SUPKEM, the challenges of the years from 2000, particularly the relationship between Muslims and the state, and the position of SUPKEM in its role as a leadership group.

***

In November 2019, SUPKEM was in the news for uncharacteristic reasons. Its then incumbent chairman, Yusuf Nzibo, had been suspended from his position. This action was unprecedented in the history of the organisation: never before had a coup d'état against the leadership of SUPKEM been successfully executed. Leadership squabbles were common, but no chairman of the organisation had ever been deposed. Aware of this, Nzibo responded, as expected, that 'it was unconstitutional to depose the chairman'. He complained that he was being falsely accused of bad leadership even when an internal audit had absolved him of any wrongdoing. Nevertheless, SUPKEM ultimately chose to install an interim chairman until fresh leadership elections could be held.

To understand Yusuf Nzibo's predicament, one needs to peel back the layers of history regarding how SUPKEM has operated in representing Muslims. First, SUPKEM was founded as a critical public forum to articulate Muslim identity in a secular state dominated by a Christian elite. Second, it emerged from a confluence of competing local dynamics that shaped its distinctive organisational structure and identity. Third, it was a key precursor of Muslims' claims against their marginalisation by the state. From its inception, SUPKEM represented a confluence of political discourse and representation strategies embedded in local Muslim socio-historical, political contestations and transformations that made its claims both a political resource and an analytical category for understanding the Muslim community in Kenya.[1]

Representativeness, referring to the legitimacy criteria for representative entities or organisations, is key in governance. International and local representative bodies are frequently criticised for their lack of representativeness (Dubin and Runavot 2013; Germain 2001; Idris and Bartolo 2000; Keohane and Nye 2001), which often appears as a cure for the legitimacy deficit of organisations. Studies tackling this issue within the framework of religious institutions are scant, although political theory has underlined elements of particular relevance such as the relationship between representativeness and democracy (Manin 2008; Pitkin 1967; Rosanvallon 1998; Urbinati 2006). Secondly, the abundance of concepts related to representativeness leads to significant confusion. Literature referring to representativeness in different contexts includes an impetus for 'civil society participation' (McKeon 2009), as a synonym for 'fair' or 'equitable' representation (Fitzgerald 2000; Sucharipa-Berhrmann 1994), or as 'democratic representation' (Kroger and Friedrich 2011; Steffek and Hahn 2010). The essential features that make up the concept of representativeness include a reliance on Fritz Scharpf's distinction between 'input' and 'output' legitimacy (1999). Representativeness is considered highly normative and

---

[1] Marieke Louis and Corine Ruwet (2016), 'Representativeness from Within: A Comparison between the ILO and the ISO', *Globalization*, DOI 10.1080/14747731.2016.1201327.

subjective, is 'always subject to review' (Urbinati 2006: 29), and depends on 'what members do about it' (Devin 2016: 92).

According to SUPKEM's history, representativeness entails the legitimacy required to influence the course of action of the organisation in the context of institutional space (national, then transnational and global) and subject matters (personal laws, hajj, constitutional review process, electoral bodies). SUPKEM's legitimate representativeness occurs through strategies of selecting actors (District Councils, Executive Committee) to be acknowledged by the organisation (top-down) and by the Muslims on whose behalf it claims to speak and act (bottom-up).

Throughout its formative years, SUPKEM's representativeness has been a functional resource for a powerful elite and a source of contestation from political and economic margins (women, professionals, ulama) that advocate for leadership reforms within SUPKEM. Two arguments are proposed in this chapter. First, the representativeness of SUPKEM is realised through the legal requirements of its constitution, primarily considered to lead to broader functional goals. This essentially consists of the regulation of relations between Muslim elites via enacting the constitution of the council. Through elections, the impetus for representativeness is expressed at the SUPKEM district level (through the selection of the most representative persons) and at the organisational level (through the composition of the Executive Committee).

The second argument focuses on the challenges in the process to redefine the representativeness that occurred from the 1990s, when some elites felt marginalised and demanded 'better representation'. These 'margins' were categories of actors, experts, advisors and civic society organisations that felt excluded from SUPKEM, a characteristic of what Matthew Holden (2009: 166) sees as an ambivalent dynamic of inclusion and exclusion. From the 1990s, the representativeness of SUPKEM became deeply rooted in this dynamic, as the organisation faced challenges to its selection criteria (determining who is and is not representative). The margins contested the representative arrangements within the organisation and challenged the overall structure of representation.

SUPKEM'S FORMATIVE YEARS, 1975–1985: CHALLENGES IN BUILDING A FUNCTIONAL REPRESENTATION

The post-independence Kenyan state developed rapidly into a one-party state. Officially, the state was secular, with constitutionally guaranteed freedom of worship and religion. In practice, it regulated religion, and forbade the formation of religiously-based political parties and encouraged the formation of state-friendly religious associations. It is against this background that Muslim associations existed. The first to be founded was the National Union of Kenya Muslims

(NUKEM) in 1968. Then, SUPKEM was founded in 1973 to consolidate efforts at promoting Muslim interests under one umbrella organisation. Among its senior officials were Muslim elites doubling as members of the Kenyan cabinet and other state functionaries.

SUPKEM's conception of representativeness was rooted in the functionalist paradigm where representation was a means of achieving the goals of the organisation. Legitimacy was assessed in a utilitarian way, in terms of the organisation achieving goals and satisfying its members. Strategically, SUPKEM's positioned task was to deal with educational, religious and social matters. Relations with the secular state played out with SUPKEM assuming the role of an intermediary between Muslims and the state – a role it played so vigorously that some Muslims felt that it fell just short of being an official mouthpiece for articulating government policies. Elites who held positions of authority in SUPKEM, including the Chairman, Secretary General and Organising Secretary, were 'secular-oriented' and state-salaried civil servants eager to have a controlling influence among their respective Muslim constituencies, and, equally, felt to be responsible for reducing any tendencies to subvert the state and its policies. To perform these roles, SUPKEM elites abhorred and avoided direct involvement in anything they deemed political. In return, they accessed state resources and were ready to redistribute some of these to their constituencies as part of efforts to maintain allegiance and legitimacy. The resources were symbolic, such as: government leaders participating in religious ceremonies; financial, where the state provided the organisation with some material benefits; or political, when the elite had access to policy-makers. Such behaviours by the leadership of SUPKEM had negative repercussions that included constant squabbling over policy issues among members. A good example of the troubles that SUPKEM experienced during its early formative years was the question of its constitution and how best to operationalise it.

During the founding years, the constitution had categorically stated the desire to turn SUPKEM into the most dominant Muslim leadership organisation. This was realised through efforts that culminated in 1976 when the elite who were associated with the state because of their employment engineered a process to devise strategies for SUPKEM to assume supremacy over the activities of other organisations. In particular, SUPKEM sought to curtail and undermine the ability of other organisations to interact with external donors. In the post-1973 constitution, the elite inserted what has come to be known as the 'clearing house clause', which gave SUPKEM the authority to 'evaluate' and approve all appeals for financial assistance to donor countries. SUPKEM facilitated this by issuing 'letters of recognition' to all delegations of leaders of organisations leaving the country in search of financial aid abroad. In 1976, SUPKEM's supremacy was guaranteed when it was officially recognised as the only organisation entitled to represent all Muslims within Kenya and to maintain links with Islamic organisations outside Kenya. This declaration was officially ratified during the annual conference held in April 1979. Apart from this, the 1976 conference adopted a proviso that established District Councils whose functions included mobilisation of participation of Muslims in their districts. The District Councils became points of liaison between the communities and the Executive Committee of the Council. After changes were agreed upon, the organisation elected its first national chairman, Maalim Said bin Ahmed, a local cleric/theologian (*alim*) famous for his religious information programme *Maswali na Majibu* (Questions and Answers), which he hosted via the national broadcaster Voice of Kenya (VoK).

SUPKEM IN THE 1980s–1990s: REPRESENTATIVENESS AS A SOURCE OF CONTESTATION

From the 1980s onwards, the Council's historical context of representativeness faced upheavals involving profound identity and legitimacy crises. Muslims accused its leadership of being corrupt and of having misappropriated donations for private gain. There were also misunderstandings between members of the Executive Committee that rendered the Council almost dysfunctional. In the Executive Committee, some members, particularly those from 'up-country', felt marginalised by their colleagues from the coast. For example, another attempt to review the constitution of SUPKEM was made in 1982, which infuriated some members of the Executive Committee who disagreed with the initiative. In a letter addressed to a member of the Executive Committee, Farouk Muslim, a prominent Muslim leader, expressed frustrations about the incessant efforts to amend the Constitution, stating:

> I found it difficult ... sometimes I could not understand the reasons for the amendments myself ... some of the amendments did not, in my view, have to be incorporated and the adoption of standing order or resolutions could have been even better. Some of the amendments are self-defeating, an example being the requirement that organizations should submit minutes to the council but that they do not have to do this if they normally do not circulate them to their own members. I also find some of the amendments unsound from a practical point of view – the formation of co-operatives for unemployed youth ... Anyhow, let us proceed to submit the amendments to the AGM at which I will be willing if that remains your wish, to explain them to participants.[2]

---

[2] Farouk Muslim to Karim Wabuti, Central Bank of Kenya, 17 June 1982.

The issue of writing a constitution for SUPKEM continued to bedevil the organisation. The matter was raised again in March 1991 during the Annual General Meeting, where a resolution was passed to review it. Ahmed Khalif, the Secretary General, wrote to affiliated organisations as follows:

> On the 9th SUPKEM AGM a major resolution was unanimously adopted that an urgent need to thoroughly review the councils constitution in order affect necessary amendments to make it relevant, consistent and responsive to the important role the council has to play in articulating and representing the needs and aspirations of the ummah. The general feeling is that the constitution as it is, is outdated and has to be overhauled if the council has to efficiently carry out and discharge the obligations, duties and responsibilities it owes the community.

In order to actualise this resolution, Ahmed Khalif continued to explain:

> All district councils to study and review the constitution and submit their proposals within three months ... Amendments proposal should be minuted in official sittings of the District branches and will be forwarded to SUPKEM headquarters for onward transmission to the amendment committee.[3]

This attempt caused further squabbles among members of the Executive Council who did not agree with some of the recommendations. For example, Bakari Baraka, Vice-Chairman of Eastern Province, thought that some recommendations included in the report of the Constitution Committee were in fact ideas favoured by the Chairman of SUPKEM. Bakari was in particular opposed to a recommendation that in his opinion would make SUPKEM ineffective by taking away the direct representation of Muslim organisations. Bakari likewise was not in favour of recommendations such as setting specific qualifications guidelines for officers in the Council, or allowing only the ulama to assume a position of leadership in the SUPKEM District Council. However, the chairman claimed he wanted SUPKEM to be led by future leaders who were committed and highly qualified for a leadership position. According to the chairman, these were not necessarily ulama but rather 'persons of great education, religious commitments and those committed to sacrifice time and resources for the union'. Eventually, SUPKEM's constitution was not changed and the status quo remained.

---

[3] Ahmed Khalif, Secretary General, SUPKEM to Chief Kadhi, Members of SUPKEM Executive Committee, SUPKEM District Chairman, Prominent Ulama, 6 March 1991, in SCKM/ADM/G/39.

'We Must Say What Is and What Is Not a Muslim Organisation'

Failure to agree on the constitution of SUPKEM led some Muslims to seek the registration of new societies without recourse to the Council. This alarmed SUPKEM, which was worried that such organisations might later become powerful and challenge the Council's authority. To hinder the continued mushrooming of Muslim religious bodies, SUPKEM wrote to the Government as follows:

> we wish to bring to your attention that most of the Muslim societies being registered by your office are not genuine Muslim organizations – some of these organizations are hiding under the cover of Muslim societies while their activities are not really religious but politics. Information received from various places where such organizations originate has revealed to us that these political organizations are not Muslim societies though they are called Muslim societies ... These organizations under the pretext of Muslim societies find ways of looking for funds from foreign Muslim organizations which caused a lot of misunderstandings and differences among local Muslims in the areas affected ... we request and advice that before any Muslim societies is registered proper investigations should be conducted to establish whether such Muslim societies are genuine or not.[4]

The Law of Succession Act: SUPKEM as Representing a Muslim Voice

Islam plays a unique role in Kenyan law and society. Before independence in 1963, parts of the coast of Kenya were under the Sultanate of Zanzibar; the Sultan had appointed representatives, including kadhis (Islamic judges) and *liwalis* (administrative officials) to ensure law and order. Kadhis in particular administered justice using Islamic shari'a principles and codes. The emergence of colonial power in 1895 ushered in a tripartite court system comprising common courts, native courts and shari'a courts. Shari'a courts, known as kadhis' courts, applied in cases involving disputes in which both parties were Muslim. After independence, kadhis' courts existed by agreement and an Act of Parliament, although post-independence kadhis' courts had their jurisdiction restricted to family law matters of Muslim divorce, succession and inheritance. From mid-1981 up to 1985, this arrangement of having Muslims guided by Islamic principles and codes in personal laws faced challenges when the state

---

[4] Mohamed Younies, National Organizing Secretary-SUPKEM to Registrar of Societies, 25 March 1994, in SCKM/TAB/S/7.

intended to consolidate all personal laws adhered to by different communities into one uniform law applicable to all. The publication of the Law of Succession Act elicited strong opposition from Muslims. Initially, SUPKEM maintained an ambivalent position, as it was unwilling to engage in politics or be seen to go against the government's wishes. While the general public was lamenting government interference in the personal laws of Muslims, SUPKEM's initial silence was puzzling to many. For months, the Council appeared less provoked. However, action was initiated by individual members of SUPKEM; their opinion opposing the government appeared in the *Daily Nation* for 21 July 1981. Sayyid Hassan bin Ahmad Badawy from Lamu wrote in support of SUPKEM to oppose the changes. Mohamed Amana from Lamu lobbied the National Council of Churches of Kenya (NCCK) through its General Secretary, saying that 'we are copying you a letter we have written to the Attorney General in which we are advising the Attorney General on the undesirable sections of the Law of Succession which go against the religion of Islam'.[5] Meanwhile, Abdulrahman Siddik, a Muslim from Mombasa, responded harshly to the editorial in the *Daily Nation* over the proposed Law of Succession Act:

> Your Editorial and the Attorney General language in the *Daily Nation* of 3rd September leaves much to be desired. I never thought that so many people remain so much ignorant about Islam and Muslims ... though we have peacefully co-existed for centuries. In Islam, there could be no Authority in person or persons when it comes to an act or law even utterances if against the Holy Quran or hadith of the Prophet. The laws of marriage (the important part of it), the law of Succession in its totality are clearly defined in the Quran and no Muslim can just brush aside such important matters, which put his very Islamic faith in jeopardy. Yourself trying to stress the importance of our parliament against the Quran is both unfortunate and shortsightedness ... the prophet Muhammad says; 'there could be no loyalty unto the creation which involves disloyalty unto their creator' ... what is required [is] that Muslims should be ruled and judged as per their clear sharia (the best so far or can you suggest a better one) and the other Kenyans should be judged as per the constitution none should be expected to be mistreated just because the majority (or their representatives such as the parliamentarians) have decided otherwise. Muslims in this country cannot be expected to have just[ice] because of their being in minority ... instead of seeing and thinking, why should people comment on other people's important matter when they can hardly see beyond what they have learnt at the mission schools ... please

---

[5] Mohamed Amana's letter to J. C. Kamau, General Secretary, NCCK, 19 August 1981.

try to understand and help us to help you in maintaining brotherhood of mankind.[6]

Other petitions included one from Harith Swaleh from Lamu to the Kenya News Agency, expressing his infuriation with reports by the Agency indicating that some Muslim countries had outdated laws that worked against women's rights and those of their children.[7] A strong push against the proposed Law of Succession Act emanated from Lamu. The Islahil Islamiyya Society under Mohammed Amana was concerned that, despite its petitions, no action had been taken, and encouraged SUPKEM to be more active in this matter by demanding that a delegation should be organised under the council: 'kwa nini yamuna majibu katika barua zote tumezileta. Twataka delegation itayarishwe na SUPKEM' (Why haven't we received responses from all the petitions we have sent? We want the SUPKEM to organise a delegation).[8] Perhaps Mohamed Amana's petitions awakened the Council, which then responded to the demands for a delegation.

In early September 1981, SUPKEM called a special meeting to address the matter. The chairman explained the fear among Muslims that the introduction of the Law of Succession Act was a step by the government in its intention to make changes to the marriage laws. He counselled Muslims to be law-abiding citizens and remain calm even as they expressed their views in the newspapers about the proposed law, because 'expression of views on any law in the country is an exercise of the democratic rights of all citizens'.[9] SUPKEM was already deciding for Muslims to seek an audience with the President and present a petition. Meanwhile, the chairman advised Muslims to 'keep away from the press and not make any statement until the petition is presented'.[10] SUPKEM appointed a committee to draft the petition. Its highlights included the concerns of Muslims over the repercussions of the draft law and how Muslims would address themselves to the President. Initially, the draft committee favoured those addressing the President using the expression 'your petitioners'. Others thought this was unfavourable, and suggested that Muslims should present themselves as 'Nyayo followers'.[11] Eventually, the committee settled on using flattering language and presented Muslims by saying in the petition: 'your Excellency, our community is known for our unswerving loyalty to you, the government and the ruling party

---

[6] Abdulrahman A. Siddik to Editor, *The Daily Nation*, in SCKM/TAB/5/7.
[7] Harith Swaleh, 2nd Vice Chairman, SUPKEM, Lamu to Senior Officer, Kenya News Agency, 3 September 1981.
[8] A letter from Mohamed Amana under the auspices of Islahil Islamiyya to SUPKEM, 20 August 1981.
[9] Minutes of the Special Meeting held to discuss a Memorandum to be presented to HE The President Daniel arap Moi on the Law of Succession. Held Saturday 12 September 1981.
[10] Ibid.
[11] i.e. those who follow a philosophy emphasising peace, love and unity.

KANU and our patriotism is proverbial, our love for you and our adherence to the Nyayo Philosophy are unquestionable.'[12] In a surprise move, the initial meeting arranged for SUPKEM to petition the President was cancelled. Instead, on 17 September 1981, Ahmed Abdalla, the Director General of SUPKEM, wrote to Ahmed Yusuf, the Secretary General of SUPKEM, disclosing that he had met the President over lunch and had presented to him a brief conncerning the Muslim disputations on the Law of Succession. Without the knowledge of other members of the Executive Council of SUPKEM, Ahmed Abdalla also wrote to the Attorney General, claiming that 'it was necessary for our side to take [the] initiative because we are the ones (Muslims) who need something from the government'. Ahmed Abdalla knew that his actions could be construed as unrepresentative, and that he could be thought guilty of insubordination and of usurping the authority of the Executive Council. He took Ahmed Yusuf into his confidence while expressing these fears:

> Please keep these documents confidential, as we do not want them to fall into the hands of those who have vowed to destroy me personally. Not that one pays too much attention to such threats but some caution is needed particularly now that SUPKEM's name has risen sky-high. Inshallah it will mark the beginning of new rigor and purposive leadership. The suggested panel of lawyers will need copies of the letter I have sent to the AG and the brief I gave to His Excellency. They should keep these close to their chests and should also feel free to suggest other additional solutions if any. What we need is commitment and public spiritedness on their part.[13]

Changes in the laws affecting communities take a long time to take effect, as interest groups are lobbied and disputes resolved. Discussions about the Laws of Succession Act and responses to petitions and queries took an agonisingly long time before the government replied. In 1983, Muslims were still lobbying the government alongside efforts to seek the guidance of 'competent' Muslims on this matter. In one such effort, the Chief Magistrate, Abdul Rauf, a Muslim, advised them that their demands were delaying the process; these appeared misconceived, and they did not appreciate the government's intentions. Abdul Rauf advised Muslims against extraneous propositions like 'wanting a specific

---

[12] An initial draft petition had been prepared by Prof. Mohamed Hyder, which was corrected by inserting some changes. Eventually a committee was selected to go through the deliberation and prepare a draft for further discussion, leading to the changes above. Members of the committee were considered experts regarding their knowledge of Islam and language and included Mohammed Hyder, Idha Salim, Jaffer, Lakha, Chaudry, Abdillahi Nassir, Ahmed Abdalla, Yusuf Ali, Shaykh Dasani, Shaykh Nassor, Mohammed Abdilahi and A. Yusuf.

[13] Ahmed Abdalla, Director General, SUPKEM to Ahmed Yusuf, Secretary General, SUPKEM, 17 September 1981.

definition of a Muslim' by urging 'the Muslim community to accept the proposed amendments and ask them to work for a definition of "Muslim" without any distinction of its concepts and meanings to avoid unnecessary confusion and complications'.[14] The concern here was that part of the Muslim community had made recommendations that would have excluded others from the definition of 'Muslim'. Abdul Rauf advised Muslims to consider the view that 'a Muslim means any person professing Islamic faith of any school or sect … introducing any other element in this definition will result in untold complexities for the courts, Kenyans and lawyers'.[15] By mid-1983, the government was still adamant about exempting Muslims from the proposed Law of Succession. In a letter to the Chief Kadhi, the Attorney General expressed frustrations with Muslim demands:

> we regret to note that our suggested amendments to the Law of Succession Act (chapter 16 of the Laws of Kenya) are not acceptable to you. Those amendments were made on our understanding of your letter of 12 June 1982 which seemed to indicate that the Muslim community was prepared to accept a compromise solution to accommodate an exception from the provisions of the Law of succession Act relating to intestacy in which case the Muslim would be governed by the Muslim sharia. It was also our understanding that the Muslim community would accept to be governed in other respects i.e. the making of wills, administration of estates etc. by the provisions of the law of succession Act. The government cannot grant Muslim community a total exception from the provisions of the Law of Succession Act. You will appreciate that the Act was passed by Parliament in which Muslim interest were fully represented. The government cannot therefore grant a total exemption to suit only a section of the community.[16]

While SUPKEM engaged the government through an exchange of letters, seeking guidance and consulting with the community, impatience was growing within SUPKEM's Executive Committee due to a lack of synergy in the Council. This came as a result of members of the Executive Council disagreeing on what strategies to use in engaging the state. For example, during a New Year event of 1982, the newly elected Secretary General of SUPKEM, Ahmed M. Khalif, had castigated the government for not responding to Muslim demands to be exempted from the application of the Law of Succession Act.[17] Khalif's action had unsettled other members of the Executive Committee. In particular,

---

[14] Abdul Rauf, Chief Magistrate to SUPKEM, 17 December 1982.
[15] Ibid.
[16] Arthur H. Buluma, Senior State Counsel, for Attorney General to the Chief Kadhi, 21 July 1983.
[17] This was reported via national radio and published in the *Sunday Nation* of 2 January 1983.

Ahmed Abdalla, the Director General, felt infuriated and warned Khalif that 'it was the practice to let the Chief Kadhi take the initiative in ascertaining Muslim opinion before a formal reply is dispatched. Our Chairman is therefore going to consult the Chief Kadhi before he returns from the Coast. This is the most constructive step to take.' The Director General also took time to advise the Secretary General that

> it is a long-standing decision of our Executive Committee that nobody issues a press statement on behalf of SUPKEM unless and until it has been considered and specifically authorized by the Executive Committee itself. The decision was taken in the interest of preserving the integrity and good name of the organization, otherwise there is danger of everybody issuing statements in its name.[18]

Interactions between Ahmed Abdalla and Ahmed Khalif signified how members of the Executive Committee jostled for control of SUPKEM. Occasionally, both spoke and acted unilaterally and claimed to represent the Executive Committee. However, the audacity of Ahmed Abdalla in pointing this out to Ahmed Khalif demonstrated differences within the Executive Committee as to how this matter needed to be approached. Ahmed Abdalla favoured a slow and controlled engagement, whereas Ahmed Khalif appeared forceful and more vigorous. Ahmed Abdalla was a public servant who favoured SUPKEM being subservient to the state. By contrast, Ahmed Khalif was a politician, a member of parliament and favoured a political approach to address this challenge; as Secretary General, he was prepared to pursue that line. In fact, in late 1983, Ahmed Abdalla was no longer communicating directly with the Secretary General but through the Executive Officer, thus signalling deep divisions and insubordination that hampered SUPKEM's efforts in the representation of Muslims. In particular, Ahmed Abdalla did not always agree with the others. For example, in October 1983 he thought the government was making every effort to resolve the matter, but that the Muslim side was delaying the solution. He praised the government and the Attorney General for formal endorsements and for willingness to restrict, in the proposed Law of Succession Act, the testamentary powers of any Muslim over what should happen to his or her estate after death. Under the proposed new amendment, if any Muslim wrote a will depriving any of his or her heirs of their share in the estate as proscribed by the shari'a then to that extent the will would be invalid and the Islamic shari'a would apply. According to Ahmed, this was a most pleasant surprise and demonstrated a genuine intention on the part of

---

[18] Ahmed Abdalla, Director General of SUPKEM to Ahmed M. Khalif, MP and Secretary General, SUPKEM, 4 January 1983.

the government to respect shariʻa and its essential requirements.[19] According to Ahmed Abdalla, the government had already offered the necessary concessions and it was now up to Muslims to show good will and accept these recommendations and end the debate.

The Islamic Party of Kenya (IPK), the Muslim Consultative Council (MCC) and the National Muslim Leaders Forum (NAMLEF)

In 1992, a constitutional provision revived multi-party politics in Kenya and opened up more space for citizens to form, join and participate in political organisations other than the ruling party, KANU. The changing political climate motivated Muslims to make efforts to redress their political positioning by becoming more assertive. Consequently, in the atmosphere of political openness and liberation, Muslims organised themselves to participate in politics by forming the Islamic Party of Kenya (IPK).[20] The government declined its registration on the grounds that it was a religiously based political party and the constitution did not allow that.

Because IPK was denied registration, Muslims felt that SUPKEM could lead in the new political dispensation, but its constitution categorically prohibited its active participation in political matters. For a while, Muslims faced a predicament. Were they to be totally oblivious and not air their views on the constitutional review process? Some Muslims thought avoiding any kind of engagement while Kenyan society was undergoing a transformation was undesirable. Muslims needed to join other Kenyans in participating in matters that affected their nation. Through consultations, a loosely established group came into existence; it called itself the Muslim Consultative Council (MCC). Members of the MCC were Muslim individuals who felt they were capable of making positive contributions to the reform process in Kenya. MCC started to agitate for a particular Muslim view, always talking in terms of 'this is the Islamic point of view' and 'this is what Muslims will contribute' in its public statements. The MCC considered itself part of the mainstream group but wanted to provide an 'alternative view' separate from the one SUPKEM was projecting. Indeed, SUPKEM continued to receive invitations to air the views of Muslims in various forums. In the constitutional review process, it was noticed that two bodies were

---

[19] Ahmed Abdalla, Director General, SUPKEM, to Al-Haj A Wabomba, Executive Officer, SUPKEM, 21 October 1983, with instruction that this information should be given to the Hon. Khalif when he came to the office.
[20] For a general history of the formation of IPK see Hassan Ndzohvu (2014), *Muslims in Kenyan Politics: Political Involvement, Marginalization, and Minority Status*, Evanston: Northwestern University Press, pp. 86–94.

now claiming to represent Muslims. Initially this appeared a strategy by the Muslims to increase their representation in the constitutional review process. In fact, the MCC re-organised itself by forming an MCC Muslim sister wing, as the voice of Muslim women, which demanded to be 'heard' separately from the 'brothers'. A strategy likely to increase the 'voices' representing Muslims, it proved fatal regarding the desire for a consolidated Muslim opinion on the process of reviewing the constitution of Kenya. Different opinions from Muslims began to emerge in response to the drafting of the Constitution of Kenya Review Act. The state, through the Attorney General, drafted the Act. Civic society was required to have an input into the draft. After a long discussion of the draft, the stakeholders agreed to nominate a committee that would redraft the Constitution of Kenya Review Act to be in line with the interest of the various stakeholders. Elected to represent Muslims was Abida Ali Aroni, a female Muslim lawyer who found herself in the review process as a representative of the MCC sisters' wing.[21] Her participation as a representative of Muslims was immediately challenged by Ahmed Khalif, who claimed he was the rightful person to represent Muslims by virtue of his being Secretary General of SUPKEM. Khalif also claimed the Council had accumulated a wealth of experience in the matter of representing Muslims, as opposed to the MCC, which he described as a 'minor and loosely formulated organization that did not have a wide experience on issues concerning Muslims'. Other Muslims did not have confidence in Ahmed Khalif, on two grounds. First, as a former KANU MP, he was associated with a political organisation accused of sabotaging the constitutional review process. Second, as Secretary General of SUPKEM he was associated with an organisation considered by many Muslims to have been inefficient in its previous representative functions. Of course, Ahmed Khalif had been in this 'game' and was not going to give up easily, so he sought to undermine MCC's choice of Ms Aroni. He claimed that, according to Islam, a woman (in this case, Abida) could not be allowed to lead the *umma* and insisted that MCC must withdraw its support for her. Ahmed Khalif's sentiments were echoed by another conservative Muslim organisation, the Council of Imams and Preachers of Islam in Kenya (CIPK), whose chairman protested the appointment of Abida, claiming that she was not a 'shaykh or a recognized leader in the Muslim community'.[22] Eventually, both CIPK and SUPKEM were unable to prevail over MCC support for Abida Aroni to represent Muslims in the drafting committee, signalling that mainstream Muslim representative groups could be challenged by other groups previously on the margins.

---

[21] Others included Abdulrahman Wandati, Murtaza Jafaar, Ahmed Khalif and Yusuf Murigua.
[22] Shaykh Ali Shee, quoted in the *East African Standard* of 1 July 1998.

The challenge posed to SUPKEM by MCC was not new; there had always been some sporadic protests against the council, particularly when it appeared to represent a government position on matters concerning Islam and Muslims. For instance, in the mid-1990s, Shaykh Ali Shee, the imam of Jamia Mosque, one of the more central mosques in Nairobi, openly defied some of the council members by arguing that SUPKEM leaders should be more democratic, rather than having leaders who always agreed with the government. The most salient protest against SUPKEM came from the Islamic Party of Kenya (IPK). The IPK was formed in January 1992, just as the Kenyan government, in response to international pressure, was legalising political parties. IPK was the main political force in Mombasa in the December 1992 elections. This party had been critical of the government's contention that there could be no religious parties, arguing that Christians led all the existing political parties. From 1992 to 1994, its unofficial leader was Khalid Balala, a fiery preacher who had returned to Kenya in 1990 from studies in Saudi Arabia. In 1992, clashes between the IPK and the government were particularly violent, with police stations and public buildings attacked and cars set on fire. Several of the demonstrators were killed or wounded by the police. Demonstrations, strikes and violence would continue until 1994 in the coastal area, especially Mombasa. In 2007, the National Muslim Leaders Forum (NAMLEF) signed a Memorandum of Understanding (MoU) with the leader of the Orange Democratic Movement (ODM) prior to the December 2007 parliamentary and presidential elections. In the agreement, NAMLEF committed to mobilising support for Odinga's presidential bid in exchange for infrastructure and educational support for marginalised areas. Odinga was probably attempting to gain political support and promote the rift between the Muslim community and President Kibaki with this agreement. Interestingly, SUPKEM denounced the pact because the Council had not been consulted and because it did not benefit all Kenyan Muslims, but only those concentrated on the coast and in the north-east. All political parties rejected the pact on the grounds that it incited religious animosity. These activities further signalled the difficulties faced by groups who claimed to be representatives of the Muslim communities in Kenya.

Conclusion

Representing the 'Muslim voice' from the perspective of SUPKEM meant justification of the legitimacy of claims to a course of action. This legitimation process was contingent on the occupation of local institutional space (national, then transnational and global) and the regulation of subject matters (personal laws, constitutional review process, electoral bodies). This chapter has deconstructed the jostling over the legitimacy to represent Muslims that involved SUPKEM and its internal disputations regarding authority. By tracing SUPKEM's evolution, this chapter has shown that the process of articulating representativeness became a functional resource for powerful Muslim elites and actors, but also a source of contestations benefiting occupants of other political and social margins (women, professionals, ulama) who subsequently advocated for reforms and challenged the representative claims of SUPKEM. A historical perspective on the organisations and the elites that have claimed to represent Muslims in Kenya suggests the presence of diverse 'Muslim voices' and 'Muslim views', making the claims of uniformity of ideas and approaches impossible.

Bibliography

Chome, N. (2019), 'From Islamic Reform to Muslim Activism: Evolution of an Islamist Ideology in Kenya', *African Affairs*. doi 10.1093/afraf/adz003.

Fitzgerald, A. (2000), 'Security Council Reform: Creating a More Representative Body of the Entire UN membership', *Pace International Law Review*, 12(2), pp. 321–65.

Hansen, H. and Michael, T. (eds) (1995), *Religion and Politics in East Africa*, London: James Currey.

Haynes, J. (1996), *Religion and Politics in Africa*, Nairobi: East Africa Educational Publishers.

Kresse, K. (2009), 'Muslim Politics in Post-colonial Kenya: Negotiating Knowledge on the Double Periphery', *Journal of the Royal Anthropological Institute*, 15(1), pp. 76–94.

Kroger, S. and Friedrich, D. (eds) (2011), *The Challenge of Democratic Representation in the European Union*, New York, NY: Palgrave Macmillan.

Mckeon, N. (2009), *The United Nations and Civil Society: Legitimizing Global Governance – Whose Voice?*, London: Zed Books.

Mwakimako, H. and Justin Willis (2015), 'Islam and Democracy: Debating Electoral Involvement on the Kenya Coast', *Islamic Africa* 7(1), pp. 19–43.

Ndzovu, H. J. (2014), *Muslims in Kenya Politics: Political Involvement, Marginalization and Minority Status*, Evanston, IL: Northwestern University Press.

Oded, A. (2000), *Islam and Politics in Kenya*, London: Lynne Rienner.

Pitkin, H. (1967), *The Concept of Representation*, Berkeley: University of California Press.

Sawad, M. (2010), *The Representative Claim*, Oxford: Oxford University Press.

Steffek, J. and K. Hahn (eds) (2010), *Evaluating Transnational NGOs: Legitimacy, Accountability, Representation*, Basingstoke: Palgrave Macmillan.

9

Muslim Networks, Public Services and Development Intervention in Post-socialist Tanzania: Between Liberalisation and Alienation

FELICITAS BECKER

INTRODUCTION

The period since around 1990 is typically seen in Tanzania as one of both political and economic liberalisation, and of increasing discontent among Muslims, but the relationship between these two developments has rarely been addressed (but see Kaiser 1996). At the level of governance, the government reduced its control over the media, privatised publicly owned companies, adopted a 'market-based' economic model and returned to multi-party elections, the first being held in 1995. As concerns grew over Islamic political activism and Islamist dissent, the landmark events included, on the political plane, the ascendance of the Civic United Front (CUF) opposition party, widely seen as at least implicitly Islamist; the controversy over Zanzibar's attempt to join the Organisation of the Islamic Conference; and the now long-running debate over the re-introduction of Islamic courts. At the level of civic unrest and repression, they included the riots around the mosque of Mwembechai, Dar es Salaam, in 1998; the involvement of Tanzanians in the Al-Qaeda-led embassy bombings the same year; the contribution of Tanzanian security services to the repression of Islamic/Islamist organisations post-9/11; and more recently, the rise and repression of the *uamsho* preaching movement in Zanzibar, which is both Islamist and separatist.

The two trends, of liberalisation and the rise of Islamic activism and protest, can thus be seen as running in parallel, with the retreat of the state from control of the public sphere in the role of facilitator of the efflorescence of Islamist activism. In discussions on Muslims in contemporary Tanzania, moreover, the shift towards political activism and dissent tends to dominate views of Islam in the country post-1990. Given the potential repercussions of Muslims' discontent in this multi-religious context, this is hardly surprising. Nevertheless, in the discussion that follows here, I seek to both qualify the impression of pervasive alienation between Muslims and the state and to examine how liberalisation may have contributed to this alienation, such as it was, in ways that were more complex than merely making space for it in the public sphere.

The discussion that follows suggests that the relation between Muslim congregations and the Tanzanian state does not fall into neat phases. Rather, it is characterised by a mixture of concurrent interactions that recur in different guises. Perhaps the most striking recurrence is that of 'working misunderstandings': situations where representatives of Muslim constituencies on the one hand, and those of state and/or donor authorities on the other, co-operate on aims that they use the same terms to define, while *interpreting* these shared terms very differently. Moreover, as will be seen, even Muslim activists who seek to define their activities in contradistinction to official and donor discourse nevertheless engage with this discourse. Historians of Africa will recognise this process, of state authorities and/or donors setting the terms of discourse, while different constituencies within society more or less discreetly reinterpret them, as of long standing, as similar processes have long been charted in colonial-era indirect rule.

To develop these thoughts, I focus on issues surrounding the delivery of HIV/AIDS services around 2010, when AIDS in Tanzania was shifting from a death sentence to a manageable condition thanks to the increasing availability of anti-retroviral drugs. Different health initiatives and different kinds of services, such as education, will be taken into account when setting HIV/AIDS services in a longer timeframe. Taking inspiration from the work of Mohamed Yunus Rafiq, also in this volume, I seek to trace a history of interaction, as well as alienation, between Muslim authority figures and state institutions. While I am mostly concerned with people involved in the delivery of basic public services, due to the prominence of appeals to, and practical attempts at, development in Tanzanian public life, this entails setting out the wider context of Tanzanian developmentalism. I then examine how a variety of Muslim networks, or social networks made up of Muslims, and a variety of authority figures have either sought to connect to the aid providers and development organisations in the 'post-statist' period since the 1990s, or, in the case of organisations with an activist Islamic agenda, have sought to define themselves in contradistinction to them.

Examination of these processes delivers three intermediate points that underpin the broader observations about recurrent stances and working misunderstandings. Firstly, despite the end of the aggressively statist model of development intervention that characterised *ujamaa*-era Tanzania, state institutions continue to interpose themselves carefully within the 'aid milieu', structuring interactions between providers and recipients of funds. There is thus no neat succession from a 'statist' to an 'NGO-driven' model in the delivery of health services. Concomitantly, and secondly, there is no uni-directional change in Muslims' stances towards and involvement in the delivery of aid interventions, the overall rise in oppositional Islamic activism notwithstanding. Rather, there are criss-crossing movements towards engagement on the one hand and rejection on the other. Third, in a context where Muslim Tanzanians need funds and aid organisations need to spend funds, the different sides in these unstable interactions become useful to each other in ways that are both asymmetrical and, nevertheless, mutual. To trace how this situation arises, it is necessary first to examine donor stances on so-called faith-based organisations in Tanzania.

A word is needed on my use of the terms 'Muslim constituencies/networks/ groups' and 'Muslim authority figures/intermediaries'. I use these relatively unspecific terms, rather than 'Muslim communities' or 'sheikhs', because they better reflect the contingent and fluid character of the groups and actors in question. It has become very evident in the period since the 1990s that Muslims in Tanzania do not constitute one interconnected community, or even series of such communities. Rather, specific groups and individuals come together in response to specific inspirations or challenges. Similarly, the people who emerge as leaders in a given context do so because they have placed themselves at specific conjunctures of the needs and preferences of Muslim constituencies on the one hand, and donors and/or government representatives on the other. For a variety of reasons, they are able to mediate between them, often in the process of what I have termed a working misunderstanding. The next section examines the context constituted by the aid world.

The 'Aid Milieu' and its Muslim Others in Tanzania

In the context of liberalisation in Tanzania since around 1990, so-called civil society organisations (CSOs) have been positioned as guarantors of a level of efficiency and accountability in social service provision that the state had failed to deliver (Semboja and Therkildsen1996; Ferguson 2006). As part of this shift, specifically 'faith-based organisations' (FBOs) have become a regular feature of the delivery of services, especially in health and education (Abrahamsen 2000; Mercer 2003; Green 2012). This chapter, however, starts from, and confirms, the observation that these organisations are at least as likely to come into being in response to donor initiatives to support and empower them as they are to pre-exist these efforts (Green et al. 2010). In other words, aid organisations' institutional framing of the social world they seek to influence encourages the emergence of particular institutional arrangements (Hulme and Edwards 1996; Igoe and Kelsall 2005).

To elaborate: in their quest for local partners to support, aid organisations confront a fluid social world and seek to divide it up into distinguishable and above all supportable entities. A variety of social actors, in their turn, seek to position themselves so as to be visible and qualify for support. For Tanzanian Christians, the Christian Social Services Commission (CSSC), made up of delegates from the major 'mainline', ex-mission churches, has been particularly successful in arranging and providing the institutional structures for co-operative ventures between long-established Christian denominations and government and international donors (Leurs et al. 2011). Less institutionalised Christian congregations, especially among the newer Pentecostal churches, do not participate in these circuits to anything like the same extent (see Dilger 2005).

Muslim congregations, meanwhile, long remained much less visible to the FBO-seeking gaze of international donors, as their informal, networked structures are harder to frame in donors' categories. This outcome forms part of a broader pattern. While Christian churches since the beginning of colonialism tended to be 'surrogates of the state' (Jennings 2008) in terms of service provision, Muslim congregations remained opaque to both colonial and post-colonial officials. Muslim clerics have never been organised into or employed by formal institutions that would parallel the integrated organisational structures of major churches such as the Anglican or Catholic churches. They traditionally depend on donations motivated by respect for their religious role, payment for specific religious services such as weddings or judgments under religious law, or entirely non-religious enterprises such as trading for their livelihoods (Lapidus 2009). Although Muslim religious experts were and are routinely involved in the dispensing of charity, they rarely became visible as representatives of formal, thus familiar, institutions to government officials' gaze.

The institutional structures of Muslim charity and education, then, have been less intelligible to the Tanzanian state than Christian ones, all the more so as Christians tended to predominate among state officials. Early on, the German colonial government investigated Muslim charitable foundations (*awqaf*) as tax avoidance schemes (TNA G 9/39:7), and the post-colonial government shut down the East African Muslim Welfare Society on charges that it lacked nationalist commitment (Nimtz 1980). Although Sufi sheikhs have long worked as teachers and healers, and Sufi chapters double as informal support networks and burial societies, neither colonial officials nor post-colonial ones treated them as potential partners in service provision. To a large extent, this is likely to be due to the lack of understanding for Muslims' organisational structures, as just set out. Moreover, Islamic education was not seen to add to its recipients' value in the labour market to the same extent as its Christian counterpart. Among Muslims, Qur'anic education was closely related to the colonial rise and post-colonial decline of Sufism, which posited an esoteric relationship between teachers and disciples and focused more on ritual and religious than on labour-market-relevant skills. Recently, reformist Muslim organisations that sought to constitute themselves on more formal lines have faced mistrust over their suspected political agendas (Loimeier 2007; Becker 2008).

This state of affairs affects a great number of people. Although religious affiliation is not covered in censuses, it is clear that Muslims form, at the least, a very large minority in Tanzania (Westerlund 1981; Ludwig 1999). Due to the close association between Christian missions and secondary education, Muslims are consistently underrepresented in secondary and higher education, and by extension in the higher levels of state administration. This marginalisation not only deepens divisions between Muslim and Christian constituencies, but also complicates interactions between Muslim organisations and Western donors, which in turn become more nervous about Islamic radicalism (Loimeier 2007; Becker 2008). Overall, then, Muslims' relationship with the 'aid sector' is weaker and more fraught than that of Christian constituencies.

Nevertheless, it is not non-existent. There is a tradition of philanthropy practised by wealthy Muslims that led to the provision of Dar es Salaam's first hospital, the Sewa Hajji Hospital, and played a crucial role in the history of Muslim education in Zanzibar (Bang 2004). Moreover, current Islamist criticism of the Tanzanian state reflects in part a sense of betrayal arising from Muslims' initially very strong endorsement of the post-colonial political project. Their alienation was gradual. For the 1960s, informants in Lindi on the southern coast remembered the most prominent Sufi leader of the time endorsing public health programmes, taking the lead in lining up for vaccination campaigns (Becker 2008). To this day, many politically quiescent Muslims would see no contradiction in such actions. To some extent, recent political activism by Muslims is driven by a generational conflict between the leaders of Muslim congregations who came to prominence in the early post-independence period and a younger cohort less invested in the national project (Becker 2006).

Some younger Muslim activists, meanwhile, find it easier to position themselves with reference to donor-compatible taxonomies of social activity than the older generation – partly, but not only, because Anglophone donors are no longer the only ones in town. Moreover, there are groups of Muslims who invoke a different social identity – such as that of 'village women' – rather than emphasising religion. For them, in some instances their religious identity can help validate and 'make visible', in the universe of aid donors, shared social practices that feed into broader livelihood strategies. They have thus been able to work with dominant notions of faith-based organisations. The following pages examine different cases of Muslims interacting with the aid industry. They highlight the tensions between donors' notions of representatives of various religions as contributors to social service delivery, and the longer-standing concerns around social co-operation, public morality and religious legitimacy that inform Muslims' social practice and charity. These tensions can be traced further in the case of services related to HIV/AIDS.

The Institutional Framework of AIDS Activism in Tanzania: PEPFAR, BAKWATA and TACAIDS

As stated above, the elaboration of a 'voluntary sector' in Tanzania is closely linked to the idea of civil society organisations as a potential answer to African states' institutional weaknesses and democracy deficits. In the following paragraphs, it will be examined in particular in relation to Muslims' participation, or lack of it, in the 'faith-based' provision of AIDS education, counselling and testing; an area where the participation of faith-based providers is built into the plans (PEPFAR 2010).

The US-funded President's Emergency Fund for Aids Relief (PEPFAR), which was established by the George Bush administration under the direct influence of American Christian organisations (Dietrichs 2007), forms an important node in the web of organisations promoting the involvement of CSOs and FBOs in AIDS service provision. In Tanzania, where Christian churches have played a well-established role in health infrastructure going back to the 'medical missions' of the colonial period, their facilities have readily fallen in line with this approach (interview with Mihayo Mageni Bupamba, AMREF office, Dar es Salaam, 2005; Hashim Kalinga, TACAIDS, Dar es Salaam, 2008). By contrast, involving Muslim organisations in AIDS education, prevention and testing proved more difficult. In part, this is due to political history: the institutionally strongest Muslim welfare organisation in the region, the East African Muslim Welfare Society (EAMWS), was shut down on government orders in 1968. This was in keeping with the pronounced 'statism' of Tanzania's government at the time, but also was plausibly connected to the strength of South Asian participation in EAMWS, which fell foul of the racial nationalism then current in the country (Westerlund 1981; Brennan 2012).

The government sought to replace and extend the functions of EAMWS with the founding of the National Muslim Council of Tanzania (Baraza kuu la Waislamu Tanzania, or BAKWATA). But, as has been repeatedly observed (see e.g. Nimtz 1980; Leurs et al. 2010), the legitimacy of BAKWATA as representative of Tanzania's Muslims has consistently remained in doubt. Moreover, its organisational structures and finances are considerably weaker than those of Christian churches, which co-ordinate their programmes with the government through the Christian Social Services Commission (CSSC) (Ludwig 1999; interview with Hashim Kalinga, Dar es Salaam, 2012). In addition, with the expansion of denominational pluralism among Tanzanian Muslims from the

1980s on and an extended phase of widespread dissension among Muslims in the 1990s and 2000s, BAKWATA became a focus of criticism by reformist, often Middle Eastern-influenced, Muslim groups, loosely summarised colloquially under the term *Ansuari* (for *Ansaar Sunna*, the companions of the way [of the Prophet]; see Becker 2008).

In this context, attempts by the African Medical Research Foundation (AMREF), an important Tanzanian PEPFAR partner, to include Muslim intermediaries in the distribution of PEPFAR funds initially encountered little success (interview with Mihayo Mageni Bupamba, Dar es Salaam, 2005). While health facilities with Muslim sponsors have become a part of the Tanzanian cityscape (Dilger 2014), Muslims not aligned with BAKWATA express concerns at the possibility of government interference with funding flows and remain distant from official AIDS policy. As for BAKWATA, its efforts have remained limited to its established role as an umbrella organisation for mosques and schools rather than health facilities (interview with Hashim Kalinga, Dar es Salaam, 2012; interview with Muhammad Hamisi Saidi, Dar es Salaam, 2012). Most Muslim groups object to what they see as the sexual permissiveness implied in official AIDS education, ironically falling in line with conservative Christian, especially Catholic, groups (Becker and Geissler 2009; Dilger and Luig 2010; Dilger et al. 2014). Although the official 'ABC' (abstinence, be faithful, use condoms) formula does commend sexual restraint, they feel that there is insufficient emphasis on the need for marriage to legitimise sexual relations. Moreover, the mere use of sexual content in AIDS education is seen as encouraging the inappropriate publicising of sexual appetites and exploits.

Since 2008, the Tanzanian government's commission on AIDS (TACAIDS) has nevertheless sought to encourage religious constituencies, both locally and trans-denominationally, to develop what it calls 'mechanisms' for the use of funds for AIDS control efforts (interviews with Hashim Kalinga, Dar es Salaam, 2008, 2012). It co-operates with the Christian CSSC and works closely with a Muslim umbrella organisation founded in response to its calls, the Tanzanian Muslim Welfare Network (TMWN). Meanwhile, Muslim groups distant from the government have also elaborated their stances on AIDS. The result is an uneven institutional landscape, with different organisational forms and different moral discourses and rationales for medical intervention coexisting and intersecting. This deserves closer examination.

BAKWATA, BAK-AIDS and their Critics

The uneasy relations between BAKWATA and its Muslim critics are played out also on the field of Muslim AIDS activism. Here, a distinction between altruistic and self-seeking behaviour comes into the conversation by way of invective, as the opposed camps question each other's motives and practices. In these circumstances, participation in the institutional practices of the aid world can be used to delegitimise opponents.

With encouragement from TACAIDS, BAKWATA itself initiated its own programme on AIDS, known as BAK-AIDS, or BAKWATA AIDS project. By 2015, it operated in Kilwa, Dar es Salaam, Tanga and Mtwara, among other places, relying on a mixture of Bakwata's official structure and locally recruited volunteers. In 2019, BAK-AIDS was recruiting staff for work in further rural locations with the help of USAID funding. While it described itself as a 'Faith-Based Organisation (FBO) implementing HIV programs to support Tanzania Government efforts to reduce the rate of HIV pandemic', the posts were described as 'Economic Strengthening and Livelihood Officers'. Their remit was to supervise 'Empowerment Workers' and 'National Peer Educators' in their efforts to map economic strengths and weaknesses, run programmes for disadvantaged youth, train and recruit participants for 'village savings and loan schemes' and roll out 'monetary literacy' education programmes (Tanzania-jobs.com, 2018). Direct references to HIV/AIDS patients or the ways of transmission or prevention of the illness, then, were conspicuous by their absence. In effect, BAK-AIDS focused on general livelihood support with interventions very similar to those run by non-religious or Christian NGOs – and indeed fully compatible with a market-based, liberalising approach to development (Becker 2019).

This manner of sidestepping the more controversial aspects of prevention, sexual practice and gender relevant to HIV/AIDS is in keeping with the *Mwongozo*, or 'guidance document', that BAKWATA had published in 2011 (BAKWATA 2011). In the introduction, BAKWATA reiterates its understanding of itself as the organisation for all Muslims in Tanzania. Overall, the document focuses on the need to live properly religious lives to stay safe. Condoms are not mentioned. Nevertheless, it includes language clearly influenced by standard AIDS policy: 'voluntary testing and counselling', 'combatting stigma', 'living with hope' and so on. Moreover, in keeping with official policy, the *Mwongozo* refers to AIDS as a *janga*, or 'disaster/emergency'. As HIV/AIDS is a problem of poverty and economic vulnerability a major cause of transmission, especially for women, there is no reason to disdain this indirect approach. It nevertheless indicates the persistent divisiveness of the questions of public and private morality and gender relations involved in HIV/AIDS.

Muslim organisations distant from BAKWATA, meanwhile, have elaborated their stances on AIDS rather differently. At one of the larger Dar es Salaam religious centres unaffiliated with BAKWATA, the Masjid Sheikhat Issa in Magomeni, the centre's *msimamizi* (manager), Bakari Ali, indirectly challenged Bakwata on its definition of AIDS as a *janga*. Moreover, he connected BAKWATA's inability to advise or speak for Tanzanian Muslims at large to its dependence on state funding, in contrast to the Masjid Sheikat's ability to survive on voluntary contributions from believers. Explicitly referring to Bakwata's use of the term *janga* in his comments, he challenged the organisation's policies, implying that they reflect the beliefs of a partisan minority who pay insufficient attention to the Qur'an. Without denying the value of anti-retroviral treatment (he asserted, in fact, that HIV-positive believers at his mosque were encouraged to seek it and that it had helped in the recovery of many), he insisted that

> Muslims believe, according to their book ... that there is no illness for which there is no medicine ... They disagree with the explanation given elsewhere that AIDS has no cure ... AIDS has a cure. What is its cure? It is to avoid those dirty matters that the Almighty God has prohibited ... [Only] if you have left the Prophet and God's teachings[,] ... now you will see AIDS as a disaster ... Ninety-nine percent of Muslims understand that AIDS is not a disaster ... They consider it an illness ... but an illness with a cure; its cure is the teachings we have in our book. (Interview, Dar es Salaam, 2012)

Not unlike BAKWATA, however, he limited the Masjid's role to providing advice; the 'experts', *wataalamu*, who provide tests, counselling and treatment, were to be found elsewhere. But Ali asserted that BAKWATA could not claim to speak for the Muslim community on AIDS because its leaders were economically self-seeking, including in response to this health crisis:

> They have received [the plans for faith-based provision of AIDS services] as a means to put their lives in order. If you bring them such means, they sort out their own lives ... I don't think they can provide good leadership ... They are not trustworthy ... They were the first Islamic organization [in Tanzania]. They could have provided an example ... as concerns provision of charity ... but you will find that they imitate us ... [Among Muslims,] if someone has wealth, he will donate some of it, for fear of God – if you have three cars, you give one over to the mosque ... BAKWATA had houses that were given as *waqf* [a charitable contribution], eighty of them, here in the city ... If you ask now, they don't have even five ... Where did they go? ... They are given everything by the government ... because they are a department that the government built in order to control us others out here. (Interview, Dar es Salaam, 2012)

The uneasy relations between BAKWATA and its critics in the Muslim community are thus played out over issues of funding and stewardship for the goods BAKWATA inherited from its predecessor EAMWS. BAKWATA acknowledges that it does have *miradi*, or income-generating schemes, including real estate, although the organisation is somewhat vague about its finances. As for the financing of the Sheikhat Issa Islamic Centre, Bakari Ali was open about the fact that it owed its existence, in its present form, to a generous patron in Abu Dhabi, although the day-to-day running of the centre depended on voluntary work and donations. He explained that the school run by the mosque could be considered an income-generating activity because the students pay school fees that are used to maintain the school building and also other parts of the complex. Yet he emphasised that while menial employees, such as the building caretaker and night watchman, were paid, many of the people involved in its core religious and educational activities, including himself, did not draw salaries, but 'had their livelihoods elsewhere'.

An exemplary religious leader, in this perspective, is one who depends on a mixture of charity that is a direct response to the leadership he provides, and this-worldly livelihood strategies that are kept separate from religious interests. This view is not limited to reformist Muslim groups explicitly critical of BAKWATA, like Bakari Ali's. The Sufi centre at the former residence of the Shadhili Sheikh Nuruddin, now deceased, is supported by a tiny shop run by his widow, selling little more than tea leaves and sugar, out of a shed backing onto his courtyard. His young followers proudly assert that they run the Sufi order, both its day-to-day activities and the annual festivals of *mawlid* and *ziara*, on a mixture of *miradi* (such as this shop and the transport of vegetables to urban markets) and contributions from the faithful (interview with Omari Mkwawa, Dar es Salaam, 2012).

Bakwata's vagueness regarding its own finances suggests that critics like Bakari Ali are winning the public argument. While, in 2000, a researcher was told that BAKWATA had received financial assistance from the Middle East (Lange et al. 2000), I was told that its financing was all Tanzanian. Financial support from the government appears nevertheless likely, as it was in fact set up with government support and endorsement, Evidently, financial independence from government enhances the legitimacy of Muslim organisations in present-day Tanzania. That said, the problem does not lie only in mistrust of the state. Rather, the non-state or, in the case of many donor organisations, effectively para-statal bodies that are supposed to aid 'faith-based' providers to step into the gaps left by faltering state provision carry with them very specific assumptions about the 'proper' organisational structures, employment practices, funding streams and moral discourses of such providers. While Sheikhat Issa was a group that actively sought to distance itself from the state, it also found itself positioned at a distance from the non-governmental sector due to the latter's specific expectations and habits. Meanwhile, elsewhere, the government actively tried to bridge the distance between Muslims and AIDS service providers.

Government-brokered Rapprochement between the Aid Industry and Muslim Organisations: TACAIDS and TMWN

Not all Muslim activists seek to keep their distance from the aid world to the same extent as the Sheikhat Issa mosque. In response to the initial call for the establishment of a funding-deployment mechanism among Muslims, a variety of Muslim groups other than BAKWATA met in Dar es Salaam in October 2008 at a hotel owned and run by Muslims in the Kariakoo neighbourhood. I was invited to attend as an observer. The participants were concerned about the recognition of Muslim networks and organisations as equal players with the institutionally stronger Christian ones, and more broadly with Muslim history as an integral part of Tanzania's history. Yet while some participants were ready to sacrifice inclusion in the TACAIDS orbit to the assertion of these political stances, others pragmatically accepted the need to learn 'donor speak' and interact with the aid world.

Attendance at this conference was mixed. Some attendees were religious activists with uncertain professional status, very committed to their voluntary work whether or not it supported their livelihoods. Others had professional status intelligible to donor organisations, and combined their religious orientation with specialised knowledge in law, education or social work. The former resembled the economically independent sheikhs described above; for them, non-religious economic activity was compatible with their status as religious community leaders. For the latter, their status as committed Muslims in a sense added value to their professional profile and enhanced their potential value as religious figures capable of mediating between Muslim constituencies and the aid world. For example, Sheikh Issa Othman, who has served on the central committee of the Tanzania Muslim Welfare Network (TMWN), has worked as a consultant for Western aid organisations on the development of educational material on AIDS for use among Muslims (interview with Issa Othman, Dar es Salaam, 2008). He remains active in health-related NGO interventions (Health Promotion Tanzania 2019). This second group was also more readily accepting of the need to speak donors' language, both literally (in that they were more likely to speak English well) and metaphorically (by adapting jargon, dress styles and manners familiar to donors).

Yet in spite of TACAIDS's technocratic, inclusive and apolitical language, its relations with religious groups were shot through with politics. When TMWN was set up in 2009, its general secretary was a former BAKWATA official. In the mid-2010s, TMWN's leadership combined ex-BAKWATA personnel with people from the younger, more Anglophone and donor-friendly generation. For the younger Muslim professionals, opting into TMWN was not simply a 'charitable' choice but also a political one: an attempt to build a linkage with officialdom separate from BAKWATA. The loose 'network' structure means that local groups with fairly diverse doctrinal stances can opt into or out of it, and by 2012 TMWN had grown into a country-wide organisation. Nevertheless, TACAIDS has complained of tensions caused by the tendency of individual Muslim leaders to question the motives of TACAIDS as well as one another, and to demand funding directly for their specific constituencies (interview with Hashim Kalinga, Dar es Salaam, 2012; see also TMWN 2010). Here, the accusation of *kutafuta maslahi*, seeking a livelihood (through participation in TACAIDS-sponsored activities), came into play.

TMWN's AIDS-related activities, moreover, remained largely subsidiary to its core programmes, the running of mosques and schools. In 'donor speak', AIDS education and counselling was 'mainstreamed' into general pastoral and educational activities. Muslim involvement in anti-AIDS measures does not extend to the hosting of test centres or counselling services of the kind once hoped for by AMREF (interview with Mihayo Mageni Bupamba, Dar es Salaam, 2005). AIDS education in this context continues to exist in a grey area where religious activism forms part of a bundle of livelihood strategies. For some religious activists, TMWN aided professionalisation strategies that enhanced their visibility in the aid world, while for others it probably bolstered their standing in more inward-looking networks of religious notables. These personal agendas have combined with the more explicit political stances of Muslim groups outside BAKWATA to both enable and constrain the interaction between TACAIDS and Muslim constituencies. The dynamics of Muslims' engagement with TACAIDS, then, escape the standard donors' accounts of civil society.

The Rapid Funding Envelope (RFE) for HIV/AIDS in Tanzania and the 'Framing' of Local Actors

Somewhat ironically, given that TMWN came about partly in response to a call by TACAIDS to provide ways of deploying financial resources through Muslim agencies, TACAIDS officials, reflecting the impact of the post-2008 funding crush on the Tanzanian as well as other governments, had moved by 2012 to discourage Muslim organisations from seeking funding directly from them. Instead, they positioned themselves as facilitators for bids for funding from other organisations. In the mid-2010s, their main path to funding lay through participation (along with the Zanzibar AIDS Commission [ZAC], TACAIDS's counterpart in Zanzibar) in the so-called Rapid Funding Envelope for HIV/AIDS (RFE), which is financed by nine bilateral donors (from the United States and northern Europe) and one Dutch private foundation.

The RFE constituted a new departure in the management of anti-AIDS campaigns. The financial oversight was provided by the management consultancy

Deloitte-Touche, whose logo (unlike those of the donors involved) featured prominently on the website (www.rapidfundingenvelope.org), and the involvement of TACAIDS and ZAC was mediated through a US-based charity called Management Sciences for Health. The donors in question thus appeared to have handed a significant degree of control over their contributions to a combination of private and Tanzanian government interests, though presumably the fact that they provided, and could withhold, the funds safeguarded their influence. The steering committee, in its turn, transmitted much of the responsibility for planning activities to the non-governmental and civil society organisations bidding for funds. In effect, rather than the government or its donors drawing up plans, the organisations seeking funds provided plans for the funders to pick and choose from.

The RFE's choice of projects to fund once again highlighted the way participation in CSO activity has come to form part of diversified livelihood strategies that go well beyond the provision of social services. Among the recipients of RFE grants for activities related to AIDS education, stigma reduction and care for AIDS sufferers and orphans, have been both Catholic and Lutheran dioceses, a department of the University of Dar es Salaam, and a department of the Muhimbili national hospital. The list of RFE's beneficiaries also indicates that some Muslims are now successful in accessing funds as representatives of civil society groups – but not necessarily on the basis of their identity as Muslims. One chapter of BAKAIDS based in the Muslim coastal town of Kilwa obtained funding for a project to train 'trainers of trainers' – a typical category of civil society intermediaries in the aid industry – in combating stigma.

Another recipient, the Masasi Women's Development Association (MAWODEA), was an even clearer example of the ability of applicants to frame their activities in accordance with donor demands. Based in the provincial town of Masasi, a religiously mixed settlement in a poor, predominantly Muslim region (see Ranger 1979), this organisation presented its overall aim as one of 'combatting poverty' and its activities as providing training on financial management, business development and entrepreneurship, including the construction of thirty-six solar driers for fruit and vegetables, and the training of 1,683 women in their use (see RFE 2006–14). Its AIDS-related programme was described as one of nutritional education and care for people living with HIV/AIDS, including the 'training of trainers' through workshops and the production of printed information material. From the information provided, it was not clear whether the solar drier trainees were self-identified as people living with HIV/AIDS, although given the prevailing climate of secrecy around AIDS it is unlikely that this number of people would come forward under this rubric. Evidently, then, the civic activity of providing nutrition education for people living with HIV/AIDS was allied to more entrepreneurial and profit-driven activities. Workshops in themselves typically provide income in per diem form.

The grant to MAWODEA thus again highlights the ability of diverse social constituencies, Muslim ones included, to 'frame' their activities in accordance with the specifications of donors. This is not the same as saying that such groups 'mislead' their sponsors, any more than the sponsors dictate their terms to the grantees. Rather, what takes place is best understood as a form of negotiation. The civil society group undertakes to provide civil society activities in terms desirable to the donor, and the donor quietly accepts the likelihood of further unstated agendas being involved. With the small-town women who obtained funding through MAWODEA, donors' notions of faith-based 'civic engagement' as a choice made by individual, autonomous citizens run up against the social world of cultivators for whom co-operation is an essential part of survival. The line between disinterested, altruistic or religiously motivated work and self-interested economic activity here becomes more of a grey area. Nevertheless, the policy framework of the post-statist period here shapes the self-representation of Muslims, rather than merely making space for them.

At present, with the Rapid Funding Envelope closed, the search for funding has moved on. Current support from USAID is mediated through an international development NGO headquartered in Washington, PACT. The language in which BAK-AIDS's PACT-funded activities were framed, quoted above in the section on BAKWATA and its critics, is entirely consonant with current development jargon in Tanzania (Becker 2019, Chapter 8). On the one hand, then, Muslim aid recipients represent and structure their activities so as to make them compatible with technocratic orthodoxies. On the other, and perhaps hopefully, the increasing salience of Islamophobia in American public life has not prevented American funders from extending grants to explicitly Muslim recipients. To an extent, it appears, the mainstream Muslims represented by BAKWATA have arrived in the mainstream of development intervention.

Conclusion

In the account given here, the useful fictions and mis-descriptions that I have referred to as 'framing' above have emerged as central to the working misunderstandings between donors and Muslim constituencies, and thus to the participation of Muslims in the governance of developmental health interventions. As with Mitchell's (1988) influential use of the term, it refers to 'ways of looking at' a social world: the implicit perceptions that operate in conjunction with explicit discourses. These ways of seeing spread within institutional frameworks and among individual actors, and influence what they accept as real, valid and relevant. But while Mitchell sees framing as the work of powerful strangers on the

Egyptian scene, in the present case the process of framing helps officials manage a particular mixture of strength *and* weakness. While donors dictate the English-language terms and hold the purse strings, they also need results; thus they need acceptable intermediaries. They are under pressure to demonstrate effectiveness, and they have to get along with state authorities as well as aid recipients. In the case of RFE, the practical and discursive 'framing' of aid practice and African aid recipients in terms of 'civil society organisations' allowed the different aims and interests of petitioners, administrators and donors to converge in terms that *look* clear on paper, whatever the indeterminacies on the ground. Thus all sides compromised, and all obtained something out of the exchange (Green 2012, 2014).

These 'working misunderstandings' surrounding the interaction between donors and 'faith-based' Muslim constituencies form part of a long tradition of Africans adopting particular public personas so as to link up to foreigners with resources and power. They establish a faint yet suggestive resemblance between today's aid officials and colonial administrators of yore, ever seeking to identify legitimate leaders (then, of 'tribes', as now of 'civil society') (see Pels 1996). Consequently, we find, at the interface of Muslim networks on the one hand and donors and funders on the other, a variety of configurations of activism, self-interest and service, and a variety of religious figures with idiosyncratic forms of legitimacy. Sheikh Issa Othman, fluent in English, well-connected in the aid 'scene', but also credible as a Muslim activist, was a kind of 'faith-based' intermediary who conformed well to the expectations that schemes such as RFE implicitly posit. Meanwhile, Bakari Ali, the volunteer-manager, an activist but not a religious specialist, at Masjid Sheikhat Issa, is perhaps best understood as working his way towards the status of elder in his chosen Muslim community: a patron in the making, drawing on funding from outside the development machine. In contrast to Issa Othman, his strategy depends on his keeping a distance from 'Western' funding streams and models of organisation; his role remains invisible to donors on the Anglophone aid scene.

In a manner observed by Brown and Green (2015), these religious figures move between representing a community to the aid world and helping to manage it from a vantage point within that world. They are intermediaries who have to actively manage their credibility with their constituencies. This involves adopting stances, sometimes explicitly, sometimes implicitly, on a plethora of ethical, social and political issues, from condom use to the political status of Muslims in today's Tanzania. These ramifications of their positions make clear how much is elided by the concept of the 'faith-based organisation' when it is posited as denoting plucky members of civil society, doing their bit for accountable service delivery. The issue is not that people like Othman do not contribute to both civic involvement and service delivery as donors understand them; they may well do so (though this is not to be taken for granted). But they do so within a force field of religious, social and political divisions, as well as personal aims, convictions and needs. Personal legitimation, political partisanship and livelihoods are all in play.

The observer may be tempted to ask what is gained by stating that donors' discursive framings elide these factors, given that the Tanzanian Muslim partners in these interactions rarely appear in a position to explicitly challenge the framings, manipulating them instead. One answer is that acknowledging these undercurrents helps 'de-normalise' donor speak, identifying it as a specific political and ideological practice, rather than a neutral description of African realities and humanitarian desiderata. Acknowledgement of this political character, in turn, makes clearer that these discursive framings, willingly or not, contribute to the process of state-making in Africa. Observed carefully, they allow us to see that the constituencies involved in and responding to this process are more diverse than narrowly focused political accounts of African states would suggest (see Abrahamsen 2000). In other words, despite their conflicted, at times alienated, relationship with the Tanzanian state, Muslim constituencies are active players.

Both the powers (sometimes unwitting) of donors *and* their limits become evident when one examines the interaction between Muslim networks and AIDS-related funders seeking channels of faith-based provision. Bakwata's and TMWN's documents on AIDS and the institutional structures supported by the RFE all show the effort to engage with and become acceptable within donors' framing of Tanzanian society, 'civil society' activism and aid provision. But there are limits to this adaptability, as is evident, for instance, in the silence of all these publications and organisations on condom use, despite its centrality in the European anti-AIDS campaigns that served as templates (Iliffe 2006). Donors' framings, in other words, have real effects on institutional practice, but they cannot simply override the religious or ideological commitments of the Tanzanian actors involved. While donors in many ways dictate the terms of the engagement with their Tanzanian constituencies, they also have to make themselves complicit in their redeployments of them. Donors' power here seems peculiarly unstable.

Returning to the issue raised in the introduction, of political and economic liberalisation in Tanzania doing more than merely 'making space' for Islamic activism, the substance of this claim is now clearer. Muslim authority figures, activists and congregations interacted with donor institutions pursuing various refractions of neoliberal policy programmes in a process of negotiation, borrowing, crossover and occasional rejection. While the Muslim parties to the interaction largely maintained their distance from positions proposed in the aid world that signalled social liberalism in matters of gender and the family, organisations like BAK-AIDS and MAWODEA have bought into the language of personal entrepreneurialism and financial responsibility. And yet, whether individualisation is the method or effect of their projects on the ground is an open question; the Masasi example hardly makes it likely. The fungibility of the prescriptions emanating from the aid world is intrinsic to their influence.

These observations highlight the necessity for caution when examining how neoliberal ideology and interventions work themselves out in Africa (Ferguson 2006). 'Neoliberalism' is not always a giant bestriding contemporary Africa, imposing a narrow yet destructive agenda for state roll-back and so-called free markets (Harvey 2007). Rather, it is likely that some of the European donors involved in an operation like the RFE have priorities in sympathy with European notions of social democracy. Conversely, the rhetoric of individual entrepreneurialism appears to have become if anything stronger in Tanzania in the 2010s, even as it lost some of its triumphalism on the world stage in the aftermath of the financial crisis. Yet even if civil society initiatives are conceived of as an alternative to state provision, TACAIDS's role shows that the government remains closely involved. In the case of MAWODEA, neither donors nor the central government had direct oversight of the group's actual activities, and the women involved had some choice, both in whether to get involved and in how to do so. The framing of the operation as a civil society venture provided a rationale for the provision of funds, whose enabling effects may well have outweighed any constraints imposed by the 'CSO' label. In this sense, the category of CSO was very useful to these rural women.

For aid recipients with an explicitly reformist Muslim identity, meanwhile, alternatives to funding streams 'tainted', so to speak, by their association with the Tanzanian state were clearly welcome, as in the example of the Sheikhat Issa mosque complex. For them, the 'mainstream' aid world was, as it were, not 'non-governmental' enough, as they were clearly aware of the Western provenance of its funds, protocols and prescriptions. Muslims without a reformist agenda, however, were able to pursue opportunities, and provide benefits, here. As is evident in Sheikh Issa Othman's 'straddling' of these worlds, considerable effort and skill were needed for brokerage between them. Nevertheless, the passages made by the likes of Issa Othman serve as a reminder that development intervention and religious practice arguably have more in common than is always appreciated. After all, both are ways of confronting uncertain futures and the painful limitations of imperfect lives.

Bibliography

Interviews
Ali, Bakari. Interviewed at Sheikhat Issa Mosque, Magomeni, July 2012.
Bin Juma, Mze. Mingoyo, 9 August 2000.
Hamisi, Bi Kombe. Lindi-Mapinduzi, 24 October 2003.

Kalinga, Hashim. Tanzania Commission on AIDS (TACAIDS), Dar es Salaam, October 2008 and July 2012.
Lipyoga, Bushiri Bakari. Rwangwa-Dodoma, 9 October 2003.
Mageni Bupamba, Mihayo. AMREF Tanzania, Dar es Salaam, 13 June 2005.
Makolela, Issa. Rwangwa-Likangara, 3 September 2003.
Mbwana Maalim, Hassan, Shehe. Lindi-Ndoro, 5 November 2000.
Mfaume, Mwalimu. Kilwa-Pande, 19 June 2004.
Mkwawa, Omari. Shadhili Center, Udoe Street, Kariakoo, Dar es Salaam, July 2012.
Mwichande, Mohamed bin Saidi. Kilwa-Masoko, 17 June 2004.
Othman, Issa, Sheikh. Blue Pearl Hotel, Dar es Salaam, June 2008.
Saidi, Muhammad Hamisi. BAKWATA, Dar es Salaam, 26 July 2012.
Zubeiri, Fadhil. Lindi-Mikumbi, 24 July 2000.

Archival material

Tanzania National Archives (TNA), TNA G9/39, German-period correspondence on religious movements.
Tanzania National Archives (TNA), TNA G 9/39:7, Letter from Bezirksamt Kilwa to Government, Dar es Salaam, 25 September 1897.

Books and periodicals

Abrahamsen, Rita (2000), *Disciplining Democracy: Development Discourse and Good Governance in Africa*, London: Zed Books.
Ahmed, Chanfi (2008), *Les conversions à l'Islam fondamentaliste en Afrique au Sud du Sahara*, Paris: L'Harmattan.
Amin, Ash (2005), 'Local Community on Trial', *Economy and Society* 34, pp. 612–33.
BAKWATA (National Muslim Council of Tanzania) (2011), 'Mwongozo on AIDS', Dar es Salaam: BAKWATA.
Bang, Anne (2004), *Sufis and Scholars of the Sea: Family Networks in East Africa*, London: Routledge.
Becker, Felicitas (2006), 'Rural Islamism during the "War on Terror": A Tanzanian Case Study', *African Affairs* 105 (421), pp. 583–603.
Becker, Felicitas (2008), *Becoming Muslim in Mainland Tanzania*, Oxford: Oxford University Press.
Becker, Felicitas and Wenzel Geissler (eds) (2009), *AIDS and Religious Practice in Africa*, Leiden: Brill.
Becker, Felicitas (2019), *The Politics of Poverty: Development and Policy-Making in Tanzania*, Cambridge: Cambridge University Press.
Brennan, James (2012), *Taifa: Making Nation And Race in Urban Tanzania*, Athens: Ohio University Press.
Brown, Hannah and Maia Green (2015), 'At the Service of Community Development: The Professionalization of Volunteer Work in Kenya and Tanzania', *African Studies Review* 58(2), pp. 63–84.
Dietrichs, John W. (2007), 'The Politics of PEPFAR: The President's Emergency Plan for AIDS Relief', *Ethics and International Affairs* 21, pp. 277–92.
Dilger, Hansjoerg (2005), *Leben mit AIDS: Krankheit, Tod und soziale Beziehungen in Afrika*, Frankfurt: Campus Verlag.

Dilger, Hansjoerg (2014), 'Claiming Territory: Medical Mission, Interreligious Revivalism, and the Spatialization of Health Intervention in Urban Tanzania', *Medical Anthropology* 33, pp. 52–67.

Dilger, Hansjoerg and Ute Luig (eds) 2010, *Morality, Hope and Grief: Anthropologies of AIDS in Africa*, Oxford: Berghahn.

Ferguson, J. (2006), *Global Shadows: Africa in the Neoliberal World Order*, Durham, NC: Duke University Press.

Geertz, Clifford (1971), *Islam Observed: Religious Development in Morocco and Indonesia*, Chicago: University of Chicago Press.

Glassman, Jonathon (1995), *Feasts and Riot: Revelry, Rebellion and Popular Consciousness on the Swahili Coast, 1856–1888*, Oxford: James Currey.

Goebel, Jan, Martin Gornig and Hartmut Haeusserman (2010), *Polarisierung der Einkommen: die Mittelschicht verliert. Wochenbericht des DIW no. 24/2010*, Berlin: Deutsches Institut fuer Wirtschaftsforschung.

Green, Maia (2014), *The Development State: Aid, Culture and Civil Society in Tanzania*, Oxford: James Currey.

Green, Maia (2010), 'Making Development Agents: Participation as Boundary Object in International Development', *Journal of Development Studies* 46(7), pp. 1,240–63.

Green, Maia (2012), 'Anticipatory Development: Mobilising Civil Society in Tanzania', *Critique of Anthropology* 32, pp. 309–33.

Green, Maia, Claire Mercer and Simeon Mesaki (2010), *The Development Activities, Values and Performance of Non-governmental and Faith-Based Organisations in Magu and Newala Districts, Tanzania*, Working Paper 49. Birmingham: Religions and Development Research Consortium.

The Guardian (2011), 'Clegg Admits Parental Job Boost Amid Crackdown on Unpaid Internships', 5 April.

The Guardian (2012), 'Internships Should Be Subject to Labour Market Rules, Says Social Mobility Tsar', 30 May.

Harvey, David (2007), *A Brief History of Neoliberalism*, New York: Oxford University Press.

Health Promotion Tanzania (2019), https://www.healthpromotiontanzania.org/index.php/en/

Hulme, David and Michael Edwards (eds) (1996), *NGOs, States and Donors: Too Close for Comfort?* Basingstoke: Macmillan.

Hyden, Goran (1981), *Beyond Ujamaa in Tanzania: Underdevelopment and an Uncaptured Peasantry*, Berkeley: University of California Press.

Igoe, Jim and Tim Kelsall (eds) (2005), *Between a Rock and a Hard Place: African NGOs, Donors and the State*, Durham, NC: Carolina Academic Press.

Iliffe, John (2006), *The African AIDS Epidemic: A History*, Cambridge: Cambridge University Press.

Jennings, Michael (2008), *Surrogates of the State: NGOs, Development and the State in Tanzania*, Bloomfield, CT: Kumarian.

Kaiser, Paul (1996) 'Structural Adjustment and the Fragile Nation: The Demise of Social Unity in Tanzania', *The Journal of Modern African Studies* 34(2), pp. 227–37.

Lange, Siri, Helge Wallevik and Andrew Kiondo (2006), *Civil Society in Tanzania*, Bergen: CMI Report R 2000.

Lapidus, Ira (2012), *Islamic Societies to the Nineteenth Century: A Global History*, Cambridge: Cambridge University Press.

Leurs, Robert, Peter Tumaini-Mungu and Abu Mvungi (2011), *Mapping the Development Activities of Faith-based Organisations in Tanzania*, Religions and Development Working Paper 58. Birmingham: University of Birmingham.

Loimeier, Roman (2007), 'Perceptions of Marginalisation: Muslims in Contemporary Tanzania', in Rene Otayek and Benjamin F. Soares (eds), *Islam and Muslim Politics in Africa*, London: Palgrave McMillan, pp. 136–56.

Loimeier, Roman (2009), *Between Social Skills and Marketable Skills: The Politics of Islamic Education in 20th Century Zanzibar*, Leiden: Brill.

Ludwig, Frieder (1999), *Church and State in Tanzania: Aspects of a Changing Relationship*, Leiden: Brill.

Mercer, Claire (2003), 'Performing Partnership: Civil Society and The Illusions of Good Governance in Tanzania', *Political Geography* 22, pp. 741–63.

Mitchell, Timothy (1988), *Colonising Egypt*, Berkeley: University of California Press.

Mosse, David (2011), *Adventures in Aidland: The Anthropology of Professionals in International Development*, Oxford: Berghahn.

Nimtz, August (1980), *Islam and Politics in East Africa*, Minneapolis: University of Minnesota Press.

Pels, Peter (1996), 'The Pidginisation of Luguru Politics: Administrative Ethnography and the Paradoxes of Indirect Rule', *American Ethnologist* 23(4), pp. 738–61.

PEPFAR Tanzania (2010), *COP Report*. www.pepfar.gov.

Perlin, Ross (2012), *Intern Nation: How to Earn Nothing and Learn Little in the Brave New Economy*, London: Verso.

Phillips, Lynne and Suzan Ilcan (2004), 'Capacity-Building: The Neoliberal Governance of Development', *Canadian Journal of Development Studies/Revue canadienne détudes du développement* 25(3), pp. 393–409.

Ponte, Stefano (1999), *Farmers and Markets: Policy Reform, Agrarian Change and Rural Livelihoods in Tanzania*, London: Hurst.

Ranger, Terence (1979), 'European Attitudes and African Realities: The Rise and Fall of the Matola Chiefs of South-East Tanzania', *Journal of African History* 20, pp. 69–82.

Rapid Funding Envelope for AIDS in Tanzania (RFE) (2006–14), *Awards Summary, Rounds 0–4*, www.rapidfundingenvelope.org.

Savage, Mike et al. (2013), 'A New Model of Social Class: Findings from the BB's Great British Class Survey Experiment', *Sociology* 47, pp. 219–50.

Schneider, Leander Gunther (2014), *Government of Development: Peasants and Politicians in Postcolonial Tanzania*, Bloomington: Indiana University Press.

Semboja, Joseph and Ole Therkildsen (1996), *Service Provision under Stress in East Africa: The State, NGOs and People's Organizations in Kenya, Tanzania and Uganda*, Portsmouth, NH: Heinemann.

Seppaelae, Pekka (1998), *Diversification and Accumulation in Rural Tanzania: Anthropological Perspectives on Village Economics*, Uppsala: Nordisk Afrikainstitutet.

Stebbins, Richard (1996), 'Volunteering: A Serious Leisure Perspective', *Nonprofit and Voluntary Sector Quarterly* 25, pp. 211–24.
Tanzania-Jobs.com (2018), Advertisement for BAK-AIDS Field Officers, https://www.tanzania-jobs.com/jobs/medical-healthcare/economic-strengthening-and-livelihoods-officerjob-atbakwata-national-hiv-aids-program-bak-aids-career-opportunity-in-tanzania-20083/
Tanzania Muslim Welfare Network (TMWN) (2010), 'Katiba [constitution] 2010', Dar es Salaam: TMWN.
Tripp, Aili Mari (1997), *Changing the Rules: The Politics of Liberalisation and the Urban Economy in Tanzania*, Berkeley: University of California Press.
Von Freyhold, Michaela (1979), *Ujamaa Villages in Tanzania: Analysis of a Social Experiment*, London: Heinemann.
Westerlund, David (1981), *Ujamaa na dini: A Study of Some Aspects of Society and Religion in Tanzania, 1961–77*, Stockholm: Almquist & Wiksell.
Williams, S. et al. (2013), *Globalization and Work*, Cambridge: Polity Press.
Urbinati, N. (2006), *Representative Democracy: Principles and Geneology*, Chicago: University of Chicago Press.

10

Shehes *and the* State: *The Role of Muslim Religious Leaders in Public Health Governance in Rural Tanzania*

Mohamed Yunus Rafiq

Both in the past and the present, religious leaders and institutions have played a vital role in state public health governance programmes in rural sub-Saharan contexts. This chapter examines the use of Muslim religious figures in two public health programmes in rural Tanzania to promote the use and knowledge of family planning and maternal and child health (MCH) services. First, I explore how projects have imagined the roles and identities of the rural religious figures they wish to recruit to implement their programmes. I then shift to how these rural Muslim religious figures imagined their own roles while negotiating with project-created roles and identities. Lastly, I present how villagers, who are the ultimate recipients of these programmes, evaluate the efficacy of using religious leaders in them. I argue that the process of using rural Muslim religious figures as low-level implementers in these programmes entails simplification, where some of their roles and identities are amplified and others marginalised to create an alignment with project goals. The present incorporation of Muslim religious figures in public health programmes offers a productive lens through which to engage with local and global debates and practices around secularism, public health governance and post-socialist state–society relations.

Introduction

It was time for noonday prayer. Shehe Mbwana and I were strolling down a mud road heading to the mosque. Shehe Mbwana is a community ambassador (CA, locally known as *Mabalozi wa jamii*).[1] CAs are members of the village

---

[1] Some names of projects, places and persons have been changed to protect their identity.

selected by the village government and the Mama na Mwana (Mother & Child) project to promote maternal and child health (MCH). That day, I had met Shehe Mbwana after a three-hour meeting where the CAs had presented their implementation progress to project facilitators. As we talked, I addressed him with the label that the project facilitators had used in the meetings, *shehe*, which was translated as 'religious leader'. After several such affirmations, Shehe Mbwana slowed down, turned to me, and said, 'I am not a *shehe*, I am a Qur'an teacher for children. I teach small children *alif baa* [Arabic alphabets] and *duas* [supplications] that they can use in their prayers. My deceased father, on the other hand, was a *shehe* and trained many individuals in this village.' Shehe Mbwana took several steps, his head reclined, then said in a calculated way, 'I guess, you people can call me *shehe*, I could be one. It's OK.' We walked silently for a few minutes before arriving at the mosque.

This interaction took place in one of six pilot villages in rural Tanga district where a project for improving MCH, known as Mama na Mwana, was being implemented. While Tanzania did not achieve the previous MCH targets from the Millennium Development Goals (MDGs), which ended in 2015, public health projects like Mama na Mwana continue to work towards the national and international goals of reducing infant and maternal mortality included in the new Sustainable Development Goals (SDGs) for 2030. The project established in 2015 used randomised control trial design to test the hypothesis of whether the selection of a subset of community members who are empowered to identify and implement solutions to MCH programmes could improve the quality of services using existing resources. To identify the problems and solutions regarding MCH services, the Mama na Mwana project recruited and trained this subset, which included religious leaders, traditional birth attendants, teachers, retired government workers, respected elders and representatives of civil organisations.

This chapter examines how health projects in rural Tanzania imagine and construct the category of religious leaders (*viongozi wa dini* in Swahili) from a diverse group of religious actors in rural Tanzania. Such projects construct religious leaders as health intermediaries responsible for the implementation of health programmes, such as family planning and maternal and child services, on their behalf. However, these categories of religious actors are not easily available for mobilisation by the project in its public health governance strategies. In the above quotation, Shehe Mbwana questioned the label *shehe*, which was used by project facilitators to mean Muslim religious leaders. He then explained how it did not fit him and explained who qualifies for that label. Then, on further reflection, he acknowledged, 'I guess you people can call me *shehe*.' This moment encapsulates a key process that entailed the construction of religious leaders as health intermediaries, the way subjects viewed themselves, and the negotiations involved in accommodating their new identities and roles created by the project. As I will show, projects' imaginations about religious leaders entailed a simplification of their identities and roles in order to create an alignment with their goal to increase use and knowledge of MCH services. In this chapter, I continue to use the label '*shehe*' because it is the term most commonly used to refer to Muslim religious figures; however, my use is informed by the term's varied uses.

In establishing or renewing old relationships with their intended communities, states and NGOs have continuously engaged in the process of constructing new citizen identities through various development programmes (Biehl 2005; McKay 2016; Nguyen 2010). Julia Elyachar has called this form of identity formation 'projects of incorporation', which includes assigning titles and roles and conducting training for the intended recipients (Elyachar 2005). Using various terms, such as therapeutic, biological and client–activist citizenship, scholars have shown how states, NGOs and development organisations are fashioning emergent relations and institutions, which have sometimes never existed before (Nguyen 2010; Petryna 2013; Robins 2006). In Vinh-Kim Nguyen's study of anti-retroviral treatment (ART) access in Burkina Faso, he observed recipients using confessional techniques, such as disclosing their positive status and crafting narratives about their suffering and responsibility, promoted by these agencies to signal their new identities (Nguyen 2010; Ong and Collier 2004). Nguyen suggests that while confessionary technologies were introduced by the nexus of state and international health agencies, recipients came to adopt them as their own idiom and set of practices for demanding ART services (Nguyen 2010; Ong and Collier 2004). By adopting new identities, ways of speaking, and modes of interaction, such as training or counselling sessions, Burkina Faso HIV patients embodied the identities the NGOs tried to inculcate in them.

While citizens adopt NGO-created labels to access care and services, at other times, NGOs rely on well-positioned individuals in the community to implement their own programmes. This position of being in between the project and the larger population has led Nancy Hunt to call these individuals 'middle figures', who make up a select group of villagers tasked with realising project goals on the ground (Gluckman 1949b; Hunt 1999). This is especially common in health-related programmes. Recent ethnographies on development work in sub-Saharan Africa show that state agencies continue to employ doctors, clinicians and nurses to provide biomedical care, opening new possibilities for career mobility and at times creating novel forms of public health governance (Nguyen 2010; McKay 2016; Livingston 2012). Whereas these authors focus on public and private medical staff recruited from the local population to service the goals of health NGOs, my research examines how health projects recruit so-called community leaders as health intermediaries in rural contexts. The former were sought because of their medical and health expertise, while the latter – Muslim religious leaders – were recruited because of their cultural and social capital, such as their ability to reach the masses and speak in ways that resonate with their constituents' sensibilities.

This form of public health governance has colonial antecedents. During British rule in Tanzania (1916–61), the village headman was expected to help mobilise his constituents for hygiene and sanitary work on behalf of the colonial state. He acted as an intermediary between the colonial state and the larger population because he possessed supposedly unique socio-cultural capital. Yet, the headman, like the present religious leaders, remained a volunteer, despite carrying out the political task of managing and co-ordinating public health measures at the local level. He was not considered a government employee (Gluckman 1949a; Mamdani 1996). Currently, health intermediaries, such as religious leaders, are recruited from their home villages but are involved in public services, a sector closely associated with the government. Yet like their colonial forebears, they are considered volunteers, and apolitical. Especially in the sub-Saharan context, the lines between religion, politics and the civic spheres remain porous. Because of the legacy of missionary institutions during the colonial era and the history of the paternal provider state in the post-colonial period, citizens view religious institutions and the providers of social services as essentially state-like, as entities representing the state or carrying out some characteristic functions of the state (Hearn 1998; Ludwig 1999).

This chapter is divided into three major sections to anchor my argument that the process of recruiting Muslim religious leaders, or *shehes*, entailed simplification, in which some of their roles and identities were amplified and others minimised to advance project goals. In the first section, I detail how project designers and representatives imagined *shehes* primarily as authority figures and orators, a view that deviated from *shehes*' lived realities. If rural Muslim figures were indeed simplified, what were their non-project roles and identities? Furthermore, how do they evaluate and negotiate their new roles as project *shehes*? The second section illuminates the questions and negotiations that rural Muslims had to make. The last section provides villagers' perspectives on and evaluations of the new role Muslim religious figures took in increasing knowledge and use of health services.

Research Methods and Settings

Between 2014 and 2016, I conducted a multi-sited ethnographic research project in three villages in the Morogoro district and six villages in the Tanga district in Tanzania. The villages were rural, primarily engaged in subsistence and commercial agriculture, and had inhabitants of varied ethnic and religious backgrounds. In both my research sites, I examined the now-established convention for the state and NGOs in Tanzania and other sub-Saharan contexts to use religious leaders to help implement public health programmes. In my Morogoro research site, located in south-central Tanzania, I followed the Connect project, whose goal was to increase knowledge and use of family planning.

I observed each stage of Connect's family planning project, including the recruitment of participants, training, creation and implementation of solutions, and follow-ups. I observed training in six villages, which included a total of forty-five village health representatives (VFTs; *wawakilishi wa afya ya jamii* in Swahili). I then observed how the representatives implemented family planning solutions. My aim was to understand how they interpreted the training and modified the programme to suit local realities. In addition to observing the training, I interviewed the three *shehes* who were involved with the project and five others who were not involved but who lived in the research areas. To understand how villagers received the project, I interviewed more than thirty villagers, both men and women, from different religious, ethnic and demographic backgrounds. I also interviewed the project staff to understand the history of the project and its goals, and their rationale for using health intermediaries, who included religious leaders. These staff members included the project manager, project supervisors and facilitators.

In rural Tanga villages, located in the coastal region of north-eastern Tanzania, I followed the Mama na Mwana project, whose aim was to improve MCH in a region with high infant and maternal mortality (Fig. 10.1). In Tanga, I used similar research procedures as in Morogoro, which included observing the training of CAs in six villages, delivery of solutions in the community, and a follow-up meeting, where project staff assessed the CAs' work (Fig. 10.2). Moreover, I interviewed six project-related *shehes* and four non-project-related *shehes*, as well as forty villagers from mixed religious, ethnic and demographic backgrounds.

Lastly, to gain an impression of the larger milieu in which the *shehes* were situated, I observed and participated in community activities, such as weddings, agricultural work, neighbourhood meetings and *maulid nabi* (celebrations of the Prophet's birthday).

Constructing Rural Religious Figures as Project Intermediaries

The project designers imagined that every village had an influential religious leader. This view was evident in the recruitment process. In both projects, the project staff requested that the village government include religious leaders in the subset of community members who they were recruiting for health intermediary positions. These health intermediaries were known for using different labels in these rural villages: CAs in Tanga and VFTs in Morogoro. Project

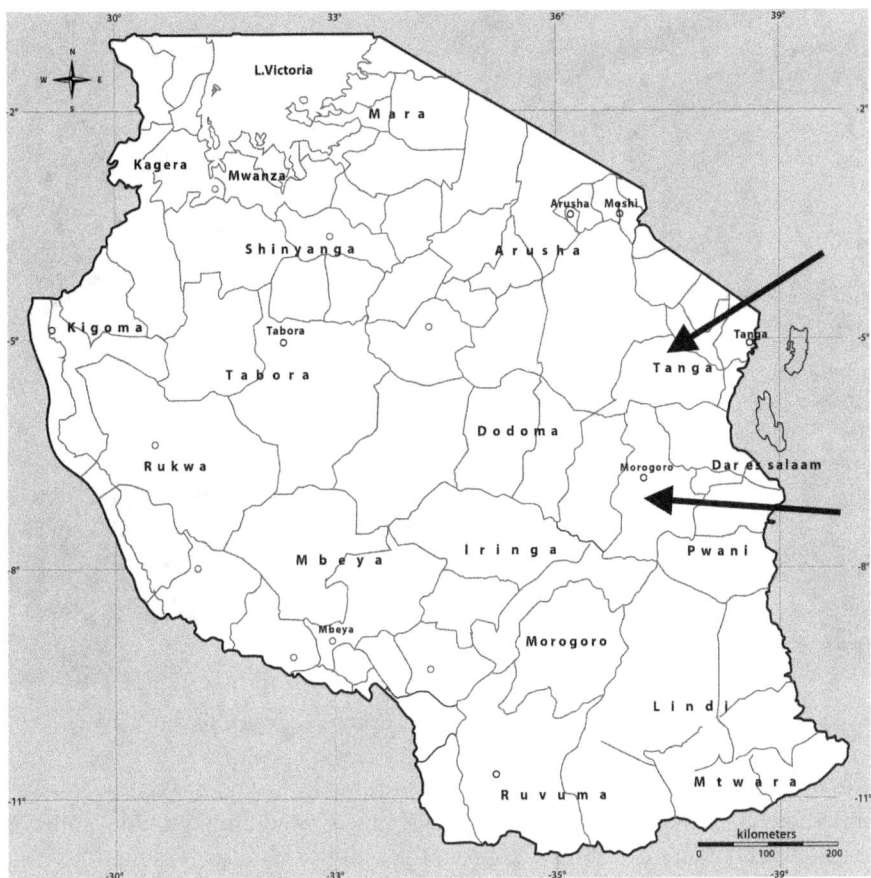

Figure 10.1 Map showing the Tanga and Morogoro districts in Tanzania. Courtesy the author.

facilitators gave health intermediaries this label to distinguish them from other villagers, who did not have training on family planning and were not mandated to increase its knowledge and use. Titles like CA and VFT signalled to other villagers that the members of this select group were the official implementers of the health project at the village level.

This is how recruitment typically worked: the project staff, which included field managers, researchers and facilitators, would visit the village government to introduce themselves and provide the relevant documents, such as research approval and a letter from the district and regional governments. Project staff briefed the village government about the project goals and requested a list of the people they wished to work for them, such as traditional healers, midwives, religious leaders, teachers and retired government officers. Though the list was

Figure 10.2 CAs in training in rural Tanzania. Courtesy the author.

provided by the project staff, the work of recruiting the first pool of candidates was undertaken by village government officials. Project staff often provided a list of values and characteristics they sought in these individuals, such as their 'having a history and heart of serving the community', being 'hardworking and truthful' and being 'someone with the spirit of volunteerism'. In Morogoro, project staff explicitly used the term 'religious leaders' (*viongozi wa dini* in Swahili) during recruitment, whereas in Tanga, project designers and project managers used the term 'informal leaders' (*viongozi wasio rasmi* in Swahili) in their documents and discourse. The field facilitators had to specify to village government officials that by 'informal leaders' they also meant religious leaders. Field facilitators' use of various terminologies to name and recruit religious leaders is not merely an issue of choice. Instead, it reveals how religious leaders are relegated as figures who are apart from the government and political matters regardless of the fact that the public codes their role and action as state-like and political. The term 'formal leaders' signals government and politics, while 'informal leaders' suggests civil culture and an apolitical sphere. The use of these varied terms that avoid the entanglement of religion and politics aligns with Tanzania's formal policy of separation between church and state.

Religious Leaders (VIONGOZI WA DINI): Not Always Equal to SHEHES

Project staff's use of the term 'religious leader' (*viongozi wa dini*) was problematic, especially when it was used synonymously with *shehe*.[2] When project staff spoke of *viongozi wa dini*, they were referring specifically to religious leaders, which is the literal meaning of the Swahili term. However, almost all the Muslim individuals recruited under the project could be *shehes*. The label '*shehe*' is multi-faceted in a way that is not apparent in this generalised use, and can be used to describe a wide range of roles, relationships and identities. In the local Tanzanian context, a *shehe* can be a madrasa teacher, a marriage counsellor, a popular and religious person, an elder, a leader, a dear friend, a healer, a politician and/or an imam. Although *shehes* were recruited by public health projects in their capacity as religious leaders, they were not the only Muslim figures in their communities, nor were they leaders in the way the projects imagined.

While the use of the term *shehe* is malleable in its local usage, the degree of its flexibility decreases depending on institutional usage and context. Muslim professionals have distinct categories for their practice; therefore, they may not agree with collapsing these categories into one another. The categories of Muslim religious figures include *kadhi*, *ulema*, *imam*, *ustadhi*, *khatib* and *mufti*, and each has a specific expertise and domain of influence. For example, a kadhi (a judge) can be a *shehe*, taken here to mean a respected person; however, being called a *shehe* does not equate with being a kadhi. Few project facilitators knew about these distinct types of expertise and roles because they were mostly Christian, urban and university-educated. Moreover, the term 'religious leader', *viongozi wa dini*, has been used so frequently in politics, and *viongozi wa dini* are employed so frequently in development practice, that the role of the *viongozi wa dini* has become a development convention, and the very ubiquity of this role has meant that the term's original meaning of religious leader has become obscured. Notwithstanding its conventional nature, projects operate in short time cycles of a maximum of three years, which means they do not have the time to understand the history, social and cultural dynamics that underpin these religious roles and identities on the ground. In these situations, the use of *viongozi wa dini* makes it easier to hit the ground running with work.

As a consequence, when the field facilitators lumped all the religious actors into the category '*shehe*', they conflated a wide range of Muslim figures into one, ignoring areas of expertise such as law or theology, and local understanding of the term. Equally, while Tanzania did not achieve the previous MCH targets stemming from the Millennium Development Goals (MDGs), which ended in 2015, public health projects like Mama na Mwana continue to work towards

---

[2] I use the label *shehe*, following Felicitas Becker's usage (2008).

the national and international goals of reducing infant and maternal mortality included in the new Sustainable Development Goals (SDGs) for 2030. Field facilitators also downplayed Muslim religious figures' other roles and identities, such as being farmers, healers, marriage counsellors, politicians and teachers of the Qur'an. Not knowing or ignoring the diversity of these local identities, whether intentional or not, not only misidentified the religious figures but also foreclosed synergies that could have been forged between *shehes* and the project. For example, marriage counsellors could be useful in promoting family planning and MCH services because they engage in disputes about marriage and childcare. But if project designers and field facilitators ignored the existing identities in recruiting their imagined *shehes*, they were specific about what qualities and values they were looking for. Field facilitators sought individuals who were authority figures who had access to the community and had speaking skills via which they could engage with their constituents. I use James Scott's term 'simplification' to describe this discursive and institutional process that was used in reconstructing these *shehes*, where some of their roles and identities were amplified while others were marginalised to fit with project goals (Scott 1999). For example, *shehes*' roles as healers, marriage counsellors and politicians were downplayed, while their supposed leadership roles were highlighted.

Imaging Rural *Shehes* as Charismatic Weberian Figures

Project staff were in search of a Weberian charismatic leader: someone who had authority over people due to his knowledge of scripture and therefore had cultivated a following. In *Economy and Society*, Max Weber describes charismatic leaders as individuals who can inspire, influence and lead their followers by virtue of their exceptional personal qualities, derived from both human and supernatural sources (Weber 1978). One key quality of these charismatic leaders is that their legitimacy remains tied to an active population that recognises their authority, heeding their calls and acting on the basis of their dictates. A charismatic leader is someone with 'wealth in people', as Jane Guyer puts it (Guyer 1995). They possess the kind of social capital that some of the development projects I studied imagined would be essential for introducing health programmes into the community.

Repeatedly, during project meetings, facilitators extolled *shehes* in ways like this:

> *Shehes* are closer to their followers than any other leaders. Muslims come to pray five times a day, the *shehe* is there, who sees them and leads them in prayers. During Friday prayers, where big crowds come to pray, Muslims' eyes and ears are directed at the *shehe*. What he says everyone can hear. No one

has connections to the Muslims like the *shehe*. (Mwanajasi, project facilitator speaking to the VFT, Morogoro, 2014)

Project members perceived *shehes'* authority and the access they had to their own community. During daily prayers and group congregations in the mosque, this ideal *shehe* was assumed to be able to speak with their congregants in an 'easier' way than others; the congregants pursued the *shehe* rather than the *shehe* pursuing them. Through these repeated social contacts, a degree of authority was thought to be established and maintained: a *shehe* is imagined as having access to Muslims five times a day and access to even bigger groups at Friday prayers.

There are several reasons why it was problematic to assume that *shehes* are leaders or possess charismatic qualities. The Muslim figures in these projects were almost all exclusively from rural, agricultural areas. Only one of the nine sites in the two projects was a peri-urban area. In these mainly agricultural villages, mosque attendance varied greatly. Most days, there were only around five congregants. That was on a good day. Sometimes, I was the only person behind the imam, the prayer leader. *Shehes* from Sewa and Mafu villages in Tanga complained that it was a challenge to convince Muslims from their villages to conduct the obligatory prayers in congregation. Friday prayers, which are obligatory for men to perform in congregation, drew much larger crowds (twenty to twenty-five people in rural Tanga), but not all Muslims attended, especially during the planting season. The ebb and flow of traffic to the mosque was seasonal.

The *shehes* I interviewed, such as Mbwana, a community ambassador from Maba Village in Tanga, spoke about the 'problem' of reaching fellow villagers with the MCH messages they have developed. During a meeting between CA, including Shehe Mbwana, and the project facilitators, Shehe Mbwana expressed his disappointment: 'Mosques are empty during the planting season, the fields are far away, you don't have time to come and pray and then return to the farms. People eat and pray there.' When Kafupi, a female project facilitator, asked him about Friday prayers, he replied, 'It's the same problem. People come to pray and then quickly rush back to their farms. There is no time to speak to them – that's why it has been difficult to educate Muslims and their *shehes* on maternal and child health.' This scenario points to several complications surrounding the idea of the *shehe* as a person with unique access to an active population.

It is interesting to note that Shehe Mbwana referred to the low attendance at daily prayers at the mosque as 'a problem'. It is the reality for rural villagers like Mbwana that they spend most of their time on distant farms, especially during the planting season. Islamic dictates have accommodated these daily realities in relation to prayers. According to *fiqh*, Islamic law, Muslims can pray on their farms without going to the mosque.³ The exception to this is the congregational prayer held on Fridays. Not attending the mosque for daily prayers is not a religious problem and does not indicate one's level of religious commitment. So why did Shehe Mbwana present the issue as a problem?

Shehe Mbwana spoke of low attendance as a problem largely due to the context of our exchange and his understanding of what it meant for the health project's intended goal of reaching a wider population. This exchange occurred during a follow-up meeting, when the VFT reported on its progress in promoting family planning. One approach that Shehe Mbwana and his fellow VFT members developed involved speaking to Muslims in the mosque about family planning. But this was not successful, since mosque attendance was low. In this sense, then, the low attendance *was* a problem: the people who were supposed to get the message did not attend. This was a problem for the project, not for the community, since low mosque attendance was a norm, especially during the rainy seasons. Importantly, though, this way of framing villagers' lack of attendance at daily prayers affected the way *shehes* regarded their own community's practices. The mosque was regarded as the primary site where Muslims congregated and the place where messages about public health could best be delivered. Though Muslims did use the mosque to meet, more often they gathered on the stairs and veranda after prayers to catch up on the latest news and sip coffee, and there were rarely more than five people at these gatherings.

My aim here is not to imply that religious individuals with authority over large groups of people do not exist, but just to make clear that the charismatic *shehes* who were sought in both Tanga and Morogoro did not readily exist in the villages where project facilitators worked. Rural *shehes* did have a certain influence on the local people, but only in the way teachers, nurses and village government officials did. They were consulted on marriage issues, resolved domestic problems and conducted public ceremonies such as *maulid nabi*, the Prophet's birthday celebration. Yet project staff imagined and circulated a discourse about *shehes* that reconstructed them indiscriminately as speakers for the Muslim community and leaders with unparalleled access to village populations. The *shehes* I met had little in common with the Egyptian televangelist Amr Khaled, described by Asef Bayat in *Making Islam Democratic*, nor were they like the late Habib Swaleh, a religious scholar in Lamu, whom Abdul Hamid El-Zein writes about in *The Sacred Meadows*. However, even assuming that followers of the late Shehe Habib Swaleh acted on his messages in making decisions about health or other social issues, this supposition of his influence cannot be fully substantiated (Bayat 2007; Zein 1974). Patients' decision-making processes are

---

³ I am grateful to Professor Sherine El Hamdy for explaining the stance of Islamic *fiqh* concerning work and obligatory prayers.

complex, varied and often contradictory (Rapp 2000). In addition, scholars have shown that *shehes* are sometimes objects of ridicule and remain contested within local settings (Khan 2012; Gilsenan 1996).

Project members uncritically assumed that the title *shehe* meant 'leader', someone with a unique degree of access to the Muslim population. Such statements reinforce prevailing Orientalist tropes about Muslims and Africans as collective societies and accessed through their leaders, with little individual agency for people to decide their own social and political trajectories (Said 1979; Green 2014). In this regard, field facilitators presented *shehes* as uncontested individuals with unprecedented access to the population, whose statements can lead to thinking and behaviour change. Such framing of *shehes* ignores the divisions, politics and diversity of opinion between villagers, including religious figures themselves. Despite their small population, many Tanzanian villages are socially, religiously and ethnically diverse spaces marked by cleavages and fissures, just like anywhere else. In the villages where I did my research, villagers did not speak in one voice; they were part of village politics and contestations that shaped their allegiances, interests and support (cf. Becker 2006). Muslim religious figures were also not immune from these cleavages, because of their intricate local kinship, residential and institutional ties.

Shehes as Orators: Changing People's Thinking and Influencing Actions

Another aspect of the project staff's perception of *shehes*' authority concerned their supposed oratory skills, which were thought to directly resonate with their congregants' sentiments and beliefs. *Shehes*' messages and speeches do in fact have a moral resonance with the Muslim faithful (Miller 2007). Several scholars have investigated the role of sound – such as the Qur'anic recitation of popular *shehes* – in the cultivation of religious piety and ethical sensibilities among ordinary Muslims (Hirschkind 2009; Miller 2007; Caton 1993). Project members in Morogoro and Tanga also placed great weight on *shehes*' supposed ability to mould, attune and focus Muslims' attention on family planning issues through their language style, which incorporates Islamic references and verbal aesthetics. In the following statement, Mwanajasi expressed how the inclusion of religious leaders as health educators changes how the community comprehends and responds to health messages:

> The good thing about the VFT is that you have different people working together; you can not only fill the gaps in what your fellow has said, but when you have religious leaders, such as the *shehes* and the pastors, the whole issue is given more weight. The religious leaders have a way of speaking to people

that speaks to their beliefs. (Mwanajasi, project facilitator speaking to the VFT, Morogoro, 2014)

Project facilitators in Tanga, in addition to describing religious leaders' ways of speaking as truthful and non-political, suggested that this stems from the 'inner qualities' of their firm religious convictions:

> Religious leaders do God's work and they are God's people. They don't do blah blah; what they say is the truth and what has been prescribed in the sacred books and sayings of the prophets. They are not businessmen and politicians. They tell you things the way they are. We need to respect them and tell them about our project the way it is. If we explain ourselves well, then they will also understand us because they don't beat around the bush; if it's something they agree with they will support it, and if it's something that goes against their values, they will reject it. (Kafupi, project facilitator, Tanga, 2015)

In these statements, both Kafupi and Mwanajasi anticipated that rural Morogoro and Tanga villagers' responses to the *shehes*' speech would be more focused, changing their thoughts and actions and leading them to reflect on the association between their faith, the content delivered and their relationship to the *shehe*. Like Mwanajasi, Kafupi saw this distinct way of speaking to be an embodiment of their inner religiosity and conviction.

Due to these qualities, religious leaders were thought to add 'weight' to people's decisions to adopt family planning services. It was imagined by project facilitators that *shehes*, as well as other religious leaders, had a distinct way of speaking, perhaps infusing their talk with religious passages that resonated with people's feelings and moral beliefs. But religious leaders that I worked with rarely infused their messages with biblical or Qur'anic passages. Seeing this omission, I asked several *shehes* who were involved in the project why they did not explicitly incorporate Qur'anic passages or prophetic sayings. Shehe Raja, from Kindi, told me that it was not necessary because the issue of MCH was significant on its own and did not need to be amplified with religion. He added that one could force the issue by appealing to religious teachings, but such action was unnecessary.

The field facilitators seemed to be referring to the work of a full-time imam (rather than *shehe*) when they spoke of someone with authority and connections to the masses. But rarely, if ever, did the term 'imam' emerge in the project discussions or training. Although a full-time imam and an ad hoc imam may have the same prayer functions, such as leading obligatory prayers, the fact that they are selected with their congregants and render their services on a full-time basis confers on them the leadership qualities that the project sought. In mosques, when a community cannot hire a permanent imam, any Muslim with basic knowledge of the Qur'an can act as an imam. In most of the villages where I lived in Tanga and Morogoro, the imams were not permanent. When the time of prayer approached, the congregated Muslims quickly asked each other who could lead the prayers. Through nomination or volunteering, an imam emerged and led the prayers. This figure is very different from the one Mwanajasi seemed to intend. Imams in the village served the needs of the congregation temporarily, having only a basic Qur'anic education and no authority beyond what they have over the people they lead in prayer at that particular time. Even if, hypothetically, an imam had a following of villagers, it would still be a stretch to assume that his authority would change people's thinking and behaviour towards health. Such assumptions narrowly describe clients' complex trajectories of care, which are not merely about access to information but are tied to other structural factors such as access, cost, distance and history of health services.

'I am Not a *Shehe*': Religious Figures' Self-representations

In this last section, I consider how *shehes* perceive and evaluate their roles and identities in conjunction with the new relationships forged within the project. As I have shown, the term '*shehe*' is multifaceted and dynamic, changing with times and conditions. Despite the fluidity of the term, at certain times and in specific local contexts its meaning congeals. For example, villagers use the term to refer to specific people who have certain characteristics and relations that they associate with being a *shehe*. Furthermore, as my examples show, Muslim religious figures who use the term are themselves aware that such a category can have more defined boundaries when used in certain interactional and social contexts.

At several points during my fieldwork in Morogoro and Tanga, my informants identified moments when they operated within these boundaries, and others when they sensed that they had moved beyond them. Muslim individuals I worked with described boundaries that existed prior to and during the project's entry into the community. Scholars have shown that categories such as race or ethnicity are highly contextual, at times porous and at times gaining fixity (Barth 1970; Cohen and Odhiambo 1992; McIntosh 2009). They have also shown that identities are always in the making: in- and out-members constantly dispute and negotiate their membership within a certain ethnic or cultural group – in this case, the one encompassed by the term *shehe*. Muslim religious figures that I worked with showed this awareness of locally established boundaries and of when these boundaries shifted. Sometimes they accepted the label *shehe* and at other times they qualified its use, pointing to other people in their local setting who better fitted the label and its functions. This is not to say that all project staff were ignorant of *shehes*' multiple roles. Rather, projects chose to amplify certain roles and identities and marginalise others to achieve their goals. Because of this, there existed a 'misalignment' between the *shehes*' traditional roles and functions and the projects' expectations.

Shehes' presentation of who they were, as expressed both by themselves and through their interactions with others, departed from the simplified definition of the *shehe* promoted by the project. What follows is Shehe Hassani's own impression of his role within the project. Shehe Hassani was one of the several 'religious leaders' (*viongozi wa dini*) who had been recruited to form the VFT group. This twelve-member group was composed of teachers, village government officials, traditional birth attendants, traditional healers, representatives of NGOs, Christian bishops and pastors, and influential leaders (*wazee mashuhuri*). VFT members like Shehe Hassani were trained to identify community barriers to family planning through the participatory approaches (PA) method, and thereafter to develop social action plans. At the end of the training, they became implementers and educators of the community on family planning services. Each village (there were three in total) developed its own action plan to promote family planning services in their area. A special section of the district government called the community health management team (CHMT) trained the VFT in basic family planning education and in PA methods and strategies for community engagement.

To better understand religious leaders and get away from the confines of the project meetings, I arranged to meet Shehe Hassani at his residence outside Ifakara town. Shehe Hassani belonged to a VFT from Mtakuja village. Upon seeing me, he ordered one of his sons to put a wooden bench near a big fig tree growing near the porch of his house for our conversation. I sat on the bench, and after a few minutes the *shehe* joined me and we exchanged greetings. Though I had interacted with Shehe Hassani many times at the village health representatives and follow-up meetings, I had never met with him alone. People constantly greeted Shehe Hassani as they passed; he waved in reply. They did not call him *shehe*, but referred to him by his name, Hassani.

We sat outside sipping our tea after our late-afternoon lunch. I asked Shehe Hassani how he got involved in the family planning project and about his Islamic training. He responded:

> I wasn't appointed by the village. The village government called our *shehe* and asked him to join the family planning project. Our *shehe* is a very busy man, being one of the main *shehes* of the town, and he is constantly moving. Sometimes he is called by the district commissioner, other times he has to attend BAKWATA [the National Muslim Council of Tanzania] meetings in other districts, in addition to his farming obligations. One day, word was

sent for me to go see him, and when I met him in his house, he asked me to represent him at the project. I agreed. That's how I got to know you. So, they chose me as a *shehe*, but I work at the mosque as a marriage counsellor.

In the project meetings, the chairman and village executive officer presented Hassani to us as a religious leader, and he described himself in all meetings as a *shehe*. To me, how he spoke and dressed defied the image of a *shehe* ingrained in my mind and what I knew of *shehes* from the urban areas in which I had worked. I remember being disappointed by my first impression of Hassani when I met him in the meetings. I had expected to meet someone who dressed in *khanzu* (long robes) or other symbolically Islamic attire, like an embroidered *kofia* (a Swahili-style hat worn by many imams and *shehes*), and had a beard. However, Shehe Hassani's hair was short; he was clean-shaven and wore a blue button-down shirt, neatly ironed and tucked into grey striped trousers. A pen rested in his right shirt pocket, making him appear like a government officer or a teacher rather than a *shehe*. When he spoke in the meetings, his speech was not sprinkled with any Islamic references, which is an oratorical style associated with the religiously learned. He used the Swahili that everyone else used. In short, one had to know Shehe Hassani personally to know that he really was a *shehe*. Within the project, his role was strictly meant in the narrow sense of the term – namely, religious leader.

Shehe Hassani perhaps registered my surprise about his work as a marriage counsellor. He asked me if I knew what marriage counsellors do. While it is not rare to hear about marriage counsellors in Tanzanian cities, this was the first marriage counsellor I had met in rural Tanzania. Like many in Tanzania, I regarded marriage counselling as a profession often practised in the United States and Europe or perhaps large cities like Dar es Salaam. I did not associate it with rural and peri-urban areas in southern Tanzania. I replied to Shehe Hassani that I knew what marriage counsellors do, but he nevertheless gave me a brief description of his work. He said that he had a small office at the *msikiti wa Ijumaa* (Friday mosque) where he spoke to couples about marriage and domestic issues for four hours a day from Monday to Friday.

To learn more about his Islamic education and whether he had qualifications in Islamic law, I asked Shehe Hassani if he had training as a kadhi (Islamic judge), they being usually known to arbitrate marriage and inheritance cases. He replied that he had never had such training; however, he advised couples using his experience and Islamic principles such as respect for each other (*heshima*), upholding justice (*haki*) and cultivating patience (*subra*). I asked him if he sometimes led prayers at the mosque or taught madrasa for adults or children. He said he did not, and added that there was an imam who has been appointed by the head *shehe* to lead both the *faradh* (obligatory prayers) and Friday prayers in his absence.

Shehe Hassani's account shows that he was not the *shehe* that the project was imagining: an authoritative figure and a point of access to a population. Instead, his account of his identity and role differed from the one that most of us – the project facilitators and myself – thought we knew. Shehe Hassani introduced himself to me as a marriage counsellor. However, Hassani never denied that he was a *shehe*. He had a sense of the boundary that existed locally between his profession as a marriage counsellor and the role of a *shehe*. Over the several months we worked together, he never told us about his work as a marriage counsellor, nor did anyone ask. So why did he think it was important to tell me about his work as a marriage counsellor when we met privately? Notably here, his profession as a marriage counsellor aligned with family planning services because it required didactic messaging with couples. Did the district *shehe* appoint Shehe Hassani as a substitute because of this compatibility? Shehe Hassani never pointed out to project staff how much his profession aligned with their goals.

Shehes' Self-representations: Meetings Away from the Project Spaces

We may consider one further example of an individual who was thought by the project staff to embody the role of a *shehe* but who identified himself as a Qur'an teacher in a different interactional context. The story of Chambi is somewhat different from the stories of Shehe Hassani and Mbwana. Shehe Chambi's case offers a perspective on someone who did not satisfy field facilitators' conception of a *shehe*. He never became a VFT member. This story is also relevant because, whereas in the cases of Shehe Mbwana and Hassani their identity as *shehes* was somewhat easily discernible, Shehe Chambi's tensions and uneasiness in embodying the role were less noticeable. Shehe Chambi's uneasiness with the term *shehe* or *kiongozi wa dini* was not explicitly articulated in his speech, but rather evidenced in how he conducted himself in project meetings. To demonstrate this uneasiness, let us consider Chambi's participation both in project-sanctioned interactions and in private interactions in other contexts.

Shehe Chambi was from the rice-growing village of Sawa in rural Morogoro. He was one of Sawa's village health representatives, who worked to educate the public about the importance of family planning and increase its utilisation in the area. The first time I met him was during the initial Sawa project meeting, where the project facilitators, members of the CHMT and project staff presented their initial findings. These findings, following the principles of the participatory approach (PA) aimed at involving the community in all levels of the planning and implementation of health services, included the community's own views on why they supported or opposed family planning, the availability of these services, and ways to improve access. The selection of religious leaders thus falls under the principle of equal representation of all stakeholders.

Shehe Chambi attended the presentation of the baseline findings, along with other 'religious leaders', such as John, the Protestant pastor from the Tanzania Assemblies of God, and the representative of a local Catholic priest from Sawa Parish named Deogratus Kinene. Also present were project facilitators, including two members of the project, a project leader and six members from the CHMT. The project had designated these six members of the CHMT the district representatives (DRs; *timu ya wilaya* in Swahili). DRs trained participants and ran the meetings, while project facilitators monitored the work and provided background information about the project. I therefore refer to them also as 'facilitators'.

The presentation of the baseline findings was followed by a discussion with the members who were present. The CHMT members expressed their views on why these services were scarce in their community and reacted to the reasons given in the baseline findings. Then the invited guests (around thirty individuals, including a *shehe*) intended to nominate twelve members who would form the VFT team. The VFTs would then receive training on family planning and on how to create and implement these plans in their community. The meeting started with an introduction of the facilitators and invited guests. Shehe Chambi sat close to John and Deogratus. The meeting was conducted at the village government's meeting hall, a structure built of fired bricks, a material and style very common in rural southern Tanzania.

During the initial meeting, Shehe Chambi sat silently and listened to the baseline findings. As time went by and the discussion period began, Mwanajasi, a senior facilitator, began asking the invited guests questions. Several other invited guests gave their views and opinions on why young girls become pregnant out of wedlock and why people continued to have many children. Some of the reasons given for the high fertility rate were that children are used as labour in rice farming and cattle keeping.

Mwanajasi sat down and let Umize, a female facilitator with significant experience in family planning, take over the second session. This is when Umize turned to Shehe Chambi and his fellows, saying, 'We have our religious leaders here today. Let's hear what they have to say about family planning.' Deogratus stood up, wearing blue pants and shirt and a plastic cross around his neck. In his left hand, he held a blue notepad and a pen provided by the project. He said, 'We have instructions from our leadership to provide family planning services. We teach and advise many of our congregants and patients about family planning services. We use the calendar method and we have been using and teaching it for some time now.' Umize interrupted, 'But you don't provide condoms or the pills?' Deogratus responded calmly, 'No, we don't provide condoms or pills in our dispensary.' Umize interjected again, moving closer to Deogratus, 'So you don't provide family planning services?' Somewhat surprised but maintaining his calm, Deogratus reiterated, 'I guess you can say that we don't provide modern family planning services, but we have our own family planning services that have been approved by our leaders (*wazee*). If someone needs the calendar method, we provide those services and those that want modern methods we instruct them to go to Mangu health centre.' 'So you don't provide modern family planning services?' Umize probed again. 'No, we don't', Deogratus replied, sitting down.

Standing in the same spot, Umize then turned to Shehe Chambi saying, 'Now, *shehe*, what can you add?' Shehe Chambi, who had spoken little since his morning introduction, stood up and said sheepishly, 'I agree with everything that my fellow just said' – turning and pointing to where Deogratus sat. He then immediately sat down with his head downcast. Umize was dissatisfied and looked at Shehe Chambi as if she could force him to provide more information by giving him a piercing stare. Shehe Chambi just sat there and picked at his notebook, flipping through the empty pages. He looked very young in comparison to most of the *shehes* I had come to know, and like other rural *shehes* I met, he did not possess the symbolic markers often associated with an urban Tanzanian *shehe*.

I have provided this extended snapshot of the first meeting in Sawa village in rural Morogoro to show the interactional context in which Chambi presented himself as a *shehe*, a role he did not perform well from the perspective of the project staff. The meetings also show how he was constructed through discourse as a religious leader. Facilitators called these three individuals 'religious leaders' and called Chambi a *shehe*. Next, I connect the interactions that I observed in the meetings regarding my suggestion that the identity of a Qur'an teacher exists somewhat separately from that of project-idealised *shehes*, and that this identity (which includes Qur'an teachers) is marginalised in the context of public health projects. Below, I present another of my interactions with Shehe Chambi, outside the context of the meeting and on his own turf.

I went to meet Shehe Chambi for an interview and to interact with him outside the context of the project, where I could ask questions and observe and learn about him away from the other VFT members. I met him at his home. We walked to the grass-thatched madrasa next to his home and knelt as we entered. At the end of the structure was a blackboard supported by wooden legs where Shehe Chambi wrote his Qur'an lessons. Imprints of the last lessons were still visible.

We sat down and started talking. I asked him to tell me about his work. He spoke serenely. 'I am a teacher of the Qur'an, I teach small children how to read the Qur'an, and perform prayers correctly. These are children from my *mtaa* [neighbourhood], but I also have children from other neighbourhoods.' I tried to ask him questions about the family planning project, but even after probing several times, he spoke very little about it. He said that I should talk to John, a Christian VFT, as he was the person who had taken on the responsibility of organising the religious leaders to promote family planning in the area. Shehe Chambi simply awaited his instructions. Most of his conversation, in which he spoke animatedly and at length, was centred on the problems involved in educating Muslim children in rural areas, such as the lack of books, parents ignoring the importance of religious education, and the lack of a modern madrasa building. He requested that I appeal to other Muslims to donate materials to build a modern fired-brick and zinc-roofed madrasa. I realised then that he was more of a *mwalimu wa kuruani* (Qur'an teacher) than the kind of *shehe* the project needed, and other interactions with Shehe Chambi further suggested this.

This example and others that I have provided demonstrate that individuals like Chambi saw their identity as *mwalimu wa kuruani*, which was markedly different from the project-assigned role as a *shehe* that signified a religious leader. Although the local use and meaning of the term *shehe* was fluid, there were certain limits to the acceptable contexts and uses of the term. There are other practical and theoretical implications to draw from the preceding examples concerning the project's attempts to simplify the role of the *shehes*. The project's attempt to co-opt religious leaders revealed both epistemic and cultural gaps; it sought to institutionalise the role of religious leaders despite the fact that they were individuals (such as Shehe Chambi) who did not see themselves as *shehes*, even though when Shehe Chambi was with the project he identified as one. This process revealed the project staff's distinct perception of religious leaders. The project's view of *shehes* was a certain kind of 'gaze', to use Michel Foucault's term, which contrasted with how the *shehes* existed on the ground as well as how Muslims conceived of that role (Foucault 1994).

As noted in the previous sections, the meaning of the term *shehe* is diverse and complex, and in certain contexts it congeals to refer to specific people and activities. In order to create a fit between their goals and the everyday identities and roles of these *shehes*, the staff members of both projects I studied engaged in a process of reconstruction, transforming these *shehes* into the kind of religious leader figures the projects wanted them to be. As we have seen, the projects' staff sought to flatten the diverse and locally specific use of the term to create a new, singular definition that complemented their goals. *Shehe* came to mean simply a religious leader: someone with access to a certain population and the authority and oratorical skill to influence that population's attitude and behaviour.

Villagers' Impressions of Religious Leaders' Efficacy

Interviews conducted as part of the assessment of Connect's family planning project in April 2016 revealed two findings about how villagers perceived religious leaders' role in family planning. Several villagers interviewed in Igi Village reported that the inclusion of religious leaders as VFTs signalled to them that neither religion nor religious leaders were against family planning. To them, the inclusion of religious leaders within the VFT team conducting household and market educational sessions indicated that religious leaders endorsed and allowed the use of family planning. Religious leaders' mere participation or appearance was a statement that villagers, and especially the followers of the particular faith, could use family planning. Several villagers I interviewed, both men and women, repeated this statement. It is interesting to note that the interviewees emphasised religious leaders' presence as an index of permissibility rather than quoting or explaining what their presence signalled to them: that they could use family planning services. It was satisfactory for villagers to just see the religious leaders' presence and participation in these campaigns. One reason, perhaps, why the villagers did not quote or recall religious leaders' actual statements about their endorsement of family planning had to do with religious leaders' own attitudes in these educational campaigns. Several religious leaders interviewed in Igi Village, both Christians and Muslims, preferred to speak about the dangers and moral implications of engaging in illicit sex, becoming a teenage mother and contracting diseases like sexually transmitted diseases and HIV/AIDS. These conversations are safe topics, because the topics are widely spoken about by everyone, and most people would agree, for instance, that HIV/AIDS is dangerous. In contrast, religious leaders refrained from speaking about using condoms because they were afraid this might be construed by their constituents as encouraging pre-marital sexual relations.

Whereas some villagers associated *shehes*' presence within VFT teams as an endorsement, others noted that they trusted religious leaders, which shaped how they received the family planning message. Rose, a twenty-six-year-old female from Igi Village testified, 'People respond well to them because religious leaders have 99 per cent trust from the community. For example, if I meet a *shehe*, I immediately believe what he tells me is not lies because he has faith. So, when he accompanies WAJA [community health workers], I expect what I will be told will be truth as compared to if I see a government official because I don't know about their faith or behaviour.' Rose notes that they see religious leaders as people of faith and therefore as being truthful. She also suggests that there is a kind of a transference that happens with the association of religious leaders with other VFTs and with family planning solutions. When religious leaders accompany other VFT members like community health workers, the latter are enabled or encouraged to also speak the truth. Rose claimed that if religious leaders accompanied a community health worker, it was unlikely the worker would lie. Lastly, she noted that she did not have the same level of trust in other leaders, such as government officials, because she did not know about their behaviour or leadership ethics. These statements suggest that family planning messages become efficacious or at least well received because villagers associate the presence of religious leaders with truth and valid information.

These findings have theoretical and practical implications. First, they suggest that even when there was a misalignment between the type of religious leaders the project imagined and how these leaders existed on the ground, the projected religious leaders were effective. The project *shehe* were not as successful in using the mosques to pull huge crowds; they did not explicitly translate the family planning ideas into religious terms, as in linking to *sunna* or hadith. But for some villagers, like Rose, the presence of *shehe* and other religious leaders signalled that religion and religious leaders are not against family planning. Arguably, the presence of religious leaders lowered the psychological and social barriers for some people to seek these services. Moreover, if villagers trusted religious leaders, it suggests they were more open to listening to VFTs' advice on family planning services. Despite these positive responses, two years after the end of the intervention, it would be best to consider these statements as perceptions and desires rather than as concrete evidence of increased use and knowledge of family planning. Besides, during the 2016 end-line assessment, only Igi villagers were interviewed, which means the results cannot be generalised to the other two sites.

Moreover, religious leaders are not the only hindrance to family planning use and knowledge. Other constraints include availability, spousal disapproval, distance to services, side effects, and national policies on family planning, which sometimes presents itself as in favour of family planning and sometimes as against. Lastly, modern family planning strategies are not the only methods available to villagers. In our interviews, villagers preferred to use a combination of family planning methods, which blended the biomedical and traditional methods, such as the calendar, the Billings ovulation method and medicinal plants.[4]

Conclusion

In this chapter, I have focused on how two public health projects in Tanzania, Mama na Mwana in Tanga and Connect in Morogoro, co-opted *shehes* to introduce social and technological changes into the realm of health to reach the larger population. I described how project staff imagined and constructed a new figure of the *shehe* to increase knowledge about and utilisation of health services. For religious leaders to perform their work as authority figures, as educators, as access points to the community, and as individuals who can legitimise the

---

[4] This method involves the evaluation of cervical mucus to predict ovulation.

project in the eyes of the larger population, the role of the *shehe* had to be simplified. The simplification process worked by amplifying certain of the *shehes*' roles and identities and marginalising others to ensure a fit with project goals.

Projects sought religious leaders with social capital, such as access to the members of their community, and the oratorical skills necessary to educate and convince their followers to use the promoted health programmes. Project members called Muslim religious leaders *shehes*, a term that, as we have seen, not only refers to various roles and identities in general, but can also have specific local meanings and uses. While a *shehe* might be a traditional healer, an elder, an educated person or a close friend, project representatives in my study restricted the use of the term to mean a religious leader. Such a move marginalised their other roles and identities contained in the traditional and quotidian uses of the term and amplified a univocal definition of the term: that of being a religious leader, even in cases where these individuals might not have identified as such. Reducing diversity to enhance the legibility of subjects is a key feature of the simplification process manifested in these projects.

The process of simplification also led project staff to overlook local and specific uses of the term *shehe*, which as we have seen is not always fluid. At times, *shehe* refers to specific people and specific roles and relations with the community. The project-constructed *shehe*, a figure that had access to Muslims and possessed oratorical skills and social capital, did not exist in the way the project imagined. *Shehes* in the village were basically ad hoc imams, who led prayers and had what can be called a moderate knowledge of Islam.[5] However, Muslim figures like marriage counsellors and madrasa teachers were also given this label. These individuals felt the need to qualify their pre-existing identities without negating the project's etic category. Shehe Mbwana, for example, denied for a moment that he was a *shehe* and defined himself as a Qur'an teacher, then subsequently agreed he could be a *shehe* for us – that is, for the purposes of the project.

Yet even when the project utilises and promotes local knowledge and authority, these skills and social capital are translated through project terms and metrics. Some aspects of *shehes*' roles and identities are amplified, while others are minimised. But this process cannot be seen as merely reductive – flattening the diversity with no effects on the recipients, the implementers or the project. The projects' promotion of local knowledge and its re-packaging to align with its goals produce new forms of knowledge and expertise. *Shehes* in my projects were both hailed as authority figures and, at the same time, given training on how to identify and implement health solutions, an experience they appreciated.

---

[5] A witch hunter called Lambalamba accused Shehe Raja's mentor of being a witch because of his knowledge of certain verses and religious books that could be used to make amulets.

How projects conceptualised local knowledge and re-organised it suggests that we should not take local expertise as a given, but rather as something that is produced and negotiated during the encounters between development projects and their intended stakeholders. In other words, expertise has different meanings for different actors that seek them. It is not a form of knowledge that is a priori available for mobilisation, even when discourse and politics cast *shehes* as entrenched and natural.

Bibliography

Barth, Fredrick (1970), *Ethnic Groups and Boundaries: The Social Organization of Culture Difference*, Oslo: Universitetsforlaget.

Bayat, Asef (2007), *Making Islam Democratic: Social Movements and the Post-Islamist Turn*, 1st edn, Redwood City, CA: Stanford University Press.

Becker, Felicitas (2006), 'Rural Islamism during the "War on Terror": A Tanzanian Case Study', *African Affairs* 105(421), pp. 583–603, https://doi.org/10.1093/afraf/adl003

Becker, Felicitas (2008), *Becoming Muslim in Mainland Tanzania, 1890–2000*, Oxford: Oxford University Press.

Biehl, João (2005), *Vita: Life in a Zone of Social Abandonment*, 1st edn, Oakland: University of California Press.

Caton, Steven C. (1993), *Peaks of Yemen I Summon: Poetry as Cultural Practice in a North Yemeni Tribe*, Oakland: University of California Press.

Cohen, David William and Atieno Odhiambo (1992), *Burying SM: The Politics of Knowledge and the Sociology of Power in Africa*, Portsmouth, NH: Heinemann.

Elyachar, Julia (2005), *Markets of Dispossession: NGOs, Economic Development, and the State in Cairo*, Durham, NC: Duke University Press.

Foucault, Michel (1994), *The Birth of the Clinic: An Archaeology of Medical Perception*, New York City: Vintage.

Gilsenan, Michael (1996), *Lords of the Lebanese Marches: Violence and Narrative in an Arab Society*, Oakland: University of California Press, http://www.amazon.com/Lords-Lebanese-Marches-Violence-Narrative/dp/0520205901

Gluckman, Max (1949a), 'Africa – The Village Headman in British Central Africa', *Africa, International African Institute* 19(02), http://journals.cambridge.org/action/displayAbstract?fromPage=online&aid=7886934&fileId=S0001972000029235

Gluckman, Max (1949b) 'The Village Headman in British Central Africa', *Africa* 19(2), pp. 89–106.

Green, Maia (2014), *The Development State: Aid, Culture & Civil Society in Tanzania*, Melton, UK: James Currey.

Guyer, Jane (1995), 'Wealth in People as Wealth in Knowledge: Accumulation and Composition in Equatorial Africa', *Journal of African History* 36(1), pp. 91–120.

Hearn, Julie (1998), 'The "NGO-isation" of Kenyan Society: USAID & the Restructuring of Health Care', *Review of African Political Economy* 25(75), pp. 89–100, https://doi.org/10.1080/03056249808704294

Hirschkind, Charles (2009), *The Ethical Soundscape: Cassette Sermons and Islamic Counterpublics*, New York: Columbia University Press.

Hunt, Nancy Rose (1999), *A Colonial Lexicon: Of Birth Ritual, Medicalization, and Mobility in the Congo*, Durham, NC: Duke University Press.

Khan, Naveeda (2012), *Muslim Becoming: Aspiration and Skepticism in Pakistan*, Durham, NC: Duke University Press.

Livingston, Julie (2012), *Improvising Medicine: An African Oncology Ward in an Emerging Cancer Epidemic*, Durham, NC: Duke University Press, https://books.google.com/books?hl=en&lr=&id=nKfswD9goqMC&oi=fnd&pg=PR7&dq=improvising+medicine+livingston&ots=8MQLdNxU-Z&sig=-sd_MMzvLMSGiEEGBfIMdZTxYa4

Ludwig, Frieder (1999), *Church and State in Tanzania: Aspects of Changing Relationships, 1961–1994*, Leiden: Brill.

Mamdani, Mahmood (1996), *Citizen and Subject: Contemporary Africa and the Legacy of Late Colonialism*, Princeton, NJ: Princeton University Press.

McIntosh, Janet (2009), *The Edge of Islam: Power, Personhood, and Ethnoreligious Boundaries on the Kenya Coast*, Durham, NC: Duke University Press, http://dx.doi.org/10.1215/9780822390961

McKay, Ramah (2016), 'The View from the Middle: Lively Relations of Care, Class, and Medical Labour in Maputo', *Critical African Studies* 8(3), pp. 278–90, https://doi.org/10.1080/21681392.2016.1233504

Miller, Flagg (2007), *The Moral Resonance of Arab Media: Audiocassette Poetry and Culture in Yemen*, Harvard Center for Middle Eastern Studies.

Nguyen, Vinh-Kim (2010), *The Republic of Therapy: Triage and Sovereignty in West Africa's Time of AIDS*, 1st edn, Durham, NC: Duke University Press.

Ong, Aihwa and Stephen J. Collier (eds) (2004), *Global Assemblages: Technology, Politics, and Ethics as Anthropological Problems*, 1st edn, Hoboken, NJ: Wiley-Blackwell.

Petryna, Adriana (2013), *Life Exposed: Biological Citizens after Chernobyl*, Princeton, NJ: Princeton University Press.

Rapp, Rayna (2000), *Testing Women, Testing the Fetus: The Social Impact of Amniocentesis in America*, 1st edn, Abingdon: Routledge.

Robins, Steven (2006), 'From "Rights" to "Ritual": AIDS Activism in South Africa', *American Anthropologist* 108(2), pp. 312–23, https://doi.org/10.1525/aa.2006.108.2.312

Said, Edward W. (1979), *Orientalism*, 1st edn, New York City: Vintage.

Scott, James C. (1999), *Seeing Like a State: How Certain Schemes to Improve the Human Condition Have Failed*, New Haven: Yale University Press.

Skovgaard-Petersen, Jakob (1997), *Defining Islam for the Egyptian State: Muftis and Fatwas of the Dār Al-Iftā*, Leiden: Brill.

Weber, Max (ed. Roth Guenther and Claus Wittich) (1978), *Economy and Society: Outline of Interpretive Sociology*, Berkeley: University of California Press.

el Zein, Abdul Hamid M. (1974), *The Sacred Meadows: A Structural Analysis of Religious Symbolism in an East African Town*, Evanston: Northwestern University Press.

11

Facing Change at the Margins of the Kenyan Nation: The Promise of the Lamu Port

CHARLOTTE KNOTE

This chapter takes you to the small island of Lamu: nestled in the clear blue waters of the Indian Ocean between the other islands of the archipelago, Lamu[1] is surrounded by the mangrove swamps of Kenya's northern coastline, in close proximity to both the Somalian border and the Kenyan mainland. Since 2001, Lamu's old town, 'the oldest and best-preserved Swahili settlement in East Africa', has been a recognised UNESCO world heritage site (UNESCO.org 2001). The majority of Lamu Island's 25,000 inhabitants are of Sunni Muslim faith and the predominant Islamic culture is, inter alia, a central aspect in constituting people's identity. Life on the island is structured, on the one hand, by the rhythm of the five daily prayers, and on the other by the phases of the moon. Since the 19th century, Lamu has functioned as a major Islamic centre for Muslims from all over East Africa who come on pilgrimage here to the annual *maulid* celebrations (Amidu 2009). Up until today, Lamu's Swahili culture has shown strong influences of the Indian Ocean trading networks with the Arabian and the Southern Asian subcontinents, as seen in the language, religion, architecture and literary traditions as well as in clothing and fashion, culinary art, popular culture and migration patterns.

Thus, within the Kenyan national context, Lamu has maintained a unique position, not only in the geographic periphery but also socio-economically, culturally and politically. For many centuries, life on Lamu has evolved around

---

[1] Throughout this chapter I use 'Lamu' interchangeably with 'Lamu Island'. When referring to 'Lamu Town', 'Lamu County', 'Lamu District' or the 'Lamu Archipelago' I will specifically designate it as such.

and in harmony with the sea. The people situate themselves within this islandscape,[2] and through their strong historical ties to maritime livelihoods and trading networks they have always been directed more towards the sea than to the mainland (see also Prins 1965 and Middleton 1992). Lamu's small community has depended mainly on small-scale tourism and fishing, which in turn depend on the archipelago's rich natural resources such as its well-preserved coral reefs, significant marine and wildlife biodiversity, dense mangrove forests and white sand beaches. Lamu's oft-cited 'magical' character and its hospitable atmosphere are not only evoked through its idyllic landscape and mystical old town but also rooted in the peaceful Islamic culture of its people.

Only a few kilometres from Lamu Island on the mainland, around the villages of Hindi and Magogoni between dense mangrove forests and a stone's throw away from Lamu's neighbouring island of Manda, one finds a vast construction site of a mega-port. The proposed deep-sea port at Manda Bay is planned to have thirty-two berths surrounded by an enormous infrastructural area that will contain an international airport, an oil pipeline and refinery, and three resort cities in Lamu, Isiolo and Turkana. Despite initial efforts, the progress of the construction has been heavily delayed over the last years. Nevertheless, as of mid-2020, the completion of the port's first three berths was expected by the end of the year (Kagai 2020).[3] When completed, the port will act as a hub for the inter-regional Lamu Port–South Sudan–Ethiopia Transport (LAPSSET) infrastructure corridor that is meant to connect the coast to inter-regional highways, oil pipelines and railway lines reaching all the way to South Sudan and Ethiopia, with a total cost estimated at 25 billion US dollars. It is the Kenyan government's flagship project for its Vision 2030 scheme and, as East Africa's biggest port, is expected to boost Kenya's economic growth and trade.[4] Apart from the port project, there have been further efforts to explore and drill for oil and gas at sites close by (Praxides 2019). On 26 June 2019, the government's intention of building a potential 1,050-megawatt coal power plant was halted through a ruling of the Kenyan court after the plan had been met with strong opposition from local and international environmental activists (Namwaya 2019).

In 2012, I spent four months in Lamu to conduct ethnographic fieldwork, researching how the local population perceived the planning and construction

---

[2] 'Sea, coast and land all contribute to an island's character. The use of the term *islandscape* is advocated as the only term which encompasses all of the constituent components of an island, in a holistic manner.' Vogiatzakis et al. 2017: 1.

[3] In fact, as of this writing, only the first of the three berths have been completed. Most delays over the years were linked to security concerns, budget cuts and political discrepancies among the regional stakeholders involved. Lamu County has repeatedly suffered under violent attacks by al-Shabaab militia in the mainland area close to the port site. Mwita 2020; Nyagah et al. 2017.

[4] LAPSSET Official Website (n.d.), see also Lamont 2013.

of this mega-project[5] and in what way they supported or criticised the impact it would have on their lives. The research also dealt with the question of how the port construction links to perceptions of historical injustices within the marginalised Muslim coastal community.[6] During fieldwork, I conducted around thirty semi-structured interviews with people from different actor groups, who were directly or indirectly affected by the port in their livelihood strategies. All belonged to the community of Lamu Town or the port site, and included elders and religious authorities, tourist guides and dhow operators, European expatriates and hotel owners, domestic workers, businessmen, farmers, politicians, fishermen and mangrove cutters, activists and conservationists.[7] In addition, I spoke informally to many people about the expected effects of the Lamu port while following the public debates in their initial stage via participant observation at different events related to the upcoming construction of the port and in everyday life. The majority of my research participants had a Swahili, and specifically Bajuni, background, were male and aged between 25 and 65. When referring to the people of Lamu I am aware that their identities are contested and subjective and encompass individual complex negotiation processes that draw on different sets of ethnic, religious and cultural aspects of belonging, such as being Swahili, Bajuni, Muslim, coastal, Kenyan, maritime, cosmopolitan, and urban, and at the same time are often constituted through distinction from 'others'. By providing examples from my ethnographic material I demonstrate how the construction of this infrastructural mega-project was being negotiated in Lamu's everyday life. By illustrating some of the central narratives I encountered regarding the threats and promises ascribed to the port as articulated by the research participants, I show how these point towards a shared perception of the islanders' social and political positioning at the margins of the Kenyan nation-state.[8]

More than ten years after the port's initiation, construction is progressing, although in no way as quickly as initially planned. Since the data that is used in this study dates from the official beginning of the project in 2012, the material should be considered a snapshot of Lamu facing the construction of the new

---

[5] Mega-projects are large-scale, transformational, complex ventures taking a long time to develop and build, involving multiple public and private stakeholders and impacting millions of people. Typically, their estimated cost is more than US$1 billion (Clegg et al. 2017; Flyvbjerg 2014).

[6] The political marginalisation of the coastal Muslim population has been widely addressed in previous years. See e.g. Willis and Chome 2014; Ndzovu 2014; Soares and Otayek 2007.

[7] The demography of Lamu County comprises roughly 123,000 people with different ethnic communities such as Bajuni, Orma, Aweer, Kore Maasai, Mijikenda, Pokomo, Somali, Bohra, Kamba and Kikuyu, among others. The Bajuni, whose origins can be traced back to different Bantu and Arab groups, constitute the majority of the islands' population, with around 25,000 inhabitants. The majority of the people indigenous to Lamu Town are largely 'Swahili' – a contested term that usually refers to East African coastal people who share Swahili as a first language and Islam as markers of common identity. For a brief overview of the debate on Swahili identity see Ray (2018).

[8] See also Das and Poole (2004) and Clifford and Marcus (2010).

port as an example within the course of historical events. Even though the port's construction had not properly started in 2012, political discourses and conflicts had emerged already and indicated a need for careful consideration of the local perspectives and interests. By seeing the port as a complex mega-project that is a site of contested sense-making and power relations (Clegg et al. 2017), I aim to show how these inherent dynamics are reflected in the lived experiences and imaginations of the people of Lamu. I argue that, among Lamu's community, the discourses and debates about the port project elicit perceptions of inequitable power relations within the Kenyan nation-state.[9] These perceived experiences of social and political injustices thus manifested my interlocutors' identity formation.

Promise of Change Evoking Hopes and Dreams

On Friday 2 March 2012, a short while after I arrived in Lamu, the groundbreaking ceremony of the LAPSSET port took place with the former heads of state of the three countries involved – Kenya, Southern Sudan and Ethiopia – being present: former Kenyan president Mwai Kibaki, former prime minister Raila Odinga, former president Salva Kiir of Southern Sudan, and the late former Ethiopian prime minister Meles Zenawi. Later, I heard on the news that during the inauguration ceremony President Kibaki had said to the guests: 'I have no doubt that this day will go down in history as one of the defining moments when we made a major stride to connect our people to the many socio-economic opportunities that lie ahead' (BBC News Africa 2012). At that time, it seemed as if the port construction was close to a breakthrough and that this event would mark the dawn of new beginnings. The atmosphere in Lamu was lit up with both excitement and tense anticipation of massive changes ahead. I had heard about the event in conversations and in the national news, where the port was marketed as a project bringing an economic upswing for the Kenyan nation and the Kenyan people, as well as a boost for all the regional economies involved.

One day before four of East Africa's presidents met at the bleak sandy stretch of the port's construction site on the mainland to celebrate their common visions of national growth and progress, I witnessed how around 200 community members flocked to Lamu Town to protest against the launch. The gathering started with a long prayer meeting, followed by a public demonstration through Lamu Old Town, singing the Kenyan national anthem, holding up signs and chanting '*Haki yetu!*' ('Our rights!'). The crowd gathered at the sea front's jetty, where they cut down the banner welcoming guests to the launching project. The protest was organised by Save Lamu, a coalition of community-based

---

[9] For a thorough analysis of the situation of the port in Lamu that looks at more recent political developments, see Chome (2020a, 2020b).

organisations in Lamu County.[10] They called for a boycott of the launch event since it was set on Friday, the holy day of rest and of congregational prayers for the Muslim community. In a written statement, they voiced their criticism of the project and addressed the port's 'lack of an environmental impact assessment and mitigation plan, the lack of community participation and consultation, lack of access to information, threats to traditional nature-based livelihoods and the failure to recognise local individual, community and public ownership of land'.[11]

The launch day can be read as an allegory for the conflicting interests between the government of Kenya and Lamu's population: While the president advertised the port as benefiting all its citizens, celebrating its launch with pomp, the majority of the local Muslim civil society, represented by Save Lamu and the protesters, felt deliberately excluded from the event as it coincided with their Friday prayer times (as criticised by the group: Save Lamu 2012a). Save Lamu, as the voice of those who would be most directly affected by the port's impact, was asking for community participation and mitigation plans, while the public authorities just followed through with their intended agenda. Later, I read in the Kenyan *Daily Nation*[12] about the promises given by the former prime minister Raila Odinga to Lamu's community:

> This project will change lives here. We are looking at a project with the capacity of the port of Dubai. The land you are talking about is just a drop in the ocean compared to the benefits you will get … Luck knocks once, not twice, and today, luck is knocking on the doors of people of Lamu. As a friend of the people of Lamu, I want to urge you to embrace this project. The benefits will far outweigh the monetary compensation you are asking for.

The trope of 'Lamu as a second Dubai' was something that reverberated immediately in conversations I had. Most people on the Swahili coast whom I spoke to knew Dubai as a place of luxury and prosperity. Many had family members who had lived in the Arab Emirates, or if they had had the privilege of travelling abroad they might have travelled through Dubai on their way to Europe or Asia, remembering the monumental airport that shows off the city's wealth. The promise to make Lamu like Dubai, with the implication of bringing jobs and economic growth to the region, provoked ideas of a utopian image of a better life that many had been longing for. These long-unfulfilled desires also linked to the

---

[10] The group was being supported by Muslims for Human Rights (MUHURI) and the Coast Peoples' Forum.
[11] See Save Lamu's Press Statement on the Launching Ceremony of the Lamu Port (2012).
[12] 'Kenya: Lamu Port Will Change Lives, Says PM', *Daily Nation*, 21 February 2012. https://allafrica.com/stories/201202211375.html

glorified shared memory of the golden Swahili past[13] that people often referred to. The people of Lamu had not only been suffering from the poor economic situation but many were also engaging in a 'nostalgic discourse' and a 'sense of bereavement', as described in Hillewaert's ethnography of Lamu Town.[14] These concern not only the cultural history of the wealth of Swahili city-states, but also the perceived loss of forgotten traditional practices, as threatened by social transformation.

Inspired by the launch event, the circle of young dhow operators with whom I had spent the day kept on talking about the port and what it would entail for their future. I had been accompanying a group of young Swahili men in their twenties who worked in the dhow business, assisting them on sailing trips and attempting to learn Swahili sailing practices. Among them, it felt as if the sudden excitement and imagining of the event had cleaved a space for only positive sentiments to prevail. They started picturing themselves in their newly envisioned lives as managers and millionaires. All of them had also been suffering due to dwindling tourist numbers caused by the travel bans that many European countries had issued after two kidnappings of foreign tourists in Lamu County the previous year (Chonghaile 2012). Lamu's economic situation was only slowly recovering from the attacks, and thus people were struggling to earn a decent living. This vulnerability, I argue, combined with poorly imparted information about the port's impact, constituted one reason why many of Lamu's inhabitants were gladly accepting the Kenyan government's promise, like these young dhow operators, despite its anticipated downsides that were also addressed publicly by organisations such as Save Lamu. While Save Lamu was advocating the social and legal concerns on behalf of the local people there were ambivalent reactions towards the promise of the port among the population and even within the initiative. The positive effects, as anticipated by my interview partners in the visions stated above, concentrated on the hope of benefiting economically from the port, such as through job and income opportunities, improved infrastructure, increased business opportunities and, thus, better living standards. At the same time, the scale of the negative impacts on the region's ecological and cultural heritage was addressed by individuals and community organisations such as Save Lamu.

Effects on Natural Resources and the Call for Participation

The Lamu port not only creates competition over land and resources, but its impact on the local environment is expected to transform historical livelihoods

---

[13] See also Curtin (1983); Romero (1997); Ylvisaker (1979).
[14] See Hillewaert (2013: 156) and Chapter 3, as well as Hillewaert (2019).

irreversibly. With fishing, tourism and small-scale farming being the three pillars of Lamu's economy, restricting the people from practising those would deprive them of their current base of existence.

During my fieldwork I had met several members of Save Lamu; they were the main stakeholders in mobilising and educating the community to claim their legal rights related to the port project. One of their activists told me about the expected impact on marine livelihoods. She claimed that since 70 per cent of the indigenous community were relying heavily on local resources, which the port would jeopardise, people would therefore have no way of surviving:

> For instance, you've got all of the area that is going to be chopped up, where fishermen are not gonna be able to go. The Dodori creek area is going to be a no-go zone. That's the place for all fishermen here. For all kinds of shrimps, fishing, the mangroves that are being cut down. You saw photographs of what they did just to put in the launching, which was nothing! Just a launch of the site! They desecrated the mangroves that were there. Those were all the nesting areas, for all the fish and crabs and shrimps and so forth. So that's going to be a big blow to fishermen here … How are they going to assist fishermen who will now not be able to use the waters like they used to? … What are they doing about it?[15]

The environmental threat being addressed here is not only the limited access fishermen have to traditional fishing sites but also the ecological devastation through the dredging of grounds, and thus the extinction of vast mangrove forests, coral reefs, and nesting areas as habitats for rare species. Asking whether the fishermen will be assisted in getting access to alternative fishing grounds or different techniques shows that this activist believes the government is responsible for offering support. While I was in Lamu, no action had been taken to involve the fishermen in the feasibility study or an environmental impact assessment, which would have been an easy way to improve the community's sense of participation.[16] This existential menace was one main concern that contributed to the community's sense of anxiety. I noticed that many local people often did not realise the extent of the negative impacts the port would have on their livelihoods, either due to a lack of information or because of other existential worries weighing heavy on their outlook on life. Nevertheless, the complexity of reasons why people would support or oppose the port represented a mixture of

---

[15] Interview with Rabia (pseudonym) in English, 9 May 2012, Lamu Town.
[16] In May 2018, the Malindi High Court ordered the government to compensate 4,600 displaced Lamu fishermen with a total sum of 1.76 billion Kenyan shillings. Further demands for compensation are ongoing.

different propositions coming together, and was even shifting among individuals and groups over time.

As the Save Lamu members had told me, in January 2009 the Kenyan government had announced its plans publicly in a 'port sensitisation meeting', although through this the information was only given in one direction without the option to participate in the decision process. Instead of the government consulting with locals about the feasibility of such a massive project, the information that plans were already being implemented was simply shared. The father of a friend of mine, a Bajuni Muslim who had lived both in Lamu and in Germany, expressed strong disappointment over the ways in which the government had been introducing the project:

> They were not informed, the people of Lamu. Those who had already been planning it, they only came now to explain it to us. They did not come to ask for our advice ... Now the people of Lamu know nothing. Because, if they knew, they would not approve ... They do not cooperate.[17]

He, as well as others, mentioned that the port's initial plans had existed since the 1970s, but that the community had not been informed or included in any decision-making processes. This exclusion was a major source of growing distrust and the main reason why many of those I spoke to had a strong sense of being marginalised as a community. This was not unique to Lamu, but was a shared perception of many coastal Muslims in Kenya. There was a general incomprehension as to why in developmental aspects the coast was lagging behind other regions of Kenya, despite the economic potential its rich natural and cultural resources offered, as well as its popularity among tourists. Most coastal community members felt neglected by the government as they were lacking opportunities and did not profit from the region's achievements. This notion is deeply rooted in an ongoing positioning of the coastal Muslims within the Kenyan state. A Kenyan coast study from 2013 shows that overall life quality diverges significantly between different members of society,[18] while people asserted that the economic achievements of the region would only benefit outsiders. As John O. Oucho explains, many political tensions in East Africa stem from the more or less randomly drawn frontiers of colonialists, in which ethnic loyalties sharply conflict with national loyalties and thus start 'rocking the foundations of

---

[17] Interview with Muhsin (pseudonym), 25 February 2012, Lamu Town. (Original Swahili quotation: 'Hawakujulishwa, watu wa Lamu. Wao walikuwa wameshapanga wao, sasa wamekuja kutuelezea. Hawakuja kutoa mashauri kwetu ... Sasa watu wa Lamu hawajui kitu. Maana, kama watu wa Lamu wajua hawangekubali ... Hawashirikiana.')

[18] The 'Kenya coast survey' conducted by Wolf, Muthoka and Ireri (2013) supports my observations in which respondents claim that governance failings such as 'bad/greedy leaders' or 'government discrimination' were perceived as being the main obstacles to development.

nationhood' (Oucho 2002: 7). In the case of Kenya, religion plays an additional role in these disruptions, as the state, although nominally secular, is 'in practice a Christian state' as 'its political culture is infused with Christian language and imagery' and the 'political and administrative elite have been overwhelmingly Christian' (Mwakimako and Willis 2014). This adds to the shared distrust felt among coastal Kenyans towards state institutions, and people have started to question their identification as Kenyan citizens in opposition to their common identity as coastal Muslims. One movement that built upon these notions of alienation politically was the Mombasa Republican Council (MRC), which demanded a secession of the coast in the demarcations of the pre-colonial ten-mile coastal strip of the Sultanate of Zanzibar. During my fieldwork, its slogan '*Pwani si Kenya*' (the coast is not Kenya) was widely read and heard in the region and brought up questions of national, ethnic and religious belonging and a calling for a renegotiation of citizenship in the social and political sphere.[19] As Kai Kresse also points out in his book (2018), 'the past present continuous' experience of Kenya's coastal Muslims being dominated by external rule is still shaping public discourse, as well as their self-identification in a dichotomy of 'wapwani' (people of the coast) versus 'wabara' (up-country people).

The Swahili – A Drop in the Ocean?

Besides the predicted environmental changes through ecological damage and questions of access and ownership of natural resources, the other major expected change was the influx of labour migrants entailing an enormous impact on the demographic structure of Lamu.[20] Every one of my research participants was sure that the port would bring social and cultural changes to the island, but the extent to which this would affect people's lives was interpreted differently. While some were mainly hoping for their economic situation to improve in the shape of better jobs, others were afraid that the port might completely eradicate the existence of the local community.

Applying the same metaphor that Raila Odinga had used in his speech during the launch event to relativise the locals' fear of losing land, Mzee Hussein Soud, an Islamic scholar and the chairman of the Lamu council of elders, visualised his fear of being outnumbered by up-country migrants:

---

[19] See Willis and Gona (2012); Shauri and Wanjala (2017); Mahajan (2016); Goldsmith (2014); Mwakimako and Willis (2014).
[20] According to the feasibility study, the port would bring over one million labour migrants, not only to complete the construction work but also to fill the emerging posts within and outside the port complex. See: Japanese Port Consultants & BAC/GKA JV. 2011. Study for LAPSSET Corridor FS & Lamu Port MP & DD: 1151.

> With the coming of LAPSSET, instead of today (we're having about 100,000 people),[21] by the time that LAPSSET is ready, we shall have, it is estimated, there will be more than 1.5 million people here. Probably the Swahili themselves will be just a drop in the ocean.[22]

The use of this maritime image conveys a feeling of being submerged, invisible and meaningless, indicating that the prevailing fear of powerlessness against the authorities would be exacerbated by becoming an even more marginalised minority.

This perception of being marginalised links into the commonly heard narratives of historical injustices on the Kenyan coast, as many were afraid that the government would continue to ignore the interests of coastal Muslims, something they had experienced since the time of independence. Lamu's vulnerability and its position at Kenya's political margins had resulted from people's struggles with the post-colonial state's institutions, as I discovered throughout my fieldwork in various expressed notions of distrust towards the Kenyan government.[23] One of the main concerns expressed within Lamu's community was that the Kenyan government, run by a majority of up-country and mostly Christian politicians, was not representing the community's interests,[24] and that the Swahili coast, despite its high economic potential in general, was suffering badly from low education rates, youth unemployment, drug abuse and radicalisation tendencies.

Linked to this pervasive sense of a post-colonial history of political neglect as second-class citizens, another major pressing issue mentioned in many of my conversations that was also officially addressed by Save Lamu was that of land adjudication. In its statements, the Save Lamu initiative flagged up repeatedly that, starting in the 1970s, there had been a number of settlement schemes in Lamu County implemented by former president Jomo Kenyatta, in the area of Hindi and Magogoni, close to where the port is being constructed today. Between 1974 and 1996, the government settled about 40–45,000 Kikuyus from Tanzania and Central Province to farm the lands there (Save Lamu 2012b; Hoorweg 2000). A Bajuni man in his fifties, Mohamed Ali, also known as Mwalim Baadi, was a well-known and respected elder and retired schoolteacher

---

[21] According to the census of 2019, Lamu County has a population of 144,000 inhabitants, with Lamu Island at around 25,000 (KBS 2019).
[22] Mzee Hussein Soud in the video 'Who I am Who We Are – Lamu' (20:12). https://www.youtube.com/watch?v=dCcnyrpyqJg This video was produced as part of an art project by Wambui Kamiru and Xavier Verhoest to explore how ideas of 'Kenyan-ness' and nationhood are embodied through senses of identity. See also: https://ke.boell.org/2014/01/23/who-i-am-who-we-are
[23] See also Ndzovu (2014); Prestholdt (2014).
[24] See also Kresse's concept of the 'double periphery': for many coastal Muslims, national politics are equal to up-country politics that 'seek to keep the coast weak and internally divided'. The one side of the periphery describes the coastal Muslims' perceived status as 'second-class citizens'; the other side refers to the Muslims' position within the global Muslim *umma* (Kresse 2009b, 2012).

in Lamu Town. He was dedicated to his work in an environmental conservation CBO and had also been politically active. He explained to me:

> If you look at the demography and if you look at the political angle of these settlers being imposed in Lamu from Central province there are several issues imagined. One is the economic issue: they are given more preference in development issues than the local indigenous population. There is more infrastructure injected into these four–five settlement schemes than ... what is being implemented in the local indigenous areas. There is the political issue: already these settlers now control the political scene ... as far as the local government is concerned ... Now a major threat is being posed by this big project, called Lamu Port. If the five settlement schemes have imposed in the county a population that is non-indigenous of 45,000 people from Central Province into Lamu District and negating the local indigenous population their economic right, their social welfare, their political rights, and even their constitutional rights, what will the port do? Definitely, according to my CBO, the impact would be even worse.

This statement once more shows that many people in Lamu had lost trust in their government to operate in the public interest of the local community and that people were afraid of historical injustices being repeated. Among those of my interlocutors who knew of these settlement schemes, most were convinced that they were laid out intentionally in order to gain influence over the indigenous population, and some even stated that this was intended with a future port construction in mind. Although one may challenge that perception, Lamu seems to be the only county with a non-indigenous population of nearly 50 per cent (Otieno 2014). This conviction of being the victims of repeated injustices coupled with a lack of political representation and a lack of control over land and resources led to an attitude of political apathy among many young people, which was consequently reflected in low voter turn-outs later on. They felt discouraged and saw no prospects for their own future under these conditions.[25]

Coastal Muslim Citizenship and Identity

Though social change is nothing new to the Kenyan coast, and Lamu's hybrid culture and society is rooted deeply in migration from foreigners and transcultural exchange over several centuries, more recent prospects of change in the post-colonial state have stirred bigger controversies as people feel increasingly afraid of becoming a liminal minority. Migrants from up-country are often seen

---

[25] See also Cottrel-Ghai et al. (2013); Willis and Chome (2014); Mwakimako and Willis (2016).

as benefiting outsiders at the coast. Overall, the rigid division of Lamu's society along ethnic and religious lines as seen in everyday life is alarming, especially in the light of the recurring tensions concerning the country's elections and the general political situation in Kenya.

In conclusion, like other large-scale development projects,[26] the Lamu port increased political tensions and grievances between national and local interests as it threatened vulnerable livelihoods and challenged the spatial, social and cultural islandscape of the Lamu Archipelago. As shown in the statements of my research participants, for some people the new mega-port meant a promising chance for a better life in a time of economic despair, while others perceived it mainly as a threat to the culture and traditions of an already marginalised community. What the people of Lamu read into the government's promise always carries a subjective component: how each person situated him- or herself within these narratives of marginalisation is linked to their personal experiences and identity as members of a Muslim island community within the Christian-dominated post-colonial Kenyan state, and to a shared cultural memory of a better life in pre-colonial history. My research shows that the political discourse stirred by the promise of the port and the resulting tensions also led to a renegotiation of my research participants' national, cultural and ethnic identities, facing the imbalance of power and the continuation of historical injustices as performed by the Kenyan state. The practices of governance and the political engagement of state and non-state actors continue to be shaped and defined by this post-colonial history of fundamental tensions that in turn are perpetuated by certain dynamics of hope and distrust in which people become further entangled.

While the port construction has been progressing slowly, the region remains vulnerable and discussions among coastal Muslims and state authorities continue over new projects that yet again raise questions regarding their environmental impact and the distribution of benefits. The Kenyan government is continuing its endeavours to develop the country into an advanced technological and modernised state, but many questions concerning the ownership of land and resources and the actual concession of constitutional rights to the local population still need to be addressed. It will take combined efforts to enable Lamu's future generations to overcome the ongoing tensions in order to benefit from both the archipelago's sustained natural and cultural heritage and the promise of modernity and development.

---

[26] The promise of development and its entailing change every so often evokes 'landscapes of anticipation, desire, anxiety and conflict' among local populations (Jamali 2013).

Bibliography

Amidu, Assibi A. (2009), 'The Role of Islam in the Political and Social Perceptions of the Waswahili in Lamu', in Kjersti Larsen (ed.), *Knowledge, Renewal and Religion: Repositioning and Changing Ideological and Material Circumstances Among the Swahili on the East African Coast*, Uppsala: Nordiska Afrikainstitutet, pp. 236–60.

BBC News Africa (2012), 'East Africa Port Project Launched'. *BBC News*, 2 March, sec. Africa, http://www.bbc.com/news/world-africa-17231889

Chome, Ngala (2020a), 'Land, Livelihoods and Belonging: Negotiating Change and Anticipating LAPSSET in Kenya's Lamu County', *Journal of Eastern African Studies* 14(2), pp. 310–31.

Chome, Ngala (2020b), 'Local Transformations of LAPSSET – Evidence from Lamu, Kenya', in Jeremy Lind, Doris Okenwa and Ian Scoones (eds), *Land, Investment & Politics: Reconfiguring East Africa's Pastoral Drylands*, Melton, UK: James Currey.

Chonghaile, Clar Ni (2012), 'Judith Tebbutt Kidnapping Puts Kenya's Tourism into Decline', *The Guardian*, 21 March. World News, http://www.theguardian.com/world/2012/mar/21/judith-tebbutt-kidnapping-tourism-decline

Clegg, Stewart R., Shankar Sankaran, Chris Biesenthal and Julien Pollack (2017), 'Power and Sensemaking in Megaprojects', *The Oxford Handbook of Megaproject Management*, Oxford: Oxford University Press, p. 238.

Clifford, James and George E. Marcus (2010), *Writing Culture: The Poetics and Politics of Ethnography*, Oakland: University of California Press.

Cottrel-Ghai, Jill, Yash P. Ghai, Korir Sing'Oei and Waikwa Wanyoike (2013), *Taking Diversity Seriously: Minorities and Political Participation in Kenya*, Minority Rights Group International London.

Curtin, Patricia Romero (1983), 'Laboratory for the Oral History of Slavery: The Island of Lamu on the Kenya Coast', *The American Historical Review* 88(4), pp. 858–82.

Das, Veena and Deborah Poole (2004), *Anthropology in the Margins: Comparative Ethnographies*. SAR Press, https://muse.jhu.edu/book/24179

Flyvbjerg, Bent (2014), 'What You Should Know About Megaprojects and Why: An Overview'. SSRN Scholarly Paper ID 2424835, Rochester, NY: Social Science Research Network, http://papers.ssrn.com/abstract=2424835

Goldsmith, Paul (2014), 'Constitutional Reform and Minority Exclusion', *Indigenous People in Africa: Contestations, Empowerment and Group Rights*, 85.

Hillewaert, Sarah (2019), *Morality at the Margins: Youth, Language, and Islam in Coastal Kenya*, New York City: Fordham University Press.

Hillewaert, Sarah (2013), 'Between Respect and Desire: On Being Young, Pious, and Modern in an East African Muslim Town', University of Michigan, https://deepblue.lib.umich.edu/handle/2027.42/97892

Hoorweg, Jan (2000), 'The Experience with Land Settlement', in Dick Foeken and R. A. Obudho (eds), *Kenya Coast Handbook: Culture, Resources and Development in the East African Littoral*, Münster/Hamburg/London: Lit Verlag, pp. 309–25.

Jamali, Hafeez A. (2013), 'The Anxiety of Development: Megaprojects and the Politics of Place in Gwadar, Pakistan', Crossroads Asia Working Paper Series 6, Bonn: Competence Network Crossroads Asia: Conflict – Migration – Development, https://hdl.handle.net/20.500.11811/129

Kagai, Danson (2020), 'Launch of Lamu Port's First Three Berths Set for December', https://www.constructionkenya.com/762/lamu-port-project-underway/

Kenya Bureau of Statistics (2019), Kenya Population and Housing Census Volume I: Population by County and Sub-County, November.

Kresse, Kai (2009), 'Muslim Politics in Postcolonial Kenya: Negotiating Knowledge on the Double-Periphery', *The Journal of the Royal Anthropological Institute* 15 (January), pp. S76–S94.

Kresse, Kai (2012), 'On the Skills to Navigate the World, and Religion, for Coastal Muslims in Kenya', in *Articulating Islam: Anthropological Approaches to Muslim Worlds*, Muslims in Global Societies Series, Dordrecht: Springer, pp. 77–99.

Kresse, Kai (2018), *Swahili Muslim Politics and Postcolonial Experience*, Bloomington: Indiana University Press.

Lamont, Mark (2013), '"The Road to Sudan, A Pipe Dream?" Kenya's New Infrastructural Dispensation in a Multipolar World', in *African Dynamics in a Multipolar World*, Leiden: Brill, pp. 154–74, http://booksandjournals.brillonline.com/content/books/b9789004256507s011?crawler=true&mimetype=application/pdf

LAPSSET (n.d.) 'Lamu Port – LAPSSET Corridor Development Authority', http://www.lapsset.go.ke/projects/lamu-port/

Mahajan, Nidhi (2016), 'Lamu, A Battleground of Memory and Aspiration', in Léonie Newhouse and Tau Tavengwa (eds), *The Corridor: How the East African Corridor Spanning the Indian Ocean from Somalia to South Africa Is Being Radically Re-Shaped*, Capet Town: Cityscapes Magazine and the Max Planck Institute for the Study of Religion and Ethnic Diversity, pp. 9–13, https://cityscapesmagazine.com/projects/the-corridor

Middleton, John (1992), *The World of the Swahili: An African Mercantile Civilization*, New Haven, CT: Yale University Press.

Mwakimako, Hassan and Justin Willis (2014), 'Islam, Politics, and Violence on the Kenya Coast', *Observatoires Des Enjeux Politiques et Securitaires Dans Le Corne de l'Afrique*, Note 4.

Mwakimako, Hassan and Justin Willis (2016), 'Islam and Democracy: Debating Electoral Involvement on the Kenya Coast', *Islamic Africa* 7(1), pp. 19–43.

Mwita, Martin (2020), 'Poor Infrastructure, Regional Politics Derail New Port Facilities', *The Star*, 17 March, https://www.the-star.co.ke/business/kenya/2020-03-17-poor-infrastructure-regional-politics-derail-new-port-facilities/

Namwaya, Otsieno (2019), 'Tribunal Stops Kenya's Coal Plant Plans', *Human Rights Watch*, https://www.hrw.org/news/2019/07/01/tribunal-stops-kenyas-coal-plant-plans

Ndzovu, Hassan (2014), *Muslims in Kenyan Politics: Political Involvement, Marginalization, and Minority Status*, Evanston: Northwestern University Press.

Nyagah, Thomas, James Mwangi and Larry Attree (2017), *Inside Kenya's War on Terror: The Case of Lamu*. London: Saferworld, https://saferworld-indepth.squarespace.com/inside-kenyas-war-on-terror-the-case-of-lamu/

Otieno, Julius (2014), 'History of Mpeketoni and Link to the Internally Displaced', *The Star, Kenya*, http://www.the-star.co.ke/news/2014/06/17/history-of-mpeketoni-and-link-to-the-internally-displaced_c956226

Oucho, John O. (2002), *Undercurrents of Ethnic Conflicts in Kenya*, Leiden: Brill.

Praxides, Cheti (2019), 'Firm Explores for Gas in Lamu Again', *The Star*, https://www.the-star.co.ke/counties/coast/2019-08-09-firm-explores-for-gas-in-lamu-again/

Prestholdt, Jeremy (2014), 'Politics of the Soil: Separatism, Autochthony, and Decolonization at the Kenyan Coast', *The Journal of African History* 55(2), pp. 249–70.

Ray, Daren (2018), 'Defining the Swahili', in Stephanie Wynne-Jones and Adria LaViolette (eds), *The Swahili World*, Abingdon: Routledge, pp. 67–80.

Romero, Patricia W. (1997), *Lamu: History, Society and Family in an East African Port City*, Princeton, NJ: Wiener.

Save Lamu (2012a), 'Lamu Community Members Protest and Boycott Launch of Lamu Port', blog, 1 March, https://www.savelamu.org/lamu-community-members-protest-and-boycott-launch-of-lamu-port/

Save Lamu (2012b), 'Memorandum on Historical Land Injustices in Lamu, Presented to: The Truth Justice and Reconciliation Commission (TJRC)'.

Shauri, Halimu and Stanley Wanjala (2017), 'Radicalization and Violent Extremism at the Coast of Kenya: Powerful Voices of Coexistence, Are They Being Heard?', in Kimani Njogu and Irine Cege (eds), *Meeting of Cultures at the Kenyan Coast*, Nairobi: Twaweza Communication, pp. 145–54.

Soares, Benjamin F. and René Otayek (2007), *Islam and Muslim Politics in Africa*, 1st edn, Palgrave Macmillan.

UNESCO.org (2001), 'Lamu Old Town', UNESCO World Heritage Centre, https://whc.unesco.org/en/list/1055/

Vogiatzakis, Ioannis, Maria Zomeni and A. Mannion (2017), 'Characterizing Islandscapes: Conceptual and Methodological Challenges Exemplified in the Mediterranean', *Land* 6(1), p. 14.

Willis, Justin and Ngala Chome (2014), 'Marginalization and Political Participation on the Kenya Coast: The 2013 Elections', *Journal of Eastern African Studies* 8(1), pp. 115–34.

Willis, Justin and George Gona (2012), 'Pwani si Kenya? Memory, Documents and Secessionist Politics in Coastal Kenya', *African Affairs* 112 (446), pp. 48–71.

Wolf, Thomas, Samuel Muthoka and Margaret Ireri (2013), 'Kenya Coast Survey: Development, Marginalization, Security and Participation', *Journal of Eastern African Studies* 8(1), pp. 115–34.

Ylvisaker, Marguerite (1979), *Lamu in the Nineteenth Century: Land, Trade, and Politics*, Boston University, African Studies Center.

Part III

Law

12

Beyond an Impasse: Rule of Law and the Kenyan Kadhis' Courts

Susan F. Hirsch

In recent decades, rule of law has gained popularity as a key feature of development initiatives and civil society campaigns directed against tyrannical leadership. In these instances, rule of law is conceptualised broadly as a set of elements that underpin democratic governance, such as procedural fairness and equal treatment under the law. Rule of law is a controversial category, not least because of its use in promoting Western interests as much as the values associated with democracy. Yet critics are hard pressed to deny the centrality of rule of law to stable governance, and its appeal to anyone who rejects tyranny. Concerns about rule of law have also animated commentators who worry about whether Islamic law or any religious legal tradition is compatible with it (see e.g. Gutmann and Voigt 2018). Claims of a fundamental incompatibility feature prominently in situations where the legal integration of Muslim personal law into secular systems is being contemplated, such as in Europe where Muslim populations are growing. Similar discourse has emerged in the United States, where calls to ban shari'a law in several American states have used the justification of protecting rule of law (see e.g. Darian-Smith 2013, Moore 2010).[1] My aim is to highlight the Kenyan kadhis' courts as an example that challenges the assumed conflict between rule of law and Islamic law.

This chapter lays out a framework for thinking about governance, religious courts and rule of law. Where others view as problematic the inclusion of religious family law within a broader secular system, I take seriously the provocative possibility that state recognition of religious family law can enhance

---

[1] It is worth noting that no one was attempting to use or institutionalise Muslim law in those US jurisdictions.

rule of law. My argument draws on the scholarship of Hussein Ali Agrama, whose ethnography of secular and religious courts in Egypt encourages us to think beyond a secular/religious chasm to appreciate that the two types of court are both grounded in rule of law commitments (Agrama 2012). The tendency for public debate and scholarly writing to focus on irreconcilable differences between secular state law and religious law reflects what Agrama (2012) has termed 'an impasse' in our thinking about law in contemporary states (see also e.g. Cesari 2013; Cesari and McLoughlin 2005). Strident debates over these questions circumscribe the ability of commentators and politicians to appreciate the governance opportunities in situations where diverse normative orders come together (Moors 2003). Agrama and others who have written about rule of law and Islam offer ways 'beyond the impasse' that characterises so much debate (see e.g. Emon 2016; Massoud 2013).

My long-standing research on Kenyan kadhis' courts also influences my approach to legal integration, rule of law and Islamic family law. The Kenyan kadhis' courts handle marriage, divorce, inheritance and personal status (Hirsch 1998, 2010). Women bring the majority of claims, and, as demonstrated in my earlier research, they generally win.[2] My contention is that, as a result of reforms related to Kenya's adoption of a new constitution in 2010, the kadhis' courts operate in new ways that enhance rule of law, especially as experienced by Kenyan Muslims, and that these shifts offer new opportunities for governance in Kenya's pluralistic democracy.

In the following section, I first define rule of law and then explore the often-assumed impasse between Islamic law and rule of law. Following a short section focused on Agrama's writing, I analyse how the Kenyan kadhis' courts have come to embody rule of law commitments through the judicial reform sparked by the adoption of the 2010 Constitution of Kenya. The chapter's penultimate section addresses a thorny issue related to rule of law: namely, the requirement that authority figures be viewed as legitimate in a rule of law regime. This requirement prompts scrutiny of the Kenyan kadhis as key figures of governance, state law and religious law, who navigate a dual and shifting position as religious authorities and judicial officers. The increasingly secularised nature of their authority poses challenges and opportunities for governance, religious identity and rule of law. The chapter concludes by mentioning areas for future research and endorsing the Kenyan kadhis' courts as an exemplar for other countries that are struggling to recognise religious minorities.

---

[2] My research on the Kenyan kadhis' courts began in the mid-1980s and continued through the 1990s. For various reasons, including a personal tragedy experienced during the 1998 bombings in Kenya and Tanzania, I did not conduct research in East Africa for many years (Hirsch 2006). Beginning in 2016, my research has been funded by a National Science Foundation research grant from the Law and Social Sciences Program; SES-155639.

A Persistent Impasse

Scholarship that views Islamic law and rule of law as antithetical is generally produced by scholars whose expertise focuses on law and governance in secular states. As an example, such scholarship routinely includes assertions such as 'the interpretation of Sharia as divine in combination with the refusal to adopt a modern interpretation of the Qur'an is the main reason for concern about the incompatibility of Islam with the rule of law' (e.g. Gutmann and Voigt 2018; see also Kuran 2010). Emon (2016) asserts that, for several reasons, only rarely does scholarship on Islamic law consider the concept of rule of law in a less than dismissive manner. First, scholars of rule of law and scholars of Islamic law tend to travel in different circles, including at universities. Second, rule of law is generally promoted to majority-Muslim countries as a Western creation with politics and preconditions that position Islamic law as inadequate, thus exemplifying what Teemu Ruskola (2002) calls 'legal orientalism', a tendency to rank legal traditions from an unexamined, ethnocentric position. The third reason, which Emon emphasises over the others, contends that 'the idea of bringing together sharia and rule of law is problematic when each term of art remains highly contested and thereby subject to dispute' (Emon 2016: 38).

Although Waldron (2002) characterises rule of law as an 'essentially contested' concept, its key features are generally identified as fairness, access to justice, non-arbitrariness, order and predictability (see e.g. Heckman, Nelson and Cabatingan 2009; Tamanaha 2004). The American-based World Justice Project (WJP), which takes as its mission the expansion and promotion of the rule of law worldwide, measures perceptions of the rule of law as defined through four universal principles (e.g. Botero et al. 2012):

1. The government and its officials and agents as well as individuals and private entities are accountable under the law.
2. The laws are clear, publicised, stable and just; are applied evenly; and protect fundamental rights, including the security of persons and property.
3. The process by which the laws are enacted, administered and enforced is accessible, fair and efficient.
4. Justice is delivered in a timely manner by competent, ethical and independent representatives and neutrals who are of sufficient number, have adequate resources and reflect the make-up of the communities they serve. (www.worldjusticeproject.org)

These principles are reflected in many approaches to the rule of law in the large scholarly literatures that it has spawned. Other topics include the nature of rule of law, its relation to governance and neoliberalism, the consequences of the absence of rule of law, the relation between rule *of* law and rule *by* law, and rule of law promotion (see e.g. Carothers 2006; Ginsburg and Moustafa 2008; Humphreys 2012). Critical perspectives are also important in identifying the elitist and Western-centric nature of much rule of law scholarship and development initiatives focused on rule of law (see e.g. Rajah 2015). Those voicing concerns over top-down rule of law projects point out their tendency to serve donors' needs, rather than securing access to justice for the public (see e.g. Ghai and Cottrell 2010). For people positioned on all sides of the issue, rule of law promotion can be undertaken as an ethical calling with the aim of striving for justice as a social value.

Rule of law scholarship focuses almost exclusively on state-level secular law, and scant attention has been paid to how rule of law or ideas about rule of law are shaped by and in relation to religious law and customary law (cf., Isser 2011; Grenfell 2013). When rule of law promotion focuses on bringing states into line with international community standards, religious personal law is often ignored, marginalised or dismissed as too antithetical to rule of law to engage. The law and development projects in post-conflict settings have struggled to address the significant on-the-ground interest in customary or religious legal practices (Grenfell 2013). For instance, in postwar Afghanistan, informal and religious legal options are the most readily available and dependable avenues for seeking justice (Barfield, Nojumi and Thier 2011), yet in such circumstances an impasse between religious and 'rule of law' systems is often assumed.

In public debate in Europe and North America, state recognition of religious law is often depicted as distinctly the opposite of support for rule of law. Frequent mention of the impasse between Muslim family law and rule of law characterises debates over the legal integration of Muslim populations (see, generally, Joppke and Torpey 2013). Attention is directed, for instance, to concerns over: (a) the incompatibility of religious and secular approaches to law; b) the politics of state support for certain religions and not others; and (c) the uneven, potentially discriminatory, treatment of certain populations under religious law. All three of these concerns were raised in the acrimonious debate over Kenya's 2010 Constitution, during which constitutional recognition of the kadhis' courts was depicted as inevitably compromising fundamental rights, such as equality of treatment for women (see e.g. Cussac 2008; Ghai 2010; Mwangi 2012; Tayob 2013; Committee of Experts on Constitutional Review 2010). Such impasse thinking stands in the way of policy-making and scholarship that takes account of the actual challenges and effects of the legal integration of religious minorities.

Beyond the Impasse

Agrama calls into question the routine assumption of impasse at the meeting point of secular and religious normative orders. Instead, he makes the provocative assertion that rule of law, a concept foundational to the modern state, can serve to ground both secular and religious normative orders and does so in most places where shariʻa-based law is used (see also Hallaq 2005, 2013; Ferrari 2002; Naʻīm 2008). Agrama's position is based on his ethnographic research on religious and state courts in Egypt. The position of shariʻa as the constitutional basis for all law in Egypt leads to the typical conclusion that secularism has little or no space in the Egyptian state. However, Agrama finds that assumptions central to secularism, specifically the right of a liberal subject to freedom of belief, underpin the operation of both religious and secular courts and the legal interpretations in their decisions. His analysis of cases of apostasy reveals that individual religious belief is protected while actions based on that belief (i.e. those communicated externally through writing or speech) can be scrutinised by both religious and state courts for their concordance with law, including shariʻa. This leads Agrama to conclude that even in Egypt's *fatwa* courts, religious belief is treated as a duality with internal and external dimensions. The individual liberal subject, with rights to an internal belief that cannot be questioned by the state, thus serves as the starting point for both religious and secular law. When apostasy is communicated externally, judgments and punishments are justified by the need to preserve public order, which, Agrama reminds us, is a fundamentally liberal notion.

Agrama's approach invites consideration of the similarities between secular and religious normative orders. Identifying a broader range of examples of such connections is a promising direction for scholarship and policy, especially given the increasing demands for legal integration of religious minorities (see also Peletz 2015). My contention is that legal integration through religious family law produces more discourse about, more understanding of, and more opportunity for enacting rule of law commitments, even though this outcome is seemingly the opposite of what might be predicted by the pervasive emphasis on the purported impasse at the meeting place of secular and religious normative orders.

As an anthropologist, my interests go beyond examining the institutional arrangements related to the legal integration of religious law to explore people's experiences of those initiatives and to ask: how does the legal integration of religious courts foster what I call 'rule of law consciousness' or perceptions of procedural fairness, non-arbitrariness, non-discrimination, and access to legal personnel and institutions? Relatedly, my interest extends to the rule of law consciousness held by judicial personnel and other actors in legal contexts, as well as in public discourse. In a study of the broader concept of legal consciousness, Moore (2010) demonstrates that multiple influences, including religious leaders and media, shape legal consciousness among members of Muslim minority communities in the United States and the United Kingdom. Osanloo (2003) demonstrates that legal consciousness for Iranian women fuses a globally circulating 'rights' discourse with the Islamic Republic's interpretation of shari'a. These studies preclude any simple conclusions about how legal integration initiatives focused on Muslim family law might stimulate or shape rule of law consciousness.

After constitutional, legislative and judicial reforms, connections between the kadhis' courts and Kenya's secular state are more explicit, robust and complex (Hirsch 2018). The kadhis' courts operate amid an 'entanglement' of moral registers through which 'the varied forms and meanings of Islamic ethicolegal traditions' are articulated and negotiated (Hefner 2016: 4). Islamic law can be viewed as 'contingent and conjunctural', subject to the influence of other normative discourses, including those of the state. My argument is that legal integration of Muslim family law through the Kenyan kadhis' courts is a site for the state's rule of law promotion. This claim depends on considering not only how the substantive and procedural entailments of the legal system embody rule of law principles, but also the ways in which rule of law consciousness is being furthered, as discussed in a later section. Speaking broadly about recent reforms, one kadhi explained to me: 'In other countries they are Sharia-fying the constitution, but here in Kenya we are constitutionalising the Sharia.'

Enhancing Rule of Law through Legal Integration and Judicial Reform

Enhancing Kenya's commitment to rule of law was explicitly identified as a goal by Chief Justice Willy J. Mutunga and others seeking to justify a programme of judiciary transformation after passage of Kenya's 2010 Constitution (Mutunga 2011). The Judiciary Transformation Framework (2012–16) was a comprehensive plan to reform all elements of the delivery of justice in Kenya. This section highlights elements of rule of law that bear the impact of the reforms: specifically, clarity of laws, access to justice, procedural efficiency and fairness in both substance and procedure.

Laws are clear, publicised and stable

As a result of reform, the laws themselves are more clearly articulated in written law and publicised by the media. Relevant changes include passage of a new Kadhis' Courts Act and the Marriage Act of 2012. The crafting of procedural and evidentiary rules specifically for the kadhis' courts has the combined effect of enhancing rule of law and embracing Islamic legal practice. Engaging the kadhis in the reform process through rewriting and publicising laws and rules demonstrates attention to rule of law. Arguably, clear, publicised and stable laws and rules create a more predictable experience for those who use the courts or otherwise seek justice, as well as for those who work in the legal system.

Justice is accessible and efficient

In the post-2010 Constitution period, the number of kadhis' courts has grown from fifteen to over fifty. With the reach of the kadhis' courts extending well beyond the coastal region and Nairobi, which have historically had the largest concentrations of Kenyan Muslims, access to justice is more efficient and regular for the majority of Muslims, who also benefit from the construction of new courthouses nationwide. The expansion and professionalisation of court clerks and other staff also mean that information about kadhis' courts is more readily available than in the past. Efficiency is enhanced as well by requiring uniform maintenance of case files and other records. Similar to the magistrates' courts, the kadhis' courts experience audits and other evaluations that emphasise the need for efficiency and fairness, while promoting the reduction of case backlogs.

Justice is fairly delivered and protects fundamental rights

Fairness is difficult to determine, as unsuccessful claimants often have difficulty believing that they received fair treatment. With respect to sectarian differences, some Muslims are being treated more fairly than in the past. In deciding cases and presenting their reasoning, the kadhis tend to draw on a wider range of Islamic legal principles than previously, when their focus was primarily guided by the Shafia sect of Sunni Islam. Specifically, their rulings include legal interpretations from across the schools of Islamic law and jurisdictions in Malaysia, South Africa and India. As a result, Kenyan Muslim communities with roots in South Asia, Shirazi (Persian) and other Shia contexts can find recognition within the broader community of co-religionists. Kadhis find that legal interpretations from other sects have been useful not only in accommodating the diverse population of Kenyan Muslims but also in addressing certain thorny contradictions that arise between Muslim law and the Kenyan constitution. For instance, if the decision is made to appoint a female kadhi, the rationale will likely cite the Hanafi school of law, which has affirmed Muslim women's capacity to serve as judges (Hashim 2015). The ability of non-Muslim attorneys to practise in kadhis' courts is evidence of the fairness of those institutions, especially as it relates to protecting fundamental rights, such as non-discrimination on the basis of faith.

The fundamental rights at issue in questions of fairness, equal treatment or discrimination are those articulated prominently in the constitution and include 'human dignity, equity, social justice, inclusiveness, equality, human rights, non-discrimination and protection of the marginalized' (Art. 10 (2) (b) Constitution of 2010). At the same time, the kadhis' courts are the only Kenyan judicial body permitted to limit the right to equality 'to the extent strictly necessary for the application of Muslim law before the Kadhis' courts' (Art. 24 (4)). Article 24(4) paves the way for contraventions of fundamental rights that could emerge through the application of particular aspects of Islamic law, such as the differential treatment of men and women based on gender in matters of, for instance, inheritance or polygamy. The broad strokes of the constitution leave some room for issues to be challenged in court.[3]

For those who believe that they have been treated unfairly in a kadhis' court, as well as those who fear negative treatment, another avenue for achieving justice is available in Article 170 (5) of the 2010 Constitution, which establishes that the jurisdiction of the kadhis' courts 'shall be limited to the determination of questions of Muslim law relating to personal status, marriage, divorce or inheritance in proceedings in which all the parties profess the Muslim religion and *submit to the jurisdiction of the Kadhi's courts*' (emphasis mine) (Kenya 2010). The 'submission clause' was added late in the constitutional drafting process and over the objections of leaders in Kenyan Muslim communities, including some kadhis. To omit it would have involved the state in violating rights endorsed elsewhere in the constitution, such as the free practice of religion and the freedom of individuals to change their religion or their religious practices. The submission clause option comports with and supports rule of law by guaranteeing these individual freedoms, even as it establishes religious courts for a specific community. Yet, the addition of the clause breaks with a past history that made religious courts virtually the only option provided to Muslims seeking to address family law issues, an approach that community leaders felt should be retained in the new constitution. By explicitly widening the ethico-legal options available to Muslims, and introducing the notion that Muslims need not seek religious

---

[3] One instance involves a woman who was divorced through a *talaka* delivered to her and registered by an agent of her husband, as per court procedure. Under Muslim family law as practised in Kenya, a *talaka* is the expression of a husband's unilateral intention to divorce his wife. It can also be called repudiation. The husband need provide no reason, and the *talaka* becomes effective when delivered orally or in written form by the husband or his agent in the presence of a witness. A *talaka* is subsequently registered in a kadhis' court, and both parties receive certificates. When the woman mentioned above received the *talaka*, she asserted the right to be heard in a kadhis' court. In an example of constitutionalising shari'a, the kadhi reopened the matter, arguing that broad Islamic principles of justice and fairness justify protecting fundamental rights, such as equality. His decision has been appealed on grounds of a husband's unilateral right to divorce through *talaka*.

solutions to family law disputes, the presence of the submission clause calls attention to the state's secular institutions and moral registers as options for Muslims. In light of the prior history and the unsuccessful efforts to keep the clause out of the constitution, the power of the state to shape the ethico-legal palette is also made clear.

The submission clause also poses a challenge to Muslims who might be tempted to seek legal remedy in civil courts. Anecdotal instances of 'forum shopping' in the civil courts involve claimants who converted from Christianity to Islam when marrying under Islamic law and then wanted out – of both the marriage and the religion – at the time of divorce. Anticipating that more Muslims might choose to bypass kadhis' courts, one non-Muslim High Court judge said wryly, 'Well, we'll just have to see if they like the other system better.'

Judicial authorities are competent, ethical, independent and accountable

The Judicial Transformation process elevated kadhis to the level of magistrates with respect to their position in the judiciary, salary, access to training and benefits as judicial officers. Two types of kadhis can be appointed, Kadhi 1 and Kadhi 2, in addition to the higher ranks of Deputy Chief Kadhi and Chief Kadhi. The position of the Chief Kadhi and the Deputy Chief Kadhi have undergone similar improvements in compensation, benefits, training and prestige. The Chief Kadhi's position is equivalent to that of a High Court judge. If they are not already university graduates, kadhis are encouraged to seek further study and credentials beyond their qualifications related to Muslim law. The kadhis attend the same trainings as magistrates and judges. Efforts to professionalise the kadhis influence how they will be judged with respect to competence – a key element of rule of law. Arguably, the decision to treat kadhis similarly to other judicial officers appears to influence how they understand themselves – particularly recently appointed kadhis – and how others, such as fellow magistrates, might view them and their role in legal matters.

It is beyond the scope of this chapter to speculate on whether the kadhis are judged as ethical, independent and accountable. It is worth noting that the kadhis were not vetted by the Judges and Magistrates' Vetting Board, which from 2012 to 2016 investigated the extent to which judicial officers were guilty of political influence or other acts that disqualified them for service.

Implications

One implication of judicial transformation is that the kadhis' courts are no longer positioned by the state as wholly different from or subordinated to other courts; in short, they are no longer treated as second class. Being tied more closely to the broader legal system could bring its own negative responses, if the magistrates' courts, for instance, are viewed as lacking rule of law. However, my point is that the kadhis' courts are positioned such that it will be difficult to marginalise them as 'other' to a putatively more legitimate legal apparatus.

Another implication is that Kenyan Muslims might come to view themselves differently as a result of their interactions with the kadhis' courts. Closer legal integration might encourage Kenyan Muslims to understand themselves differently as citizens of Kenya. Among the changes would be their view of the state. To the extent that individual Kenyan Muslims recognise the state's role in supporting the courts and appreciate the commitments to rule of law afforded through the kadhis' court, then an altered sense of themselves as Muslim Kenyan citizens might be encouraged. Elsewhere, I have argued the following:

> As the Kadhis' courts become further integrated into the broader Kenyan legal system, and more Muslim Kenyans become aware of, and make use of these services, an increasing number of individuals will have the experience of connecting to the state through a process that also affirms their religion. The sense that they have the same entitlement to legal services in the area of personal law as do other Kenyan citizens, yet can receive those services in a way that recognises religious difference, may be meaningful for an increasing number of Kenyan Muslims, as access to justice through the Kadhis' courts expands to new regions and becomes more predictable and reliable. Arguably, for Kenyan Muslims this experience is an example of the unity in diversity aspired to in the Constitution and a counterpoint to the discrimination that Muslims have long faced. (Hirsch 2018)

The effects would likely be experienced by women to a greater extent than men, given women's greater use of kadhis' courts. My aim is not to judge whether it is good or appropriate that the kadhis' courts are being shaped by rule of law and other commitments of judiciary transformation. As a non-Kenyan, this is not for me to say. However, it is important to appreciate that the changes provide an example of legal integration that might serve Muslim minorities in other countries, even though thorny issues remain. The next section tackles one of these, while also identifying unexpected opportunities for governance made possible by increased attention to rule of law.

Legitimate Authorities, Rule of Law and Governance

A key element of rule of law is the requirement that the authorities who administer the law be viewed as legitimate (see e.g. Gowder 2016). Their legitimacy depends in part on the relation between the legal regime and the governance structure. In a chapter on shari'a and rule of law, Emon conceptualises rule of law as a 'claim space' in which to articulate arguments about justice (Emon 2016: 53). These arguments provide clues about the 'conditions and boundaries that define the claim space of what counts as legal for a particular rule of law system' (ibid.). It follows, then, that examining the operation of kadhis' courts sheds light on the governance structure in which the courts sit and, more specifically, about who counts as a legitimate authority.

Among the thorny issues forecast above is whether non-Muslims are legitimate authorities in kadhis' courts. No non-Muslims have been appointed as kadhis, yet non-Muslim judges have always heard appellate claims. Appeals of kadhis' court decisions are reviewed by High Court judges, who are joined in their deliberations by the Chief Kadhi, unless the lower court decision was made by him and another kadhi serves in his place. Challenges to the legitimacy of appellate judges on the basis of religion have been raised at times, and such challenges influence overall perceptions about the legitimacy of the kadhis' courts. The appointment of women as kadhis raises other legitimacy issues (Hashim 2015). Although attempts have been made to appoint women as kadhis, these were blocked by protests from powerful community members. Several kadhis believe that it will happen in the coming years as the pressure to conform to fundamental rights increases.

As the role of the kadhi shifts from religious authority to judicial officer, the structure of Kenyan Muslim leadership is also transforming. As kadhis become more highly educated and professionalised, they tend to become less connected to the broad range of people in local religious communities. Thus, their ability to gain recognition as local leaders decreases. At the same time, the recognition of kadhis as judicial officers influences their status as members of the group of magistrates and judges with whom they train and collaborate. Those kadhis who possess both a secular law degree and credentials in Muslim law may, in future, be called on to hear matters in magistrates' courts as well as in kadhis' courts. Dual appointments would increase kadhis' influence. The increased status afforded kadhis might boost other efforts to use religious law or religious values in, for instance, alternative dispute resolution or courtroom settings. Anecdotally, some Christian women have asked about access to the kind of justice rendered in kadhis' courts to alleviate their personal struggles more effectively than is possible through civil court proceedings.

With many new kadhis hired, and veteran kadhis adjusting to the changes, the struggle over what constitutes legitimate authority is only beginning. Will the kadhis uphold rule of law as Muslim jurists or as technocratic judicial officers? How different are these two options? In his study of Islamic law courts in Malaysia, Peletz (2015) notes that the implementation of Islamic law through reformed 'modern' procedures offers a vehicle for the state to shape citizens as Muslim legal subjects who conform to state-sanctioned behaviour. Thus the judiciary serves the state's ends in new, legitimate ways. It remains to be seen whether particular interests of the state or national values are reflected in the decisions of the Kenyan kadhis. Are their decisions affirming the unity in diversity of Kenya's constitution or a set of neoliberal values that better serves the state's governance aims?

Conclusion

Several lines of research follow from the analysis above. The first would centre on how the kadhis' courts actually perform with respect to rule of law. In addition to the state's judicial audits, what is needed are scholarly appraisals of the function and achievements of the courts as they relate to family life, claimants' experiences and perceptions, divorce and reconciliation rates, and broader effects on citizenship, identity and governance. A second line of inquiry would examine how Kenyan Muslims come to think about the state, and to experience its role in their lives, through their encounters with the kadhis' courts.

Scholarly attention to the integration of religious minorities is of great importance at the current moment when the number of people on the move – whether displaced by conflict or migrating to seek new political status or economic opportunity – exceeds all previous measures. The integration of Muslim minorities is a policy imperative in many contemporary democracies. By building theoretical understanding of family law's role in the legal integration of minority religious communities, my aim is to contribute to the broader policy discussion in Kenya, the United States, EU nations and elsewhere. As they adjust to a period of significant reform, the Kenyan kadhis' courts offer a compelling model for other contexts where minority Muslim populations reside and where states are willing to pursue unity in diversity. What can be said about the Kenyan example? The strong influence of Christianity in Kenya has not been diminished after over a century of state recognition of Muslim law. Thus, the kadhis' courts are an example of religious law coexisting in a vibrant modern, multi-religious state and enhancing the relation between Kenyan Muslim citizens and their government. Legal orientalism and lack of interest in examples from the Global South might stand in the way; however, if the kadhis' courts can be appreciated as sites for rule of law enhancement, then this deepened relationship should be of interest to many countries with diverse populations.

Bibliography

Agrama, Hussein Ali (2012), *Questioning Secularism: Islam, Sovereignty, and the Rule of Law in Modern Egypt*, Chicago: Chicago University Press.

Barfield, Thomas, Neamat Nojumi and J. Alexander (2011), 'The Clash of Two Goods: State and Nonstate Dispute Resolution in Afghanistan', in Deborah Isser (ed.), *Customary Justice and the Rule of Law in War-Torn Societies*, Washington, DC: United States Institute of Peace Press, pp. 159–92.

Cesari, Jocelyne (2013), *Why the West Fears Islam: An Exploration of Muslims in Liberal Democracies*, 1st edn, *Culture and Religion in International Relations*, New York, NY: Palgrave Macmillan.

Cesari, Jocelyne and Seán McLoughlin (2005), *European Muslims and the Secular State*, Network of Comparative Research on Islam and Muslims in Europe, Aldershot, Hants/Burlington, VT: Ashgate.

Committee of Experts on Constitutional Review (2010), Final Report of the Committee of Experts on Constitutional Review, Nairobi, Kenya.

Cussac, Anne (2008), 'Muslims and Politics in Kenya: The Issue of the Kadhis' Courts in the Constitution Review Process', *Journal of Muslim Minority Affairs* 28(2), pp. 289–302. doi: 10.1080/13602000802303227.

Darian-Smith, Eve (2013), *Laws and Societies in Global Contexts: Contemporary Approaches*, New York: Cambridge University Press.

Emon, Anver M. (2016), 'Shari'a and the Rule of Law', in Robert W. Hefner (ed.), *Shari'a Law and Modern Muslim Ethics*, Bloomington and Indianapolis: Indiana University Press, pp. 37–64.

Ferrari, Silvio (2002), 'Islam and the Western European Model of Church and State Relations', in W. A. R. Shadid and P. S. van Koningsveld (eds), *Religious Freedom and the Neutrality of the State: The Position of Islam in the European Union*, Leuven/Sterling, VA: Peeters, pp. 6–19.

Ghai, Yash (2010), 'Why Kenya's Constitution Should Recognize Kadhi's Courts', *Pambazuka News*, 29 April, http://www.pambazuka.org/governance/why-kenya's-constitution-should-recognise-kadhis-courts

Ghai, Yash and Jill Cottrell (eds) (2010), *Marginalized Communities and Access to Justice*, New York: Routledge.

Gowder, Paul (2016), *The Rule of Law in the Real World*, New York, NY: Cambridge University Press.

Grenfell, Laura (2013), *Promoting the Rule of Law in Post-Conflict States*, Cambridge: Cambridge University Press.

Gutmann, Jerg and Stefan Voigt (2018), 'The Rule of Law and Islam', in Christopher May and Adam Winchester (eds), *Edgar Elgar Handbook on Rule of Law*, Cheltenham and Northampton: Edward Elgar, pp. 345–57.

Hallaq, Wael B. (2005), *Authority, Continuity, and Change in Islamic Law*, digitally printed 1st pbk edn, Cambridge/New York: Cambridge University Press.

Hallaq, Wael B. (2013), *The Impossible State: Islam, Politics, and Modernity's Moral Predicament*, New York: Columbia University Press.

Hashim, Abdulkadir (2015), 'Eligibility of Appointing Female Qadis Between Islamic Religious Norms and the Provisions of the Constitution of Kenya, 2010', *The Law Society of Kenya Journal* 11(1), pp. 63–82.

Heckman, James J., Robert L. Nelson and Lee Cabatingan (eds) (2009), *Global Perspectives on the Rule of Law*, Abingdon: Routledge-Cavendish.

Hefner, Robert W. (2016), *Shari'a Law and Modern Muslim Ethics*, Bloomington: Indiana University Press.

Hirsch, Susan F. (1998), *Pronouncing & Persevering: Gender and the Discourses of Disputing in an African Islamic Court*, Language and Legal Discourse series, ed. William M. O'Barr and John M. Conley, Chicago: University of Chicago Press.

Hirsch, Susan F. (2006), *In the Moment of Greatest Calamity: Terrorism, Grief, and a Victim's Quest for Justice*, Princeton: Princeton University Press.

Hirsch, Susan F. (2010), 'State Intervention in Muslim Family in Kenya and Tanzania: Applications of the Gender Concept', in Shamil Jeppie, Ebrahim Moosa and Richard Roberts (eds), *Muslim Family Law in Sub-Saharan Africa: Colonial Legacies and Post-Colonial Challenges*, Amsterdam: Amsterdam University Press, pp. 305–29.

Hirsch, Susan F. (2018), 'Religion and Pluralism in the Constitution: Expanding and Transforming the Kenyan Kadhis' Courts', in *The Constitution and Pluralism in Kenya*, Nairobi: Katiba Institute, https://www.katibainstitute.org/religion-and-pluralism-in-the-constitution-susan-f-hirsch-professor/

Isser, Deborah (2011), *Customary Justice and the Rule of Law in War-Torn Societies*, Washington, DC: United States Institute of Peace Press.

Joppke, Christian and John Torpey (2013), *Legal Integration of Islam: A Transatlantic Comparison*, Cambridge, MA: Harvard University Press.

Kenya, Government of (2010), Constitution of Kenya, 2010, Nairobi: Government of Kenya.

Kuran, Timur (2010), 'The Rule of Law in Islamic Thought and Practice: A Historical Perspective', in James J. Heckman, Robert L. Nelson and Lee Cabatigan (eds), *Global Perspectives on the Rule of Law*, Abingdon, UK/New York: Routledge, pp. 71–90.

Massoud, Mark Fathi (2013), *Law's Fragile State: Colonial, Authoritarian, and Humanitarian Legacies in Sudan*, Cambridge Studies in Law and Society, Cambridge: Cambridge University Press.

Moore, Kathleen M. (2010), *The Unfamiliar Abode: Islamic Law in the United States and Britain*, New York: Oxford University Press.

Moors, Annelies (2003), 'Public Debates on Family Law Reform Participants, Positions, and Styles of Argumentation in the 1990s', *Islamic Law and Society* 10(1), pp. 1–11.

Mutunga, Willy J. (2011), 'Progress Report on the Transformation of the Judiciary', *Kenya Law*, 24 October, http://kenyalaw.org/kenyalawblog/progress-report-on-the-transformation-of-the-judiciary/files/13492/progress-report-on-the-transformation-of-the-judiciary.html.

Mwangi, Oscar Gakuo (2012), 'Religious Fundamentalism, Constitution-making and Democracy in Kenya: The Kadhis Courts Debate', *The Round Table* 101(1), pp. 41–52. doi: 10.1080/00358533.2012.656026.

Na'īm, 'Abd Allāh Aḥmad (2008), *Islam and the Secular State: Negotiating the Future of Shari'a*, Cambridge, MA: Harvard University Press.

Peletz, Michael G. (2015), 'A Tale of Two Courts: Judicial Transformation and the Rise of a Corporate Islamic Governmentality in Malaysia', *American Ethnologist* 42(1), pp. 144–60. doi: 10.1111/amet.12122.

Rajah, Jothie (2015), '"Rule of Law" as Transnational Legal Order', in Terence C. Halliday and Gregory Shaffer (eds), *Transnational Legal Orders*, Cambridge: Cambridge University Press, pp. 340–73.

Ruskola, Teemu (2002), 'Legal Orientalism', *Michigan Law Review* 101(1), pp. 179–234. doi: 10.2307/1290419.
Tamanaha, Brian Z. (2004), *On the Rule of Law: History, Politics, Theory*, Cambridge: Cambridge University Press.
Tayob, Abdulkader (2013), 'Kadhis' Courts in Kenya's Constitutional Review (1998–2010): A Changing Approach to Politics and State Among Kenyan Muslim Leaders', *Islamic Africa* 4(1), pp. 103–24.
Waldron, Jeremy (2002), 'Is the Rule of Law an Essentially Contested Concept (in Florida)?', *Law and Philosophy* 21(2), pp. 137–64.
World Justice Project (n.d.) 'Advancing the Rule of Law Worldwide', https://worldjusticeproject.org/files/14275/worldjusticeproject.org.

13

The Law of Evidence Applicable in the Kadhis' Courts of Kenya: A Study of Two Decisions by Kadhi Abduljabar, Kadhis' Court Nairobi at Upper Hill

Tito Kunyuk

Introduction

Kadhi Abduljabar Ishaq Hussein and I joined the judiciary of the Republic of Kenya late in 2012 to serve as kadhis (Islamic judges) in one of the most pronounced recruitments of kadhis in Kenya's recent history. My first interaction with Kadhi Abduljabar was in 2010 when I visited my former college, Thika College of Sharia and Islamic Studies (now called Umma University), to speak to students doing their BA degrees in Sharia and Islamic Studies. He was a student then and I would interact with him and other students, holding academic discussions late into the night, which were frequently focused on the geopolitics of the Middle East. After we joined the judiciary, our discussions started to focus exclusively on the kadhis' courts, the present laws applicable in the courts, and the kind of jurisprudence practised by the kadhis in their respective locales. Evidence law has frequently featured in many of our discussions. This chapter concerns the status of evidence law applicable in the kadhis' courts of Kenya today, with particular emphasis on two case decisions from the Nairobi kadhis' court that reflect Kadhi Abduljabar's thinking on the law of evidence.

The chapter is divided into two sections and a conclusion. Section one addresses the history of evidence law in the kadhis' courts of Kenya. Section two focuses on the two cases heard by Kadhi Abduljabar.

Islam and Evidence Law from the Past to the Present

Islamic law looms large in contemporary discourses surrounding the relationship between law, religion and the state. Since the end of the Cold War up to the post-9/11 era, many scholars, legal practitioners and policy-makers across the world have taken a deeper interest in the shariatisation of politics, a phenomenon premised on a real or imagined competition between religion and the secular, especially in spaces where Muslim populations are concentrated (Tibi 2008). With the rise of constitutionalism in African states such as Kenya, the debates on the accommodation of public religion in governance and public institutions has been heightened. Recent contestations on the constitutionality of the kadhis' courts of Kenya (Cussack 2008; Mwangi 2012) and the wearing of Muslim headscarves (*hijab*) in Kenyan schools are examples of such (on hijab see *Methodist Church in Kenya* v. *Mohamed Fugicha & 3 others* [2019] electronic Kenya Law Reports eKLR).

Kadhis' courts applying Islamic law have existed in Kenya since pre-colonial times (Mwakimako 2010: 110). While much attention has been given to assessing the historicity of kadhis' courts and the intellectual tradition of kadhis in Zanzibar and Kenya, few scholars have explored the development of Islamic law as a regime of law in a state governed by a constitution and state laws passed by its parliament. In fact, it is uncommon to find Islamic law or decisions from the kadhis' courts as a subject of legal commentary in law books and law journals published in Kenya today. This chapter therefore uses the law of evidence applicable in the kadhis' courts of Kenya as a window into assessing the broader relationship between Islamic law and other laws in a court setting. It particularly looks at whether the evidence law used in the kadhis' courts is purely a product of classical rules extant in manuals of Islamic jurisprudence (*fiqh*) or is a hybrid of Islamic and codified laws of Kenya.

A number of terms are used to signify evidence in the Arabic language. These include *hujjah*, *daliil*, *burhan*, *sultan* and *bayyinah*. All these terms have appeared in the Qur'an and hadith in different contexts (See Qur'an 11:96; 2:211). The term *bayyinah*, however, is frequently used to signify courtroom evidence. A majority of Muslim jurists have used the term to exclusively refer to witness testimony (*shahadah*) and the manuals of Islamic jurisprudence contain chapters named *Kitab-al-Shahadah* (see e.g. Rushd 1999), which typically explain rules of evidence.

Evidence in Islamic law is given primarily by admission or confession (*iqrar*), witness testimony (*shahadah*) and oath (*yameen*), and there are detailed rules in Islamic legal texts concerning each of these methods of discharging evidence (Masud et al. 2012: 25–8). Each case requires a specific type and threshold of evidence. Of note in the discharge of evidentiary burden is the need for *tazkiya* of witnesses, a process of screening witnesses in order to gauge their competence to discharge the burden of proof (Abualfaraj 2011: 149–50).

With the onset of the nation-state and the rise in the movement for codification of Muslim law, shari'a courts in Muslim majority states and some Muslim minority jurisdictions with a significant Muslim population like Israel adopted civil or common law rules of evidence in the administration of justice. Malaysia, for example, has the Syariah Court Evidence (Federal Territories) Act of 1997, which defines the law of evidence applicable to proceedings in or before any shari'a court in Malaysia. The Act further provides for the substance of evidence law to be used in the shari'a courts and the procedures of taking evidence in these courts.

When Kenya was colonised and the coast of East Africa was made a British protectorate in 1920, the Sultan of Zanzibar, who had dominion over the coastal strip, made arrangements with the British on behalf of the inhabitants of these areas that Muslim-based institutions of power and authority, such as the kadhis' courts, would continue to operate (Mwakimako 2008). The Sultan retained the power to appoint the kadhis (Anderson 1954).

The problem of which regime of evidence law was applicable in the Muslim subordinate courts in the Protectorate was a subject of contestation as early as the 1930s. Anderson (1954) notes that the case of *Baraka Binti Bahmishi* v. *Salim bin Abed Busawadi* (1939) turned on the interpretation of Section 11 of the Courts Ordinance, 1931. This section stated:

> Subject to the provisions of this Ordinance and to the rules of court, all Courts shall follow the principles of procedure laid down in the Civil Procedure Ordinance and the Criminal Procedure Code, so far as the same may be applicable and suitable.

Anderson further observes that in a case prior to the *Baraka* case, the words 'so far as the same may be applicable and suitable' were construed as allowing the use of Islamic rules of procedure and evidence since the matter was litigated in an Islamic court, and the officers presiding over it were qualified only in their law and not the colonial law. Moreover, the territorial jurisdiction of the courts was still under the Sultan's dominion and therefore the Islamic law of procedure and evidence was applicable.

The judge handling the *Baraka* case, however, disallowed the use of Islamic rules of procedure and evidence in the kadhis' courts by holding that if 'the Legislature did not intend Muslim Subordinate Courts to be bound, in normal circumstances, by the statutory rules of evidence and procedure, it should have said so clearly'. The judge further noted that the Indian Evidence Act of 1872, having been applied to Kenya by the East Africa Order in Council of 1897 and retained by the East Africa Order in Council of 1902 and again by the Kenya Colony Order in Council 1921, should be deemed binding on all courts, Islamic or otherwise.

Mwakimako (2011) cites a similar ruling by Justice Thacker on the appeal case number 11 of 1941. The Mombasa Law Society raised concerns over such decisions, since almost all decisions from the Islamic subordinate courts could be challenged on the grounds that the kadhis did not correctly apply the rules of procedure and evidence. This, according to the Mombasa Law Society, would occasion difficulties for litigants before Islamic courts. Most kadhis were not trained in the codified laws, and did not know English.

Zanzibar and Kenyan kadhis' courts have shared a pre-colonial and colonial history and even the provisions of the Kenyan Kadhis' Courts Act on evidence mirror those of the 1985 Zanzibari Kadhis' Act (see Stiles 2009: 137), at least up to 2017 when the new Kadhis' Courts Act No. 9 of 2017 of the laws of Zanzibar was introduced. Stiles' study of the Mkokotoni court in Zanzibar reveals the role of *shehas* (local administrators) and *wazee* (elders) as frequent witnesses in the court. Giving testimony, Stiles argues, not only produced evidence but also 'reflected state, community and familial webs of power and influence' (p. 131). The elders, *shehas* and 'local kadhis' (*kadhi wa mtaa*) tried to solve disputes before they reached the state-appointed kadhis who presided over the court. Witnessing was the primary means of giving evidence at the Mkokotoni court, as is evident in the cases *Hamza* v. *Kombo*, *Mpaji* v. *Jafari* and *Fatuma* v. *Omari* analysed by Stiles. Some cases were also settled through the use of oaths, as in the custody case between Aisha and Seifu, where Seifu eventually swore an oath that the children were his and he would take them and take care of them. Kadhi Hamid, after noting no objection from Aisha, ruled for Seifu.

The Kadhis' Courts Act of 1985 required kadhis of Zanzibar to apply the evidentiary rules without discrimination on the grounds of religion, gender and ethnicity. This provision is seemingly at variance with the *fiqh* rules governing evidence in classical Islamic law and is testimony to how the modern state limits the application of Islamic law. Although these provisions existed, some kadhis like Shaykh Hamid were not aware of the requirements for witnessing as outlined in the Act and therefore were ready to apply their own understanding of Islamic law rules pertaining to evidence (Stiles: 194). In some other cases, the kadhis would avoid application of the strict rules of evidence by incorporating *shehas* and elders in decision-making. Any agreements arising from such interventions were considered valid and enforceable. This helped the kadhis to strike a balance between their role as government officials on the one hand and their religious function in the community on the other (Stiles: 193).

While Stiles' work was primarily based on her study of the happenings in and outside the Mkokotoni court, Stockreiter's (2015) work was centred on studying kadhis' court documents from the early 20th century written in Arabic, which were sourced from the Zanzibar National Archives. She also studied marriage and divorce certificates, certificates for manumission of slaves, deeds for sale, and other documentary evidence produced in the courts during the colonial period relevant for proving a case. Stockreiter argues that, as early as 1899, regulations allowing for every witness to be heard and cross-examined regardless of religion and gender were in place. This was part of the reforms introduced by the British that targeted the perceived lack of procedure and impartiality in the kadhis' courts and was seen to have had an influence in subsequent legislation regarding the kadhis' courts.

Somewhat earlier, Hirsch (1998) conducted pioneering work on Kenyan kadhis' courts in Mombasa and Malindi. In her work, she noted that the kadhis' unfamiliarity with the provisions of the Evidence Act somewhat explained their reluctance to dispense with some Islamic evidentiary rules even as the Kadhis' Courts Act required them to. On the basis of her work in these courts, Hirsch argued that Kenyan kadhis have always contested the jurisprudence of superior courts concerning the application of Islamic rules of evidence in the kadhis' courts. This ambivalence, as I shall argue shortly, still persists among the Kenyan kadhis to date. One of the rules Hirsch cited was the requirement for screening of witnesses (*tazkiya*) before they testified. This requirement, she notes, was dispensed with in favour of their questioning of witnesses in court (Hirsch: 131). This particular rule is also ignored in Kenya's kadhis' courts today.

LEGISLATION GOVERNING EVIDENCE IN THE KADHIS' COURTS OF KENYA

The constitution and evidence in the kadhis' courts

Article 2(3) of the Constitution of Kenya 2010 stipulates that the constitution is the supreme law of the land and that any laws that are inconsistent with it are void to the extent of the inconsistency. This overarching provision draws the jurisdictional boundaries of the law of evidence that is to be applied in the kadhis' courts. Where there are rules of evidence in Islamic law that could be deemed contrary to the constitution, such rules, when pointed out by superior courts, should not be employed in the kadhis' courts since their use would be tantamount to perpetuating an illegality. Another provision on evidence in the constitution is Article 50, which enumerates the general principles concerning the production of evidence in Kenyan courts. These include the right to be represented by an advocate of one's own choosing; the right to remain silent and not to testify during proceedings; the right to be informed in advance of the evidence of the accuser and to access such evidence; the right to adduce and challenge evidence; and the right to have the assistance of an interpreter. These are fundamental rights concerning the use of evidence rules in court and they guide the kadhi in the administration of justice.

The Evidence Act and the Kadhis' Courts Act

Both the Kadhis' Courts Act (Cap. 11, Rev. 2012) and the Evidence Act (Cap. 80, Rev. 2012) recognise that the Islamic law of evidence is the applicable law in the kadhis' courts. Section 2 of the Evidence Act states:

> This Act shall apply to all judicial proceedings in or before any court other than the Kadhis' Court, but not to proceedings before an arbitrator.

Section 6 of the Kadhis' Courts Act states the following:

> The laws and the rules of evidence to be applied in the Kadhis' Court shall be those applicable under Muslim law provided that:
> I. all witnesses called shall be heard without discrimination on the grounds of religion, sex or otherwise;
> II. each issue of fact shall be decided upon an assessment of the credibility of all the evidence before the court and not upon the number of witnesses who have given evidence;
> III. no finding, decree or order of the court shall be reversed or altered on appeal or revision on account of the application of the law or rules of evidence applicable in the High Court, unless such application has in fact occasioned a failure of justice.

Taken at face value, the law of evidence applicable in the kadhis' courts is essentially Islamic law. However, I argue that this does not preclude the Evidence Act from being applied by presiding kadhis. First, the restrictions put by the Kadhis' Courts Act in the use of Islamic rules of evidence in the kadhis' courts suggest the aim of expanding the scope of evidence law in order to address contemporary challenges and concerns in the administration of justice. For example, the number, gender and religion of witnesses are an important aspect of evidence law in classical Islamic courts, yet the same may not work seamlessly in today's multi-religious Kenyan society where if a next-door neighbour were to be barred from being a witness in the court, an injustice could be occasioned. Second, kadhis' cases may be appealed to the High Court. Section 6(iii) of the Kadhis' Courts Act provides that no order or decree shall be reversed or altered on the sole ground that the kadhi used rules of evidence ordinarily applied in the High Court – that is, in the Evidence Act – in deciding the matter, unless the way the rules were used occasioned a failure of justice. I argue that there is no better licence for the kadhi to use the Evidence Act in the kadhis' courts than this provision. For example, Sections 83–95 of the Evidence Act address presumptions concerning certified documents, records of evidence, law reports and certified copies of foreign judicial records. There are not such detailed provisions on presumptions in the Kadhis' Courts Act or in the corpus of classical Islamic law, and thus a kadhi would face a dilemma accepting such evidence if the Kadhis' Courts Act did not indicate, albeit subtly, that he could use the Evidence Act in evaluating the evidence before his court.

The Two Cases

Kadhis' courts are classified as subordinate courts in the Constitution of Kenya and the decisions emanating from them have no precedential value; hence they are ordinarily not reported in the Kenya Law Reports (KLR). However, there has been an agreement in recent times between the kadhis and the National Council for Law Reporting (NCLR) concerning publishing kadhis' decisions in the Kenya Law Reports. Reporting cases allows public access to decisions in the kadhis' courts and improves the public's knowledge of the law applicable in the kadhis' courts. It also gives judges hearing appeals from the kadhis an idea of their legal reasoning and assists judges in considering appeals with some knowledge of what really happens in the kadhis' courts. However, this section will use unreported cases, since at present we do not have a significant number of reported cases to draw data from.

There are currently forty-seven kadhis' courts in Kenya, with most of them forming part of the law court stations created through gazette notice by the Chief Justice, which may include a Magistrate's Court, a High Court, or even a Court of Appeal. There also exist a few standalone kadhis' courts where the kadhi is the administrative head of the station. The Nairobi Kadhis' Court is one of the standalone courts. It is located in the Upper Hill area of Nairobi.

There are currently fifty-four kadhis spread across the country. Some stations, like Mombasa Kadhis' Court, are staffed by four kadhis; the Mombasa court includes the Chief Kadhi of the Republic of Kenya. The Nairobi Kadhis' Court has two kadhis: Hon. Sukyan Omar Hassan, who is the Deputy Chief Kadhi of the Republic of Kenya, and Hon. Abduljabar Ishaq Hussein, a Senior Resident Kadhi. Both have qualifications in shari'a and in common law, and the Deputy Chief Kadhi also holds a Master of Laws from the University of Nairobi. He also has the honour of being the first kadhi to be admitted to the roll of advocates after passing his bar exams.

In Kenya, kadhis, like magistrates and judges, are appointed by the Judicial Service Commission (JSC) after undergoing a rigorous application and interview process. Article 170(2) of the Constitution of Kenya requires the person to be appointed as kadhi to profess the Muslim religion and to possess 'such knowledge of the Muslim law applicable to any sects of Muslims as qualifies the person, in the opinion of the Judicial Service Commission, to hold a Kadhis' Court'.

It is apparent from the recruitments since 2005 that the JSC has appointed individuals with a basic degree in Islamic law or a related discipline to the office of the kadhi in a marked departure from the previous practice of appointing them from the lay Muslim clergy. Most kadhis now, including Abduljabar and me, are graduates from Muslim universities in Kenya, Uganda, Sudan, Egypt, Saudi Arabia and Pakistan, among others.

Much of the work of kadhis entails the hearing and the determination of questions of Islamic family law regarding personal status, marriage, divorce and inheritance. Other roles include solemnisation of Muslim marriages and registration of marriages and divorces as per the Marriage Act 2014. The Chief Kadhi still retains the role of announcing the onset of the Ramadan fasting period and Eid celebrations, although that is not considered part of his judicial duties.

Kadhi Abduljabar has been at the court since mid-2014. At the time of writing, he was probably the youngest of the kadhis, and he joined the judiciary in 2012 at the age of twenty-four. He was posted first to Kitui, some ninety kilometres east of Kenya's capital Nairobi, but was then assigned to Kibera Law Courts in Nairobi, where he also started to hear cases at the Upper Hill Court. Shortly after this, he was transferred to work full-time with the then Deputy Chief Kadhi, Hon. Radhid Ali Omar, until the latter's retirement in 2018.

Since we joined the bench as colleagues and peers, Kadhi Abduljabar and I have been sharing decisions from our courts and we have had several intellectually stimulating discussions on the future of the laws applicable in the kadhis' courts. Because I was researching evidence law, I asked him to share with me some of his thoughts on the nature and the future of evidence law in the kadhis' courts. He sent me thirty of his decisions. In this chapter, I focus on two of these, to show the relationship between the kadhi's knowledge of the laws governing evidence and the intervening priorities of handling evidence during adjudication. All the decisions sent to me were delivered between 2013 and 2019 and are written in English.

Case 1: Mariam Sheibani Salim & Another *v.* Hassan Ramadhan, *Civil Suit No. 3 of 2013, Nairobi Kadhis' Court*

Halima, a daughter to the petitioners, died and left behind a daughter, a husband (Hassan, the respondent herein) and the two parents (the petitioners herein). The petitioners sought orders for inheritance of Halima's property and permanent custody of Halima's daughter, who was at the time under the actual custody of Hassan, whom they regarded as her putative father. The petitioners' contention was that Halima and Hassan were not legally married and, as per Islamic law, the product of such a relationship would have a matrilineal kinship. They argued that their daughter was actually married to one Khamis

Chibendo – not to Hassan – and they were not aware of any divorce between them. The petitioners testified, and two witnesses were called to testify in support of their case. A picture dated 8 May 2010 was produced as evidence of the day of Halima's marriage to Chibendo.

Hassan denied the petitioners' allegations that he was not Halima's lawful husband and called one witness to support his defence. He argued that he married Halima in presence of her brother Said, who acted as a guardian in place of her father, who was away at the time. He claimed that Halima's mother consented to the marriage. Furthermore, he claimed that a divorce letter dated 19 May 2010 and authored by Chibendo was presented during the marriage ceremony as evidence of Halima's divorce from the first marriage. The same letter was produced in court as evidence. A marriage certificate issued by a Sheikh Ali Darani, Assistant Registrar of Marriages and Divorces in Mombasa, was also produced as evidence of Halima's marriage to Hassan. The veracity of this marriage certificate was not disputed by the parties. The respondent urged the court to take judicial notice of the legal documents produced before court and to dismiss the case.

After assessing the evidence before court, Kadhi Abduljabar made a finding that the marriage between Halima and Hassan was legally valid and therefore Hassan was entitled to the custody of the daughter and to a portion of the deceased's inheritance, according to the law. In making the determination, Kadhi Abduljabar referred to two provisions of the Evidence Act of Kenya: Section 59, which states 'No fact of which the Court shall take Judicial notice need be proved'; and Section 60(d), which states the 'public seal of Kenya, the seal of all courts of Kenya and all seals which any person is authorised by any written law to use' as matters that the court should take judicial notice of. The certificate of marriage bore the seal of the Assistant Registrar of Marriages and Divorces, who is an officer authorised and gazetted by law to solemnise marriages and issue marriage certificates. The certificate of marriage, once certified as authentic, was enough to prove the fact of marriage between the Halima and Hassan as per Section 59 of the Evidence Act.

Case 2: Abdullahi G. Chogorsa v. Sororo S. Sori, *Civil Case No. 84 of 2017, Nairobi Kadhis' Court*

In the second case, the plaintiff sought a declaration that the unilateral divorce letter he issued on 6 January 2017 was valid and that the two last-born children of his wife were a product of illicit affairs of the defendant with another man, and were therefore illegitimate. He also sought orders for the issuance of a divorce certificate, the division of matrimonial property, and the deduction of the value of assets squandered by the defendant from her rightful share of matrimonial property.

In her statement of defence, the defendant did not object to the dissolution of the marriage. However, she asked that the petitioner be compelled to provide maintenance for the defendant and their children and to pay alimony to the defendant. Petitions for alimony are rare in the kadhis' courts, since parties usually ask for award of either *eddah* (the period within which a divorced woman or a widow is forbidden to remarry) maintenance payments or a *mat'aa* (compensation payment) upon divorce.

The plaintiff argued that he unilaterally divorced the defendant after discovering that their two youngest children, N and W, could have been sired by a man named Muhsin, as was evident in the Kadhis' Court Nairobi Miscellaneous Case No. 276 of 2017. In this particular case, Sororo had sued Muhsin over his claims that he had entered into a marriage with her while Chogorsa was away in Saudi Arabia. Although the kadhi in the *Muhsin* case ruled that the marriage certificate produced by Muhsin was fake, this did not deter Kadhi Abduljabar from ruling that the children N and W were born out of wedlock and that the unilateral divorce by the plaintiff was therefore valid.

In ruling for the plaintiff, Kadhi Abduljabar wrote the following: 'Save for the fact that the two youngest minors were born within the subsistence of the marriage, there is no serious rebuttal by the defendant against those grave allegations of extra-marital affairs. The defendant also did not rebut the evidence that the two youngest minors were sired as a result of extra-marital affairs.'

The kadhi quoted *fiqh* positions on the presumption of paternity after divorce. The general rule in Islamic law is that the paternity of the child belonged to the marital bed, meaning that the child is attributed to the father if the child was born during the marriage – this is known as the *walad lil firash* ('the child belongs to the marital bed') principle. This principle, the kadhi argues, can be invoked if the child was born six months after the marriage, or within ten months after dissolution of the marriage (for Shi'a), within two years of dissolution (for the Hanafi), or within four years of dissolution (for the Shafi'i and Maliki). The kadhi, however, did not decide the question of paternity on the basis of the *walad lil firash* principle, for reasons to be given shortly.

The kadhi also quoted Section 118 of the Evidence Act to show the circumstances under which the principle of presumption of paternity could be applicable. The section provided that 'the fact that any person was born during the continuance of a valid marriage between his mother and any man, or within two hundred and eighty days after its dissolution, the mother remaining unmarried, shall be conclusive proof that he is the legitimate son of that man unless it can be shown that the parties to the marriage had no access to each other at any time when he could have been begotten'.

Kadhi Abduljabar, in my opinion, departs from the *walad lil firash* principle in two ways. First, the plaintiff's allegations that the defendant had extramarital relations and bore two children from these relations went unchallenged. If there was any sort of challenge, the plaintiff would have been required to provide evidence for his allegations. Second, the kadhi took judicial notice of the presence of case No. 276 of 2017, in which Sororo wanted to exonerate herself from allegations that she had contracted another marriage in the absence of her husband. The fact that she was the one who filed the application against Muhsin points, in my opinion, to the existence of relations between them, and this might have swayed the decision in Chogorsa's favour, hence dispensing with the presumption of paternity principle.

Analysis

The two cases not only reflect the approaches kadhis use when they grapple with the question of the relationship between Islamic law and codified state laws, but they also represent recent attempts at redefining what is meant by something being 'Islamic' (see Shahab 2016). Shahab argues that any meaningful conceptualisation of Islam must come face to face with the 'capaciousness, complexity, and often outright contradiction that obtains with the historical phenomenon that has proceeded from the human engagement with the idea and reality of divine communication to Muhammad' (2016: 6).

The corpus of Islamic law has been re-interpreted and reformulated in various societies in tune with the needs of the specific societies and in response to the level of Islamic scholarship within the same communities. In so far as kadhis determining matters in courts of law are concerned, Al Qarafi, the 13th-century Maliki jurist, argued that the office of the kadhi includes 'the power to originate judicial rulings in controversial areas of law or those areas of law that are amenable to legal controversy if the case is a novel one with no prior legal opinion or decision being given in respect of it' (Al Qarafi and Fadel 2017:177).

Article 20(3)(b) of the Constitution of Kenya 2010 requires courts to 'adopt the interpretation that most favours the enforcement of a right or fundamental freedom'. This provision applies to interpretation of all laws including the laws of evidence applicable in the kadhis' courts of Kenya.

In almost all the decisions of fellow kadhis that I have perused, I have seen little or no interrogation of the laws governing evidence in the kadhis' courts. It seems to be almost a given that the classical Islamic rules of evidence operate seamlessly with the codified state laws. However, as we have seen in the two cases above, Kadhi Abduljabar has expanded the scope of evidence law applicable in the kadhis' courts to include specific provisions of the Evidence Act and any other law that is, in the opinion of the kadhi, relevant to meeting the ends of justice. In the *Maryam Sheibani* case, Kadhi Abduljabar anchors his determination of the question of the validity of divorce on the doctrine of judicial notice in the Evidence Act, whereby he ruled that documents bearing seals of courts are presumed to be valid. In the *Abdullahi Chogorsa* case, he cross-referenced the substance of Islamic law with provisions of the Evidence Act on the presumption of paternity to emphasise the fact that Islamic law and state law can work in harmony with each other.

Conclusion

In her analysis of evidence laws in the kadhis' courts, Hirsch argued that the Kadhis' Court Bill of 1967 resolved the ambiguity of conflicting case decisions arising from the fluctuating application of Muslim rules of evidence. The Bill, in her opinion, resolved this by decreeing that Islamic evidentiary principles would apply in the kadhis' courts with three provisos: (1) that all witnesses be heard without discrimination on grounds of religion, sex or otherwise; (2) that facts must be determined on the credibility of evidence rather than on the number of witnesses; and (3) that the application of the Evidence Act is not subject to reversal on appeal (1998: 131). However, it appears that even with the three provisos, the ambiguity was never resolved and the uncertainty as to which regime of evidence law was applicable in the kadhis' courts persists.

I agree with Kadhi Abduljabar that the scope of evidence law applicable in the kadhis' courts of Kenya extends to the use of the Evidence Act as a necessity in adjudication in order to fill the legal lacunae left by the lack of codification of Islamic law in Kenya. This interpretation, in my view, accords with the position of some of the revisionist scholars of the 12th and 13th centuries, such as the Hanbali polymath Ibn Qayyim al-Jawziyya, who defined *bayyinah* (evidence) as 'a name for everything that renders the truth clear and proves it' (2013: 76).

Bibliography

Abualfaraj, M. (2011), 'Evidence in Islamic law: Reforming the Islamic Evidence Law Based on the Federal Rules of Evidence', *Journal of Islamic Law and Culture* 13(2–3), pp. 140–65.

Al Jawziyya, I. (2013), *I'laam al-muwaqqi'iin 'an Rabbil 'aalamiin*, 1st edn, Beirut: Dar Ibn Hazm.

Al Qarafi, S. and Fadel, M. (2017), *Criterion for Distinguishing Legal Opinions from Judicial Rulings and the Administrative Acts of Judges and Rulers*, NH: Yale University Press.

Anderson, J. N. D. (1954), *Islamic Law in Africa*, London: HM Stationery Office.

Cussack A. (2008), 'Muslims and Politics in Kenya: The Issue of the Kadhis' Courts in the Constitutional Review Process', *Journal of Muslim Minority Affairs* 28(2), pp. 289–302.

Hirsch, F. Susan (1998), *Pronouncing and Persevering: Gender and the Discourses of Disputing in an African Islamic Court*, Chicago: University of Chicago Press.

Masud, M. K. et al. (2012), 'Qadis and their Courts: An Historical Survey', in M. K. Masud et al. (eds), *Dispensing Justice in Islam: Qadis and their Judgements*, Leiden: Brill, pp. 24–8.

Mwakimako, H. (2008), 'Kadhis' Courts and Appointment of Kadhis in Kenya Colony', *Religion Compass* 2(4), pp. 424–43.

Mwakimako, H. (2010), 'Conflict and Tension in the Appointment of Chief Kadhi in Colonial Kenya', in S. Jeppie et al. (eds), *Muslim Family Law in Sub-Saharan Africa: Colonial Legacies and Post-Colonial Challenges*, Amsterdam: Amsterdam University Press, p. 110.

Mwakimako, H. (2011), 'The Historical Development of Muslim Courts: The Kadhi, Mudir and Liwali courts and the Civil Procedure Code and the Criminal Procedure Ordinance c. 1963', *Journal of Eastern African Studies* 5(2), pp. 329–43.

Mwangi, O. G. (2012), 'Religious Fundamentalism, Constitution-Making and Democracy in Kenya: The Kadhis' Courts Debate', *The Round Table* 101(1), pp. 41–52.

Rushd, Ibn (1999), *The Distinguished Jurist's Primer: A Translation of Bidayat al-mujtahid*, Reading: Garnet.

Shahab, A. (2016), *What Is Islam: The Importance of Being Islamic*, Princeton: Princeton University Press.

Stiles, Erin E. (2009), *An Islamic Court in Context: An Ethnographic Study of Judicial Reasoning*, New York: Palgrave Macmillan.

Stockreiter, Elke (2015), *Islamic Law, Gender and Social Change in Post-abolition Zanzibar*, New York: Cambridge University Press.

Tibi, B. (2008), 'The Return of the Sacred to Politics: The Case of the Shariatization of Politics in Islamic Civilization', *Theoria* (115), pp. 91–119.

14

Courts within Courts: Kadhis and their Courts in the Kenyan Judicial System

Abdulkadir Hashim

In Kenya, kadhis and their courts have, since the pre-independent period up to the present, occupied a peculiar position relative to that of other religious and customary courts in East Africa. Since independence, the accommodation of kadhis' courts in Kenya in the mainstream judicial system has revealed the recognition of religious courts in a modern conventional, plural legal setting where Muslims are in the minority.

This chapter examines the status and position of kadhis' courts in Kenya in order to provide a comparative legal history and an analysis of the application of Muslim personal law in a plural legal system. In Kenya, this has resulted in contestations and conflicts between the kadhis' courts and the conventional courts in the post-colonial period. The chapter thus shows the interplay between politics and religion in the post-colonial context. The chapter also demonstrates the connection between politics and religion in Kenya, and how the state negotiated with its citizens for the creation of religious spaces. The government of Kenya managed, through various constitutional processes, to retain the kadhis' courts despite opposition from some churches.

Criticism of the kadhis' courts and accusations that the government of Kenya favoured Muslims by retaining kadhis' courts in the mainstream judicial system were raised during the constitutional review process in 1997 and the referendum process. However, kadhis' courts managed to survive the turbulence of the time and were retained in the Constitution of Kenya 2010.

Despite the challenges facing kadhis and their courts in Kenya, kadhis' courts in post-independence Kenya can serve as a model for other countries in East Africa with substantial Muslim minorities who seek recognition of Muslim religious courts and Islamic personal law. This chapter shows this potential by explaining Kenya's emerging comparative jurisprudence between judges in secular courts and kadhis in Islamic courts on issues of child custody, matrimonial property and succession.

Constitutional Debates over Kadhis' Courts: Christian Reactions and Muslim Responses

The constitutional review process triggered heated debates on kadhis' courts that led to arguments and counter-arguments between different groups of Christians and Muslims. Some Christian churches opposed the inclusion of the kadhis' courts in the new constitution. Muslim organisations represented by their umbrella bodies, such as the Supreme Council of Kenya Muslims (SUPKEM) and Jamia Mosque in Nairobi, not only reacted by advocating for the retention of the kadhis' courts in the constitution but also sought more powers and privileges for kadhis and their courts. For instance, the Muslim umbrella bodies asked for the expansion of the structure of the kadhis' courts to include a High Court and a Court of Appeal specialising in adjudicating Muslim cases on appeal from the kadhis' courts as opposed to subjecting appeal cases from kadhis' courts to the High Court of the Court of Kenya.

The controversial debate on kadhis' courts brought together church organisations representing many mainline churches, including the Catholic Church, the National Council of Churches of Kenya (NCCK) – the umbrella organisation of the Protestant churches, including the Anglican and Methodist churches – and the Kenya Church, an umbrella body of forty evangelical Christian groups including Christ is the Answer Ministries (CIAM), Jesus Is Alive Ministries (JIAM) and Neno Evangelical Ministries.[1]

The main contention of the Christian evangelical groups was that kadhis' courts, as religious courts, were not a constitutional issue and therefore should not be a subject of discussion in the constitution review process. Essentially, the Christian evangelical groups argued that kadhis' courts as religious entities should not have a place in a secular state like Kenya.[2] The Kenya Church, which was at the forefront of opposing the inclusion of kadhis' courts in the constitution, pointed out that 'the personal laws of these two minority religious

---

[1] Kahumbi Maina (2011), 'Islamophobia among Christians and its Challenge in Entrenchment of Kadhis Courts in Kenya', in Abdulkader Tayob and Joseph Wandera (eds), *Constitutional Review in Kenya and Kadhis Courts*, Centre for Contemporary Islam: University of Cape Town, p. 49.

[2] S. Mbithi Kimeu (2011), 'Historical and Legal Foundations of the Kadhi's Courts in Kenya', in Abdulkader Tayob and Joseph Wandera (eds), *Constitutional Review in Kenya and Kadhis Courts*. Cape Town: Centre for Contemporary Islam, University of Cape Town, p. 29. To support this argument, a church organisation referred to Section 10 of the Harmonized Draft Constitution, which stated that 'the State shall provide equal treatment to all religions', arguing that retention of kadhis' courts in the constitution would favour Islam and elevate it into a state religion. The Federation of Churches in Kenya, Christian Concerns in the Constitution (unpublished document).

(Muslims and Hindus) cannot be given a constitutional recognition in the total exclusion of all other religions in Kenya and especially of the mainstream Christian religion which comprises over 80% of the population'.[3]

In 2004, Reverend Jesse Kamau of the Presbyterian Church of East Africa and twenty-five members of the clergy filed a case challenging the constitutionality of the kadhis' courts. They argued that Kenya was a religiously plural and multi-cultural state and that the existence of kadhis' courts funded by the state amounted to segregation, sectarianism and discrimination. The clergy further argued that Article 66 of the Constitution of Kenya 1963, which entrenches kadhis' courts, infringes on their constitutional rights to equal protection under the law as elaborated in other articles of the constitution. Therefore, they argued, Article 66 is discriminatory, unconstitutional and should be expunged from the constitution.

In response to the grounds raised in the case filed by Reverend Kamau, the High Court declared in May 2010 that Article 66 of the Constitution of Kenya 1963 was unconstitutional and discriminatory. The High Court also held that any form of religious courts could not form part of the judiciary in the constitution as it violated the doctrine of separation of state and religion. Despite declaring the unconstitutionality of Article 66, the High Court noted, 'it is not the court's role to expunge it [Article 66]. It is the role of Parliament and the citizenry in a referendum.'[4]

The Muslim umbrella bodies responded to the Christian opposition to kadhis' courts by arguing that the kadhis' courts were entrenched in the Constitution of Kenya 1963 as a result of agreements signed between the Sultan of Zanzibar and the first Prime Minister of Kenya, Jomo Kenyatta, in 1963.[5] These organisations also argued that the Kenyan constitution is based on Christian values and that the constitution and laws of Kenya thus reflect the Judaeo-Christian origins and beliefs of the colonial masters.[6] Hence, Muslims in Kenya deserve a similar recognition with regard to Muslim personal law in the constitution.[7] The Muslim umbrella bodies further advocated for increasing the number of kadhis' courts throughout the country, for kadhis' jurisdiction to be extended to civil

---

[3] The Kenya Church, Recommendations to the Constitution of Kenya Review Commission on the Proposed Draft Constitution of the Republic of Kenya, Nairobi, December 2002.
[4] *Rev. Jesse Kamau & 25 others v. Attorney General* [2010] eKLR.
[5] Muslims were represented by their religious umbrella organisations, which included, *inter alia*, the Supreme Council of Kenya Muslims (SUPKEM), the Muslim Task Force on Constitutional Review based at the Jamia Mosque in Nairobi, the National Muslim Leaders Forum (NAMLEF) and the Muslim Consultative Council (MCC).
[6] Muslim Task Force (2003), 'The Muslim Position: A Response to the Kenya Church Concerns', Nairobi (unpublished).
[7] Ibid.

and commercial matters, and that a separate structure of appeals be established for Islamic law.[8]

Conflicts and Tensions between the High Court and Kadhis' Courts

The submission clause of Article 155 of the Revised Harmonised Draft Constitution (RHDC) that was adopted by the Article 170(5) of the Constitution of Kenya 2010 gave an option to Muslim litigants to submit to the jurisdiction of the kadhis' courts. This paved the way for conflicts between the High Court and the kadhis' courts. The conflicts manifest in cases where litigants file appeals at the High Court against kadhis' decisions. Section 65 (1) of the Civil Procedure Act (Chapter 21) states that 'an appeal shall lie to the High Court (c) from a decree or part of a decree of a Kadhi's Court, and on such an appeal the Chief Kadhi or ... two other Kadhis shall sit as assessor or assessors'. Section 5 of the Kadhis' Court Act states that 'A Kadhi's court shall have and exercise the following jurisdiction, namely the determination of questions of Muslim law relating to personal status, marriage, divorce or inheritance in proceedings in which all the parties profess the Muslim religion; *but nothing in this section shall limit the jurisdiction of the High Court or of any subordinate court in any proceeding which comes before it*' (emphasis added).

An interesting result of the conflicts between the High Court and the kadhis' courts is the emergence of a novel comparative judicial jurisprudence by judges and kadhis. We find this comparative judicial jurisprudence on issues that include, *inter alia*, jurisdiction of kadhis' courts on matters related to division of matrimonial property between divorced Muslim spouses, child custody, and matters of succession and administration of the estates of deceased Muslims.

In the case of *Genevieve Bertrand* v. *Mohamed Athman Maawiya and Anor* [2104], the Court of Appeal of Kenya explained the criteria for interpreting the jurisdiction of the kadhis' courts: 'Thus the jurisdiction of the Kadhi's Court is determined by the existence of three factors. That is the subject matter of the claim or dispute, the party's Muslim faith, and the party's submission to the jurisdiction of the Kadhi's Court.'[9]

Judges of the High Court of Kenya interpreted the above decision of the Court of Appeal with divergent opinions that led to conflicting judgments. For example, the case of *S.H.H.* v. *M.H.Y* [2015] involved a dispute between divorced Muslim spouses regarding submission of Muslim litigants to the

---

[8] *The People's Choice, The Report of the Constitution of Kenya Review Commission* (Short Version) (2002), pp. 54–5.
[9] *Genevieve Bertrand* v. *Mohamed Athman Maawiya and Anor*, Malindi Civil Application No. 24 of 2013 [2014] eKLR.

jurisdiction of the kadhis' courts. A judgment delivered by Justice Meoli of the High Court of Kenya gave the Muslim litigants the option not to submit to the jurisdiction of the kadhis' courts. Justice Meoli held that 'a party who professes the Muslim faith *may opt not to submit* to the jurisdiction of the Kadhis' Court'[10] (emphasis added).

Contrary to the above decision, a judgment of the High Court delivered by Justice Kimaru declined to give Muslim parties the option not to submit to the jurisdiction of the kadhis' courts. In the case of Ashraf Abdu Kassim v. Karar Omar & 3 others [2014], Justice Kimaru of the High Court declined to accept the argument that a person professing the Muslim faith has an option of either submitting or refusing to submit to the jurisdiction of the kadhis' court. Justice Kimaru held that 'The *raison d'etre* for the recognition of the Kadhis' Court by the Constitution was the demand by Muslims that matters relating to personal status, marriage, divorce and inheritance be governed by Islamic Law. Disputes involving persons of Islamic faith can only be determined by the Kadhis' Court because the holders of the office of Kadhi are required under Article 170(2) of the Constitution to be persons who profess the Muslim religion.'[11]

The Custody of Children

Article 170(5) of the Constitution of Kenya 2010, which limits the jurisdiction of kadhis' courts 'to the determination of questions of Muslim law relating to personal status, marriage, divorce or inheritance in proceedings in which all the parties profess the Muslim religion and submit to the jurisdiction of the Kadhis' courts', opened the door for interpretation that caused conflicts between judges and kadhis. A key question that has faced the kadhis' courts was whether matters related to custody of children are included in the term 'personal status'.

In the case *Amin Mohammed Hassan v. Zahra Mohammed Abdulkadir* [2009] appealed at the High Court of Kenya, the appellant argued that the kadhis' courts had no jurisdiction to hear and determine any dispute concerning children and that the proper court for such a case is the Children's Courts.[12] The former Chief Kadhi, Sheikh Hammad Kassim, gave his opinion as an assessor at the High Court that kadhis' courts had jurisdiction to hear such matters so long as the parties before it professed Islam. Commenting on the case, Justice Sergon of the High Court also held that the issue of the custody and maintenance of children was properly heard before the kadhis' courts. The judge further held that issues touching on maintenance and custody of children fell into

---

[10] S.H.H. v. M.H.Y. [2015] eKLR, Matrimonial Cause No. 1 of 2015.
[11] *Ashraf Abdul Kassim v. Karar Omar & 3 others* [2014] EKLR, Succession Cause No. 689 of 2010. *In the Matter of the Estate of Maryam Juma Kibanda (Deceased)*.
[12] *Amin Mohammed Hassan v. Zahra Mohammed Abdulkadir* [2009] eKLR.

the category of personal status and therefore it was not right to claim that the kadhis' courts had no jurisdiction to hear and determine the issue.[13]

In the case of *Abdirahman Mohamed Abdi & Nasar Ali Bashir* v. *Adan Yussuf* [2013], the appellants appealed at the High Court of Mombasa against the former Chief Kadhi, Sheikh Hammad Kassim, by arguing that he had no jurisdiction to hear and determine an issue relating to the paternity of the child in question. The issue raised before the court was whether the kadhi had jurisdiction to decide on the issues of paternity and custody of a minor child. Justice Mutuku stated: 'I have no doubt in my mind that the parties were correctly before the Kadhis' Courts for determination of those issues … My view therefore is that paternity and custody of the child in this case are incidental to the issues of marriage and divorce between the Appellants and thus it falls under the jurisdiction of the Kadhis' Courts.'[14]

The decisions of the High Court in these two cases, *Amin Mohamed Hassan* v. *Zahra Mohamed Abdukadir* and *Abdirahman Mohamed Abdi & Nasar* v. *Adam Yusuf*, extended the jurisdiction of kadhis' courts to include custody of children. Contrary to these two decisions of the High Court, Justice Maraga of the High Court of Kenya disqualified the jurisdiction of kadhis' courts in dealing with custody of children, and held: 'Kadhi court has no jurisdiction to deal with custody of children. That jurisdiction, it is contended, is vested in the Children's Courts.'[15] A similar approach was adopted by Justice Muchelule in the case of *S.M.H.* v. *S.A.A.* at High Court in Kisumu [2013], who held, 'My understanding is that the Kadhi's Court is properly seized of the divorce matter, but may not deal with the issues of custody and maintenance of the children. These issues are not among those in respect of which the Constitution and the Act have donated jurisdiction to the Kadhis' Court. These issues can only properly be dealt with by a children's court under the Children Act No. 8 of 2001.'[16]

In the case *H.M.M.* v. *K.J.D.* at the High Court in Mombasa [2014], the defendant objected to the jurisdiction of the kadhis' court in child custody matters. The trial kadhi who had originally heard the case held that 'Under Islamic law, questions of custody and maintenance of children fall and is specifically provided for under personal status. It is also the direct result of divorce.' The defendant was aggrieved by the kadhi's decision and appealed to the High Court. The appeal was heard in the presence of the current Chief Kadhi, Sheikh Ahmed Al-Mohdhar, who held: 'I am of the opinion that the Kadhi's Court has

---

[13] Sukyan Hassan Omar (2015), 'The Jurisdiction of the Kadhis' Courts in Kenya on Children Related Matters', LL. M dissertation, Faculty of Law, University of Nairobi.
[14] *Abdirahman Mohamed Abdi & Nasar Ali Bashir* v. *Adan Yussuf*, Civil Appeal 13 of 2012, eKLR [2013].
[15] Miscellaneous Civil Application No. 903 of 2005, High Court at Mombasa, *Republic* v. *Kadhi Sheikh Twalib and Arif Ramadhan Karama Interested Part, Ex Parte* [2005] eKLR.
[16] *S.M.H.* v. *S.A.A.*, Kisumu High Court Misc. 125 of 2013 [2013] eKLR.

no jurisdiction in determining children matters as there is nowhere any written laws of Kenya which gives Kadhi jurisdiction over children matters.'[17] The High Court adopted the Chief Kadhi's opinion, and Justice Odero held that '[n]o mention is made in either the Constitution or in the Kadhis' Court Act to custody and/or maintenance of children ... I am of the opinion that the Children Act grants exclusive jurisdiction over all children matters including custody and/or maintenance only to Judicial Officers who are gazetted under the said Act. The Kadhi is not a judicial officer gazetted to handle children matters.'[18]

In an earlier case of Z.H.Z. v. S.D.S. at High Court in Mombasa, Justice Odero made an argument similar to the Chief Kadhi's opinion that the kadhis' court has no jurisdiction in child custody matters. He argued as follows:

> The cited law [Constitution and Kadhis' Court Act] makes it clear that the jurisdiction of the Kadhis' Court is to matters of personal law e.g. marriage, divorce and inheritance. No mention is made of children's matters like custody access and/or maintenance of children of a marriage ... It is only in a children's court and with reference to the Children Act that decisions respecting custody, access and/or maintenance of children can properly be made.[19]

The case of G.S.A. v. A.S.A. at the High Court in Nairobi [2014] involved issues of child custody and maintenance. The appellant, a mother, argued that her children from a previous marriage were of tender ages and therefore she was apprehensive about placing the children under the custody of their father, who was married to another wife. The father argued that the appellant had remarried and therefore he could not leave his children under the custody of a man who was a stranger to his children. In a subordinate court, the trial kadhi had granted custody of the children to the father. The mother was dissatisfied with the kadhi's judgment and appealed to the High Court in Nairobi. On appeal, Justice Musyoka held:

> Affairs concerning children are governed by the provisions of the Children Act, No. 8 of 2001. The said statute is of universal application. It applies to Kenyan citizens and residents alike, irrespective of their ethnicity, race or creed. I have not encountered any provision is that law which exempts Muslims from the provisions of the Act.[20]

---

[17] H.M.M. v. K.J.D, High Court Civil Appeal No. 15 of 2013 at Mombasa, [2014] eKLR.
[18] Ibid.
[19] Z.H.Z. v. S.D.S., Mombasa High Court Civil Appeal No. 45 of 2013 [2014] eKLR.
[20] G.S.A. v. A.S.A., Nairobi High Court Civil Appeal No. 53 of 2013 [2014] eKLR.

In his ruling, Justice Musyoka examined both the Children Act and Article 170(5) of the constitution, which explains kadhi court jurisdiction, and doubted that the courts could rule on custody matters since they were not specifically given such a jurisdiction: 'From the wording of Article 170(5) of the Constitution it would appear that the Constitution has not granted jurisdiction to the Kadhi's court over matters touching on custody and maintenance of children. It is doubtful therefore whether the Kadhi's court can grant custody and maintenance orders over children.' Noting the 'tender age' of the children, he ordered that they remain with their mother.

Contemporary kadhis in Kenya have adopted the criteria of best interests to safeguard the welfare of children. This novel approach demonstrates the emergence of a comparative jurisprudence in the kadhis' courts as opposed to the traditional trend adopted by previous kadhis who based their decisions on classical Muslim jurists.

Division of Matrimonial Property after Divorce

The division of matrimonial property among Muslim parties after divorce is another area that has raised conflicts of jurisdiction between judges and kadhis in Kenya. Muslim litigants are caught between two scales of justice. On the one hand, in matters related to matrimonial property involving Muslim litigants, the parties are bound by the provisions of the constitution on equal rights and obligations at the time of the marriage, during the marriage and at the dissolution of the marriage. On the other hand, qualification clauses exempt Muslim litigants from the application of such provisions.

The Constitution of Kenya 2010 provides for exemption clauses excluding Muslim law from its provisions creating legal lacunae, which have raised conflicts and tensions in judicial decisions issued by judges and kadhis. For instance, in the Chapter of the Bill of Rights under a section on limitations of rights and fundamental freedoms, Article 24(4) states:

> The provisions of this Chapter on equality shall be qualified to the extent strictly necessary for the application of Muslim law before the Kadhis' courts, to persons who profess the Muslim religion, in matters relating to personal status, marriage, divorce and inheritance.

The Marriage Act of 2014, which is applicable to all citizens of Kenya, provides the entitlement of equal rights of spouses during marriage and at the dissolution of such marriage. Section 3(2) of the Marriage Act 2014 states: 'Parties to a marriage have equal rights and obligations at the time of the marriage, during the marriage and at the dissolution of the marriage.' Section 3(2) of the

Marriage Act 2014 is a replica of Article 45 (3) The Constitution of Kenya 2010.

However, the Marriage Act qualifies Section 3(2) by exempting Muslims from the provision on equal rights and obligations. Section 3(4) reads: 'Subject to subsection the parties to an Islamic marriage shall only have the rights granted under Islamic law.' Furthermore, Section 3 of the Matrimonial Property Act 2013 states: 'A person who professes the Islamic faith may be governed by Islamic Law in all matters relating to matrimonial property.'

Before the enactment of the Matrimonial Property Act 2013 and the Marriage Act 2014, the applicable law in cases related to matrimonial property for all litigants in Kenya was the Married Women's Property Act of 1882 in the United Kingdom. In the case of *Essa v. Essa* (1996), the Court of Appeal in Kenya was called upon to adjudicate on the distribution of the matrimonial property acquired during the marriage between spouses who contracted an Islamic marriage.[21] Justice Omolo of the Court of Appeal held that the Married Women's Property Act of 1882 was an act of general application, and applied equally to Muslims and non-Muslims in Kenya.[22]

The applicability of the Married Women's Property Act of 1882 to Muslim litigants was then challenged in *R.M.M. v. B.A.M.* [2015]. The main issue in the appeal was the question of how property acquired during the subsistence of a valid marriage should be dealt with following the dissolution of a Muslim marriage. At the High Court in Mombasa, the appellant, the divorced wife of the respondent, narrated how she had met and married the respondent in 1972 under Kamba customs before she became a Muslim. Their marriage was then regularised by a kadhi under Islamic law in 1995. Two children of the marriage were born between 1972 and 1996. The marriage broke down and they separated, leading to a formal divorce in 2007. Hence, the appellant claimed that she was entitled to a declaration that the properties acquired during the subsistence of a valid marriage between her and the respondent, her former husband, were owned between them jointly.

The respondent denied that they were married in 1972, but asserted that they were married under Islamic Law of Marriage and Divorce in 1995, and that that marriage was registered in 1999. He also denied that there was a Kamba customary marriage as the appellant had alleged, and that therefore the two children were born out of wedlock in 1976 and 1985. However, he nevertheless recognised them as his daughters and took care of them. The respondent thus

---

[21] *Essa v. Essa* (1996) EA 53.
[22] These cases include, *inter alia*, *Neema Nungari Salim v. Salim Ali Molla* eKLR [2006] and *Amin O. Abdulkadir v. Ravindra N. Shah* eKLR [2006].

concluded that there was no property acquired by both of them during their marriage that could be divided.

After considering the pleadings and the evidence placed on record, Justice Maureen Odero at the High Court in Mombasa held that there was no marriage under Kamba customary law between the appellant and the respondent between 1972 and 1995. Justice Odero further held that since the marriage was regularised by a kadhi under Islamic law in 1995, the applicable law on the distribution of matrimonial property acquired during the parties' marriage was Islamic law. Justice Odero stated: 'For these reasons I find that the Married Women's Property Act 1882 which of necessity envisages a monogamous union is not applicable in this case. The Plaintiff ought to have sought relief in the Kadhis Court under Cap 156. For this reason I do dismiss this suit and decline to grant the prayers sought.'[23]

The wife was dissatisfied with Justice Odero's decision in the High Court, and she appealed the decision at the Court of Appeal in Nairobi. The Court of Appeal quashed the High Court's decision by Justice Odero and held that the trial court had erred. The Court of Appeal ordered that the matter be remitted back to the High Court for re-hearing of the matter and be placed before any Judge of the High Court other than Justice Maureen Odero.

The challenge facing the post-divorce division of matrimonial property acquired during the subsistence of a Muslim marriage is due to the lack of a definitive legal position of Muslim classical jurists on the extent of division of matrimonial property after divorce. This is coupled with the lack of a clear definition by courts in Kenya on the extent of the indirect contribution of a wife to the acquisition of a matrimonial property.

The proponents of giving a share of matrimonial property to a divorced Muslim wife rely on verses of the Qur'an that prohibit oppression among spouses.[24] They compare division of matrimonial property with partnership (*sharikah*) where properties of spouses are merged and in the event of divorce each spouse is entitled to a proportionate share of his or her contribution. Take, for example, the case of *Hussein Sheikh Bashir v. Hassida Mohamed Ali* heard at the kadhis' court in Nairobi 2014. The parties had married in 1977 and divorced in 1999. The defendant (the wife) requested that the matrimonial property in the case be awarded to her to the exclusion of the plaintiff (her former husband) on the grounds that she had taken care of her husband's mental and emotional well-being before, during and after the purchase of the suit property. The kadhi gave a share of one-eighth of the matrimonial property to the wife on the basis

---

[23] R.M.M. v. B.A.M. [2015] eKLR, Civil Appeal No. 267 of 2011, Waki, G. B. M. Kariuki, Mwilu, M'inoti & Murgor, JJ. A.
[24] E.g. Qur'an Chapter 65 verse 6.

of her taking care of her husband's mental and emotional well-being during and after the purchase of the property. The kadhi held: 'It is now generally accepted that where most Muslim women are not employed or in salaried employment contribution does not necessarily mean cash payment. It is sufficient if as a result of division of labor, the spouses perform different functions all of which enhance the good of the family including the acquisition of matrimonial property.'

However, opponents of giving a divorced Muslim wife a share of the matrimonial property hold that such a move may unlawfully infringe on the rights of other legal heirs.[25] Opponents also argue that there is no clear legal authority on the division of matrimonial property among Muslim parties after divorce. Some Muslim jurists have opined that a wife's taking care of her husband's mental and emotional well-being is not part of her matrimonial obligation and does not amount to a contribution in the distribution of the matrimonial property. For instance, Imam Taqi al-Din Ahmad Ibn Taymiyyah (d. 728 AH) held that it is obligatory upon a wife to serve her husband according to the custom of her peers.[26] Imam Muhammad Abu Zahra quoted the evidence of the wives of Prophet Muhammad (peace be upon him) and the wives of the companions who undertook matrimonial duties in serving their husbands. Imam Abu Zahra concluded that it is obligatory for a wife to undertake matrimonial duties towards her husband according to her peers.[27] Imam Ibn Al Qayyim noted:

> It cannot be assumed based purely on what is held in hand or having authority over a name by having the name on a land title and the likes becoming the rights of only a single person if the property is acquired during the duration of the marriage, in fact its existence is of no consequence. In relation to this, an allusion can be made to the appliances in the house and other properties for example a house, a piece of land and the likes that are acquired during the time when both are still husband and wife unless there is proof to show that the properties were divided or the rights of each one separately.[28]

In recent years, kadhis in Kenya have delivered judgments related to the division of matrimonial property between Muslim litigants. In the case of *Amin Hassan Mohamed v. Yussuf Adan Abdullah*,[29] the court held that 'on the issues of the matrimonial house, the Court holds that it is a matrimonial property acquired during the continuity of the short-lived marital bond ... I hereby judge

---

[25] E.g. Qur'an Chapter 2 verse 188.
[26] Taqi al-Din Ahmad Ibn Taymiyyah, *Majmu al Fatawa*, vol. 33, pp. 58–9.
[27] Muhammad Abu Zahra (1957), *Al-Ahwal al-Shakhsiyyah*, Cairo: Dar al-Fikr al-Arabi, p. 167.
[28] Ibn Al Qayyim (1961), *al-Turuq al-Hukmiyyah Fi al-Siyasah-al-Shariyyah*, Cairo: Matba'ah Al-Madani, p. 24.
[29] Unreported, Kadhi's Court Case No. 143 of 2014 at Upper Hill, Nairobi, 2015.

for the plaintiff herein ½ share of the matrimonial property.' Similarly, in the case of *Hanifa Mohamed Nur v. Ahmed Duale Osman*[30] the court ordered the Respondent to pay the outstanding balance of US$ 15,000, this being the share of the petitioner in the matrimonial property.

Succession and the Administration of Estates of Deceased Muslims

Conflicts in succession matters and the administration of estates of deceased Muslims also arise in the decisions of various High Court judges due to apparently conflicting provisions of the Law of Succession Act. Section 2(1) of the Act provides for the universal application of the Act and states: 'Except as otherwise expressly provided in this Act or any other written law, the provisions of this Act shall constitute the law of Kenya in respect of, and shall have universal application to, all cases of intestate or testamentary succession to the estates of deceased persons dying after the commencement of this Act and to the administration of estates of those persons.'

However, Section 2(3) of the Law of Succession Act exempts deceased Muslims from the application of the Act on testamentary or intestate succession. The Section states: 'Subject to subsection (4), the provision of this Act shall not apply to testamentary or intestate succession to the estate of any person who at the time of his death is a Muslim to the intent that in lieu of such provisions the devolution of the estate of any such person shall be governed by Muslim law.'

Section 2(4) of the same Act endorses the application of administration of estates of deceased Muslims by the Act. The Section provides: 'Notwithstanding the provisions of sub-section (3) of the provisions of part VII relating to the administration of estates shall where they are not inconsistent with those of Muslim law, apply in case of every Muslim dying on or after 1 January 1991.'

Ironically, Section 48(2) of the same Act gives the kadhis' courts the jurisdiction on 'any other question arising under the Act', which may be construed to include the administration of deceased Muslims. The Section states: 'For the avoidance of doubt it is hereby declared that the Kadhi's courts shall continue to have and exercise jurisdiction in relation to the estate of a deceased Muslim for the determination of questions relating to inheritance in accordance with Muslim law and of any other question arising under this Act in relation to such estates.'

The above sections of the Law of Succession Act have resulted in conflicting decisions of the High Court on the jurisdiction of kadhis' courts on handling succession matters of Muslim parties and administration of estates of deceased Muslims. For example, in the case of *Re the Estate of Ismail Osman*

---

[30] Unreported, Kadhi's Court at Nairobi, 2015.

Adam (Deceased), Noorbanu Abdul Razak v. AbdulKader Ismail Osman [2009], the Court of Appeal upheld the choice of Muslim parties to submit to the kadhis' court or to file succession proceedings in the High Court. However, the Court of Appeal clarified that despite the fact that the High Court has the jurisdiction to entertain succession matters to related Muslims, the High Court is bound to apply Islamic law. The Court of Appeal held:

> There should not be any confusion between the jurisdiction of the High Court to entertain a dispute relating to testamentary or intestate succession to estates of Muslims and the substantive law applicable in the High Court in such disputes ... However, if the High Court assumes jurisdiction to the estate of a deceased Muslim, then by virtue of section 2(3) [of the Law of Succession Act], the law applicable in the High Court as to the devolution of the estate is the Muslim law and not the Law of Succession Act.[31]

In the case of *Rashid Zahran v. Azan Zahran & 4 others* [1999] at the High Court in Mombasa, the appellant raised an objection that the kadhis' courts did not have the jurisdiction to adjudicate on matters that related to the administration of estates of deceased Muslims and that the respondent did not obtain letters of administration from the kadhis' court. Justice Ibrahim of the High Court of Kenya in Mombasa held: 'Upon consideration, this court finds that letters of administration is not a requirement under Islamic law for the purpose of inheritance of succession proceedings.'[32] In the case of *Zog'llo Zolleyn aka Alis Said Ahmed v. Abdalla Said Ahmed* [2014], Justice Odero recognised the jurisdiction of the kadhis' court handling matters relating to the administration of the estates of deceased Muslims, and stated:

> It is conceded by both parties that probate proceedings regarding the estate of the deceased Fatuma Hassan are already in progress before the Kadhi's Court ... The matter ought to proceed on the first instance before the Kadhi and only if any party is dissatisfied with the manner of probate in the Kadhi's Court, then the matter may move upon appeal to the High Court.[33]

Justice Kimaru of the High Court in Nairobi adopted a similar approach in the case of *Re. Estate of Maryam Juma Kibanda (Deceased) Ashraf Abdul Kassim v.*

---

[31] *Re the Estate of Ismail Osman Adam (Deceased), Noorbanu Abdul Razak v. AbdulKader Ismail Osman*, Mombasa Civil Appeal No. 285 of 2009.
[32] *Rashid Zahran v. Azan Zahran & 4 others*, Civil appeal No. 55 of 1999 at the High Court of Kenya at Mombasa (unreported).
[33] *Zog'llo Zolleyn aka Alis Said Ahmed v. Abdalla Said Ahmed* [2014] eKLR, Succession Cause No. 467 of 2013.

Karar Omar & 3 others, [2014] that was taken for an appeal at the High Court over a dispute on a petition for the grant of letters of administration intestate by the kadhis' court. Kimaru J. held: 'In the premises therefore, this court holds that the parties to these proceedings being Muslims, and the deceased having been a Muslim, the dispute between them shall be referred for hearing and determination by the Kadhis' Court.'[34]

Contrary to the above decisions on giving jurisdiction to kadhis' courts to grant letters of administration for estates of deceased Muslims, *In the Matter of: The Estate of S.P.B. – Deceased R.B. & others and A.S.B. & others* [2014], Justice Muriithi declined to allow the kadhis' court to adjudicate a succession matter after one of the parties had refused to submit to it. Muriithi J. held:

> I find that the High Court has jurisdiction to entertain the application by the Petitioners in this case. The issue of the applicable law will fall for consideration, as observed above, when the court determines the prayers for administration and distribution of the Estate.[35]

Conclusion

Kadhis' courts have occupied a significant place in the Kenyan judicial system. Despite the trials and tribulations of the kadhis' courts, these judicial-cum-religious institutions have survived and have stood the test of time. Kadhis' courts were retained in Kenya after going through a complex historical trajectory that culminated in their entrenchment in the Constitution of Kenya 1963. With the constitutional reform process, controversies over kadhis' courts re-emerged in the mid-1990s and triggered heated debates that led to Christian reactions and Muslim responses. The existence of the kadhis' court in Kenya and its incorporation in the constitution have faced objections, particularly from some Christian churches during the constitutional review process in 1997 and the referendum in 2005. Kadhis' courts survived these constitutional challenges and were retained in the Constitution of Kenya 2010.

This chapter has shown the significance of religious entities in a secular state and the role of the state in handling contentious constitutional issues in a multi-faith society. The Kenyan experience in dealing with kadhis' courts demonstrates the discourse of religion and politics in a pluralist society with contentious religious underpinnings. The retention of kadhis' courts shows how

---

[34] *Re. Estate of Maryam Juma Kibanda (Deceased) Ashraf Abdul Kassim v. Karar Omar & 3 others* [2014] eKLR.
[35] Succession Cause No. 301 of 2014 In the Matter of: The Estate of S.P.B. – Deceased.
1. R.B. 2. R.G.O. and A.S.B. (2 Years) and 1. H.S.B. 2. A.S.B., R.B. & R.G.O. v. H.S.B. & A.S.B. [2014] eKLR.

the state managed to strike a balance between the politics of accommodating religious minorities (Kenyan Muslims) by incorporating the kadhis' courts in the constitution on the one hand, and, on the other hand, coping with the politics of neutralising criticisms raised by some Christian groups who opposed the entrenchment of kadhis' courts in the constitution.

The conflicts and tensions between judges and kadhis in courts could be partly attributed to the legacy of colonial perceptions of kadhis and their courts. The wholesale adoption of Common Law principles by conventional courts, which ignore Islamic law rules, and the application of Islamic law rules by the letter by kadhis' courts, which disregard Common Law notions of justice, could be another source for conflicts. A possible solution to ease the tension between judges and kadhis seems to lie in formulating comparative jurisprudence that will incorporate the best of both worlds: Kenyan common law and Islamic law.

The chapter has demonstrated the interesting scenarios that engage judges and kadhis on matters of Muslim personal law in the Kenyan courts. This situation resulted in a constructive engagement between two arms of the judiciary – the judges and the kadhis – that in turn has set the stage for an emerging comparative jurisprudence within a pluralistic society.

Contemporary emerging issues touching Islamic personal law can no longer be dismissed, but rather need to be approached and responded to with a comprehensive juristic vision highlighting the ultimate objectives of Islamic law (*maqāsid al-sharī'a*). There is a need to formulate new approaches in developing a confident and constructive Muslim jurisprudence that will respond to emerging challenges.

Contemporary kadhis in Kenya have adopted a progressive approach that encourages the flexibility and adaptability of the Muslim law of personal status, compatible with present times but according with the ultimate objectives of Islamic law and its higher values. Decisions of kadhis that are based on the best interests of children in cases of child custody, and the awarding of a share of matrimonial property to Muslim wives who have made either direct or indirect contributions in marriage, demonstrate the emergence of a comparative jurisprudence in the Kenyan courts.

The chapter underscores the need for a progressive comparative jurisprudential approach that promotes the flexibility and adaptability of Islamic law, which will in turn assist in responding to emerging legal issues facing Muslim litigants in the Kenyan courts. It advocates for the harmonisation of Islamic law with common law principles, without necessarily sacrificing the intended objectives and values of the two legal systems.

15

The Case of the Stubborn Heir: State and Non-state Actors in Zanzibar's Kadhis' Courts

Erin E. Stiles

Introduction

In order to address the governance theme of the conference that was the inspiration for this volume, this chapter examines the interplay of state and non-state actors in various kinds of disputes in rural Islamic courts in Zanzibar. In nearly all of my previous writing about Islamic courts in Zanzibar, I have addressed marital disputes, focusing specifically on maintenance and divorce cases. In much of this work, I have looked at patterns in judicial reasoning. More recently, I have considered the interplay of various kinds of authority figures and different normative orders in the plural legal landscape of rural Zanzibar (2018). This chapter compares my findings on marital disputes with what I am learning about inheritance disputes. After describing how Islamic courts, known as kadhis' courts or *mahakama ya kadhi*, are incorporated into Zanzibar's legal system, I will briefly review what I have referred to elsewhere as the three-stage process of resolving marital disputes (Stiles 2009, 2018). Then, I will draw parallels with how people manage inheritance disputes both inside and outside of the kadhis' courts, using one inheritance case as an example. The focus in this chapter is not so much on judicial reasoning or decision-making in inheritance disputes as on the interplay of different kinds of authority-wielding actors in the process of resolving such disputes.

Throughout, I highlight the practices and perceptions – or, in the language of the original call for papers for the foundational conference, the 'attitudes and activities' – of everyday people in order to highlight the relationship between Muslims and state governance in the context of rural Zanzibar. Elsewhere, I describe this approach as 'legal pluralism from the ground up' (2018). I find that in rural areas of Unguja, Zanzibar's largest island, the process of disputing is viewed by lay people, scholars, government actors and legal professionals as involving matters that are not simply under the formal jurisdiction of the kadhis' courts, which they are, but as matters which many types of authorities and many normative ideas inform. In Ido Shahar's recent discussion of the usefulness of legal pluralism for understanding Islamic courts, he observes that '*shar'ia* courts often constitute only one element ... in much broader decentralized, socio-legal fields, and Islamic law is frequently practiced in parallel to other, non-shari'a bodies of law' (2008: 116). In Zanzibar, both state and non-state actors, and both religious and non-religious actors, are expected, and are eager, to weigh in at various points in the handling of personal status disputes. I argue that the interplay of state and non-state actors in Zanzibar shows that Islamic law is not practised in parallel with (in Shahar's terms) but in conjunction with other bodies of law (such as secular magistrates' courts) and other types of legal authority (such as elders or government-appointed community leaders). I argue that the various types of expertise that are consulted in the managing of disputes, rather than being viewed by people as competing legal regimes, are seen as mutually supportive routes to the restoration of harmonious relationships between people.

I have not conducted extensive fieldwork in Zanzibar for several years, so this chapter draws primarily on data collected during around twenty-four months of field research carried out between 1999 and 2008. Most of my research took place in the kadhis' court in the fishing village of Mkokotoni in northern Unguja and in the rural communities surrounding the court.

Islamic Courts and the Legal Landscape of Zanzibar

Zanzibar, as a semi-autonomous archipelagic state of Tanzania, has a semi-independent legal system. Unlike on the Tanzanian mainland, Islamic courts are incorporated into the legal system through the 1984 constitution. The structure and jurisdiction of the courts is laid out in the Kadhis' Courts Act of 1985, which established ten to fifteen district kadhis' courts for Zanzibar, and an appeals process through a Chief Kadhi; final appeals rest with the High Court of Zanzibar. According to the constitution, the president of Zanzibar appoints kadhis on the basis of their knowledge of and expertise in Islam. Section 6.1 of the 1985 Act established the jurisdiction of the courts and reads as follows:

> A Kadhis' Court shall have and exercise jurisdiction in the determination of questions of Muslim law relating to personal status, marriage, divorce or inheritance in proceedings in which all the parties profess the Muslim religion.

Since the vast majority of Zanzibar's population is Muslim, the kadhis' courts handle most personal status matters.

In 2003, *The Written Laws (Miscellaneous Amendments) Act. No. 4* amended the Kadhis' Courts Act in a number of minor ways. However, the make-up and jurisdiction of the courts remained essentially the same. The 2003 Act established more specific required qualifications for a person to be appointed as a district or appellate kadhi, or as one of the legal scholars who advise the High Court in matters of appeal beyond the Chief Kadhi. The appointment procedure also changed slightly in the Act, in that the president would appoint kadhis in conjunction with a Judicial Services Commission kadhi.[1] The Act renewed the jurisdiction of the kadhis' courts, and specifically gave the courts jurisdiction over child custody 'for the time being'. Prior to 2003, this was a confusing issue in the courts; no one seemed sure about whether kadhis' courts or magistrates should handle such cases. In the chapter in this volume by Abdulkadir Hashim, the author describes the controversy around this same issue in contemporary Kenya. The Act also sets an upper limit on the amount of maintenance that could be claimed in the kadhis' courts. The courts also had jurisdiction over Islamic charitable endowments known as *wakf* (Ar. *waqf*) and inheritance cases when all parties were Muslim:

(1) Every District Kadhi shall have and exercise Jurisdiction in the determination of matters of Islamic laws relating to:-
    (i) personal status, marriage, divorce, guardianships and subject to the provisions of any other law for the time being in force, the custody of children in cases all the parties are Muslims.
    (ii) Wakf or religious charitable trusts, gift inter vivos and inheritance in cases all parties are Muslims; and
    (iii) Claims of maintenance, where such claim is for a lump sum of not exceeding Five hundred thousand shillings or for a periodical payment to be made at a rate not exceeding fifty thousand shillings per month, in cases all parties are Muslims.

In Act no. 9 2017, the 1985 Kadhis' Act was repealed and replaced by a new Kadhis' Act, which re-established the District and Appellate Kadhis' Courts. The Act outlines the exclusive jurisdiction of the kadhis' courts over the following:

(a) marriage, divorce;
(b) personal status;

---

[1] See Section 2 of The Written Laws (Misc. Amendments) Act. No. 4 of 2003.

(c) maintenance and custody of children;
(d) *wakf* and religious trusts, grants and gifts inter vivo;
(e) wills and inheritance;
(f) divisions of matrimonial assets if there is actual contribution;
(g) any other matter in respect of which jurisdiction is conferred to the Kadhis' Court by any written law.

In addition, the new Kadhis' Act sets out the criteria for being appointed as a district, appellate or chief kadhi, and the primary criterion is holding a bachelor's degree in Islamic shari'a from a recognised university. The Act also made some additional change to the function of the courts. For example, the Act establishes a provision for mediation, and outlines the role of the mediator.

Today, there are ten Islamic district kadhis' courts in Zanzibar, a deputy chief kadhi on Unguja, and an appellate kadhi on Pemba; both are subordinate to the Chief Kadhi, who is subordinate to the High Court and the Chief Justice. All kadhis are thus direct employees of the state, and receive a salary. According to the constitution, like all judges in Zanzibar, kadhis may not be members of political parties, although they maintain the right to vote. Today, all kadhis are trained in the Shafi'i *madhhab*, which is the dominant Islamic legal school of thought in coastal East Africa. During my early research, most kadhis I interviewed told me that although they were Shafi'i, they would make an effort to use another *madhhab* if disputants were of another *madhhab*. The Zanzibari state regulates procedural law in the kadhis' courts, but not substantive law as relates to personal status. The Kadhis' Act states that procedure will be the same as in other subordinate courts unless or until the Chief Kadhi and Chief Justice determine otherwise. The Kadhis' Act also states that Islamic rules of evidence shall be applied in the kadhis' courts, but establishes that witnesses must be heard without 'discrimination based on religion, sex, or otherwise' and that assessment of facts must be based on the credibility of evidence provided rather than on the number of witnesses. There is no family or personal status law code in Zanzibar; thus in terms of substantive law, kadhis make judgments according to their knowledge and understandings of the Islamic legal tradition.

State and Non-state Actors in Muslim Marital Disputing in Rural Unguja

As noted, I have written previously on the interplay of various kinds of actors and authority figures in managing marital disputes in rural Zanzibar as evidencing a certain kind of pluralism (2018, and briefly mentioned 2009: 131). For the purposes of this chapter, I will briefly relate some of the key points I made on this subject to set the stage for a comparison with the process of inheritance dispute management. It is important to note that these observations reflect dispute resolution in rural northern Unguja, and that dispute processing in the urban centre of Zanzibar Town might look somewhat different. In northern Unguja, people commonly recognise a three-step process of managing a marital dispute in the present day (people will note differences in the past when elders did nearly all the management of such disputes); the steps in the process involve both state and non-state actors, and both religious and non-religious authorities. I should note that the population of northern Unguja is almost entirely Muslim, so I will be discussing Muslims throughout the chapter, even if I do not specify. There is widespread agreement between both the authority figures themselves and the lay people on the process: (1) if a married couple is disputing, first they take their problem to the *wazee*, the elders. If *wazee* are unable to reconcile the couple or solve their problem, then it is taken (2) to a government-appointed community leader called a *sheha*. If the *sheha* fails to solve the problem, then the matter is taken to a state-appointed kadhi in the kadhis' court. As one woman explained it to me: 'Everyone goes [to the elders] – even the *watu wazima* (adults). If the elders fail, then they go to the *sheha*. But the *sheha* is not someone of the law. No, the *sheha* just gives out a paper sending you to the kadhi' (Stiles 2018: 107).

Shehas have long had a role in dispute processing in Zanzibar, as noted by historians (Ingrams 1931; Stockreiter 2008), and they were most recently established as part of the governing structure of Zanzibar by Act No. 11 of 1992. The Act replaced the political districts called 'branches' that were established in Zanzibar after the 1964 revolution with districts called '*shehias*' and designated *shehas* as the chief executives of the *shehias* (Stiles 2009). The Act states that *shehas* are responsible for 'the settlement of all social and family disputes arising in that area in accordance with the customary laws of that area'. Unlike kadhis and other judges whom the law prohibits from joining political parties,[2] *shehas* can be members of a political party. In northern Unguja at the time of my research, most were affiliated with the ruling party, and the common understanding was that only loyal party members were appointed as *sheha*.

Sometimes, disputants may also consult with a *kadhi wa mtaa*, a locally recognised expert in Islam or 'neighbourhood kadhi'. The *kadhi wa mtaa* is not, however, regarded as a mandatory part of the disputing process, but as an optional voice of expertise in Islam that some may call upon (see Stiles 2009 for more on *kadhi wa mtaa*).

As I have written elsewhere, rural Zanzibaris view the elders, *shehas* and kadhis as having different kinds of legally relevant knowledge, and drawing

---

[2] Article 97. 'It is hereby prohibited for a Judge of the High Court (including the Chief Justice), Magistrates of all grades Registrar, Acting Registrar, Deputy Registrar and Assistant Registrar and all Kadhis (together with the Chief Kadhi) to join any political party save only that he shall have the right to vote which is provided for in Article 7 of this Constitution.'

their authority from different sources (2018). Elders, the first step in the process of disputing, have authority as senior members of the family, and draw on their affection for their children and concern for their welfare in handling disputes. The state appoints *shehas*, but they do not have any formal expertise in law. Rather, they draw on their knowledge of the local community, local norms and interpersonal relationships. The kadhis must be experts in Islamic law, but are also associated with the state: they are appointed by the state and their decisions are binding and thus final in a way that the reconciliation efforts of elders and *shehas* are not.

These three types of authority figures draw on different types of knowledge and different sources of expertise. Some are salaried appointments of the state and some not, yet Zanzibaris understand all of them to be compulsory steps in dispute resolution. This was consistent across all people I worked with. At each stage in the disputing process, disputants would be reminded of the previous steps and asked if they had fulfilled them. A *sheha* would ask a woman if she had already talked to her elders, and the kadhis' court clerks would ask potential litigants if they had a letter from the *sheha* confirming that he (or rarely, she) had been consulted. Regularly, the kadhi with whom I worked most closely called in *shehas* and elders to advise on cases opened with him. In terms of work on legal pluralism, it seems interesting to me that these very different kinds of authorities – elders, *shehas*, kadhis – are not 'forum shopped' by Muslims in rural Zanzibar, or consulted as alternatives to one another, but are rather regarded as ranked, obligatory steps in the widely agreed-upon process of managing marital disputes (Stiles 2018: 123). Therefore, they are not an 'either/or' set of choices in resolving disputes but an 'also-and', or actually not really a 'choice' at all, but rather a widely accepted structure for handling disputes that draws sequentially on different types of authority and different fora (Stiles 2018). For the purposes of this volume, it seems important to note that this framework does not draw contrasts between types of authority (community, state, Islamic) or juxtapose Islamic and non-Islamic, state and non-state, but rather acknowledges a series of compulsory steps in the process of dispute resolution; steps that take disputants in and out of the state.

Managing Muslim Inheritance Disputes

Now let me turn to some preliminary thoughts on inheritance disputes among Muslims living in the same part of Unguja. During my years of research in Zanzibar, I collected court cases on inheritance and engaged in a number of conversations and interviews on the subject, but it was never the primary focus of my research, and it is only recently that I have turned to examining these materials on inheritance disputes.

As noted previously, the 1985 Kadhis' Court Act and the 2003 amendments to it give the kadhis' courts jurisdiction over inheritance cases when all parties are Muslim. Zanzibar has also had a Wakf Commission for some time, most recently re-established as the Wakf and Trust Commission in Act No. 2 of 2007. According to the letter of law, the Commission is charged with administering the estates of 'deceased Muslims' under a number of conditions, such as dying intestate, leaving a will, or designating the Commission as administrator of the estate. In addition, I have heard that there are *wakf* and inheritance officers appointed in various parts of Zanzibar, but I have not yet had the chance to talk with one. Since I have not encountered anyone who had made use of the Commission, I will not discuss it further in this chapter.

I found widespread agreement in this part of Unguja that property is generally divided according to Islamic rules of inheritance or through an informal personal arrangement among heirs. Most people explained that this process was simple; one acquaintance, for example, told me: 'We just follow *sheria za dini* to divide it [property] so there are no problems.' A *sheha* told me that people just tend to agree among themselves how to use the property, the trees or the land and often do so without argument or without recourse to the laws of division. He explained that in the case of a dispute or a complex division question arising, people would probably go to a *kadhi wa mtaa* to ask for help.

During the period of my extended field research, only a few inheritance cases were opened in the Mkokotoni court. I remember once asking some acquaintances why there were so few, and the jesting reply, which of course contained an element of truth, was along the lines of 'Because we are poor! There is nothing to dispute over!' In the years for which I have court records, 1979–2005, an average of forty to fifty cases were opened per year in the Mkokotoni court; the vast majority were maintenance claims or suits for divorce brought by women (Stiles 2009). In this period, the number of inheritance cases opened per year ranged from zero to five, with an average of only 1.3 per year. However, these figures reflect only cases that were opened. Sometimes, disputants brought inheritance questions or problems to the kadhi without opening a case. In these situations, the kadhi played an advisory role. The advisory role might be quite extensive and take up several hours of the kadhi's time. However, it leaves no paper trail – court documents and kadhi notes were not usually produced unless a case was formally opened.

MKO 23-00: A Stubborn Heir

Now, let me briefly examine one of the few inheritance cases opened during my time in the Mkokotoni court. The case was brought by a young man I will call Juma, from a village about one hour by bus from the court. Juma's father had died the previous year, and his family was 'late', as he put it, in distributing his property to the heirs. Juma came to court many times, sometimes with other family members, and sometimes alone. We talked together on one of his early visits. I learned that he was twenty-three years old, and had two wives but not yet any children. When he died, Juma's father left behind three wives and sixteen children; Juma was the only child of his mother. He told me that he had opened the case so that everyone would inherit his or her share. He explained that the family had not yet divided the property, and it was causing many problems. He told me he did not know exactly how much money or property there was, but he knew that there were several houses, various household implements and money. The only property he named specifically aside from the houses were various books – some in Arabic, some in Swahili, and many of them used in his father's work as a *mganga*, or healer. When I remarked on the large number of heirs, Juma explained that this was exactly why he had opened the case: so the property could be divided fairly among them.

After his father's death, Juma said, his elder brother had not gone to elders to help with the division of the property, so he had approached that brother. However, the brother refused to see the elders about the division of property, and the elders failed to divide the property themselves. At the time of our conversation, Juma had opened a case and had been to court about ten times, but many of the respondents had never shown up. I asked him if he had visited the *sheha* and he said he had. He told me that, before coming to court, he had visited the *shaykhs* (meaning local religious experts such as the *kadhi wa mtaa*), his elders and the *sheha*, and that they had all sent him to the kadhi. Juma took the unusual step of going straight to the Chief Kadhi (this was odd in terms of procedure, since the Chief Kadhi only hears appeals cases). The Chief Kadhi met with him, but told Juma not to make trouble by coming there first, and so sent him back to the district kadhi at the Mkokotoni court. In our conversation, it became clear that the main problem was the stubborn elder brother, who refused to see anybody about the division of property, which is why they had all sent Juma to open a case with the kadhi, who could compel the brother to act. Juma also told me that the *sheha* had sent him elsewhere because he knew that the Islamic division of property was more than he could handle.

I discussed Juma's case with the chief clerk, Bwana Fumu, who confirmed that the problem was the stubbornness of the elder brother. In Fumu's view, it was not a complicated case. He told me that the court knew what property there was to divide, who the heirs were, and how to divide the property according to the law. However, the elder brother was obstinately refusing to go along with the process of dividing the property, and so they opened a case to summon him. However, he never responded. Because there had been so much trouble getting the one older brother and some of the other heirs to court, the kadhi and court staff eventually decided to go to the family's village themselves to meet with all the parties involved. I did not go on this trip, but the journey was successful, and the property was divided in a way that the court and their heirs found acceptable.

Although Juma told me several times that he was not the only plaintiff, the *madai*, or plaintiff's claim, was written up with him as the only *madai*, claimant, and with ten *wadaiwa*, respondents, listed. This was most likely due to the decision of the clerks, who frame nearly all of the cases opened in the court in a way they find appropriate. The claim stated that Juma's father had died several months earlier and left several kinds of property, including three houses, numerous kinds of goods, and 70,000 Tanzania shillings, and that the ten respondents named needed to prove in court that they were indeed the heirs of the property they were holding. There was no counter-claim on record, reflecting the fact that the court and Juma had trouble convincing the defendants to show up together as a group. There was also no written decision, because the matter was decided out of court. The kadhi's notes on the case are rather brief, and record simply the many occasions on which Juma and some of the respondents showed up, the frequent postponing of the case, and a comment on the fact that the property was divided successfully. He also noted that the *sheha* of the *shehia* in which the litigants lived approved and recorded the division of property; however, he did not record any details of the division.

For the purposes of this chapter vis-à-vis the goals of the book, there are a couple of interesting things about this case. One is simply the fact that a case was opened: in some of the other inheritance disputes that I witnessed, a formal case was never opened, even when the matter seemed complicated to me, as in determining who the legal heirs were. In this one, however, the kadhi deemed it necessary because a key elder brother would not participate in the normal mode of dividing property within the family and community. Thus, Juma approached the kadhi as the state authority with the most power to compel compliance by issuing a summons and possibly making a binding decision about the property. The case was not opened because it was a complicated division or a dispute over who was an heir, but simply because one heir refused to participate in the division of property.

There are also noteworthy parallels in the process of managing marital disputes and inheritance disputes in rural northern Unguja. In both situations, disputants and others recognise many types of community, religious and state actors as having relevant expertise in and authority over managing disputes. Although all generally regard the process of managing such disputes as in accordance with *sheria za dini*, or religious law, only state and neighbourhood kadhis have Islamic expertise. As with the management of marital disputes, we see that the state-appointed kadhi is something of a last resort to be approached when other options for dividing the property have failed.

Discussion

What can the analysis of disputing in Zanzibar contribute to this volume's primary aim of exploring the relationships between governance and Muslims in East Africa? Zanzibar is quite different from Kenya, mainland Tanzania and Uganda, in that Muslims are in the overwhelming majority. Zanzibar's constitution establishes the kadhis' courts, and they are the only court option available to Muslims for handling issues of personal status. Perhaps most clearly from the examples presented in this chapter, we see that Muslims in rural parts of Zanzibar (and perhaps in urban areas too) tend to view the state-established kadhis' courts as the final rung on a ladder of resolving disputes. The courts are not an alternative to other modes of handling disputes, but rather part of a process that incorporates state and non-state actors and institutions, religious and non-religious authority and knowledge bases. Disputing wives and husbands end up at the kadhis' court when the elders and the *shehas* have failed to reconcile the couple or solve their problems. At this point, my work on inheritance is somewhat preliminary, but the limited data that I have indicates that although there may not be as formal a recognition of a tripartite process, there is a clear understanding that kadhis, *shehas*, shaykhs and elders all have a role to play in handling disputes. Again, from the materials I draw on in this chapter, there is no indication that these are seen as alternative authorities, competing knowledge bases, or different legal regimes that would result in significantly different outcomes; rather, they seem to represent a sort of sequential pluralism. As I have described elsewhere, people certainly differentiate between these actors and institutions in terms of their expertise, and may admire or disrespect the individuals who hold various offices (such as kadhis and *shehas*), but I have not found general patterns indicating the expectation of different kinds of results or settlements. People seem to regard the differences as complementary, not competitive. Moreover, even the most politically minded critics of the ruling party, many of whom are devout Muslims suspicious of the ruling party's ties to mainland Tanzania, tend to share the view of the steps required in disputing. In both cases, people regard the kadhi as the final resort when other attempts have failed.

However, in the case of inheritance, I suspect further research might show that this is not the whole story, and this will be the subject of my next research project. Recently, a project undertaken by Zanzibar's Ministry of Lands, Housing, Water and Energy and the non-profit Vitongoji Environmental Conservation Association (VECA) in Chake Chake, Pemba, tried to tackle the phenomenon known as 'property-grabbing', in which a widow's male relatives try to claim property to which she would otherwise be entitled. The phenomenon is well documented on the Tanzanian mainland and elsewhere in East Africa (Izumi 2007; Ezer 2006; Mwenda, Munda and Mivola-Mwenda 2005), but has not been extensively documented or researched in Zanzibar. The outreach campaign aimed to teach women about marital property, property rights and inheritance rights. However, the VECA director let me know that the project had lost funding and had therefore been discontinued.

I do not yet know how widespread such practices are in Zanzibar, but during a brief exploratory trip I made to Zanzibar in 2019, several people confirmed to me that property grabbing was a problem in both rural Zanzibar and in the urban context of Zanzibar Town, and that heirs were often hesitant to pursue claims, for various reasons. In 2016, the Thompson Reuters Foundation reported on the practice in northern and southern Unguja, citing that community leaders in rural areas were telling widows that 'local norms' prevented them from inheriting property from their husbands (VECA used the term *mila na desturi* to describe the practice). According to Islamic laws of inheritance, which are theoretically in use throughout Zanzibar, widows inherit from their deceased husbands. The Reuters report encouraged me to rethink an incident from the Mkokotoni court from over ten years ago. One day, two elderly women and a number of their relatives came to the court. The dispute was about who should have inherited three houses after the death of an elder. Shaykh Hamid, the kadhi, in asking for clarification, framed it in terms of rights to inheritance. The kadhi listened, advised and eventually determined that the party had divided the inheritance correctly. The women's inheritance rights had not been violated, so there was nothing he could do for them.

Later, the kadhi told me that the party had first come to him some time ago when their grandfather had died, and he had helped them divide the property according to the *sheria za dini*. Now, he explained, the men were trying to take back the property of the women, who were understandably very angry. The kadhi told me that they needed to open a civil case in the magistrate's court, because this was no longer a dispute over inheritance, by which he meant a determination of the heirs or division of property, but rather a dispute over property, and over who owned what. I do not know if they opened a case in the magistrate's court.

To conclude, I would like to suggest that in going forward with academic exploration of the relationship between Muslims and the state in East Africa, we foreground what governance means in practice and at the local level. By looking at the processing of disputes, we see how governance plays out in day-to-day life.

Bibliography

Benda-Beckmann, Franz von (2002), 'Who's Afraid of Legal Pluralism?', *Journal of Legal Pluralism* 47, pp. 37–83.

Benda-Beckmann, Kebeet (1981), 'Forum Shopping and Shopping Forums: Dispute Processing in a Minangkabau Village in West Sumatra', *Journal of Legal Pluralism* 19, pp. 117–59.

Berger, Maurits (1999), 'The Shari'a and Legal Pluralism: The Example of Syria', in B. Dupret, M. Berger and L. al-Zwaini (eds), *Legal Pluralism in the Arab World*, The Hague: Kluwer Law International, pp. 113–24.

Bowen, John R. (2003), *Islam, Law and Equality in Indonesia: An Anthropology of Public Reasoning*, Cambridge: Cambridge University Press.

Bowen, John R. (1998), 'Law and Social Norms in the Comparative Study of Islam', *American Anthropologist* 100(4), pp. 1,034–8.

Caplan, Pat (2015), 'Two Weddings in Northern Mafia: Changes in Women's Lives since the 1960s', in Erin E. Stiles and Katrina D. Thompson (eds), *Gendered Lives in the Western Indian Ocean: Islam, Marriage, and Sexuality on the Swahili Coast*, Athens: Ohio University Press, pp. 85–116.

Caplan, Pat (1995), '"Law" and "Custom": Marital Disputes on Northern Mafia Island, Tanzania', in Pat Caplan, *Understanding Disputes: The Politics of Argument*, London: Routledge, pp. 203–21.

Dean, Erin (2013), '"The Backbone of the Village" Gender, Development, and Traditional Authority in Rural Zanzibar', *Journal of Contemporary African Studies* 31(1), pp. 18–36.

Dupret, Baudouin (2007), 'Legal Pluralism, Plurality of Laws, and Legal Practices', *European Journal of Legal Studies* 1(1), pp. 1–26.

Ezer, Tamar (2006), 'Inheritance Law in Tanzania: The Impoverishment of Widows and Daughters', *The Georgetown Journal of Gender and the Law* 7(599), pp. 599–662.

Griffiths, John (1986), 'What Is Legal Pluralism?' *The Journal of Legal Pluralism and Unofficial Law* 24, pp. 1–50.

Izumi, Kaori (2007), 'Gender-based Violence and Property Grabbing in Africa: A Denial of Women's Liberty and Security', *Gender and Development* 54 (March), pp. 11–23.

Keefe, Susi (2015), 'Being a Good Muslim Man: Modern Aspirations and Polygynous Intentions in a Swahili Muslim Village', in Erin E. Stiles and Katrina D. Thompson (eds), *Gendered Lives in the Western Indian Ocean: Islam, Marriage, and Sexuality on the Swahili Coast*, Athens: Ohio University Press, pp. 321–53.

Merry, Sally Engle (1988), 'Legal Pluralism', *Law and Society Review* 22(5), pp. 869–96.

Merry, Sally Engle (1990), *Getting Justice and Getting Even: Legal Consciousness among Working Class Americans*, Chicago: University of Chicago Press.

Merry, Sally Engle (2013), 'McGill Convocation Address: Legal Pluralism in Action', https://lawjournal.mcgill.ca/article/mcgill-convocation-address-legal-pluralism-in-practice/

Middleton, John (1992), *The World of the Swahili: An African Mercantile Civilization*, New Haven: Yale University Press.

Mwenda, Kenneth K, Judge Florence N. M. Munda and Judith Mvula-Mwenda (2005), 'Property-Grabbing under African Customary Law: Repugnant to Natural

Justice, Equity, and Good Conscience, Yet a Troubling Reality', *George Washington International Law Review*, 37, pp. 949–67.

Shahar, Ido (2008), 'Legal Pluralism and the Study of Sharia Courts', *Islamic Law and Society* 15, pp. 112–41.

Shahar, Ido (2013), 'Forum Shopping between Civil and Shari'a Courts: Maintenance Suits in Contemporary Jerusalem', in Franz von Benda-Beckmann, Kebeet von Benda-Beckmann, Martin Ramstedt and Bertram Turner (eds), *Religion in Disputes: Pervasiveness of Religious Normativity in Disputing Processes*, London: Palgrave Macmillan, pp. 147–64.

Shahar, Ido (2015), *Legal Pluralism in the Holy City: Competing Courts, Forum Shopping, and Institutional Dynamics in Jerusalem*, Farnham: Ashgate.

Stiles, Erin E. (2009), *An Islamic Court in Context: An Ethnographic Study of Judicial Reasoning*, New York: Palgrave Macmillan.

Stiles, Erin E. (2014), 'The Right to Marry: Daughters and Elders in the Islamic Courts of Zanzibar', *Islamic Law and Society* 21(3), pp. 252–75.

Stiles, Erin E. (2015), 'An Unsuitable Husband: Allegations of Impotence in Zanzibar', in Erin E. Stiles and Katrina D. Thompson (eds), *Gendered Lives in the Western Indian Ocean: Islam, Marriage, and Sexuality on the Swahili Coast*, Athens: Ohio University Press, pp. 245–68.

Stiles, Erin E. (2018) 'How to Manage a Marital Dispute: Legal Pluralism from the Ground Up', University of California, *Irvine Law Review* 8, pp. 101–22.

About the Contributors

Felicitas Becker is Professor in the Department of History at Ghent University.

James R. Brennan is Associate Professor in the Department of History at the University of Illinois Urbana-Champaign.

Abdulkadir Hashim is Senior Lecturer in Sharia and Islamic Studies at the University of Nairobi.

Susan F. Hirsch is Vernon M. and Minnie I. Lynch Chair of Conflict Resolution and Anthropology at George Mason University.

Charlotte Knote is a Research Fellow at the Leibniz-Zentrum Moderner Orient, Berlin.

Kai Kresse is Professor of Social and Cultural Anthropology at Freie Universität Berlin, and Vice Director for Research at Leibniz Zentrum Moderner Orient (ZMO), Berlin.

Tito Kunyuk is a kadhi in the Kenyan Judiciary.

Kjersti Larsen is Professor of Social Anthropology at the University of Oslo.

Mark LeVine is Professor and Chair of the Program in Global Middle East Studies, Department of History, University of California, Irvine.

Hassan Mwakimako is Associate Professor of Islamic Studies at the Department of Philosophy and Religious Studies, Pwani University.

Hans Olsson is Marie Curie Fellow at the Centre for African Studies, University of Copenhagen.

About the Contributors

Jeremy Prestholdt is Professor in the History Department of the University of California, San Diego.

Mohamed Yunus Rafiq is Assistant Professor of Anthropology, NYU Shanghai and Global Network Assistant Professor, NYU.

Erin E. Stiles is Professor in the Department of Anthropology, University of Nevada

Farouk Topan is Professor Emeritus at the Aga Khan University, Institute for the Study of Muslim Civilisations, London.

Halkano Abdi Wario is Senior Lecturer in Religious Studies at Egerton University, Kenya.

Index

Abdalla, Abdilatif
   Kenya: Twendapi?, 54
Abdalla, Ahmed, 192, 194–5
Abdirahman Mohamed Abdi & Nasar Ali Bashir v. Adan Yussuf, 296
Abdullahi G. Chogorsa v. Sororo S. Sori, 286–8, 289
Africanisation, 147–9
Agrama, Hussein Ali, 264, 267
ahl al-hall wa-l-'aqd (those who loosen and bind), 31–2, 40–1, 42, 44
aid/aid organisations, 200–15
AIDS services, 200, 204, 205–12, 222
al-Qaeda, 58
Algeria, 30
Ali, Bakari, 206–8, 213
Ali, Mohamed, 254–5
alienation, 49, 50, 62, 63, 77, 99n, 200
All-Muslim National Union of Tanganyika (AMNUT), 112, 122–32
Amana, Mohamed, 190, 191
Amin, Abubakar, 103–4
Amin, Haj, 40, 42, 43
Amin Mohammed Hassan v. Zahra Mohammed Abdulkadir, 295–6

Amina Hassan Mohamed v. Yussuf Adan Abdullah, 301–2
AMNUT (All-Muslim National Union of Tanganyika), 112, 122–32
ANC (Tanganyika African National Congress), 129–30
Anderson, J. N. D., 280
Ang'elei, Ikal, 46
Ansâr Sunna, 165, 173
Aristotle
   Politics, 26
Aroni, Abida Ali, 196
Ashraf Abdu Kassim v. Karar Omar & 3 others, 295
Auda, Jasser, 84
authoritarianism, 30
authority, 41

Baadi, Mwalim, 254–5
BAK-AIDS (BAKWATA AIDS project), 206, 212, 214
BAKWATA (National Muslim Council of Tanzania [Baraza kuu la Waislamu Tanzania]), 12, 138–9, 140, 204–8
BAKWATA AIDS project (BAK-AIDS), 206, 212, 214

Balala, Khalid, 56
Bang, Anne, 154
Baraka, Bakari, 188
Baraka Binti Bahmishi v. Salim bin Abed Busawadi, 280, 286
bin Ameir, Hassan, 119–20, 137–8, 139
bin Juma, Hussein, 117
BRAVE (Building Resilience Against Violent Extremism), 69–71, 78–9, 81–4, 85–8 Building Resilience Against Violent Extremism (BRAVE), 69–71, 78–9, 81–4, 85–8
Butt, Shahid, 99n

CAs (community ambassadors), 220–1, 224–6f
CCM (Chama Cha Mapinduzi), 137, 145, 165, 166, 167, 174
Central Society of Tanganyika Muslims, 114, 115, 117, 129
Chama Cha Mapinduzi (CCM), 137, 145, 165, 166, 167, 174
Chambi, Shehe, 236–7, 238–9
Chamwenyewe, Mohamed Saidi, 122, 123, 124
Chaurembo, Abdallah, 137–8, 139
Christian Social Services Commission (CSSC), 202, 204, 205
Christianity
 kadhis' courts (Kenya), reaction to, 292–3
 Kenya, 33, 39, 61, 253
 Tanganyika, 120–1, 122, 125, 131
 Tanzania, Catholic family planning, 237–8
 Tanzania, Christian organisations, 202, 204, 205
 Zanzibar, 146–7, 156, 161, 163–4, 165–6, 167–75
CIPK (Council of Imams and Preachers of Islam in Kenya), 196
citizenship, 83, 148

Civic United Front (CUF), 165, 166, 167, 174, 199
civil society organisations (CSOs), 201, 204, 211, 215
civil war, 73–4
Coast Peoples Party (CPP), 53
coastal Muslims (Kenyan), 3, 49–50, 52, 63
 alienation in, 49, 50, 62, 63
 counter-terrorism, 58–62
 exclusion, 55, 252, 254
 identity, 253
 IPK, 55–9
 MRC, 59, 253
 political engagement, 54–9
 politics, 54, 63
 rejectionism, 59, 63
 repression, 58–9
 as second-class citizens, 72–5, 92, 252, 254
 separatism, 51–4
 UMA, 57
coastal strip (Kenyan), 2–3, 51–4, 72, 73–4
 MRC, 59, 73, 74, 253
colonialism
 coastal strip, 50–1
 Kenya, 2, 50–1, 72–3, 74
 Tanganyika, 113, 126
 Tanzania, 121, 202, 223
community ambassadors (CAs), 220–1, 224–6f
Constitution of Kenya Review Act, 196
'Constitution of Medina', 26
conversion, 171
corruption, 35, 36–7, 41, 134
Council of Imams and Preachers of Islam in Kenya (CIPK), 196
counter-radicalisation programmes (Kenya), 69–88, 101
counter-terrorism (Kenya), 58–62, 77
 counter-radicalisation programmes, 69–88, 101
 see also P/CVE

coups d'état, 28–9
CPP (Coast Peoples Party), 53
CSOs (civil society organisations), 201, 204, 211, 215
CSSC (Christian Social Services Commission), 202, 204, 205
CUF (Civic United Front), 165, 166, 167, 174, 199

Dar ul Islam, 82–3
democratisation, 30
devolution, 34–6
Discipline and Punish (Foucault, Michel), 28
discursive space, 92–109
   Elimika na Stambuli! ('Get Educated with Stambuli!') (radio programme), 102–7, 108
   Friday Bulletin, The (pamphlet), 94, 96–102, 107 108
   Pwani FM, 107–8
divorce/marital disputes, 270n, 271, 286–8, 298–302, 309–11
domestic space, 108
drums, 118–19

EAMWS (East African Muslim Welfare Society), 11–12
   Tanganyika, 112, 113, 133–4, 135, 137–8
   Tanzania, 112, 138–9, 140, 204
East Africa, 25, 252–3
   Muslim history in, 25–6, 33
East African Muslim Welfare Society (EAMWS) *see* EAMWS
Economy and Society (Weber, Max), 228
education
   Tanganyika, 120–1, 122, 123–4, 125–6, 130–1, 137
   Tanzania, 202–3
   Zanzibar, 4–5, 150–3
Egypt, 31, 267

elders, 310–11, 315
Elimika na Stambuli! ('Get Educated with Stambuli!') (radio programme), 102–7, 108
equality, 269–70; *see also* inequality
Essa v. Essa, 299
Essajee, Abdullatif, 99n–100
ethnic territorialism, 52–3
extremism, 43, 60, 78, 79–83, 101; *see also* militancy; P/CVE

faith-based organisations (FBOs), 201, 202, 204, 206
families, 107–8, 287, 295–8
Fatuma v. Omari, 281
FBOs (faith-based organisations), 201, 202, 204, 206
festivals, 114–19, 138, 139, 140
Foucault, Michel
   Discipline and Punish, 28
   Psychiatric Power: Lectures at the College de France, 1973–74, 29
framing, 212–13, 214
Friday Bulletin, The (pamphlet), 94, 96–102, 107 108
Friends of Lake Turkana, 45–6
Fumu, Bwana, 313
Fundirkira, Abdulla, 112, 132–7
Fundirkira, Nassoro, 132, 133

Genevieve Bertrand v. Mohamed Athman Maawiya and Anor, 294
Germany, 72, 121, 202
Githongo, John, 97
governance
   colonial forms, 27
   post-colonial forms, 27
   pre-colonial diversity, 27
   definition of term, 26
   state power, 27–8
Great Britain
   coastal strip, 3, 53
   colonialism, 72, 74
G.S.A. v. A.S.A., 297–8

Hamza v. Kombo, 281
Hanifa Mohamed Nur v. Ahmed Duale Osman, 301
Hassani, Shehe, 234–6
Helgoland–Zanzibar Treaty, 72
Hirsch, Susan, 93, 282, 289
HIV/AIDS services, 200, 204, 205–12, 222
H.M.M. v. K.J.D., 296–7
human rights, 73, 77
  Muslims, 59, 60, 63, 71, 94, 96
Hussein, Abduljabar Ishaq, 278, 284, 285, 286, 287–9
Hussein, Sukyan Omar, 284
Hussein, Yahya, 122, 135, 136
Hussein Sheikh Bashir v. Hassida Mohamed Ali, 300–1
Hyder, Mohamed, 105

ibn Taymiyya, 32, 83
identity, 222
  coastal Muslims, 52–4, 253
  Lamu Island, 247, 256
  Muslim, 49, 50, 56, 57, 62–3, 95–6
  *shehe*s, 222, 227, 228, 230–5, 238, 242
  Tanzania, 203
  veil, the, 143
  Zanzibar, 147–50, 155, 161–2, 163–4, 167, 168, 169–70, 172, 173
Idris, Mohammed, 78n, 98, 99n
imams, 232–3
In the Matter of: The Estate of S.P.B. – Deceased R.B. & others and A.S.B. & others, 304
inequality, 73, 74–5
  coastal Muslims, 51, 72–5, 92, 252, 254
  Muslims, 71, 73, 74–5, 86
  terrorist profiling, 97–8, 99, 100–2
  see also equality
inheritance, 302–4, 311–16
institutions, 11–14
  Lamu Port (Kenya), 246–56

representativeness, 184–5
SUPKEM (Kenya), 34, 36–7, 183–98, 292
Tanzania, 199–215, 220–43
IPK (Islamic Party of Kenya), 55–7, 195, 197
irrigation, 41, 43–5
Islam (Kenya), 25, 26, 189, 288
  ahl al-hall wa-l-'aqd (those who loosen and bind), 31–2, 40–1, 42, 44
  BRAVE, 69–71, 78–9, 81–4, 85–8
  counter-radicalisation programmes, 69–88
  custody of children, 295–8
  Dar ul Islam, 82–3
  divorce/marital disputes, 270n, 271, 286–8, 298–302
  extremism, 43, 78, 79–83
  jurisprudence, 84–5
  Lamu Island, 245
  land of, 84–5
  law, 263, 265, 266, 268, 269, 278–9, 280–9, 291–305
  pure, 39–40
  succession and estate administration, 302–4
  terrorism, 58–9
  see also kadhis' courts (Kenya); Muslims (Kenya)
Islam (Tanganyika), 112, 113, 114–22
  festivals, 114–19, 138, 139, 140
  politics, 125–6
  see also Muslims (Tanganyika)
Islam (Tanzania), 112–13, 139–40, 199, 202–3
Islam (Zanzibar), 144, 149–54, 156, 162, 164–6, 168, 171–3
  bida'a, 5
  education, 4–5, 150–3
  kadhis' courts, 14–15, 189, 281–2, 306–16
  law, 14–17, 189, 281–2, 306–16
  reformism, 144, 145, 147–9, 151, 152–3

Salafism, 150, 151, 154
Sufism, 149–50, 152, 153–4
see also Muslims (Zanzibar)
islam mondain (Islam in the present world), 2
Islamic Centre of Lodwar, 33, 38–45
Islamic College/Muslim Academy, 4–5
Islamic Divorce in the 21st Century: A Global Perspective (Stiles, Erin and Yakin, Ayang Utriza), 17
Islamic Party of Kenya (IPK), 55–7, 195, 197
Islamic state, establishing an, 82–3

Jamiatul Islamiyya, 113
Jaysh al-Ayman, 80
jihad, 68–9, 79–80, 81–3, 88
 debates, 106–7
Jihad for All Facebook page, 68–9
Journey to Extremism (UNDP), 77
Juma (inheritance plaintiff), 312–14

kadhi wa mtaas, 310–11, 315
kadhis' courts (Kenya), 14, 189, 264, 266, 268–74, 284, 291–305
 Abdirahman Mohamed Abdi & Nasar Ali Bashir v. Adan Yussuf, 296
 Abdullahi G. Chogorsa v. Sororo S. Sori, 286–8, 289
 Amin Mohammed Hassan v. Zahra Mohammed Abdulkadir, 295–6
 Amina Hassan Mohamed v. Yussuf Adan Abdullah, 301–2
 appointment/roles of khadis, 284–5
 Ashraf Abdu Kassim v. Karar Omar & 3 others, 295
 Baraka Binti Bahmishi v. Salim bin Abed Busawadi, 280
 case reports, 284
 Christian/Muslim constitutional debate, 292–4
 Courts Act, 283, 284
 custody of children, 295–8
 divorce, 270n, 271, 286–8, 298–302

Evidence Act, 283–4, 286, 287, 288–9
evidence legislation, 282–4, 288–9
 Fatuma v. Omari, 281
 Genevieve Bertrand v. Mohamed Athman Maawiya and Anor, 294
 G.S.A. v. A.S.A., 297–8
 Hanifa Mohamed Nur v. Ahmed Duale Osman, 301
 High Court, conflicts with, 294–5, 296–7
 H.M.M. v. K.J.D., 296–7
 Hussein, Abduljabar Ishaq, 278, 284, 285, 286, 287–9
 Hussein Sheikh Bashir v. Hassida Mohamed Ali, 300–1
 In the Matter of: The Estate of S.P.B. – Deceased R.B. & others and A.S.B. & others, 304
 Islam and evidence law, 278–81, 282
 Mariam Sheibani Salim & Another v. Hassan Ramadhan, 285–6, 288–9
 matrimonial property, 298–302
 Mpaji v. Jafari, 281
 R.M.M. v. B.A.M., 299–300
 Rashid Zahran v. Azan Zahran & 4 others, 303
 Re. Estate of Maryam Juma Kibanda (Deceased) Ashraf Abdul Kassim v. Karar Omar & 3 others, 303–4
 Re the Estate of Ismail OsmanAdam (Deceased), Noorbanu Abdul Razak v. AbdulKader Ismail Osman, 302–3
 S.H.H. v. M.H.Y., 294–5
 S.M.H. v. S.A.A., 296
 succession and estate administration, 302–4
 Zog'llo Zolleyn aka Alis Said Ahmed v. Abdalla Said Ahmed, 303
kadhis' courts (Zanzibar), 14–15, 189, 281–2, 306–16
KADU (Kenyan African Democratic Union), 51, 53–4, 74
Kamau, Jesse, 293

INDEX

KANU (Kenya African National Union), 2, 3, 51, 52, 53, 54, 55, 56, 57, 74
   IPK, 56, 57
   UMA, 57
Karim, Abdul Wahyd, 126, 130–1, 136
Karume, Abeid A., 138, 150
KDF (Kenya Defence Forces), 76
Kenya, 78, 85
   Christianity in, 33, 39, 61, 253
   citizenship, 83
   coastal strip, 2–3, 50–4
   colonialism, 2, 50–1, 72–3
   community-building, 37–46, 108
   conflict, 36, 43
   corruption, 35, 36–7, 41
   counter-terrorism, 58–62
   devolution, 34–6
   ethnic territorialism, 52–3
   history, 72
   institutions, 34, 36–7, 183–98, 246–56, 292
   irrigation, 41, 43–5
   Lamu Island, 245–56
   land expropriation, 41, 44
   Lodwar, 33, 35, 36, 37–40, 41–2, 44, 45
   loyalty pledge, 70n
   militancy, 61, 62, 77–8, 80
   northern, 34
   poverty, 35–6, 37–8, 42
   public safety/security, 98–100
   repression, 55, 61, 62, 75, 95, 97
   Swahili, 52, 53, 54, 57, 62
   Turkana, 34–9, 41, 44, 45–6
   violence, 40, 50, 57, 58, 59, 60–1, 78, 98–100, 197
   see also Islam (Kenya): law (Kenya); Muslims (Kenya); politics (Kenya); terrorism (Kenya)
Kenya African National Union (KANU) *see* KANU
Kenya Church, 292–3
Kenya Defence Forces (KDF), 76
Kenya Muslims Charitable Society, 37
Kenya People's Union (KPU), 54
Kenya: Twendapi? (Abdalla, Abdilatif), 54
Kenyan African Democratic Union (KADU), 51, 53–4, 74
Kenyatta, Jomo, 37, 52
Kenyatta government, 54
Khalif, Ahmed M., 188, 193–4, 196
Kibaki, Mwai, 58, 75, 248
Kibaki government, 58–9
Kinene, Deogratus, 237–8
Klerruum Wilbert, 130
KPU (Kenya People's Union), 54

Lamu Island, 245–56
   environment, the, 250–3
   exclusion, 252, 254
   identity, 247, 256
   migration, 253–6
   nostalgia, 250
   second-class citizens, 252, 254
   as second Dubai, 249
   settlement schemes, 254–5
Lamu Port, 246–56
   economic potential, 249, 250
   natural resources, effects on, 250–3
   opposition to, 248–9, 250, 251–2, 253–6
Lamu Port–South Sudan–Ethiopia Transport (LAPSSET), 246, 254
land ownership, 41, 44
LAPSSET (Lamu Port–South Sudan–Ethiopia Transport), 246, 254
law, 264
   Agrama, Hussein Ali, 264
   Islam, 263, 265, 266, 268, 269, 278–9, 280–9, 291–305
   law of consciousness, 267–8
   religious law, 263–4, 266
   rule of law, 263–4, 265–6, 267, 268–74
   shari'a law, 263, 265, 266, 267

Zanzibar, 14–17, 189, 281–2, 306–16
  see also law (Kenya)
law (Kenya), 14–17
  custody of children, 295–8
  divorce, 270n, 271, 286–8, 298–302
  High Court, 294–5, 296–7, 300, 303
  Law of Succession Act, 190–5, 302
  Marriage Act, 298–9
  matrimonial property, 298–302
  rule of law, 268–72
  succession and estate administration, 302–4
  2010 Constitution, 266, 268, 269–70, 288, 294, 295, 298
  see also kadhis' courts (Kenya)
law of consciousness, 267–8
Law of Succession Act, 190–5
Lodwar, 33, 35, 36, 37–40, 41–2, 44, 45

Mahmood, Saba, 143, 172
Making Islam Democratic (Bayat, Asef), 230
Malaysia, 280
Majimbo, 3, 52
Makaburi (Abubakar Shariff), 80–1
Mama na Mwana (Mother & Child) project, 221, 224, 227–8
Mardin conference (2010), 84
Mardin *fatwa*, 83–4
marginalisation *see* inequality
Mariam Sheibani Salim & Another v. *Hassan Ramadhan*, 285–6, 288–9
marital disputes/divorce, 270n, 271, 286–8, 298–302, 309–11
Married Women's Property Act, 299
Masasi Women's Development Association (MAWODEA), 211–12, 214–15
Masjid Sheikhat Issa, 206–8
Maswali na Majibu (Questions and Answers) programme, 187
maternal and child health (MCH), 221, 224, 229, 232

maulid festivals, 114–15, 116, 117–18, 138
MAWODEA (Masasi Women's Development Association), 211–12, 214–15
Mazrui, Hammad Muhammad Kasim, 99
Mbwana, Shehe, 220–1, 229
MCC (Muslim Consultative Council), 195–7
MCH (maternal and child health), 221, 224, 229, 232
media, the, 93
  Elimika na Stambuli! ('Get Educated with Stambuli!') (radio programme), 102–7, 108
  Friday Bulletin, The (pamphlet), 94, 96–102, 107 108
  Pwani FM, 107–8
  Radio Rahma, 102
migration, 81–2, 83–4, 253–6
militancy, 61, 62, 77–8, 80; *see also* extremism
Mitchell, Timothy, 28, 29
Mohamed, Abdallah, 124, 125, 127, 129
Moi, Daniel arap, 55, 70
Moi government, 56
Mombasa Law Society, 280–1
Mombasa Republican Council (MRC), 59, 73, 74, 253
al-Momin Foundation, 38
Mpaji v. *Jafari*, 281
MRC (Mombasa Republican Council), 59, 73, 74, 253
Mtemvu, Zuberi, 117–18, 129, 130
Mtnguumwa, Yakob, 127
Muhsin, Ali, 126
Mujahideen Moments videos, 62
multi-racialism, 116–17, 118, 125, 127–8
Muslim, Farouk, 187
Muslim Academy/Islamic College, 4–5

— 327 —

INDEX

Muslim Consultative Council (MCC), 195–7
Muslims (Kenya), 25, 85, 95–6
  alienation, 49, 50, 62, 63, 77, 99n
  colonial period, 2
  counter-terrorism, 58–62
  definition of, 193
  divorce, 270n, 271, 286–8, 298–302
  dress, 97, 98
  extremist, perception as, 86–7
  history, 1
  identity, 49, 50, 56, 57, 62–3, 95–6
  inequality, 71, 73, 74–5
  internal differences, 7
  islam mondain (Islam in the present world), 2
  Lamu Island, 249
  law, 269, 270–1, 272, 285–8, 294–5
  MCC, 195–7
  mutual distrust, 93–4, 95
  Otherness, 143
  repression, 55, 61, 62, 95, 97
  as second-class citizens, 72–5, 92, 97–8
  succession and estate administration, 302–4
  terrorist profiling, 97–8, 99, 100–2
  Turkana, community-building, 38–43
  see also coastal Muslims (Kenya); Islam (Kenya); al-Shabaab
Muslims (Tanganyika), 113–14, 131
  African and non-African, 113, 115, 120, 127–8
  AMNUT, 112, 122–32, 136
  Central Society of Tanganyika Muslims, 114, 115, 117, 129
  EAMWS, 112, 113, 133–4, 135, 137–8
  education, 120–1, 122, 123–4, 125–6, 130–1
  Jamiatul Islamiyya, 113
  multi-racialism system, 116–17, 118, 125, 127–8

  political leadership, 113
  Tanganyika Society of Muslim Youth, 128
  TANU, 113
  see also Islam (Tanganyika)
Muslims (Tanzania), 1, 161, 199–200
  African and non-African, 139
  aid/aid organisations 200–15
  aid funding, 201, 204, 205, 206–8, 209, 210–15
  alienation, 200
  BAKWATA, 12, 138–9, 140, 204–8
  communities, 201
  EAMWS, 112, 138–9, 140, 204
  family planning projects, 228, 230, 231, 232, 234, 236–41
  history, 1
  HIV/AIDS services, 200, 204, 205–10
  internal differences, 7
  leaders, 201, 227–8
  Mama na Mwana project, 221, 224, 227–8
  mosque attendance, 229–30
  political roles, 112–13
  public health programmes, 221, 223, 227–8, 230, 231, 232, 234, 236–41
  sexual permissiveness, views on, 205, 207, 240
  *shehe*s, 221–2, 223, 227–32, 233–6, 238–40, 241–2
  TMWN, 205, 209–10
  see also Islam (Tanzania)
Muslims (Zanzibar), 144, 149–50, 166, 173
  belonging, 161–2, 163, 164, 169–70
  dress, 143, 154–5
  history, 1
  kadhis' courts, 14–15, 189, 281–2, 306–16
  legal pluralism, 306–7
  religious pluralism, 161–2, 170, 172, 173

stereotypes, 143, 145
Uamsho, 162, 166, 167–8, 170, 172, 173, 174
women, 143
see also Islam (Zanzibar)
Mwambao movement, 3, 51–54, 57, 59, 63
Mwindadi, Juma, 118, 119

Naida, Al-Haj Salim, 38, 39–40, 43–4
Nassir, Abdilahi, 53, 54, 102
Nassir, Shariff, 55, 92
Nassir, Stambuli A. 102–4
National Muslim Council of Tanzania (Baraza kuu la Waislamu Tanzania [BAKWATA]), 12, 138–9, 140, 204–8
National Muslim Leaders Forum (NMLF), 197
neoliberalism, 29
Ngala, Ronald, 51, 52, 54
NGO system, 42–3, 45, 222
Nguyen, Vinh-Kim, 222
NMLF (National Muslim Leaders Forum), 197
Nyayo philosophy, 70
Nyerere, Julius, 114, 120, 126, 128, 131, 135
 AMNUT, 127, 130–1
 Fundikira, Abdallah, 133, 136
 Takadir, Suleiman, 121–2
Nzibo, Yusuf, 184

Odinga, Raila, 197, 249
Otherness, 143, 145, 148, 156
Othman, Issa, 209, 213, 215

P/CVE (preventing and countering violent extremism), 69, 77–88
 BRAVE, 69–71, 78–9, 81–4, 85–8
Pakistani missionaries, 154–5
people power, 30–2, 45
PEPFAR (President's Emergency Fund for Aids Relief), 204, 205

Plantan, Ramadhan Machado, 121, 122, 123
politics, 6–11, 75
 liberalisation, 199–200, 214–15
 political action strategies, 49, 50, 63
 political contests, 50
 political engagement, 54–7, 63
 Tanganyika, 112–40
 Tanzania, 112–40, 199–200, 214–15
 Zanzibar, 143–57, 160–75
 see also politics (Kenya)
Politics (Aristotle), 26
politics (Kenya), 25–46, 49–63, 69–88, 92–109
 coastal Muslims, alienation and engagement, 49–63
 Constitution of Kenya Review Act, 196
 counter-radicalisation programmes, 69–88
 discursive space, 92–109
 grassroots governance, northern Kenya, 25–46
 IPK, 55–7, 195, 197
 MCC, 195–7
 multi-party, 195
 mutual distrust, 93–4, 95
 patronage-based system, 54
 public safety/security, 98–100
 reprisal voting, 55
 2010 Constitution, 266
 'Presidential Special Action Committee to Address Specific Concerns of the Muslim Community in Regard to Alleged Harassment and/or Discrimination in the Application/ Enforcement of the Law', 75
President's Emergency Fund for Aids Relief (PEPFAR), 204, 205
preventing and countering violent extremism (P/CVE) *see* P/CVE
property-grabbing, 315–16
protest, 30–1, 166, 167, 174, 199, 248–9; *see also* revolution

Psychiatric Power: Lectures at the College de France, 1973–74 (Foucault, Michel), 29
public health, 221, 222–3, 227–8, 230, 231, 232, 234, 236–41
public safety/security, 98–100
Pwani FM, 107–8

al-Qaeda, 58
Qur'an, 40–1, 83, 232, 300
Qur'an teachers, 238–9

R.M.M. v. B.A.M., 299–300
race/racism, 113, 120
   African and non-African (Tanganyika), 113, 115, 120, 127–8
   multi-racialism, 116–17, 118, 125, 127–8
   Zanzibar, 148
radicalisation, 43, 60, 101
   counter-radicalisation programmes (Kenya), 69–88, 101
   see also extremism
Radio Rahma, 102
Raja, Shehe, 232
Rapid Funding Envelope for HIV/AIDS (RFE), 210–11, 213
Rashid Zahran v. Azan Zahran & 4 others, 303
Rauf, Abdul, 192–3
Re. Estate of Maryam Juma Kibanda (Deceased) Ashraf Abdul Kassim v. Karar Omar & 3 others, 303–4
Re the Estate of Ismail OsmanAdam (Deceased), Noorbanu Abdul Razak v. AbdulKader Ismail Osman, 302–3
reform, 2
   Islamic reformism, 144, 145, 147–9, 151, 152–3
rehabilitation, 94
religion, 26, 85, 144
   belief and the law, 267
religious law, 263–4, 266

religious pluralism, 160, 161–2, 170, 172, 173
representativeness, 184–5, 186, 187–8
repression
   Kenya 55, 61, 62, 75, 95, 97
   Tanzania, 199
   Zanzibar, 145, 146, 150–2, 156, 167, 174
revolution, 3–4, 145, 146–7, 150; *see also* protest
RFE (Rapid Funding Envelope for HIV/AIDS), 210–11, 213
Rogo, Aboud, 60, 80–1
Rose (Igi Village), 240–1
rule of law, 263–4, 265–6
   Agrama, Hussein Ali, 264, 267
   kadhis' courts, 268
   Kenya, 268–72
   legitimacy, 272–4

Sacred Meadows, The (El-Zein, Abdul Hamid), 230
Salafism, 150, 151, 154
Save Lamu, 248–9, 250, 251, 254
secularism, 267
   Tanganyika, 113–14, 120–1, 125, 129, 131–2
   Tanzania, 139
   Zanzibar, 170–2, 174
security issues, 1–2; *see also* terrorism
al-Shabaab, 50, 58–62, 63, 75, 76, 79–80, 94
   amnesties, 94
   recruitment, 79–80
shari'a law, 263, 265, 266, 267
Shariff, Abubakar (Makaburi), 80–1
shehas, 310–11, 315
shehas, 221–2, 223, 224, 227–36, 238–9, 240, 241–2
S.H.H. v. M.H.Y., 294–5
Siddik, Abdulrahman, 190–1
S.M.H. v. S.A.A., 296
Somalia, 60, 72–3, 75, 78
Soud, Mzee Hussein, 253–4

state, the, 82
  ahl al-hall wa-l-'aqd (those who loosen and bind), 31–2, 40–1, 42, 44
  authoritarianism, 30
  control, 93
  coups d'état, 28–9
  definition of term, 26
  democratisation, 30
  Foucault, Michel, 28–9
  Mitchell, Timothy, 28, 29
  power, 27–30, 31
  power holders, 29, 31–4
  upheaval, 29, 30–1
  war, waging, 82
  working misunderstandings, 200, 213
Stiles, Erin E., 281
Stiles, Erin and Yakin, Ayang Utriza
  Islamic Divorce in the 21st Century: A Global Perspective, 17
Stockreiter, Elke, 281–2
Sudan, 30
Sufism, 149–50, 152, 153–4, 202–3
SUPKEM (Supreme Council of Kenya Muslims), 34, 36–7, 183–98
  challenges to, 197–7
  constitution, 185, 186, 187–8, 195–6
  Constitution of Kenya Review Act, 196
  establishment, 184, 186
  kadhis' courts, 292
  Law of Succession Act, 190, 191–2, 193–5
  leadership, 184, 186, 187, 193–4
  representativeness, 185, 186, 187–8
  resources, 186
  supremacy, 186–7, 189
Supreme Council of Kenya Muslims (SUPKEM) *see* SUPKEM
Swahili, 1, 5, 8, 9, 12, 14, 26, 46, 52, 53, 54, 57, 62, 72, 73, 92, 95, 102, 104, 107, 109, 118, 121, 123, 127, 138, 139, 145, 163, 168, 221, 224, 226, 227, 235, 237, 245, 247, 249, 252, 253–5, 313

Swaleh, Habib, 230
Sykes, Abbas, 131–2

TACAIDS, 205, 206, 209–11, 215
Takadir, Suleiman, 120, 121–2
TAMU (Tanganyika African Muslim Union), 115
Tanganyika, 1, 3, 5
  AMNUT, 112, 122–32, 136
  ANC, 129–30
  Central Society of Tanganyika Muslims, 114, 115, 117, 129
  Christianity, 120–1, 122, 125, 131
  colonialism, 113, 126
  corruption, 134
  EAMWS, 112, 113, 133–4, 135, 137–8
  education, 120–1, 122, 123–4, 125–6, 130–1, 137
  festivals, 114–19, 138, 139, 140
  Fundirkira, Abdulla, 112, 132–7
  multi-racialism system, 116–17, 118, 125, 127–8
  politics, 112–40
  secularism, 113–14, 120–1, 125, 129, 131–2
  self-government, 123–4
  TAMU, 115
  UTP, 117, 118
  see also Islam (Tanganyika); Muslims (Tanganyika); TANU; Tanzania
Tanganyika African Muslim Union (TAMU), 115
Tanganyika African National Congress (ANC), 129–30
Tanganyika African National Union (TANU) *see* TANU
Tanganyika Society of Muslim Youth, 128
TANU (Tanganyika African National Union), 112, 113–14, 115, 117, 118, 120, 126–8
  AMNUT, 122–3, 125, 126–8, 130–1
  Chaurembo, Abdallah, 137–8, 139

TANU (Tanganyika African National Union) (*cont.*)
  education, 121
  Elders Council, 120, 127–8, 131–2
  Fundirkira, Abdulla, 112, 132–4, 135, 136, 137
  Takadir, Suleiman, 120, 121–2
  see also Islam (Tanganyika); Muslims (Tanganyika); Nyerere, Julius
Tanzania, 225f
  aid/aid organisations, 200–15
  aid funding, 201, 204, 205, 206–8, 209, 210–15
  BAK-AIDS, 206, 212, 214
  BAKWATA, 12, 138–9, 140, 204–8
  CAs, 220–1, 224–6f
  CCM, 137, 145
  Christian organisations, 202, 204
  colonialism, 121, 202, 223
  CSOs, 201, 204, 211, 215
  CSSC, 202, 204, 205
  developmentalism, 200–1
  EAMWS, 112, 138–9, 140, 204
  education, 202–3
  establishment of, 1, 3–4, 5
  FBOs, 201, 202, 204, 206
  festivals, 138, 139, 140
  HIV/AIDS services, 200, 204, 205–12
  institutions, 199–215, 220–43
  Islam, 112–13, 139–40, 199, 202–3
  liberalisation, 199–200, 214–15
  marriage counselling, 235
  Masjid Sheikhat, 206–7
  MAWODEA, 211–12, 214–15
  MCH, 221, 224, 229, 232
  Otherness, 148
  politics, 112–40, 199–200, 214–15
  protest, 199
  public health programmes, 221, 223, 227–8, 230, 231, 232, 234, 236–41
  religion, 5–6, 160–1
  repression, 199

RFE, 210–11, 213
secularism, 139
Sufism, 202–3
surveillance, 140
TACAIDS, 205, 206, 209–11, 215
TMWN, 205, 209–10
working misunderstandings, 200
see also Muslims (Tanzania); Tanganyika
Tanzanian Muslim Welfare Network (TMWN), 205, 209–10
territoriality, 79n
terrorism (Kenya), 33–4, 58–62, 75, 78–80, 94–5
  amnesties, 94
  counter-terrorism, 58–62, 69–88, 101
  Elimika radio debate, 104–6
  Friday Bulletin, The (pamphlet), 96–100
  Hirsch, Susan, 93
  Muslim profiling, 97–8, 99, 100–2
  rehabilitation, 94
  al-Shabaab, 60–2, 75, 76, 79–80, 94
Tewa, Tewa Said, 133, 135
TMWN (Tanzanian Muslim Welfare Network), 205, 209–10
Turkana, 34–9, 41, 44, 45–6
Turkana Dawaa Muslims Organisation, 37
Turkana Inter-Religious Council, 44
Turnbull, Richard, 124, 125

Uamsho ('the Awakening'), 162, 166, 167–8, 170, 172, 173, 174
UMA (United Muslims of Africa), 57
Umize (Sawa project meeting), 237–8
UNDP
  Journey to Extremism, 77
United Muslims of Africa (UMA), 57
United Tanganyika Party (UTP), 117, 118
UTP (United Tanganyika Party), 117, 118

veil, the, 143
violence
  al-Shabaab, 50, 58–62, 63
  Kenya, 40, 50, 57, 58, 59, 60–1, 78, 98–100, 197
  Muslim leaders, 78, 98–9
  UMA, 57
  Zanzibar, 167
  see also terrorism; war

war, 73–4, 82
  BRAVE, 82–3
  civil war, 73–4
Weber, Max, 228
  Economy and Society, 228
women, 118, 143, 151
  Constitution of Kenya Review Act, 196
  divorce, 299–301
  kadhis' courts, 273
  MAWODEA, 211–12, 214–15
  property-grabbing, 315–16

Zanzibar, 1, 3–4, 5, 155
  Africanisation, 147–9
  alcohol, 147
  Ansâr Sunna, 165, 173
  autonomy, 146
  CCM, 165, 166, 167, 174
  Christianity, 146–7, 156, 161, 163–4, 165–6, 167–75
  citizenship, 148
  climate of uncertainty, 147, 155, 156
  coastal strip, 2–3, 51, 52, 53
  CUF, 165, 166, 167, 174
  diversity, 160–1, 162–3, 168, 169, 172
  education, 4–5, 150–3
  identity, 147–50, 155, 161–2, 163–4, 169–70, 172, 173
  identity, distinctions of, 149, 155, 163–4, 167, 168
  inter-religious dynamics, 160–75
  kadhis' courts, 14–15, 189, 281–2, 306–16
  law, 14–17, 189, 281–2, 306–16
  nationalism, 164
  Otherness, 143, 145, 148, 156
  Pakistani missionaries, 154–5
  politics, 143–57, 160–75
  pork, 147
  property-grabbing, 315–16
  protest, 166, 167, 174
  religion, 4–5, 149–52
  religious pluralism, 161–2, 170, 172, 173
  restrictions, 145, 146, 150–2, 156, 167, 174
  revolution, 3–4, 145, 146–7, 150
  secularism, 170–2, 174
  television, 147n
  Uamsho, 162, 166, 167–8, 170, 172, 173, 174
  United Republic of Tanzania (Union), 161, 165–6, 167, 170–2, 174
  violence, 167
  youth of, 152–3, 154–5
  ZICC, 174–5
  see also Islam (Zanzibar); Muslims (Zanzibar); Tanzania
Zanzibar International Christian Centre (ZICC), 174–5
ZICC (Zanzibar International Christian Centre), 174–5
ZNP (Zanzibar Nationalist Party)/ZPPP (Zanzibar and Pemba People's Party), 135
Zog'llo Zolleyn aka Alis Said Ahmed v. *Abdalla Said Ahmed*, 303

EU representative:
Easy Access System Europe
Mustamäe tee 50, 10621 Tallinn, Estonia
Gpsr.requests@easproject.com

www.ingramcontent.com/pod-product-compliance
Lightning Source LLC
Chambersburg PA
CBHW050201240426
43671CB00013B/2210